UP MY P

UP

MY

PARTICULAR

CREEK

2012 EDITION

Valentine Howells

www.valhowells.com

UP MY PARTICULAR CREEK

UP MY PARTICULAR CREEK

2012 Edition
Published by: Landsker Publications Ltd

Paperback ISBN: 978-0-9542732-3-1
Hardback ISBN: 978-0-9542732-4-8

Ebook Editions
Published by: Landsker Publications Ltd.

PDF Version ISBN: 978-0-9542732-8-2
E-Pub Version ISBN: 978-0-9542732-8-6
Audiobook ISBN: 978-9573001-0-1

Previously Published by Pavilion Publications as

UP THAT PARTICULAR CREEK

First published 2002
Second Edition 2004

ISBN 0 9542732 0 6

Previous Work

SAILING INTO SOLITUDE

1st Edition
Published 1966, in the U.K. by Temple Press
Published in the U.S.A by Dodd Mead & Company
(Library of Congress Catalogue Card Number 66-27273)

2011 Edition
Published by: Landsker Publications Ltd
ISBN: 978-0-9542732-2-4

UP THAT PARTICLAR CREEK

Pavilion Publications
1st and 2nd Editions
ISBN 0 9542732 0 6

(Films for BBC TV)

ALONE IN A BOAT
(Producer: John Ormond)

MINERS IN THE PINK
(Producer: Selwyn Roderick)

AN OBSESSION IN THE FAMILY
(Producer: Derek Trimby)

I, A STRANGER
(Producer: Selwyn Roderick)

VALENTINE'S NIGHT
(five part series)
(Producer: Derek Trimby)

BBC 2

THE JOLLY RODGERED SEA
(Producer: Selwyn Roderick)

CONTENTS

PAGE NOTES

Occasionally, throughout the text of *Up My Particular Creek,* reference is made to a seafaring event the reader may not be familiar with (for example; the role of the *Pilot of the Pinta*), or maybe something that is not readily understood; for instance, how the *Lays of Ancient Rome* have been allowed to stray into a seafaring narrative. In situations of this sort, information will be found in the notes which are displayed at the end of every chapter. These items have been given a page-by-page notation, and cross-indexed, in order that they may be easily located.

WHERE TO GO & HOW TO GET THERE

ANYONE living in Northern Europe and contemplating an extended small boat cruise is forced sooner or later to consider moving south, if only because the sailing season in the Baltic is limited to a few short summer months. And the same logical assessment applies to other Scandinavian and even British waters, regardless of the ameliorating effect provided by the Gulf Stream.

It's all very well spending a summer month or two exploring the beauty of the Outer Hebrides, even being tempted to extend the challenge to the Orkneys and then the Shetland Isles; but as the seasons advance, summer turns to autumn. The daytime temperatures fall, the incidence of depressions sweeping in from the Atlantic becomes more frequent, and even the hardened seaman is forced to the conclusion it *is* time to head South - leave the storm-tossed waters of the Pentland Firth, to slip along rather grandly in the lee of the British Isles.

Working your way westward.

Negotiating the choppy waters of the English Channel, with the declared intention of hauling further south.

Dropping the frost-bitten Scots and the flu-threatened Anglo Saxons astern, to head for some exotic haven, where the sun still shines, the wine seems reasonably priced, and the dreamtime of seafaring ambition is not in any way cramped by the dismal turn of seasonal events.

Spain's the place to head for, with the possibly wet and windy close-hauled passage across the Bay of Biscay planned and hopefully made good well before the onslaught of the equinoctial gales. And even then don't dawdle through October, pottering about among the Basques, charming though they may be (if you are not an ETA-targeted Spaniard),[1] but use the remaining autumn days to log more southern miles made good; pressing on, with possibly a call at La Coruña or oily old Vigo to stock up on stores while improving the look of the latitude.

From the middle 40s you may be lucky enough to pick up the Portuguese Trades. The hoped-for northerlies which are not really trade winds at all, merely the optimistic term seamen have coined for what they know they are heading for. The prospect of a favourable breeze, the sun

1

gaining warmth each day, so when you do ease sheets and run dry decked, the necessity of pulling on clammy oilskins and soggy sea boots no longer puts such a damper on proceedings.

Having got as far south as the Berlengas, the question then arises: shall we look in at Lisbon?

The Tagus is less than a day's sail further south, and after rounding Cabo da Roca you could, if you wanted to, haul away to the east'ard, while keeping close ashore to rekindle memories of Estoril and have another look at Cascais. However, before the decision is made to enter the estuary proper, perhaps it would be sensible to pause for a while, ease up for a moment, in order to take stock of the position.

When planning a cruise, dreams often crowd out reality - being the proud owner of an ocean-going yacht doesn't necessarily mean the bank balance matches the draft of the vessel. Sometimes the reverse is the case, and what seems a craft of powerful persuasion has its hoped-for cruising ground restricted to within the limit of a shrouded headland. Shrouded, because the planning hasn't been conducted in the clear light of day, the crucial decisions having been taken from the shelter of a deep armchair, when the wine's been poured and glasses emptied. It seems a pity to bring this matter up, it is after all merely (merely?) a matter of money. But when you view the wealth of Cascais, and contemplate spending time in Lisboa, the prompt's been made. A crucial item brought forcibly to your attention, that sums should be done, stubs of pencils applied to greasy scraps of paper, because the truth is, every time you tie up to a quay it's going to cost real money.

This points up another conundrum: what part of the world are we bound for?

It's all very well deciding to avoid the northern winter (heading south has always seemed sensible enough) but heading and drifting, although they may be two sides of the same coin, are really poles apart, particularly when applied to a seagoing vessel located on the eastern seaboard of the north Atlantic Ocean. Aboard a yacht which over the past month or so has been quietly trickled down from northern latitudes, and having taken this sun-seeking departure, we could, if inclined to do so, decide to over-winter at any one of a number of different locations.

For instance, go no further, and spend the off-season in Portugal; or go a little further, and gallivant in Spain.

Yet again, head for the Rock, and use that dramatic outpost to creak open another door. The possibility unfolding of exploring the southern shores of the Med, and once there, of pottering on towards Egypt, chancing the dust and dirt of Alexandria, while a little further along the coast the shade of Ferdinand de Lesseps [2] still beckons, his canal offering the absolute certainty of tropical shirt and shorts and a swim in a dirty lagoon.

See how the imagination tumbles?

Have boat, can travel - a statement which is not only axiomatic, but very much better than that, the irreducible kernel of truth.

We are not aboard a cruise ship, where every little item has had its fancy pants pressed.

Dress for dinner: spend one day here, overnight there, maybe experience the doubtful thrill of a conducted tour of the Casbah, on offer, as usual, as a supposedly risqué and certainly overpriced excursion.

This is all very well, but it isn't ocean cruising. In some ways it's little more than careless stumble bumming, because even concerned tourists, transported in the giga numbers we are getting used to, are in danger of destroying the very thing they scour the world to admire.

There's little risk of doing that when sailing your own boat - modestly equipped, it's possible to slip along leaving barely the trace of a wake. The supposedly difficult decision (which of the many hundreds of cruise ships to sign-up for) has been easily avoided. There really is no argument about abandoning the broad Atlantic, to cruise the Mediterranean, when as a child you have been raised on books with titles that resound to the bugle call of further flung adventure.

The Venturesome Voyages of Captain Voss; [3] Dwight Long's book *Cruising All Seas In The Idle Hour;* [4] to say nothing of the classic, Joshua Slocum's *Sailing Alone Around The World.* [5] The fact that few of the younger generation are aware of these volumes is neither here nor there (if they are that young and deprived, their parents may be well advised to let them cut what's left of their milk teeth on Erling Tamb's *The Cruise of the Teddy*).[6] But if you are familiar with these admittedly archaic volumes, have even read them, then taking leave of the Western Ocean to potter about in the Med, even if it is recognised as the largest inland sea in the world, seems to offer little in the way of genuine inducement.

Estoril, Cascais and Lisbon.

The Rock of Gibraltar.

Malta and Sicily.

The footballed toe of Italy.

The division of Cyprus.

The glitz of Tel Aviv: the misery of Gaza.

The wail ...

.... prompted by the claim made at the Wall of Jerusalem. [7]

All these temptations are as nothing, compared to the thrill of using an ocean as a bridge between the Old World and the New. You can't do that in the Med, which all too often is a backward looking sea; bounded not only by its shores, but also by antiquity - charming in its old-fashioned way, but will it lead to the moon?

What it may lead to, if you wander carelessly along the strands which form the southern shore of that particular sea, is having your simpleton throat cut. Not, quite reasonably, by a starving man who may be in desperate need of the money - by a gang of ruffians in the name of religious belief - butchered, not for your gold watch, but because your grandmother was rash enough to marry an Anglican church warden.

Can there be a better reason to head west, instead of east, when the cards are still face down on the table?

So it's onward and southward, from Cabo de Sao Vincent, with barely a backward glance, if you have spent formative years in more tolerant latitudes and managed, through dint of some luck and more hard labour, to have built your own boat and scrambled enough cash together to enable a start to be made.

The sensible course lies sou'sou'west, with this old-fashioned phrase being nothing for a landlubber to worry about, merely an indication that some of us were at sea before the three hundred and sixty degree compass card notation was almost exclusively applied. If you are not happy with the term sou'sou'west, try steering about two hundred and two (true), both courses being designed to bring us down to Lanzarote, the northernmost island of the group we know as the Canaries.

These bird caged islands are a natural port of call when leaving Portugal and bound south. An archipelago of volcanic origin, they lie between the latitudes of 28 and 29 degrees north, some 60 nautical miles off the African coast. There are seven islands and six other uninhabited islets, covering some 2,800 square miles, so they really shouldn't be described as (although of course they were, and perhaps will be again) a vent hole in a pie crust. Nevertheless, when taking a departure from Saint Vincent and embarked on 500 miles of short sea passage, two thousand eight hundred square miles of land does seem a large enough target to aim at - being aboard a boat you have put together yourself also offers advantage (you know what's beyond suspicion, and you also know the

4

faults that have been carelessly included) so starting from basics, the choice of rig was easy enough: a cutter preferred to a sloop.

A cutter?

A sloop?

How many masts has a schooner?

How many feet in a fathom?

What's a brig?

Where's the orlop deck?

What's the difference between a barque and a barquentine?

Is it anything to do with calling out the dogwatch?

Don't worry: the nautical jargon is simple enough when you get the hang of it. All you need to know is cutters and sloops have a single mast apiece, but rigged as a cutter, a vessel offers the benefit of two headsails, instead of the larger, solitary headsail carried by the sloop; both craft also carry mainsails, while the choice of two headsails doesn't necessarily increase the amount of sail carried, merely splits the canvas into easily managed amounts. This is handy enough when you find yourself alone in a boat, making (setting) sail and trimming canvas in a way that drives the vessel forward, then taking the decision to reduce the area on offer well before the wind pipes up. All part of the art of seamanship - simple enough to appreciate, perhaps more difficult to understand, sometimes hard to manage in the hurly burly'd pressure of events.

Midnight - a northerly gale, fetched straight from bitter arctic floes.

Frozen fingers, whip-lashed spray, the dangerous flog of wildly flapping canvas.

The sea tumultuous, loud with toppled roar as breaking crests are curled then crashed aboard the boat.

Decks awash, bilges flooded, the pump part blocked.

The vessel sinking?

Dear God Almighty: is this the way to end your days?

Not yet, because seamanship demands a sense of proportion, as well as a sense of humour. The acknowledgement, that although your boat is but a small vessel, afloat on a large ocean, a frail bottle will survive the ultimate storm in absolute safety (the trick being, of course, to keep the cork in), which is merely another way of saying, when you're aboard a small boat, it *is* advisable to keep the ocean out.

Doesn't every fool know that?

It's uppermost in every seaman's mind when sailing, or even pottering about in northern latitudes - to err there is to court disaster (a soaked

5

bunk, coupled with wet gear, leads inevitably, and much sooner than you think, to a drop in body temperature and on to hypothermia). A fine prospect, yet one which does concentrate the mind wonderfully, much in the way the click of a rifle being cocked would be hard to ignore if you were standing in front of a firing squad.

It would also be a mistake to imagine that the Old Man with the trident [8] is more forgiving than any other officer in charge of events (it even seems, at times, he's there to pose those awkward questions). Yet the examination certainly gets easier to face with every southern mile made good; that by the time you're down to the latitude of The Rock the papers are not quite so demanding, and what's been pushed over the counter is nothing more than a simple questionnaire, with boxes outlined which encourage you to place the tick in the appropriate place (because don't most of us secretly harbour the opinion, that 'multiple choice' offers the chance of a successful, even if it is a sometimes scrambled result?).

So it's with every confidence you settle her down on the previous heading, *sou'sou'west*. Not steering the boat yourself, but setting up the gear you have specifically installed to do the job for you, because nobody steers around the world, over an ocean, or even during a short sea passage. Self-steering gears or auto-helms are now commonplace aboard every seriously equipped ocean-going yacht, with the truth being, that while the helmsman's job is not always boring, it does have the built-in capacity of becoming surprisingly tedious.

The bold buck who says, '*I just love a trick at the helm*' is talking about an afternoon's jolly about a sheltered bay - not endless hours wrestling with a tiller aboard a vessel being forced to windward in the teeth of a northerly gale, where every time she slams a great deal more than spray is hurled across the foredeck. In this situation, no matter how carefully you oilskin-up and jam a sou'wester on your head, sooner or later you feel the cooling liquid trickling down the back of your neck, soaking the strip of towelling which is supposed to deal with this particularly nasty problem.

An icy stream of seawater, pinching down your vertebrae, little by shivering little, until you're sitting in an irritating puddle of salt, reduced to wriggling your bum about in an endeavour to keep what you hope is the circulation going in the frozen cheeks of your arse.

These are the stern joys of Norsemen, the hard men of the arctic.

However, when sailing about the latitude of Gibraltar, nothing so distasteful should threaten even the most apprehensive crew. In these forgiving seas, with the wind in a favourable quarter and temperatures expected in the middle sixties, it's possible to relax and ease sheets. Allow the jib and staysail both to billow out, take up the sensuous shape which appears so attractive when reaching across a moderate sea and a softly tailored breeze.

On this favoured point of sailing, there's no danger of the hull being driven under the threat of a steeply breaking crest.

No knee-deep surge of ice cold water sluiced along the side deck.

No necessity to head-duck spray as it slashes over the cockpit.

No alarming thump, as she hits the wetting tumble of yet another crest.

When broad reaching, in moderate weather, there's very little spray; with the wind abaft the beam there's hardly any noise. The slam and bang of windward work has been replaced - by a smile, that embroiders the chuckle drawn from the broadly rippled wake.

In these conditions, five hundred miles of short sea passage is something of a cakewalk. The work on deck is easy enough; a reef shaken out of the mainsail, sheets eased again, and another knot picked up.

Nothing immediately to do with rope work, merely a nautical term that arrives at the speed of a vessel, by counting the number of knots spaced at regular intervals along the line which is slipping through the bosun's gnarled old fingers. [9] A midshipman tends the sand-glass [10] so with knots counted, compared with time elapsed, they arrive at the speed of the vessel expressed in nautical miles per hour.

The fact that the length of a shore going mile has its origins in the Roman term *mille,* meaning a thousand paces (about 1,618 yards) tends to make for confusion when note is taken that in Italy, Spain, and Portugal, to say nothing of a host of other places, the miles found there range between just over three-quarters, to one and a quarter English or American miles made good, which is now agreed as being 1760 yards in length.

Small wonder then, that various Boards of Admiralty, in their collective wisdom, fixed on a nautical mile of exactly one minute of arc, measured on a great circle of the earth, [11] which turns out to be about 6,080 feet. Rather more than the shore going article - yet it does offer the advantage of remaining the same length if you are sailing away from Portugal, approaching Madagascar, circumnavigating the Outer Hebrides, or even skating across a frozen lake somewhat bitterly located in the ice bound reaches of the distant Hindu Kush.

And this isn't a case of mere semantics

When engaged on a passage, it really is important to know - not only how far you've come, but how far it is to your chosen destination - with the earlier part of the question being the easy bit of the nautical equation.

In days gone by (back as far, but not beyond our gnarled old bosun) the careful seaman trailed a log, meaning a brass rotator, equipped with carefully angled fins which impart rotary movement to the supporting length of plaited rope.

This may sound complicated, but it's nothing more than transposing measured length, into graduated rotation, both methods arriving at the speed of the vessel and, eventually, the number of nautical miles made good.

So, if you steer a course and have the gumption to take note of how far you've travelled, it doesn't really require the ability of Einstein to make a stab at your new found geographical location.

And while this is true, in a limited way, it must also be admitted there are one or two complications associated with the pursuit of seagoing navigation. Magnetic variation, deviation, leeway, drift; [12] even the inattention of a careless helmsman, all play a significant part in the conduct of affairs, so perhaps it's just as well these hurdles can be approached, and successfully negotiated, as and when the need arises.

On the way to Lanzarote the distances involved are modest enough. It's possible to find the place, being careful about the course being steered and taking regular note of miles made good; two simple disciplines, and you're going to make a successful passage.

And before anyone decries this method - declaring it too simplistic - it would be as well to remember that not so long ago, and countless generations previously, our forefathers did navigate their way about the oceans of the world in this particular way. It's only comparatively recently we've had the benefit of further scientific advance, so it's not in any way fanciful to anticipate a successful passage from Saint Vincent to Lanzarote using nothing more complicated than a compass and a careful man at the helm. Although you would indeed be foolish if, having the necessary bits and pieces and a current nautical almanac, you neglected to take those observations which enable a cautious seaman to keep a reasonable check on his tracked across the chart position; because you may need this reassurance when running towards the northern-most tip of the island.

These are somewhat odd waters: because they are located so close to the West African shore, the visibility is not always as good as it should be. Not plagued by the sort of dismal pea soup fog reminiscent of the gas-lit London streets described so graphically by Arthur Conan Doyle, but by a reduction in visibility, brought about by haze, a phenomenon we usually assume is caused by the suspension of minute particles of water vapour.

However, wondering, along with *Watson,* [13] what may have prompted the damnable haze, doesn't make the approach to this cinder of an island any easier, or safer.

The particular problem associated with this landfall is experienced because the breeze holds from an easterly direction.

This may be the self-same favourable breeze you eased sheets to a little earlier in the passage.

But as more southing is made, the wind has been blowing over a significant part of the North African land mass, some of it arid desert country, composed largely of sand and the staggering amount of droppings left by plodding lines of slack arsed camels; so you may be unfortunate enough, when making your landfall on Lanzarote, to find yourself peering through a haze of (let's hope it's nothing more than just very fine dry sand) picked up in the desert and carried over from the mainland by a wind the locals know, somewhat further south, as Harmattan. [14] A fine name for a dubious event because, in the worst conditions produced by this breeze, visibility may be reduced to no more than half-a-mile, sometimes less, so it may be possible to run aground before you have even a glimpse of the shore.

Yet all is not gloom and doom when approaching Lanzarote - the fact that the current is not setting across the vessel's track is something in your favour.

This is part of the general clockwise gyre of surface water found in the north Atlantic. A gigantic stirring of the ocean, recognised as the Gulf Stream when running up the American eastern seaboard, to meander as a body of warm water across the top of the north Atlantic, eventually turning south to slip past Portugal, Madeira, and the Islas Canarias.

To be deflected, yet again, by the spin of the globe towards the West Indies, propelled from east to west by the ever-blowing trades. The silent yet massive assist we've had under the hull of our small vessel since running down the Portuguese coast, making its presence felt by adding an unearned half-knot to the speed of the vessel. The unseen but significant influence which has consistently pushed the craft ahead of her estimated position, so that now, to the one hundred or so honest miles made good every day under sail, there's been added a further ten or fifteen very nautical miles provided by the Old Man's sleight of hand. A lift gratefully accepted during the passage - now something which should be taken into careful account when actually making the landfall. The good advice being, when dealing with Neptune, that the cautious seaman should always count the ever varying amount of his temptingly jingled change.

And there are other tricks to the trade, also worth considering.

When you're running towards your destination, it isn't sensible to plot the vessel's course to directly pinpoint your objective. To understand this adage, it may be necessary to remind those people who have been fortunate enough to shoot a high-flying pheasant (and even more so, those who have been put off by the blood lust which seems to taint the sporting opportunity) that the gun wise always 'aim off'. As does the experienced navigator, who is manoeuvring by the seat of his pants, without the benefit of the modern aids to navigation which include echo sounders, radio direction finders, facsimile weather reporting machines, satellite navigators, boat speed, together with wind speed and direction indicators, that are in turn hooked up to computers which are primed to allow for set and drift, before conveniently printing out the course to be steered and the distance remaining to be sailed. All this equipment being miniaturised and available, if affordable, to the most modest of yachts.

There have even been two significant omissions.

A radar set, which reduces the problem of zero visibility to little more than a nuisance, and a powerful radio telephone, so if you do get into trouble, you can get on the blower and summon a host of visiting firemen, represented by a team of well trained men who, if they can't solve the immediate problem, will lift you to safety using the Air Sea Rescue helicopter, which is also little more than a confident phone call away.

But what all this does to your sense of adventure, the gut-gripping twitch to your balls experienced when running, alone, in a sparsely-fitted cockleshell, towards a haze enshrouded island - this is something that you *now* know belongs, not to a game, but to a different sort of war. Under these conditions, bereft of everything but your Mark One Eyeball, it's even possible to break into something of a sweat.

We have run our distance, so the island should be showing up, bearing 5 miles on the starboard bow.

How do we know Lanzarote is on the starboard bow?

Because we have aimed-off, dunderhead.

Taken the sensible precaution of assuming we are not going to score a bull, but we will be happy with an 'inner', and remain reasonably confident that we are au fait with the essential part of the equation, which is - are we to the east, or are we to the west, of the blasted island?

In the meantime, we have run another two miles further south, maybe more, if the southern-going current has given us an even bigger lift than usual, which it could well do, because the Old Man can't resist sticking his salty finger in just to complicate proceedings (of course, as we're not *all* dunderheads, there's no doubt we're to the east'ard of the island).

Because the breeze remains drawn from an easterly direction, the course being steered has been carefully aligned to keep the vessel to the windward, the eastern side of the island, and this for several reasons. If you *know* you're to the east, and have run your distance, you can confidently alter course to the west, and be sure of making the landfall, even though lack of visibility is postponing the well-anticipated event.

There's also another consideration.

If you had, rather foolishly, allowed the vessel to fall off to the west'ard (the leeward side of the island), you would, if required to make a substantial alteration of course in order to close the shore, find yourself downwind, forced to harden sheets and beat up, with all this entails in the way of flying spray and soaking clothes - hours of unnecessary sailing before successfully gaining the lee.

One more thing.

Have you noticed the degree of irritability which has crept aboard the vessel?

The nuance that provides an appreciable, even if unappreciated feeling of tension in the air?

That the language used has become a little bit more vulgar, in style as well as flavour?

The island described as *blasted,*

People downsized as *dunderheads.*

There's even been talk of sweat being raised, when what's needed is a cool assessment of the situation in order that the decisions taken produce the required result.

What it boils down to (apart from the obvious display of human frailty, exemplified as nerves) is no matter how many landfalls you have previously made - the one you are making now is the one that's causing concern.

And there's more to this truism than at first appears.

When you're alone in a boat, there are numerous personal risks which must be faced, and to the uninitiated, it may appear they centre largely about the isolation involved in the conduct of the passage.

The reality is, few people come to grief in the middle of an ocean.

There are dangers a'plenty, of course, and many of them intensify as you approach the shore.

Tidal streams swirl round headlands.

A restriction, produced by the funnelling of a channel, increases the rate of flow, and with the acceleration, the height of the sea encountered.

A change in the depth of water dramatically alters the behaviour of an otherwise modest swell.

The broken nature of the seabed has a decisive influence on the shape and extent of an overfall, so a gale of wind, blowing over a weather-going tide, tumbled in the overfall, can produce conditions which threaten even a substantial vessel, up to and including a trawler.

And there's more, much more - but why raise the spectre? When you're engaged on a landfall, there are other things, yet perhaps just the one thing that occupies your mind.

Where *is* the blasted island?.

Another mile has been run, again to the south'ard, and it's time to make the decisive alteration of course, which should have been made half an hour earlier.

The breeze remains the same (in these latitudes, you can usually count on that) so this major alteration of compass course brings the wind over the starboard quarter, as a commanding breeze, produced not by good fortune, but by the foresight of keeping well up to the windward side of the island.

Yet another mile has been made good, this time due west, the crew peering anxiously into the haze, while wondering what's the extent of the visibility.

And this isn't as daft as it sounds.

It may appear, because you are actually *there,* you would know how far you can see.

This is not always the case.

These conditions are most deceptive.

You may be able to see a mile and a half, three miles, even four - but there's no way of measuring the density of the haze that's obscuring your vision. All you have to rely on is hard-won experience, your own appreciation of the subtle changes in wave shape and incidence which indicate we are certainly closing the shore.

The swell has become steeper; no doubt about that, there's a curl to the crests that carries an extra threat to the safety of the vessel.

The colour of the water is also significant; but the shading from the brilliant blue of an ocean, to the approaching grey of an off-lying shelf, occurred some time ago. The surrounding sea now *is* different, so we *must* be approaching the island, yet still can't see loom nor strand of the shore.

Heave-to, and take a sounding?

If we had use of an echo sounder, we would certainly switch the thing on.

But taking a sounding right now (a hand-cast leadline, used to laboriously measure the depth of the water in this particular place, after having taken most of the way off the vessel), this time-taking, even if it is a time honoured manoeuvre, isn't going to tell us much more than we already know.

We are closing the shore.

Yet still can't see, even an outline of the island.

But to be honest, there's a certain amount of unnecessary huff and puff going on here, with the truth being, there's overwrought nail biting, almost play acting, of the knicker twisting type of hysteria being indulged in, because Lanzarote isn't a place girt with a dangerous shelf of poorly marked shoal. In this regard, it can't be judged an island that's difficult to approach, as are some of the low-lying Pacific atolls, where you can run aground on the coral before you're in sight of the motu [15] which may be nothing more than a cluster of palms, clinging to the top of a half-hidden ocean-washed reef.

Lanzarote is, by comparison, a mountainous island; even though little more than a pile of sun baked cinders, the whole thing does attain an altitude of some two thousand, one hundred, and ninety-eight rather dusty feet.

Then why, in the name of all that's confidently nautical, can't we see it now?

(Patience, friend, patience) all will be revealed in the goodness of time; believe me, one more haul spent on the course being steered, and we are *guaranteed* to make a safe landfall.

This being the time-honoured response of navigators, queried down the ages; from the endlessly questioned pilot of the outward bound Pinta [16] (who was eventually right), to the over-confident gentleman attached to Admiral Sir Cloudesley Shovell's [17] homeward-bound squadron, who turned out to be disastrously wrong.

Nevertheless, those who counsel *patience* are nearly always right.

The island does show up, roughly where you expected it, yet seems closer than imagined.

13

Not much more than three miles away, shrouded in haze, which is not the same as European fog, the wind-blown African component of this landfall having reduced the island to a softly focused tint - yet somewhere there, drifting tantalisingly in and out of billowed wraith looms the outline of the shore.

Tall buildings ghost into frame, then click into focus as nothing more romantic than the thicker lipped façades of high-rise concrete cubes (just balconied hotels).

So it's time to alter course, yet again.

Stop closing the shore (we're much too close already), because quite apart from anything else, there's bosun's work which must be attended to without further gawped delay.

Making a landfall is marvellous.

A significant geographical shift, accompanied by a genuine lift to the spirit, which provides even the blasé navigator and the crew with a totally different perspective, because in these special circumstances, you are not merely looking at an island, but the embodiment of genuine achievement. It may be modest, but it's none the less real. And there's no point in being shy about this statement, it just happens to be true, of all seamen, in all ships, down every age of man.

The Phoenicians, like the Greeks, probably had a word for it. [18]

And when you've made *your* landfall, having solved the problem (posed by Davy) [19] concerned with this significant arrival, no self-respecting matelot is going to trickle into harbour without a blast on some sort of trumpet, even if he alone can hear it, because what we're involved with here is pride in seafaring tradition - and who should be shy about that?

There's a national ensign to unfurl, carefully hitch and proudly hoist to the truck of a brightly varnished flagstaff.

There's also a courtesy flag to be selected; a Spanish ensign this time, hoisted on the starboard yardarm halyard.

And then, if you're alone, this is also the time to take a few other seamanlike precautions.

You can't just sail, as bold as brass but blundering, into a strange harbour, hoping for the best - if you do, you are certain to become involved in an incident which will live in your mind forever.

If we were aboard a proper (proper?) vessel, equipped with a radio telephone, we could make contact with the harbour master's office and obtain some useful advice. However, as we're sailing in an apparently simplistic manner this option isn't open, so our approach must be made with a certain amount of forethought, leavened with a degree of seamanlike guile.

For a start, it's time to reduce sail, get the jib down on deck, and pull down a reef in the mainsail. There's plenty of wind available, and when you enter the confines of a harbour, you want to be well in control of the boat. Able to jill about under a sensible amount of canvas - not charge around as an understudied duffer, displaying all the brazen dexterity of a butter fingered juggler.

While working on deck, this is the time to heave-to, in order that the movement of the hull is restricted to not much more than an accommodating vertical response to the surge and lurch of the swell. The margin of safety is increased when way is taken off the vessel, and it's as well to remember, that what's to be done aboard this hooker has to be done by one man, who should take care to remain in control of events.

An anchor, not necessarily the best bower [20] must be got up on deck, and an adequate amount of chain faked out of the locker, both items being shackled together and arranged along the foredeck, with everything *outside* the lifelines - so all's ready to rattle out whenever the hook is needed.

There are fenders to dig out.

During the voyage, they've been crammed away in inaccessible places (in a small boat, stowage space is at a premium), but these previously awkward items are now an essential part of harbour entry, particularly aboard a short-handed vessel where, when actually coming alongside, it may be impossible to avoid inflicting a slight bump, but hopefully not a dent in someone else's nicely varnished topsides.

The fenders, and there should be plenty of them, are best hitched to the lower run of lifelines, then kept inboard, lying in the scuppers, until it's time to kick them over the side.

What else needs to be done?

The halyards need attention.

During the passage, the spare ends have been made up in tight coils, hitched to their own cleats, well out of the way of trouble. It's now time to unhitch and lay the rope out, making absolutely sure when the halyards are let slip, the sails come down immediately - not held up by a snarl (in nautical terms, a gorgeous bunch of buggers) which could prove amusing in an embarrassing way, but also downright dangerous - so after the halyards have been cleared away, it's as well to have another look around the deck to see what else needs doing.

Now the vessel is hove-to, and no longer making way through the water, this is the time to notice the log line is still dangling from the transom, its task completed, its job well done.

This essential item of equipment should of course have been hauled aboard *before* the boat was hove-to, yet strange to say it's nearly always forgotten.

It's now the only despondent thing to be found aboard the hooker, because the overall tenor remains unassailably upbeat, and the lift occasioned by the landfall is boosted still further as the staysail sheet is eased and canvas allowed to draw, setting her moving forward, closing the shore, on this last short leg of the voyage.

Previously, the self-steering gear was in use 24 hours a day, but it's now time for the skipper to take his place at the helm, and it should be recognised that having a hand on the tiller does impart more than just a sense of responsibility. Doing your own trick, you are attached in a way significantly different from the once-removed feeling associated with overlong use of an autopilot. The feeling the helm provides, far and above the purely physical task, is nothing less than emotional involvement. And this is not star-gazed claptrap, merely an honest appreciation of the joy, the very real pleasure, offered by what may look like just a piece of timber, but is in reality the medium of the message, which is, for those fortunate enough to receive it, the simple yet enduring thrill provided by a vessel as she's worked across the well-heeled spray of a breeze.

Under reduced mainsail and staysail, the boat, while not footing as fast as she would under a press of canvas, feels balanced and responsive.

She's carrying just the right amount of weather-helm, with the tiller requiring a slight upwind pressure to keep her on course (with this well-mannered vessel, if you take your hand off the tiller, she rounds up), [21] not viciously, just a sensible alteration of course which eases the momentum until the mainsail is taken aback and starts to flog - it would seem to gain attention from the inattentive helmsman. However, our gnarled old bosun would regard this, at best, as a load of over-scented soft soap, amounting to nonsensical obeisance to an inanimate object, and take it as a sure sign that, for *that* sort of crew, *of soldiers*, the time *had* come to close the shore.

For the hopefully better balanced rest of us, while the initial landfall has been successfully accomplished and the thrill savoured, there remains the problem posed by locating the port we're bound for, so what we are looking for now is Arrecife, the commercial dockage located halfway down the eastern side of the island.

It's worth recalling, the landfall was made when closing the nor'eastern tip of Lanzarote, and the assumption could be made that if we run in a sou'westerly direction, close ashore, we will sooner or later come across the port.

But enclosed within the logic is one slight reservation.

It's true, that if the landfall has been made to the nor'ard of the dock, we could indeed run down and be certain of hitting the jetty. However, if (and it really is only a very small if) *if* our landfall was significantly further south than assumed, then, should we continue to sail even further along the tempting shore, we may not end up in Arrecife, but run out of land - fall off the end of the island, which could turn out to be something of a navigational embarrassment.

This is the sort of *could be - may be* situation, which should be resolved by careful analysis of the navigational log, particularly the entries made prior to the landfall, in order to assess what degree of perhaps recurring error had crept into the calculations.

But in the less refined world of bare bum small-boat navigation,, without a satnav and devoid of any modern navigational aid, when one man is reduced to sailing by the seat of his pants and his previously mentioned Mark One Eyeball, you often find that other methods come to be relied on.

In what is sometimes laughingly described as the final analysis, the decision often turns, not on the actual numbers in the navigational log, which logically it should do - more on the gut feeling you have been developing just below your navel; the family jewels (your balls) becoming involved because there *are* occasions, such as having to proceed in dense fog towards an inhospitable shore, when a certain amount of fortitude, otherwise described as an unshakeable belief in your own judgement is a necessary part of proceedings.

So the trick here, when running along the south eastern shore of Lanzarote, looking for Arrecife, is to recall it's still possible to fall into the same sort of awkward hole Sir Cloudesley's man fell into.

All this amounts to is - a sensible degree of doubt.

The adoption of a cautious attitude.

The sort of critical look at the odds any seaman would take before he put his neck, his boat, or anything else for that matter (let alone his balls) on any sort of line; so with the precedent acknowledged, and both eyes consequently not only open, but wide open, there's nothing over-dramatically involved when approaching Arrecife.

The land being observed is cautiously judged as being no more than *maybe* that lying to the nor'ard of the port, and seems reasonably benign.

The circumstances are such that there shouldn't be the unsprung traps, of the sort which did for Shovell, anywhere near this sun and salt vicinity. The shoreline being approached is charted clear of danger, and that being the case, it's possible to sail along admiring the view.

In a small-boat sort of a way, of course, which allows for the fact that while you have taken the trouble to read the Admiral's meant for battleships advice, it's as well to remember that someone even senior (the crafty Old Man himself) could have introduced some small print of his own. The sort of trivial, maybe awkward detail which could have escaped the official hydrographer's otherwise sea eagle eye'd attention.

Regardless of this cross eyed outlook, that can be traced to the lack of sleep occasioned by the landfall, which led to this twitch of nervous tension, what drifts into view through the still hanging about haze is a further succession of high-rise structures, that eventually form the hard edged shapes of what look like more hotels.

Then, although the visibility's not good, something else slips into focus.

A structure composed of coils of pipes, snakes of ladders, the pots of many-bellied boilers. Groups of slender fingered chimneys puff silent plumes of softly whistled steam. An apparition, that blends then fades into the haze, providing only the briefest of brief sights, little more than a glimpse, nothing more than the sleight of hand involved with the finessed display of another one of Father's tantalising clues.

But now something more substantial claims the eye; another high-rise building, this time topped by a hammer-headed crane, flanked by another brace of rusty bellied boilers - but still no breakwater, let alone a port.

Can we possibly be, sou'west'ard of harbour?

It's beginning to look like it; a glance at the chart shows there are more hotels, and the *airport* is located even further along the coast.

Time to alter course.

Bring the breeze round the stern and harden sheets to sail back up the coast. An irritating prospect, with the puff recently mentioned, concerning the care which should be taken when making an unfamiliar landfall, and all come about because the strength of the current experienced during the last day's run before making Lanzarote has been underestimated.

Yet more shades of Shovell.

Although it must be said he fell grandly into the abyss by being hopelessly wrong in his longitude, which was, to give him his due, difficult to calculate without the benefit of a reliable chronometer.

But his was the luck that bottomed-out, not ours; this sail back up the coast is easy. The breeze holds a tad south of east, which means a nor'easterly course can be maintained while the crew endures this embarrassing delay.

And the harbour at Arrecife does come eventually into view, drifting from fuzzy outline to emerging detail rather slowly, because the vessel is under-canvassed and bucking what could be almost a knot of adverse current (the price which has to be paid for making such a poor landfall), so there's an air of genuine relief when the harbour entrance is at last abeam, allowing a glimpse inside the protective arm of the mole.

A commercial port.

Several trawlers.

Vessels berthed at a jetty.

Groups of gleaming white yachts, moored in front of the club house.

A few meandering bumboats.

A harbour launch, smart about its business.

A trawler entering, another leaving.

The usual nautical jumble presented for appraisal when entering a strange port, sometimes offering a degree of genuine confusion, but a view which does sustain the good sense of the previously taken decision. To reduce sail, get the boat under easy canvas, and clear of the harbour mouth while others are using the entrance; then, once the channel is clear, the crew put about the task of assessing the right approach.

This may seem little more than an exploratory run, before the breeze, into the harbour itself. A cautious tactic, which allows the skipper time to get it all in focus; and having made the judgement, tack, and make a close-hauled leg back out.

An apparent retreat, which may seem too timid for words.

It's nothing of the kind.

It's a sensible reconnaissance, that leads to the conclusion there's not much bed and board available. The commercial jetty's in use, and is in any case much too high, dusty, and dirty, to provide a comfortable overnight stay for our pride and joy of a shell.

Another possible location, amongst the moored yachts, requires careful consideration.

The smarts are close together, grouped about an inner basin, not difficult to approach, yet presenting something of a problem to anyone in charge of a vessel without an auxiliary motor. Dependent entirely on the breeze, progress is easy enough to make, but sometimes difficult to arrest, the resultant crunch being best avoided if there's a better berth to go to.

What about the fenders?

They should be left in the scuppers because, when entering harbour and intending to anchor, rather than going directly alongside, nothing looks worse than a bunch of slipshod fenders being dragged along the waterline of an otherwise shipshape vessel.

No: what needs to be undertaken now, while still outside the harbour, is another reduction in canvas.

The jib has been handed, so it can be unhanked from the forestay, stuffed in its bag, and shoved down the for'ard hatch (this rough and ready nautical housekeeping clearing away the foredeck). And getting the staysail down improves the view still further. However, this sail is left on its stay, retained on deck, immediately available if needed in a perhaps lack of wind emergency. This sensible rearrangement being undertaken well clear of the harbour entrance, and carefully upwind of it, so the boat is now under a mainsail alone and not feeling anywhere near as responsive as she did when benefiting from a balanced double-headed rig. Yet under this reduced amount of canvas, she's still able to run and reach across the breeze, even work slowly to windward, should the need arise.

The other advantage offered by the clearing of headsails is the increased arc of visibility available to the busy helmsman.

Previously, when under mainsail, staysail and jib, it's difficult to obtain a clear view to leeward, because the cut of the headsails, particularly the sweeping foot of the staysail, drags low across the foredeck. In a fully-crewed vessel this doesn't present a problem - the skipper merely instructs a reliable member of the crew to keep a sharp eye hitched to leeward, and that's the difficulty and the danger largely overcome.

However, when you're alone, this option isn't available.

The single-handed skipper who's daft enough to enter harbour under a press of canvas, is reduced to peering anxiously under the foot of a staysail which is all too often awash. In these careless circumstances, it's easy to remain blissfully unaware of an approaching vessel, and within a breathless minute, you find your backside forming buttons as a large trawler pops up from under your blindside lee and less than a boat's crunch of shouting length ahead.

There's also another seamanlike reason for this latest, penultimate reduction in sail. Apart from anything else, and perhaps rather prosaically, the vessel's angle of heel is reduced, making the stroll along the side deck easy enough to accomplish, in order to be absolutely sure, yet again, that the anchor and chain are cleared away and everything's ready to slip.

There's also the mainsail halyard to check, the spare amount taken off the cleat, and the resulting bight of rope faked out over the cabin top, all ready to run.

Has anything been forgotten?

Before returning aft, it may be as well to temporarily hitch the necessary sail ties to the topmost run of lifelines, to make sure that, when the mainsail is handed, they will be handy-by when needed to secure the flapping canvas, prior to undertaking the later, leisurely, proper harbour-job stow.

Anything else?

It may be verging on the pernickety, even seem fuss-arsed, but now is the time to dig out the ship's best heaving line.

During the passage, this special bit of monkey-fisted rope [22] has been stowed in the bosun's locker, and the uninitiated may think it might as well remain there, having assumed that because the vessel is about to be anchored, there seems little reason to expect a heaving line will be needed. But our wise old bosun would growl away at this, and insist the line be coiled down on the cockpit sole, *with the end well secured*, so that if (the self-same, endlessly-recurring, but oh so seamanlike *if*) the unexpected happens, the mad scramble to find a decent bit of rope isn't left to the ham-fisted forage of bunglers.

One last thing.

Before entering an unfamiliar port, *always* have a look at the harbour plan, which is normally displayed in a convenient corner of the large scale chart of the area. Some of the things to look for are - places designated *prohibited anchorage,* together with those seemingly innocuous lines cartographers prick in as *submarine cables*.

And there may be other items which help you decide where to go and, just as importantly, where *not* to go, with the upshot being that having absorbed this further information, you are now as well prepared to enter the confines of the port as you are ever likely to be.

Making the climb back on deck, from this valuable perusal of the chart, something which can be undertaken with confidence.

And what a pleasure it is to have done the essential bits of homework.

To know, in this nautical context, exactly what's expected, so entering harbour no longer presents a problem which becomes more intricate as the view inside the breakwater is revealed in all its complexity. Takes the shape of a familiar jigsaw, with just the one piece missing; that one piece being nothing more complicated than the vessel you are sailing towards this easy turn of events.

Could anything *be* easier?

It all fits so neatly into place.

The breeze fills the mainsail.

The boat moves ahead.

The commercial scene unfolds.

The fact that the harbour is as cluttered as it appeared to be when the initial reconnaissance took place is neither here nor there.

There is the suitable anchorage, located, so it seems, at the centre of your mind's selective eye. A place which is tucked modestly away, clear of the commercial jetty, out of the smelly reach of trawlers, within easy-going hail of white and welcoming yachts.

Inside the breakwater, the harbour presents an oily corner or two. It also offers a haven, in marked contrast to the heave of yesterday's swell, that just about forgotten movement having been cordoned off by the protective arm of the mole.

So all we have to do is manoeuvre the boat to the place where the anchor needs to be dropped, a task which seems, and is, ridiculously easy.

A reach across the breeze, while easing the mainsheet, *to slow the old tub down.*

Having spilled enough wind, a nonchalant push on the tiller, *to round the hooker up.*

Then walk, *don't hurry*, just stroll to the mainsail halyard.

Two more steps on the foredeck, *to let slip the anchor and chain.*

And while this useful item is rattling down its predetermined amount (*three times the depth of water*) just walk back and pull down what remains of the mainsail.

The sail ties are handy enough.

Anything else?

wouldn't most people look forward to a stroll on the welcoming shore ?

CHAPTER ONE: PAGE NOTES

(1) Page 1. Line 27 .... *'if you are not an ETA-targeted Spaniard'*.

The Basque separatist movement, known as *Euzkadi ta Azkatasuna* (translated as *Basque Homeland and Liberty*) is the development of an organisation that dates back to 1890, with ETA being shorthand for the subversive cadre that has fought a protracted campaign in order to secure their political ends, which are apparently not satisfied with a significant degree of autonomy, but require the creation of a separate State - a concept which the Spanish Government has so far resolutely opposed. The ETA strategy has been marked by violence that has targeted not only the Spanish establishment (Politicians, Police, Army Officers, etc) but by the use of car-bombs and other explosive devices maimed and killed innocent people, and while this resort to terror is meant to influence the political outcome, it is arguably counter-productive, quite apart from the fact that it besmirches the otherwise good name of those people who are proud to call themselves Basque.

(2) Page 3. Line 3 .... *'Ferdinand de Lesseps'*.

The French citizen who conceived and supervised the construction of the Suez Canal, the artificial waterway connecting the Mediterranean and the Red Sea. The work took 10 years, and was finally completed on November 17th 1869. The canal is 99 miles long, had initially a depth of 33 feet and a minimum width of 198 feet; vessels equipped with searchlights can traverse the waterway in approximately 15 hours.

(3) Page 3. Line 25 .... *'The Venturesome Voyages of Captain Voss'*.

One of the standard volumes in any mariner's library. The captain hailed from British Columbia, and although he may have been short of height (less than 5 feet tall) he was not short of much else, apart from perhaps an adequate supply of capital, but that didn't deter him from cruising the Pacific in a dugout canoe.

When negotiating the eastern seaboard of Australia he impressed the locals by demonstrating the qualities of his craft, and his own seafaring skills by bringing *Tilikum* over the dangerous sandbars which obstruct the entrances to many of the east coast estuaries. He used a sea-anchor, equipped with a trip line, and when the destructive breaker (an endlessly recurring threat) had passed under the hull of his small vessel, the venturesome captain 'tripped the anchor' and proceeded through the surf, no doubt waving in a confident manner to the dubious crowd on the shore.

(4) Page 3. Line 26 .... *'Cruising All Seas in the Idle Hour'*.

The author, Dwight Long, was an American citizen who completed a small boat circumnavigation prior to World War 2. He spent considerable time in the South Pacific, where he befriended a Polynesian boy, taking him on as crew; sadly, this youngster died in Europe and was buried far from home.

(5) Page 3. Line 27 ………. *'Sailing Alone Around the World'*.

The author, **Joshua SLOCUM** (1844-1909) has the distinction of being the lead figure of a whole raft of seafaring literature, this being the case because he was the first man to sail around the world alone, in a boat he built himself. Having completed the solo circumnavigation, he wrote *'Sailing Alone Around the World'*, with the volume now heading a body of work having a similar nautical background.

Captain Slocum was born in Nova Scotia, but took American citizenship early in his career, which was concerned with sail in one commercial form or another, even though he was the son of a man who earned his own hard-won living from the land. At one time Slocum had climbed the ladder sufficiently to become Master and proud part owner of the fully-rigged ship *Northern Light*, and later he owned the bark *Aquidneck*; but somewhere along the line the vessels grew smaller, until, as he says, *'times grew hard, and what was I to do?'* He was not in any doubt of his ability, declaring he had *'studied the sea, as few men have studied it, neglecting all else'*, so he found it natural to stick to the thing he knew best - shouldering the task of building his own boat, the *Spray*; and then, suitably equipped, spent three years circumnavigating the globe, supporting himself by lecturing to audiences who grew more numerous and enthusiastic as the voyage progressed.

The book he wrote is still worth reading, just as long as we keep in mind the old dog's salty inclination to gild the lily, if only just a little bit.

(6) Page 3. Line 31 ……… *'The Cruise of the Teddy'*.

This book features as Number 5 in *The Mariner's Library*, first published (1933) by Rupert Hart-Davies Ltd., 53 Connaught Street, London W 2. The author, **Erling TAMBS**, was a Norwegian writer who set out in 1928 with his wife (but no sailing experience) intending to circumnavigate the globe. His friends said of Erling, *'though he never made the same mistake twice - he never seemed to run out of mistakes to make'*; nevertheless, he was a popular figure about the Sydney waterfront, and was admired by everyone who knew him. The introduction to *The Cruise of the Teddy*, by the great Arthur Ransome, leaves you in no doubt this is first class seafaring adventure.

(7) Page 4. Line 3 ……*'the wail, prompted by the claim made at the wall of Jerusalem'*.

JERUSALEM: the settlement dates from the Stone Age, and urban development was mentioned in documents as far back as 1400 B.C.

The city was captured by David about 1000 B.C. and became the national centre for the Jews. Solomon, amongst others, built a temple, and at the time when the palatinate was part of the Roman Empire, the crucifixion of Christ took place in Jerusalem.

The Roman Emperor Titus destroyed the city in A.D. 70; but it was rebuilt by Hadrian. Some 200 years later Constantine the Great built a church on the site of the Holy Sepulchre.

For the next 1,700 years its prosperity depended largely on the influx of European pilgrims, and this practice was allowed to continue by the Arabs after they took the city in 637 A.D.. However, there was ultimately a change of policy, with Christians being treated as persona non-grata, and this prompted the First Crusade, with the outcome being that Jerusalem was recovered, and from 1099 to 1187 was the capital of a Latin kingdom. The Moslems reconquered the territory in 1517 and it became a Turkish possession until, during the First World War, British troops reoccupied it in 1917.

The present development has areas devoted to Jews, Armenians, Christians, and Mohammedans, with the Wailing Wall being sacred to the Jews and the focus of ideological differences between the religious sects. The Arabs staking their claim and designating the city El Kuds (the Sanctuary) with the mosque of Omar featuring prominently in their religious observance.

The modern state of Israel claims Jerusalem as its capital, while the Arabs, as the result of endless conflict (and massive financial and political intervention from American Jewry) have been effectively dispossessed of a significant proportion of what they regard as their ancestral lands. The other way of putting this is - that Jerusalem has been, and will no doubt remain, a flashpoint and grave example of the destructive clash of religious intolerance.

DAVID: biblical character, the youngest son of Jesse, who was anointed as Saul's successor to the kingdom, in the defence of which he slew the giant Goliath. He is regarded as the founder of the royal line to which Jesus Christ reputedly belonged.

Michelangelo's statue of David is regarded as one of the worlds artistic masterpieces.

SOLOMON: King of Israel, son of David and Bathsheba: his reign (c 974 B.C. to c 937 B.C.) was relatively peaceful and he was able to conducted extensive foreign commerce. The Old Testament book known as the *Song of Solomon* is now considered a secular poem, wrongly attributed to him.

(8) Page 6. Line 6 .... *'Old Man with the trident'*.

The *Old Man* in this instance is Neptune, the Roman god of the sea (known to the Greeks as *Poseidon*) usually represented as an elderly person, bearded, equipped with a trident, and often mounted on a dolphin - sometimes riding a monster having the head and forequarters of a horse, but with the tail and hindquarters of a fish.

(9) Page 7. Line 20 .... *'Bosun's gnarled old fingers'*.

The crewmember known as a 'bosun' should perhaps be more correctly described as a 'boatswain' - although this archaic term has fallen into disuse and been displaced by the colloquialism. The Shorter Oxford defines both terms as descriptive of a ship's officer, with special duties concerning the mustering of the crew by use of 'bosun's pipes'. However, in modern usage, the bosun is not correctly classified as a ship's officer. He is not a member of the 'after-guard', as are deck officers and certificated engineers, but is a senior member of that group which would in army terms be described as non-commissioned officers (sergeants, corporals etc.). Nevertheless, he is a important member of a ship's company, and an enduring relationship between the first mate and the bosun is a vital part of good ship management.

(10) Page 7. Line 20 .... *'a midshipman tends the sand glass'*.

The term 'midshipman' is common usage in the Royal Navy but rarely used in the Merchant Service where the approximate equivalent to an RN midshipman would be the indentured apprentice. In the Senior Service the rank falls between that of a naval cadet and a sub-lieutenant, and derives from the bygone action-station positioning of the midshipmen in the 'middle' of the vessel. In the U.S. navy the term 'ensign' equates to a midshipman.

(11) Page 7. Line 32 .... *'great circle of the earth'*.

A *great circle* is any circle that has as its centre - the centre of the earth - and as its *radius*, the distance from the centre, to the surface of the earth.

(12) Page 8. Line 16 .... *'magnetic variation, deviation, leeway, drift'*.

Magnetic variation is the angular difference between *true* north and magnetic north; it varies from place to place, and forms one of the items provided to the navigator by his charts. **Deviation** is the angular distance between *magnetic* north and the direction indicated by a compass needle, with this discrepancy being due to the vessel's own magnetic field. **Leeway** is the lateral movement of a ship to leeward (being blown across and down wind) of her desired course. **Drift** is the term applied when a vessel is carried along by a current.

(13) Page 9. Line 3 .... *'along with Watson'*.

A reference to the character created by the Scottish writer, **Arthur Conan DOYLE** (1859-1930) who was born in Edinburgh of Irish parentage. Having studied medicine, and set up practice in Southsea, he took to writing in order to supplement his income, with early work being published in *Chamber's Journal* in 1879. Although his novels were successful, his real claim to fame became the super-sleuth Sherlock

Holmes, along with his faithful but perhaps not quite so brilliant companion Doctor Watson. Having established the genre, Doyle produced a series of detective stories, some of which were serialized in the Strand Magazine between 1891 and 1893.

Conan Doyle was a man of wide-ranging talents - he supervised a mobile hospital in the Boer war (1899-1902); he also stood, unsuccessfully, for parliament, played cricket for the MCC, and championed what were at the time regarded as avant-garde projects, amongst them being a Channel Tunnel and modernisation of the then archaic laws relating to marriage and divorce.

Towards the end of his amazingly productive and well rewarded life (he was knighted in 1902) he was certainly influenced by the death of his son during the First World War. Thereafter he devoted a significant portion of his substantial fortune to the promotion of spiritualism, exemplified by his unshakeable belief that the dead can be contacted through what many of his contemporaries saw as the dubious offices of 'mediums', some of whom (many of whom), most of whom (all of whom?) turned out to be charlatans.

(14) Page 9. Line 18 ………. 'Harmattan'.

Derived from the West African term *haramata*; a dry wind which prevails during the months of December, January, and February on the coast of Upper Guinea. In extreme conditions, the air is full of red dust, with visibility badly effected.

(15) Page 13. Line 20 ………. 'aground on the coral, before you're in sight of the motu'.

The term 'motu' stems from Polynesian usage, and describes an accumulation of soil, vegetation, and palms that collectively make up an island, perched on the top of a reef, which otherwise may only break surface on the ebbing of the tide.

(16) Page 13. Line 33 ………. 'The Pilot of the Pinta'.

A reference to one of the ships, the *Pinta*, which Christopher Columbus had in his fleet of 3 small vessels on his epic voyage of discovery, having sailed from the port of Palos on August 3, 1492, looking for the New World. No doubt there were many anxious questions posed of this particular pilot, before they eventually made a landfall on what is now known as the Bahamas.

When Joshua Slocum was on his historic 1895-1898 first ever single-handed voyage around the world, he visited the Azores, and while there was generously entertained by the local population. Amongst the many gifts received by the gallant captain from the people of Horta was a plentiful supply of fresh plums, and when leaving the neighbouring island of Pico he was presented with a quantity of white cheese by no less a person than General Manning, the American consul general serving on the island. Slocum says he assumed the cheese was fit to be eaten, together with the plums; but this turned out to be a mistake. Having over-indulged, he was struck down with a bout of vomiting, so severe he was forced to take to his bunk, where he was visited by an apparition, who turned out to be *The Pilot of the Pinta*. This gent, apparition or not, proved a first rate seaman who steered *Spray* throughout the night, running before a gale of wind which raised a sea bad enough to threaten the safety of the vessel. Come morning, and having made some sort of a recovery, Slocum says he was astonished to find his vessel, having been so grossly over-canvassed, was still afloat; and further on than that, he was convinced *'Columbus himself could not have held her more exactly on the course I had previously plotted'*. Slocum's only complaint (and this really is the cap of a quite delightful story) he was *amazed*, having weathered such a storm-wracked night, prostrate in his bunk, and so dependent on the Pilot - he was amazed the phantom hadn't had sense enough to *'reduce sail, and so relieve the vessel'*.

(17) Page 13. Line 35 .... *'Admiral Sir Cloudesley Shovell'*.

Born in Norfolk, November 1650, Shovell was brought up in relatively poor circumstances; nevertheless, having joined the Navy in 1664 as a boy, he worked his way from the lower deck; with favourable patronage was promoted lieutenant in 1673, and then served in the Mediterranean with distinction, attaining the rank of captain in 1677. He was knighted for his service at the battle of Bantry Bay in 1689; in 1690 was promoted Rear Admiral of the Blue and took part in the battle of Beachy Head. In 1704 he played a significant role in the capture of Gibraltar and commanded the van at the battle of Malaga, with his only notable career failure being an unsuccessful attack on Toulon in 1707.

In the same year, on the night of October 2, when returning from the Mediterranean, and attempting a thick weather run-in from the western approaches to a landfall on the Lizard, bound ultimately for Plymouth, a navigational error brought about the destruction of a substantial part of the Admiral's fleet. The mistake was largely the result of being unable, in that age, to accurately compute a vessel's longitude. Those on board the flagship believed they were on track, when in fact they were so far adrift the squadron was set ashore, at the height of a howling gale, and in the pitch black middle of a dismal night, on one of the many off-lying reefs which surround the Isles of Scilly. The lead vessel, the *Association* and two other ships, the *Eagle* and the *Romney* were lost, virtually with all hands. Two thousand seamen were drowned, with very few men washed ashore alive, one of them being the Admiral himself.

Legend has it that a local woman, coming across Sir Cloudesley prostrate on the sand, noticed a fine emerald glinting on his finger - but instead of offering help, greed overcame compassion and this harpy murdered Shovell and pocketed the ring. She admitted the crime some thirty years later, confessing on her death bed, being unable to rest until she had surrendered her prize, which she offered as proof, not only of her disgraceful conduct but, as she then saw it, a means of contrition to set against her damnable behaviour.

(18) Page 14. Line 21 ...... *'the Phoenicians, like the Greeks, probably had a word for it'.*

Known as the *Sidonians* in biblical times, the Phoenicians founded Carthage and were recognised as the most proficient seamen of their period, journeying as far as Cornwall, where they traded for tin. Their principle export was a rich dye (Tyrian purple) named after one of their cities. Their place in history ended with the fall of Tyre to Alexander the Great in 332 B.C.

(19) Page 14. Line 23 ...... *'Davy (Jones)'.*

The seafaring term for what is assumed to be the *evil spirit of the sea*. A possible source of the phrase being *Davy* as a corruption of the West Indian word *duppy* (meaning a devil) and the name *Jones* derived from *Jonah*. The concept dates back at least to the 18th century and has become part of seafaring lore; but it also brings into question - if it's rational, in this age, to assume that the sea harbours an inverted deity of this sort?

(20) Page 15. Line 16 .... *'not necessarily the best bower'.*

The well-found seagoing vessel is equipped with at least three anchors - the *best bower* being first choice in normal circumstances - while the *second best bower* (both anchors being readily available) would be put into service should the vessel make a running moor (i.e. use two anchors). The third anchor would be lighter than the bowers (a kedge) and used primarily to warp the vessel about in lack of wind conditions, or perhaps anchor temporarily, waiting for the tide. In old-fashioned usage, the term *sheet anchor* is used to describe the best anchor aboard - the choice in dire emergency, with the description dating back to the medieval *'shute-anchor'.*

(21) Page 16. Line 29 .... *'she rounds up'.*

The term describes the reflex action of a vessel, when either close-hauled or reaching across a breeze. In these conditions, when the helmsman takes his hand off the tiller, a well-mannered boat will round up (come up into the wind) in marked contrast to those cows who pay off - thus risking an uncontrolled gybe (defined as bringing a boomed, or a loose-footed sail, crashing from one side of the boat to the other).

(22) Page 21 Line 18 .... *'this special bit of monkey-fisted rope'.*

A fanciful description for a heaving line, with the word *monkey* derived from the name of the knot tied at the end of the rope. This knot, known as a 'monkey's fist' was first described in a seaman's handbook written by Captain **E.N.LITTLE**, published in 1889, and titled *Log Book Notes* - although the knot must have been in use long before that date, even though unrecorded in earlier manuals. The knot has three parallel parts, and an experienced seaman ties a fist by casting the necessary turns around the fingers of his left hand (if he's right-handed) while keeping the middle finger and his ring finger slightly apart. He then adds three more turns at right-angles to the first three turns (and *through* the fingers which were separated) while the final three turns are wound *outside* the second three turns - but *inside* the first three turns. The knot is then worked-up (tightened) after having a piece of lead incorporated within the ball in order to provide the impetus required for the 'flight' to be successful. This may sound a complicated procedure, when in practice, it isn't all that difficult.

Anyone interested in rope work could do no better than consult *The Ashley Book of Knots*, first published in 1944 by Doubleday, Doran & Company Inc., New York, and then issued in the U.K. in 1947, and reprinted many times since by Faber & Faber Ltd., 3 Queen Square, London. W.C.1. The book, eleven years in the making, is an undoubted masterpiece, containing detailed descriptions of over 3,800 different knots, bends, splices, sinnets, and decorative rope work. If it *has* a limiting factor, it is sheer size (over 600 pages, in hard cover 11" x 9" format) so there remains a place for a handy book which can be slipped into a pocket. Amongst the dozens available *The Guide to Knots* by *Mario Bigon* and *Guido Regazzoni*, translated from the original Italian by *Maria Piotrowska*, and published by Century is not only as good as any, but better than most. The photographic illustrations are excellent, and the coverage includes sailing, fishing, camping, and climbing.

However, **Clifford ASHLEY'S** work remains supreme, displaying as it does a complete mastery of his subject, combined with a ready wit and a deft touch with a pencil (look out, particularly, for his illustrated Chapter Headings).

WHAT *NOT* TO DO WHEN YOU ARRIVE

ANY lone individual, arrived at a distant port, no matter how easy the previous down wind passage, can surely expect to experience a certain amount of - shall we just say *satisfaction*?

Regardless that the weather has been almost entirely benign, and the Old Man with his alarming trident apparently away on a rare enough holiday, the single-handed seaman would be a strange animal indeed if, after successfully running a nautical gauntlet, he found himself totally devoid of an immodest sense of achievement. Of course, whether he would be wise in this assessment of his own worth is something which could be examined at a more convenient date (with the hope that he will be forgiven for casting himself as something of a hero) - perhaps not quite on the scale of Horatius, but you do feel, while you may not have *actually* defended the bridge, you have at most certainly crossed one [1] and this in itself should be the matter of some congratulation.

However, alongside the temptation, which should be avoided if you have been fortunate enough to perceive it, there is a positive development, because the ocean wanderer, who may have been satisfied with an introspective stance, is now apt to be more aware of the gregarious side of his nature, and this is pointed up by the privacy on offer when lying anchored-off. In this relatively isolated position, you are partially withdrawn from the day to day running of the port, and it's hard to view the scene with anything less than a certain amount of detachment.

Yet the harbour is busy enough.

The previously identified 'steamers at a jetty' turn out to be sizable commercial vessels, loading and discharging cargo.

The trawlers, still coming and going, add their delicate scent of success to the otherwise busy scene, while at the other end of the spectrum, in the charmingly well mannered way which has ensured they are all upwind of the fish dock, the yachts are defensively grouped in front of the local club. A strategic deployment which prompts the thought that getting away from your own boat may be a well earned release from confinement, particularly as the craft is small, and you have just completed a passage. So it's not long before the dinghy's been inflated, launched, and the row ashore made to the accommodating jetty.

At one time Arrecife must have conveyed a hardbitten, dusty, and entrepreneurial air, because the Spaniards, who were and still are magnificent seamen, arrived here by reason of the immense variety of fish to be found about these islands - the amazingly productive waters between Lanzarote and the mainland. Nevertheless, while this hard worked industry remains, even if threatened with decline, air travel, combined with the all-embracing packaged tour, has spread its bland but distorting features, to the extent that the visitor is confronted with a series of high-rise hotels on either side of the town.

All laudable enough, of course (I suppose everyone should speak for themselves), but after you have made your number with the Port Captain, it's time for a beer and, surprise, surprise, it seems difficult to avoid the glitz and find what used to be recognised as an old-fashioned Jack Tar's bar. (2)

Yet it's worth continuing the search, moving from the main drag until the streets narrow, the cobbles roughen, and the encroaching walls display the pock marked age countless applications of slaked lime have done their best to soften in the sun.

The entrance, when you come to it, is two-part 'stabled,' and located on the shady side of the street. The lower door well enough hung, but the upper left ajar, no doubt because when closed, the fit of the two halves and the thrust of the bolt between them bars some poor soul from entry.

Inside, the room is long, blessed with a high ceiling, and slowly revolving fans that are doing their best to deal with the haze of today's tobacco smoke, the breath of yesterday's ale, and the unforgiving reek of an atmosphere produced by over-indulged consumption of the rougher sort of blood-red Spanish wine.

The customers are a mixed lot, grouped about tables of varying size and haphazardly located, they are, to a man, men - not a woman in sight, not even behind the bar, where a swarthy, apron-girt, and undeniably pot-bellied individual waits the call of his trade.

About the room, below the hum of conversation, comes the constant click of counters, and for those of sharper hearing, the softly fingered shuffle as a dog-eared knave falls quietly on a wine stained mahogany top.

Having entered, the stranger may feel somewhat inhibited - where to go presents something of a problem.

He would be pushing his luck if he elbowed his way amongst the people who are intent on protecting their cards, and the domino players are an even tighter clique, hedged about with grunts, the occasional oath, and a resigned look at the unforgiving ceiling - as a reluctant player is forced to make a move he hopes isn't going to favour his opponent over the chance he would obviously prefer for himself.

The bar top reflects the atmosphere, it is purposeful rather than inviting, consisting of a length of timber that has been haphazardly designed to do little more than support the height and weight of an elbow.

Strategically placed on this care worn altar are rows of special offerings.

Fish in place of peanuts, grey finned shapes swimming just below the surface of bowls full of sticky olive oil (a sharp-eyed seaman may notice the occasional fleck of tobacco ash) but the sardines seem healthy enough.

Above the bar, suspended from racks, but within easy reach of the barman, hang a selection of scarlet skinned salami - spotted here and there by the occasional buzz of a fly.

Behind the salami, a magnificent series of home cured hams swing from hooks that have been securely fixed to the ceiling, and the brown skinned hams display, as part of the curing and drying process, an ooze of fat which glistens with an extruded layer of salt.

The effect is overwhelming.

A festoon, not of baskets full of flowers, but a hanging garden of pig meat, amounting to a bacchanalian scene [3] enveloped by the sound of drinks being poured, and food being eaten, amid the clatter of hard-earned money about to be carelessly wagered on the reckless turn of a card.

Could Babylon have bettered it?

The ideal place for the just-arrived seaman, who is yet to be dissuaded that fortune favours the brave.

The barman is busy, serving drinks, and passing orders to his knife-wielding assistant.

A ham has been taken down from the ceiling, and is being sliced, then carefully arranged, layer after appetizing layer on plates burdened with small rolls of freshly baked brown bread. When the rolls are broken open their wheaten smell mingles with generously portioned, freshly cut, lightly cured ham.

What a combination!

Who could possibly resist it?

Yet trying to catch the barman's eye is a time-taking process, there's competition from several other customers, all of whom are locals who assume they head the queue, until at last your turn does come.

'En que puedo servile, Senor?' (not all that difficult, even if you haven't got the lingo).

In any case, a smiling request for a beer, in English, is plain speaking to an attentive barman in any commercial port in the world.

'Que cerveza apetece?' (this is problematical).

Behind the bar are rows of glass-fronted fridges, well stocked with dozens of canned and bottled ale, mostly of Spanish origin (no worries with that) because it presents the visitor with something which can be tentatively approached.

'Do you have a pint bottle of Newcastle Forest Brown?'

Now, it must be admitted this is little more than an attempt at a monoglotted joke.

Here we are, off the coast of Africa, just twenty nine degrees north of the equator, not far from the sweating Tropic of Cancer. The temperature, regardless of the slowly rotating fans, is in the upper eighties. The bar obviously caters for locals who, to say the very least, are unlikely to display an enduring preference for Newcastle Forest Brown (which as *we* all know is a northerly ale, designed to delay the onset of frostbite to the extremities of those dedicated football fans who are prepared to brave the winter blast of terraces).

So if the beer isn't suitable: why ask for it?

Perhaps for the very devil of it.

For the pleasure of delivering a throwaway line which contains an outrageous request.

The sort of remark a solitary, maybe defensive individual finds himself making when he lands in foreign parts and has yet to find his feet. Also, the request may have been prompted because there's the tinge of an atmosphere here that has nothing to do with the climate.

At first glance, this place appeared to be what was being tramped about for, yet it now seems there could be more to it than that, because while this is a seaman's bar, and as such an acceptable haven, overlaying the judgement is the doubt that a stranger may not be entirely welcome, yet the barman is doing his best.

'Newcastle Brown? Newcastle Brown? Nunca he oido hablar de la cerveza llamada, Newcastle Brown?' (not easy).

Nevertheless containing a glimmer of light, because there's a quizzical look accompanying the rhythm of the utterance which provides its own clue, with part of the telegraphed message being - maybe the world isn't quite so small as you previously assumed it to be, and also, in a satisfyingly convoluted way, that you were damned sure this side of maybe he wouldn't have heard of Forest Brown in the first place (else why ask for it?).

But it's important to get this relationship off on the right foot.

Bars and barmen are important institutions.

To row ashore, clear your papers with immigration, and then muff a chance of meeting at least some members of the local community would be nothing less than a travelling disaster. So the best thing to do is smile, then make an appreciative movement with your hand, while pointing to the nearest beer-stocked fridge, at the same time conveying, by the manipulation of an eyebrow and a facial gesture which would receive tribute from no less an actor than Gielgud [4] that you don't really mind what sort of beer you get, just so long as it's cool.

This does take a certain amount of practice, but having mastered it, it's possible to feel, when you actually get your beer, you certainly deserve it.

But is the wait worth while?

Indubitably (and get the practised boozer's emphasis just right), *indubitably*, because there's a particular tang to a first cool beer being sampled by a just-ashore seaman who's had his taste buds titivated by a thousand hard-won miles of ocean passage - even the way he lifts the sweating glass to his lips illustrates the gravity of the occasion, and included in this assessment is the strength of the beer itself.

Alcohol is funny stuff; alongside everything else, it provides those special keys that all too often should be left hanging on the protruding nails which are meant to hold together our skeleton-laden cupboards, but when removed, these masked instruments are used to try, then pick, so many diverse locks, with this well illustrated by the confident way that, now the first alcoholic sip's been taken, it's so much easier to turn around and look about the room.

The first impression was accurate enough - it *is* a large, smoke-filled joint, made just about acceptable because of the high ceiling, and the idle manner in which the slowly rotating fans are attempting to bestir the tobacco tainted air.

For the totally committed non-smoker the polluted atmosphere is an immediate turn-off, a place which should be vacated, and not a minute too soon. For the rest of us, who hate tobacco smoke, yet are prepared to accept that everyone should be allowed to go to hell in his own particular basket, what's on display is worth a second look.

The people who are playing dominoes inhabit their own well protected enclave - the sort of place where, to gain entry a stranger would need a passport, and a special visa issued and stamped by his own commonly acknowledged grandmother before he could rely on a welcome.

The card players are a more amenable lot, and amongst this group are people dotted about the tables who may not even be Spaniards.

Over in the corner, furthest away from the bar, are three individuals who appear to be playing pontoon (*vingt et un* to the rest of us).

All three are well past the first attractive flush of youth, are perhaps not all that successful in their various attempts to hold back the threat of advancing middle age. One of them is certainly not a local, sitting, but leaning back in his chair he's a distinctive figure - sandy haired, pale skinned, freckle faced, angularly framed, and from this distance, quietly but abrasively spoken, an unusual, but still recognisable combination.

Is he a Scot? (a better than even money bet).

The person running the 'bank' at this stage of their game is a neat looking man, dark haired, with a well trimmed beard and Faustian look.

He's living up to his distinctive appearance by manipulating the pack in an alarmingly professional manner - the speed with which he cuts, shuffles and distributes the cards is apt to leave the curious onlooker wondering - what else is he bound to be better than good at?

The third man sitting at the table is altogether different.

This player is boyish in appearance; he is seated opposite the banker, holding his hand of cards in front of his face; in so careless a manner that even a cross-eyed huckster would be offered the opportunity of a peek in what might be deemed the wrong direction. But what seems attractive about the personality is, he knows this to be the case, yet is easy going enough to discount the probability, and the game is proceeding pleasantly enough.

The banker, who could be a Frenchman, is asking the Scot (?) if he wants another card; but the invitation is cautiously avoided on the dubious ground that it's not actually his turn, so it's now up to the boyish-looking player.

He could be a Swede; bold forehead, blond hair, dressed in shirt and shorts; not smoking, yet seems handy enough with his elbow - with a broad smile he asks the banker to twist him a card from the deck, and almost inevitably, he's bust, but not the least disgruntled.

So it's now the turn of the Scot to chance his arm.

'I'll try just the one wee card, thank you, Jacque.'

Before the words have left his mouth what's been asked for has been flipped across, and has landed, spinning, in front of the player. In marked contrast to the deliberate movement of the recipient, who leans forward, stretches cautiously out, then uses the tip of a reluctant finger to pull the card carefully, face down, towards the edge of the table.

The way in which he manipulates his ill-concealed anxiety, towards the precipice of his anticipated failure, is not in any way relieved by the use of his thumb to expose the overhanging, dog-eared corner of the pasteboard.

He *levers* the edge of the card from the surface of the table, as if it had been *glued* there, to reveal, by way of a facial grimace, that the worst of his fears have been fatally confirmed.

'Aye, too many; only *one* too many, mind you - yet too many it is. You have the luck of the devil, Jacque, there's no mistake about that.'

Smiles all round (not quite so pronounced on the face of the Scot) who gets to his feet, throwing his losing hand of cards down, but not rudely down on the table in front of the banker, who recovers the coins just wagered and lost with a practised sweep of his hand.

'Time for another round: same again, Sven? And for you Jacque?'

Now if you are the sort of foot loose ocean wanderer who has just arrived in a foreign port, having spent several weeks at sea in something approaching uncomfortable, not to say tedious circumstances (small-boat sailing being what it is) this is not the time to recall your dear old Granny's well meant yet nevertheless limiting advice, concerning the evils of drink, knaves in the pack, entrapment by strangers, and the unspoken risks which might be involved in being smilingly invited to join them.

That cautionary tale has somehow faded, because the question that has risen to the top of *your* pack is - how do you get into the game?

The Scot is approaching the bar, as indeed he's obliged to, there being a discriminatory as well as only a limited amount of finger-beckoned table service available in this down to earth taberna. He's carrying three empty glasses, and must have somewhere to put them - by merely moving aside it's possible to create space, which is nothing less than an invitation for him to head for this section of the bar. It works like a charm, because only a gump is going to approach a counter and then, having had an opening made, ignore the opportunity so conveniently presented, the forthcoming nod of appreciation is all that's needed to get your exploratory foot in the door.

'You seem to have a nice little school going there.'

'Aye.'

This might sound monosyllabic, yet it's a long way from being a rebuff, rather to the contrary, because contained in the burr is the hint of appreciation; an acknowledgement, that it *is* a good school.

'Can anyone join?'

This is much too quick off the mark. An opening gambit which takes a risk, with the outcome depending on any one of a host of unknown prejudices (you can almost hear the wheels whirring) and while he waits for the barman's attention, what you get is a speculative glance.

'Been here long?'

He's not asking how long you've been in the bar: he knows very well you have only just arrived. He may not even be wondering how long you've been in the port; waterfront gossip being what it is the world over, he's probably put two and two together and guessed you're from the small vessel which arrived yesterday afternoon, and anchored overnight.

No: what he's actually doing is gaining the momentary second that will allow him to arrive at a personal decision - do you, a stranger, come anywhere near fitting the bill?

However, this will have to wait, because the barman has arrived.

'Quieren otra bebida? Lo mismo para todos?' (no offer of a drink from the Scot).

And you certainly wouldn't expect it, not because it would be out of character (the stage character, completely miscast as it happens, of the parsimonious kilt) but because he can see you're holding a full glass, and doesn't want to follow your gaffe with one of his own.

'Ach, anyway; come over and meet a few o'my pals.'

The walk over from the bar counter to the table located on the other side of the room may be only the matter of a few feet, but these steps allow a shoulder to be put to, and induce the well-oiled swing of a substantial door.

A door that's not crudely labelled *acceptance* - nevertheless, it does have *opportunity* written all over it (even if the letters are subliminal).

The dark haired man, the banker, turns out to be Jacque Lacombe, a Frenchman, who hails from the port of La Rochelle.

The second member of the group is Sven Carlson, all the way from Stockholm, Sweden, arrived in Lanzarote to oversee the construction of yet another hotel complex. The cautious Scot is Andrew McNeil, formerly employed by the United Nations (UNESCO) as an entomologist, with a roving brief which took him slowly and expensively around the world studying the swarming habits of locusts.

This information is not arrived at helter-skelter, in the matter of a moment. It takes time, dribbling out, after nodded introductions, the establishment of a common language, which fortunately turns out to be English - the exchange of paper money for coins about to be wagered, and half an hour of card play. An innocuous game, where nobody is going to lose his shirt, but it will be possible to end up paying more than an equitable share of the drinks, now being consumed in appreciable amounts.

The local product is a red wine that offers all the lustre associated with the best copal varnish, but the liquid, long out of the can, has perhaps been over-thinned by the addition of too much turpentine substitute. Yet Jacque will persist in downing it, while at the same time denigrating it, to the extent that nobody in the world could be in any doubt that the stuff is only just about drinkable.

'Do they cultivate vines here on the island?'

'Aye, they do. The locals are some of the most industrious people you have ever met in your life; nearly on a par wi' the good people o'Glasgow.'

'How do they manage, when there's so little rain; almost none in a dry season.'

'Zey 'arness ze dew; zere's quite a lot of morning dew forms 'ere on Lanzarote. Do you want an'ozer card?'

This is a difficult decision.

The half-arsed fist I hold amounts to the awkward figure of 16. If I take another card, and it turns out bigger than 5, the hand will be bust. If I *do* decide to chance it, shall I pay for it (so the Banker will be unable to see the value of the card being dealt) or should I opt for a twist, which will allow Jacque to deal the card face-up on the table, and allow him to assess the cumulative effect of the new card on the others previously held?

This is not as simple as it sounds.

It's serious stuff.

Nothing less than the balance of probabilities concerned with the cash involved in the purchase of another round of drinks; while outside, somewhere on this blistered cinder of an island, a hard day's toil of sunburnt men are still at work.

Labouring, throughout what seems their longer than usual evening's stint.

Sweating, to create the cunningly fashioned depressions in the bone-dry soil, so that tomorrow's life-giving dew will trickle down and moisten the parched roots of countless hectares of drought-threatened vines, in order that Jacque will be able to appreciate *zee'ard won fruit'* of their dignified but modestly rewarded labour.

Yet this is inconsequential stuff.

What's of real moment now (the product of *serious* debate) is - should I twist? Or should I buy the card on offer?

'I'll twist.' (after all, would it be wise to be profligate with resources as meagre as mine?).

So Jacque deals, with a Banker's measured response, and the card is propelled by a neat flick of the wrist to land, face up, conveniently under the tips of my apprehensive fingers (an Ace of Spades, a good card, but not the one that was needed).

Jacque's body language now displays, even though he's seated and not moving a muscle, the bugger you boldness of a buccaneer, bordello bound. However, this raffish stance is amazingly inverted, by at the same time conveying the ambivalence offered by a presumptive virgin's nothing less than enigmatic smile. A carefully constructed, totally misleading, two-faced masquerade - a look impossible to interpret, as indeed is meant to be the case, because the man is a card player of some distinction and apparently limitless guile.

But the question remains.

Shall I take another card?

And involved in this riddle is the sixty-four-dollar delight - what sort of hand has he got? Lying, in perhaps more ways than one, face down on the scrub-topped table.

As banker, he has the benefit of his first dealt, as yet unseen, pair; so he could be holding anything. With his luck, which may amount to more than meets the tyro's eye, he's almost bound to have, say, sixteen points or better; so the chances are, my tally of seventeen spots will end up a losing fist.

'I'll twist again, please, Jacque.'

He smiles, the sort of barely discernable twitch a python might usefully employ to adjust the hinge of his jaw, prior to approaching just the right size of unsuspecting kid (and the card?).

A five of diamonds.

That means I'm bust (now who could have possibly thought it?).

Top of the list is Jacque, who proceeds to dish out the same medicine to

Andrew and Sven. And having disposed of those players, he casually reveals his own hand, which turns out to be an inadequate eight of diamonds, alongside a rickety six of spades; taken together, only fourteen measly spots.

'Aye, the luck of the devil. To get away with it again. Yet I knew it, I always damned well knew it.'

'Then why didn't you stick when you had the chance?'

There's no logical answer to this sort of irritating hindsight - by far the best response is to get up and call another round of drinks. A move appreciated by Jacque, who goes to the bar and pushes the boat out still further, almost out of sight, by ordering a generous supply of smoked ham, a basket full of bread rolls, a small jar of pickled pullet eggs, another one of onions, together with a supply of the sort of rubber chunks that masquerade hereabouts under the name of pulpo (or is it calamares?).

It's worth mentioning, there's sometimes an air of conviviality associated with a waterfront bar, when what seems the central purpose of the evening is derailed, unwittingly or otherwise. Previously, a friendly game of cards and a convivial but modest sip at the sauce were centre-stage. But sometimes the gathering and not just the game is apt to develop its own momentum, and an unannounced vehicle is found to be rattling its own careless way along unpaved roads, to a place that has yet to be signposted in any sensible direction. Some of us realize a drink or three has something to do with arrival at this bizarre bus stop, and a cautious individual rarely embarks on the roller-coaster'd whoop-up, partly because of his, certainly her, degree of inbuilt reserve, not to say well-mannered sense of discretion (don't most people manage to avoid the pig-out that Bacchus not only reputedly enjoyed - but went out of his way to ceaselessly arrange in dissolute profusion?).

It takes a certain type of individual to get this sort of ball rolling, and Jacque is the viveur who is perfectly cast for the part.

Wine is no longer ordered by the measly glass, but in bottles, a cork-drawn pair at a time. And this is not the gut-wrenching local hootch previously grimaced over, but a Rioja worth bringing all the way from Spain. A tinto, robust enough to carry the traditional reliance on oak without any loss of the fruit. A wine perfectly proportioned to accompany bread, to say nothing of the jambon; and then, for the calamares (or it could even *be* the pulpo) a vinos blanco that has the more difficult task of accompanying those specialized delights.

The table top, previously amply proportioned, now seems barely up to the task.

A large plate of sliced ham upon ham upon ham holds centre-stage, with the onions, pickled eggs, and bread rolls all within easy picking reach, while dishes of calamares and the blessed pulpo take up the rest of the available space.

There's not the slightest hint of reticence now in those of us low at the trough. We tuck in, fingers were made before forks, and the sliced meat is folded into wads, then piled between the freshly broken bread; onions are scooped out of the wide-mouthed jar, and eaten as the Garden's pippins were before Eve even made a tyro's attempt at any sort of a tart.

The pickled eggs get the same treatment.

And this is just as well, because the slightly squeamish among us would be well advised to bite and swallow, and not spend too much time examining the dark line separating the yellow of the yolk, from the grey tint of what should be the pure glaze of albumen, which My Dear Old Granny (I now vividly remember) once told me was a sure indication that a hard boiled egg, in or out of a preserving jar, had spent far too long on the shelf. But apart from that, and the still to be acquired taste for the pulpo and/or the blessed calamares, the whole thing goes with a swing.

Even Sven is enjoying himself.

Have you noticed the Swedes, as well as the Norwegians, can be a trifle dour at times? There's often a degree of seriousness associated with their behaviour, which a stranger may interpret as something approaching a ring fence, meant - perhaps not to *exclude* the newcomer - just cautiously limit the scope of what might be expected to happen after the welcoming grip of a handshake. This is not a criticism that can be applied to their Scandinavian cousins, the Danes, who almost to a man (and hopefully all their women) will be suggesting a trip to *The Gardens* [5] even though they are aware you have barely the price of a drink. However, when the square-heads *do* let their hair down, you would be well advised to hang on to what little is left of your hat; an aphorism that particularly applies to Sven, who is now starting to take on the role of 'quite a big lad'.

This may seem another of those fanciful inversions of the sort that shouldn't be applied to a man of no more than average weight and build, who is certainly over forty years of age. Yet Sven can be fairly described as a big lad, because not only is he moving towards the stage where he's going to run the risk of appearing somewhat larger, and so much louder than life, he's also behaving in the manner of someone who, although middle-aged, seems determined to recapture at least some of the errors associated with the unrestrained exuberance of youth, (there are other ways of putting this), but to be fair, the unbiased observer would probably judge him to be, not drunk, just verging - perhaps about to emerge on the intrusive side of noisy.

Up to this point in the proceedings he's been a friendly, smiling sort of cove, so quietly spoken, his conversation has consisted of little more than a brief *Jah* to this, and another perhaps more guttural *Jah* to that, in reply to the sort of inconsequential chatter most of us indulge in when playing cards in a waterfront bar. But the Rioja, on top of the local wine, and who knows how many beers, has had what could be described as a modifying effect on his behaviour, and it's obvious that he now has the bit well between his teeth.

This is nothing new for the Swedes.

They have an enviable reputation as excellent seamen, and determined elbow-benders, who display the sort of rumbustiousness which allows the modest flag of caution to be displaced by the merest zephyr of a breeze, and then go on to take that wild step further, which makes quite sure there's a gale of wind in the offing.

Sven is now quaffing Rioja, breaking bread, stuffing ham, and scoffing eggs, while at the same time trying to persuade a reluctant Jacque it's time to restart the card game - and in this regard he has become loquacious, at least by Swedish standards.

'Jah.' (after another hearty slurp of the red stuff and what seems, but can't possibly be, a hunger-driven rummage amongst what remains of the jar of pickled onions).

'My turn as Banker, Jah?' (he's addressing Jacque) who is in the middle of a meal which, while it may be large, still retains the quintessentially Gallic style of a civilized repast.

'Cards! You want us to play *cards?* In ze middle of ze meal?'

'Why not?'

Jacque smiles, again, a smile of indulgence; nothing less than a beneficence bestowed on an otherwise bright child - of the sort who has asked an unexpectedly gormless question.

Our cultivated Frenchman is poised in the act of examining the label displayed on one of the bottles he previously ordered (even in the smoke filled tumult of this dockside boozer, he's thought it worthwhile to pay attention to this useful information). After reading the label, he pours a little wine; with an exploratory sniff, he's holding up a third of a glass, the better to catch the pierced tint of the liquid.

'*Labastida*? Yes. Commercial? Surely. But still a good wine; and we owe zis to *Gonzalo Rodriguez.* [(6)] A wine of zome quality, zome distinction even, at a price we can most of us a'ford. What more can a man ask?'

This seems lost on Sven, who stays true to form and comes out with what amounts to a taunt.

'What about some cards, Jacque?'

There is now a resigned air about our wine tasting Frenchman. He samples the wine again, spears a chunk of pulpo (he carries his own toothpicks, in a little plastic phial) pops the morsel into his mouth - he's evidently pleased, as his face lights in appreciation.

'Yes, yes indeed; a fine bal-ance. More zan a leetle fruit brought to ze wine, yet it's just e'nough to add real int'rest to ze meat. We must now try ze other purchase.' (as he selects another morsel) pours more wine, and savours the ensemble.

'Come on Jacque, what about the cards?'

'My dear Sven, are you a bar-bare?' (but he doesn't complete the sentence, or even the word) being content to raise an eyebrow in Sven's direction, while including the rest of us in the wink of his other twinkling eye, which isn't easy to accomplish.

But he does it to perfection.

Sven, meanwhile, is clearing table by salvaging scraps of ham, which he piles on one platter, then pulls the laden dish towards him.

'Are you going to carry on eating, Sven?'

'Jah; I must have missed lunch.'

'Don't you know if you missed a meal?'

'Is it important? This day is something of a holiday for me, Jah? Did I take breakfast? Did I take lunch? Did I take dinner? Who cares: Jah! All I know is I could eat - how do you say it in English? The back end of a horse?'

It seems hardly worth reminding him he's just worked his way through an amazing quantity of the similar end of a pig, together with a half-dozen eggs, small though they may be, and a generous supply of pickled onions, all washed down with a formidable amount of booze. And this list is illuminated, cheekily confirmed by the way in which he levers one side of his bum off his chair and lets go a careless rip of wind, with the penultimate, if not the final thought being, perhaps it's just as well for the environmentally-threatened rest of us that the table we are occupying is located directly under one of the slowly revolving fans with which this rough and ready taberna is happily equipped.

Not that this display of waterfront manners fazes Jacque in any way. Although he's not finished his meal, he proceeds to pull out a packet of cigarettes (the fatal weed that has trapped his generation) so to the reek of pickled onions is added what is hopefully not a prescient wreath of tobacco smoke, which now swirls dizzily about what remains of Sven's still pervasive, slack-arsed indiscretions.

From a distance, this may seem a doubtful combination (even at close quarters, there remain unanswered questions?) but for the people who are actually *in* the bar, especially those of us seated round the table, there are other things to occupy the mind - because Sven is not the only one who's been experiencing something of a lift.

While he and Jacque have been enjoying themselves in their own particular manner, Andrew has taken the opportunity, perhaps sensibly enough, to make a quiet trip to the bar, and has now returned with another bottle of wine, as well as a bottle of Scotch, with the way in which he's already enjoyed himself expressed in the broadening of his speech.

'Ye'll ha' to excuse me I'm afraid. Believe it or not, they di'na have a fu' bottle. Can you credit it? A place of this size, down to the very last dram. This would'na do in Glasgo', I can tell you.'

Nobody's impressed.

Sven has finished eating, and is in other more intimate ways quietening down. Jacque is still enjoying his coffin nail, but has not yet finished his meal. While I'm wondering if, in the event of the card game being resumed, it would be possible to take up something that offered more scope than the limited thrill of pontoon. This genuinely daft thought being a certain indication that I've already had, if not one too many, certainly enough to put a hopelessly rosy tint on the prospect of matching, or even approaching Jacque at his own particular game (confirmation, that enough has been seen of the bottle to make certain it's only a matter of time before the table is cleared and play resumed) taking the form, by common consent, of five-card brag. [7]

The stakes are also somewhat larger than was previously the case.

This playlet has now resolved itself into a group of men who have had a few drinks, are seated around a bar room table, and surely there's nothing exceptional in this all too simple account?

Yet what is it - with booze, bars, cards, tobacco, and the reckless consumption of food - some of which turned out to be stale.

Taken piecemeal, and with the self-righteous judgement of hindsight, wouldn't some of the items mentioned have been rejected out of hand?

And beyond that, don't we all know the dangers supposedly (supposedly?) associated with passive smoking?

And apart from that cautionary tale, the physical discomfort, if you're a non-smoker, of spending hour after dissolute hour in close proximity with people who seem intent on carelessly affecting your well-being, as well as destroying their own, would seem reason enough to up-sticks and head for the nearest door.

But the truth is, everything else being equal, or unequal, as the case may be. The truth is (always a bad sign, when '*the truth*' is manoeuvred into it) it seems these lads are quite a good bunch to be with, particularly when what can be hazily described as the partly cleared fume of an alcoholic plateau has been thankfully arrived at, with this degree of postponed debacle brought about by the so-called, probably spurious, blotting paper effect, coupled with a much more effective easing-up on the elbow, while at the same time (*just* in time, some might say) it would appear enough brains remain amazingly unfuddled to hopefully ensure we're not all about to fall flat on the sweat trickled daze of our moon shining faces.

Because I'll have you know Sir (or Madam, as the case may be) those of us present at this post prandial dingdong would claim we are *just* the sort of experienced tipplers who have, over a long and expensive stint of apprenticeship, brought the use of alcohol to what we are now convinced is the elevated state of nothing less than a serene, even if it is a slightly wobbled fart (sorry: *art*). And further on than that, we believe we exemplify this gravely drawn distinction (*oops:* an apology, really, for an uncontrolled fart of my own). Yet not to put too fine a point on it, we are all of us here convinced of the scope of our undoubted ability to keep this, what we would strenuously deny is a *far* from drunken ship afloat. So I can announce, with some degree of certainty, even if not with all that amount of clarity (or is this the reverse of the case?) that we, that's to say, my new-found friends and I haven't come here to make ourselves out to be *crass*, or indeed fools of any sort.

For a start - I have seldom seen a better card game.

Jacque, of course, the cunning old devil, thinks he's so much above the knees of the bees (the bees of the knees?) or could it be nothing more complicated than he just *thinks* he's the bee's knees?

However it turns out, when it comes to the little matter of bending a deck, I have no clouded doubt at all that my old mate Harry would have led him a devil of a dance, given half the chance that he's had.

Now there's a peculiar thing (didn't I tell you?).

Haven't I already told you?

Didn't I even *mention* my old mate 'Arry?

Another boozing chum of mine, just come happily to mind.

Dredged up from all of yester-year.

You should 'ave seen 'im when . . .

So it goes.

Time passes.

Andrew sports a small cheroot.

He's also got the whisky bottle conveniently positioned, and while he's made a token of passing it around, it has somehow emerged that he has a well-established, proprietorial interest in this particular crock.

Sven, on the other hand, has mellowed in a more likeable manner. With what turns out to be a rueful smile of acknowledgement, he has shifted his tipple back to a modest ale, having renounced the Rioja and the rotgut, as well as the mirage of the briefly-offered Scotch (so in some important points our Swede must be classed a sensible fellow?).

Not entirely, because he has otherwise thrown discretion to the wind by the way in which he plunges, risking far too much of his cash on the unlikely turn of events. Five-card brag being the sort of game (and isn't it just?) where you can bid up your hand - or what you hope you have bluffed your opponent into thinking are your prospects - regardless that the cards you're holding may be worth little more than the gut of a flickering light.

Now we all know survival in this type of school requires the sort of mental discipline that's not necessarily to hand when you need it most. The whole adventure being meat and drink to Jacque, who is in the process of amassing a sizeable pile of loot. In marked contrast to the modest stack of coins which were originally employed to fuel the initial, seemingly innocent, modest game of cards. However, a prospective sandbagging of this sort does offer a participant who is either more cautious, or just a little more experienced, the opportunity of playing a better balanced, longer waited game.

Exercising a degree of patience.

Waiting, until you have a hand which might be worth supporting. And then, having decided to gamble, limiting the stake to an amount that, should it go down the dunny, will not lead to the distressing situation where those who plunge, and lose, no longer have available the dry-mouthed price of what has now become a badly needed, but barely affordable morale supporting drink.

The trick here, of course, is *not* to lose your shirt.

This being rather fortu (*fortu'it?*), fortuitushly? Hell, just easier to accomplish, if you're seated across a table from someone who is more than happily involved in the mind embalming process of losing most of his.

Who cares?

The night wears on.

Higher grow the stakes.

Thicker grows the smoke.

Longer grows the ash on our Scotsman's small cheroot, who is pouring more the drinks (pouring *more* the drinks?).

Whatever!

Because it turns out to be Andrew who seems blessed, perhaps cursed with an iron constitushon.

Not a good thing to possess (or is it the one thing you *have* to possess?) in spades, if you become all that fond of the sauce.

Yet this is a barely perceived difficulty, hardly worth pursuing, because who are we to critishsize? He plays what he, and we . . . us *all*, would call a canny game of cards.

And to be fair, old Andrew's still the only person who can come anywhere near out toffee-nosing Jacque. It's also worth observing that while sampling his Rabbie Burning spirit, he's wise enough to restrict his alcoholic intake, with the pour of a practised hand, to no more than the sip that it takes to maintain the reel of his Scottish tune, which for a lesser endowed Sassenach would mean the reel that leads to oblivion (this flicker of truth leading to the inescapable conclusion that here we have a bald headed Banquo who knows how to balance his booze).

Didn't I tell you he's sparse on top?

It's of little consequence, because there's no doubt at all he could drink the soft-headed rest of us under his hard-headed table if we were ever daft enough to elbow our way forward to try an' even attempt it.

Not that he's likely to get such an accommodating response from Jacque, who is dealing with the call of his own bar room performance with an appropriate Francophone toot, if you consider chain-smoking and blowing the occasional smoke ring comes close enough to being the barely acceptable face of smug enough behaviour.

And it's no use complaining.

'What is ze matt'aire?'

'Are you bein' boz'aired?'

'I'll 'ave you know zat zis 'ere, is ze very fi'nest full strength Gauloise, zat *your* money can buy.'

So he's still smiling, because he's still winning, and if we continue playing five-card brag that sure as hell is bound to be the case.

There are also other things that are getting maybe a little more, certainly not much less than fuzzy round the edges.

Time being one of them.

We have all been here since God knows when (for some of us, it could be longer even than that), and this is not a blasphemous remark, merely an honest admishion that I, we, they, *us*, don't have the foggiest idea of what the faltering clock says.

In this smoke-filled bar, it could be midnight.

It could be more.

It could even be time to leave (but not before the big 'and's on ten, and the littl'un's on two) as someone once hopefully mumbled.

'So what time does this pub close, anyway?'

'I think it's sometime in October, Jah?' (and this is delivered with a genuine burst of Jah-ha-ha-ha'd laughter).

'Come on Sven, that's not a Swedish yolk, that's an Irish joke, and one that's been tip-toe'd down, all the way from Sligo.' The sort of ancient bar room quip that's been doing the smiling rounds of punters since Paddy winked his other eye for another pint of porter.

(Between you and me) it doesn't matter that Sven may not know where Sligo is, or he thinks porter has probably got something to do with a railway. It's also unlikely he's ever been tempted to tip-toe anywhere, apart from out of a boudoir. Nevertheless, regardless of this laboured analysis, he carries on chuckling, quite unashamedly wallowing in what he sees as the humour he so much admires, illuminated by the glassy eyed gleam of his finely shone sense of perception (this being another bleary eyed example of how this drunken session is developing).

But quite apart from this regrettable sally, our friend is becoming restless.

Not paying attention to his cards.

Squirming about in his chair.

Trying to get a better view of the bar - not to whistle up more booze, which certainly isn't needed, but to be able to eyeball a group who have just walked into this run-of-the-mill waterfront pub.

How he became aware of this development remains something of a mystery. He must be the proud possessor of a sixth, or even a square-head's seventh perceptive sense, because throughout the entire evening he's had his back to the business-end of this establishment. While playing cards he's been oblivious of other people's comings and goings, which in any case have been far and few between (they could even have been few and far between), not that it makes much difference, because the Big News is - the prompt of a Swedish leer has just walked in through the door.

Well, to be absolutely accurate, as near as comes close to the churlish point of an otherwise charitable appraisal, three ladies - 'of one sort or an'ozaire,' have just arrived (as Jacque is quick to observe). And these eye-catching additions are now leaning against the bar, talking to the barman, while treating us pigeon-holed customers (appraised as swivel-eyed prospectives, or back to the cards write-offs) to the jut of provocative butts.

Nothing overdone, of course, because this dockside watering hole has well-established rules of procedure. But there's something else here which casts its own particular spell. It's hard to put your finger on it, but the atmosphere now is ....

How can it feel so much *heavier* than before?

True, the smoke remains as thick as ever, perhaps even denser than that, because Jacque is still puffing away and Andrew has started another cheroot. Yet apart from this continued onslaught on the delicate tissue of other people's pipes, something else is influencing the ambience of what is now turning into quite a delectable romp.

However, it doesn't remain a mystery; in the same way that it no longer seems remarkable that Sven just *knew* the girls had walked into the joint. All that's happened is that the ceiling-mounted fans have stopped turning. If anyone would care to lean back in his chair, and risk an arse-over-tip glance upwards, it would also become curiously obvious that they have also stopped revolving, but strangely enough, the effect is precisely the same (wall to wall smoke to the door).

Can this be a *sign*?

Indeed it is.

It's the silent yet effective signal, used in this particular boozer, to drop the eye-watering hint that the time has come to go home.

There's no time-honoured shout of ... **'Time!** ... *Time Gentlemen, Please!'*

All they do here is switch the blistering fans off.

And quite effective it is, because a silence has fallen from the ceiling.

Can a *real* silence, fall from a *real* ceiling?

Indeed it can.

And it not only fell in this room, it also fell, with the clang of a resounding call to arms, in another establishment, located not all that distant, where the sign on the door doesn't say much more than it doesn't even have to. And there's nothing in any way complicated with this oblique analysis, because the rule in this pub, as Jacque explains it, is that 'Ze ladies, are not allowed to flaunt (you say in eengl'eesh, *'flaunt'*?) the tools of zey're old-fashioned trade.' There may be what amounts to a Gallic misappropriation here, but it's better to let it pass, as does everyone else, and have another look at the turn of the wheel of events, because the girls are a nice enough group - if you're possessed of that sort of appreciative eye.

High heels.

Long brown legs.

Short black skirts.

Bare midriffs, with belly-buttoned brown-eyed navels well to the eye-catching fore.

Knotted white blouses.

Tight tucked tits.

Jet-black hair and, as usual, all seeing, all knowing, highly made up *eyes.*

Loads of mascara.

False eyelashes, which are so long that if the gals looked up, and fluttered them, they'd sweep the damned soot from the ceiling

To say our lad Sven is interested, is the understatement of the weak (should it be *week*?). Not really, although it does have something to do with time, it has more to do with temptation, because from his point of view, what has previously been little more than an elbow-bent evening has now drifted on to what he hopes will become nothing less than the longer-leg'd charm of the night.

So a change of pace is in the offing.

Marking the end of the alcoholic era, and the birth of a situation which is outlined, on the one hand, by the cessation of the fans, and on the other by the risible size of Sven's newly-felt ambition, with this snide little joke providing, just possibly, a clue to the sort of bulge which now seems bent on extending the front of Sven's rather tight, very smart shorts. And perhaps prompted by this interesting development, Jacque is wrapping-up the card game.

However, it seems they are his cards; not a pack provided by the establishment, as is usually the case; but his very own deck.

And might not this well handled, tarnished little nugget have been a significant piece of information, if allowed to enter the public domain just a little earlier in evening? Not that there was anything sinister in the way he conducted the play. The important thing is, we've all had a good time, even if it cost us a couple of quid.

And what is money anyway?

But to Sven, who has just lost his shirt, the prospect of being completely skint is beginning to dawn in what we must all hope is not a mercenary manner.

He's still fidgeting, and is not content until he's moved his chair to the other side of the table, so he will have a better view of the bar - while Jacque, having stashed his deck, and his loot, is ignoring the goings-on at the counter, no doubt because he finds Sven's behaviour nothing less than amusing, perhaps nothing less than hilarious.

'What is ze mat'aire, Sven? You zeem to be getting a little 'ot aroun' ze coll'aire.'

'Jah.' (and this one word contains an honest acknowledgement), the sort of deep-throated growl a large dog would employ to establish a proprietary interest in a juicy bone, which some kind soul had just produced from under a hitherto unnoticed hat.

'You are wasting your time, my friend; ze ladies ('ow do you say eet in eengl'eesh?) zey ar' *spoken for.*'

Sven is not amused.

He doesn't *say* anything, but he doesn't really need to, the frown on his face says it all. Obviously, what he's thinking is - how can they be spoken-for, when they've just walked into the joint?

The answer, of course, is simple enough.

Lanzarote may be an island of volcanic origin, the result of a comparatively recent erection (dear me, a *genuine* Freudian slip: a comparatively recent *eruption*). But unlike Sven's bubbling testosterone, the flow has cooled sufficiently to enable a rudimentary system of communication to be established - taking the form of an intricately designed, even if sometimes woefully inadequate series of wires strung between centres of economic interest, prominent among them being this boozer and another establishment, located down the street, but well within a bawdily prompted and wildly unrighteous down to Mother Earth hail.

There's also been another development.

Not only have the fans stopped turning, some of the lights have been turned off, while others have been dimmed, and this combination of fanless ceiling and lightless wall has provided, for those of us sufficiently well-imbibed, a subterranean-like atmosphere. A *cave,* into which hooded and sack clothed figures, carrying the tools of some terrible trade have now begun to appear.

And this is the only dark way to describe it.

It's not so much a question of *who* they are - more like, what *can* they be?

Yet this drunken appraisal hardly does them justice, because, on close examination, they just turn out to be people.

Cleaners, no less; and now the customers are drifting away, these ladies have started sweeping the floor, clearing tables, collecting empty glasses, carrying them to the bar - generally bringing cheerful order out of booze and baccy chaos. Nevertheless, there's a juxtaposition here, perhaps only accessible to those of us brought to a sufficiently maudlin state by the downward push of a cork. A bleak judgement, prompted by the sight of the smiling crew of cleaners, who could be described, cruelly, as crones - apropos the giggle of girls at the counter who, whatever the rainbow drawn play they now offer, will eventually be dumped at the dismal drawn end of the road.

So what price now, the drunk's *unperceptive* eye?

Or have you got to be pissed to perceive it?

But whether it is, or it was, or it isn't, Sven is intent on improving what he wrongly perceives are his chances; without the real glimmer of hope, because with the change of pace, several trawlermen have quietly but determinedly been making their way to the bar (with Jacque's earlier prediction of *spoken-for* ladies, now taking on a much more accessible meaning).

Yet make no mistake about it, there's not what might pass for a romantic adventure anywhere in sight.

Yes, there are eye-fluttered smiles.

Yes, to a friendly arm placed on a shoulder.

Yes, even, to a murmured, but leered endearment.

There are also bums being pinched.

Breasts being ogled.

Tits being tarted.

The bottom line being that cash has already been placed (laid) on the barrel-head (maidenhead), all part of the commercial transactions which have been previously negotiated by the barman who, in this pub, while he may be doling out food and drink, is also a beer-gutted, once-removed Madam, with a money-grubbed slice of the take.

It's nothing to get alarmed about.

The system works well.

It enables the bar to operate on an acceptable level, that's close to the wind, but on a road which runs parallel to the rough and ready rule of the Law.

For rough and ready people?

Indeed we are.

If you took a hard look at the trawlermen, now arm in arm with their lady friends, it would take a bold man, or an idiot, let alone a policemen, to even *think* of coming between them and whatever amorous port they're bound for.

So, should we be concerned with Sven's well-being?

Not really: although he's lost his shirt, he hasn't scrambled his brains (not, at least, to that extent). To challenge doubt with desire he's carrying on a smiling conversation with Jacque, with the word *money* mixed in somewhere between tomorrow and the next day.

Andrew, meanwhile, is in the midst of a conversation with the barman, and for one wild moment it might be assumed our staid Scot is going to kick over the traces, or whatever they do North of the Border when this particular breeze tickles a well set up Jock in his kilt.

But all that's being talked about with the barman is the usual arrangement for what remains of Andrew's bottle of Scotch, because it seems, when he declared he was *down to the very last dram*, it was something of an evasion, there being a well established procedure in this boozer that has his 'medicinal purposes' put aside, in order that he's never going to be caught short for his essential drop of the hard stuff. A revealing snippet of information, even for a tiddly recipient, because it does tell anyone who cares to add two and two together, and get past three, that Andrew is perhaps over-fond of the sauce. That he doesn't want to be put in a position where he may have to manage without it.

Who cares?

Maybe we should all care?

Perhaps nobody cares.

The barman certainly doesn't care, all he's concerned about is we leave his establishment in an orderly manner, so goodnights are being said in several languages, with varying degrees of regret, with Jacque, as usual, apparently in control of events.

Marshalling us all to the door.

Obviously on familiar territory.

Seems to know everyone, not only the girls and the cleaners, but a significant number of locals, as well as most of the crews.

So where does that put us?

Without doubt, on what has previously been judged the down-side of the once stumbled upon entrance, both entering and leaving - because do *you* remember that particular door?

Or is it *this* particular door?

Anyway, *a door*, haphazardly located on the shady side of the street, marked by the countless applications of pock-marked lime that seemed, at the time, to have been softened by the blistering glare of the sun.

But all that has gone.

That sun has set.

Drifted off, waved farewell to, by us, the inebriates, who are doing our best to re-inhabit, if not reinvent, perhaps just get a grip on our topsy-turvy'd, just out of the reeling pub whirl'd. A world that previously had, as its ceiling, the swing of a fan, the pop of a cork, the slice of a spicy salami. But a place that has been transformed, on the turning out of the boozer, to a world that presents the billowing scud of a puff of a cloud over the gleam of a shine of a moon. An eye-catching orb which hangs above this tavern's (cavern's?) entrance (exit?) while everything else in the sky moves off in a sou'westerly direction. In eye-blurring contrast to the rough raggle-taggled, bobtailed, unsteady, yet just about stationary, raucous little mob now trickling out on the street.

Some of us belching.

Some of us farting.

Some of us, decorously or otherwise, 'adjusting our dress', having had the pleasure of making a dark splash in the loo. The rough and ready local tinto imposing its own special strain and stain on the barely adequate local system, which really shouldn't be exposed to the light of any sort of drunk or indeed all too sober day.

Now, having got some sort of a bearing on proceedings, and standing as a reasonably coherent group outside the portals of this boozer, enjoying the relief of emptying what must be the pink insides of pleasantly relaxing bladders - reached the state of near nirvana (have *you* ever had a skin full, and then enjoyed a long overdue, veritable *cascade* of a pee?).

Whatever: another problem is raising its unsteady head, because this street seems angled.

Indeed it does.

Sure enough, *up* is still up, and *down* is still down - but which is the way to the harbour?

And where have all the trawler crews gone?

The louche lads with the loop-ended lariats, that are long enough to lassoo even the loudest and lewdest of the lolled-about lasses.

Where are they now?

(*Off whoring, you fool*) while the rest of us, equipped with oval wheels and rubber axles, are not in a condition to do much more than describe the toe-tottered outline of tipthy ellipthses.

So what we need ith - thum athisistanth.

But not in double quick time.

We would surely be better off in nothing more demanding than waltz time.

And who better provide it than Jacque?

The only reasonably sober member of the party.

A beacon, no less.

He even has some of the attributes of a slowly rotating lighthouse, in an otherwise wobbly world.

A world that needs some sort of a push to get it moving in hopefully the right direction.

'Where is your boat, Val?' (*what a good question*), the *very* thought that's been buzzing about, but until this drunken minute, I haven't been able to enunciate it.

Formulate it?

Not much more than vaguely.

Enunshiate it?

Not reely coheeerently, it's remained the vague outline of a question, located somewhere well in the back of my mind.

After all, what's missing is trivial enough - just the location of the place where I live.

You see, boats are like snails (*no: sailors are like snails*).

What the hell.

What I'm *trying* to say is - *small-boat* sailors are like snails.

And if this sounds a doubtful proposition, what you should do is *think* about it; because we, of this or that particular fraternity, while not actually *carrying* our abodes about (*I like that - that bit about abodes*), yet we, even as *very* small, small-boat sailors, do have the undoubted pleasure of being able to move the old homestead about, from place to irregular place (*s'truenough, you can tie up in Manchester, and wake up in Manchuria, s'allthesame*) although whether either of these locations offers reasonable small-boat anchorage I'm not, at this moment, in a position to either confirm or deny.

Suffice it to say (now, I *don't* like that) but shove-ice it to say anyway, I still can't remember where my boat, let alone where my homestead is, although of course (indeed, very much of course, of course) I remain convinced they *must* be one and the same place; but the trouble is, I still can't remember where either of them are right now.

'Did you come ashore in a dinghy, Val?' (now there's a thought: of *course* I came ashore in a dinghy).

Why didn't I think of that before?

'Did you use the jetty steps?' (*think back:* leaving the boat; rowing ashore in a dinghy, an inflatable dinghy).

Was there a beach?

Were there steps to negotiate?

Who knows?

I can remember looking *down* on the boat (so there probably *were* steps) yet help is at hand, because even in my sozzled state I can see what's involved in rowing ashore, stepping out on a beach, and then, having sufficient elevation to be able to look *down* on the transport.

'Yes, I did tie up at some steps.' (so we all trundle off in his wake).

And here's a funny thing.

A thing *really* worth knowing.

Because if, through absolutely no fault of your own, you sometime in the future happen to find yourself temporarily (just *temporarily*, mind you) unsure of where you left your dinghy ....

Aways walk *downhill!*

Because it's just come to me - in a flash, so to speak - it may not be all that sensible to spend too much time and effort marching in the opposite direction.

Isn't this worth knowing?

The sort of useful information only acquired after a lifetime spent in a variety of vessels (bottles not excluded).

And I've just remembered something else, but I'll keep it under my hat for the moment.

Although, now I come to look for it, I haven't actually *got* my damned hat (must have left it in the pub); dear me, but never mind, because we're making real progress.

Trundling as an unsteady convoy in the wake of the escorting vessel.

Tittle-tattling amongst ourselves.

Carefree, because the navigational responsibilities have been lifted from our irresponsible shoulders.

As the lane widens, cobbles pass to paving.

Left turn, then on a bit.

Right turn, and on a bit more (but not *up* hill).

Approaching a smart boulevard where brightly-lit shop windows display long limbed, sun burnt, papier-mâché, provocatively feminine models, clothed in the briefest of brief bikinis (so I wonder what the trawler lads are up to now?).

And why, for Heaven's Sake, are these smart shop windows floodlit? At this time of what Sven previously found to be a very expensive night. Although I can hear, somewhat distantly located, the sound of thumping music - a disco of one loud sort or another, so there are revellers about.

Tourists, must be tourists, who appear to be blessed with more stamina than our small group of less than concurring heroes - nevertheless, we must be making progress towards the seaweedy side of the town, because I can smell the outline of the harbour.

Smell, the outline of a harbour?

Absolutely, it's not only as plain as a bell - it's as clear as the nose on my face.

The first faint tang and murmur of the sea, while the second faint tang and *murder* of the sea, a pervasive waft of diesel-engined drift-netter, reinforces the amazing advantage of living aboard a boat that doesn't have to bother with even the whiff of a niff of filthy infernal combustion.

And I can see her now.

My small, but delightfully unencumbered vessel.

Lying at anchor.

Shining through the loom of the gloom.

Swinging to her second best bower, just ahead of a group of commercial vessels.

'Where did you leave your dinghy, Val?' (it was at this jetty, of that I'm sure).

Peering over the top of the concrete wall, there's nothing there but the oily gleam of the lip of the steps, and that's as far as it's possible to see, because the dockside lights are still as far and few between as the same old bumbled joke, casting shadows which could hide a reluctant dinghy from a drunk's apparently attentive, yet hopelessly crass, bleary-eyed appraisal.

And still no boat.

'Don't worree; zey 'ave probably pulled 'er ashore, so az to make room for ozer traffic using ze steps.' (now that would be uncommonly good of them - if they've been generous enough to do it).

So we're casting about as tired old hounds, working by rote.

Not under the gleam of the waterfront lights, which just about illuminate the paved area on top of the jetty - in the tempting thickets cast by the shadows of dockside buildings (groups of untidy fishermen's sheds) while I'm buoyed up by that titbit of private information I previously came across, under the confines of my own hat (if I'd been wearing it at the time).

'Jah; here is a boat: over here.'

So we congregate about an inflatable that's been leant against the shadowy side of a wall (one quick glance confirming that it *is* my boat). A bit of luck, really, because there are some places in the world where a carelessly moored punt would just as likely end up in the fish hold of an about to depart trawler. To be sold at the next port of call, for a quick couple of quid, to blow on whatever (and guess what would take their short-skirted fancy at the time?).

'Sure, here is ze boat: but where are ze oars?'

'Did you leave them 'ere, Val?'

Now, this is where I can start to feel rather smug about it all.

Even though I would have to agree, I probably wouldn't have been able to find my own way, unaided, through the *brightly* lit part of the town, let alone through the dim tangle of streets that led on down to the jetty, what's allowing me a certain amount of satisfaction is the flash of insight experienced when we were in the wake of the escorting vessel. This was hardly a revelation of the magnitude experienced by Paul (or was it Saul?) on the travail to (or was it from?) Damascus, [8] but what's been stumbled over, vaguely remembered, is where I put the bits of stick us old dogs use to propel a punt (*the oars, Dear Boy, the OARS*) **I *know where they are.***

All we have to do is - return to the jetty steps; go through the motion of having just climbed them; take a drunken look around, while remaining swayingly motionless (some might call this, a simple matter of reorientation).

And 'Hey Presto' - the old grey cells click into gear (and there it is) the priceless flicker of recognition which leads the half-awash idiot, perhaps not unerringly in the right direction, nevertheless a near enough stumble towards a pile of dunnage and odd scraps of canvas that, at the time, I thought provided just the right camouflage for things which should be left more or less concealed.

Not a bad decision (taken, of course, in the sober light of day) and can it have been just that amazingly short time since rowing ashore? In order to pay such a virtuous visit to the Harbour Master's office?

It seems barely believable.

But finding the blades does allow our drunken crew to carry the inflatable to the top of the retraceable steps, and it's here that Sven drops his own particular bombshell.

We had been talking, Sven and I, when rambling down to the jetty (the tittle-tattle previously mentioned) much in the way that strangers, having spent an evening together, then find, when about to go their own particular way, they know next to nothing about each other. But as a result of this trundled-along conversation, Sven knows I sailed here, to this particular harbour, in my own particular boat (which, to a Swede, is not in any way unusual), but this apparently harmless snippet of trivial information now prompts him to pop a decidedly awkward question.

'Can we come aboard, Val; and have a look around?'

This raises a problem. To be quite honest - I've just about had it.

It's been a long hard day. I'm tired, might even be judged the worse for wear (the understatement of the escapade), it's God knows what in the morning. Just about the last thing I want to do is invite any new found friend, but shortly to be left astern acquaintance, aboard my floating home.

Yet what am I do?

Tell Sven to get lost?

Suggest coming back in the morning?

Quite apart from the fact that in another hour or so, the first faint streak of the dawn will be greying-up the eastern horizon (so it almost *is* the ruddy in more ways than one morning).

In any case, Sven has already scotched that line of retreat.

During the trickled-down walk from the boozer he told me he will soon be on his way to Sweden, ticketed aboard the 12 o'clock plane, having worked his roster round to the opportunity of two weeks well-deserved leave.

So this is the man who is now standing on the top of the jetty steps, oars in hand, ready enough to help launch my reluctant inflatable.

Then Andrew chimes in.

It seems he also wouldn't mind having a look at my nice wee boat. Only level-headed Jacque has the decency to keep his smiling mouth shut.

However, we (they) all too easily decide to have a look at my boat.

Carefully negotiating the slippery steps, to launch the dinghy and steady her, prior to embarkation.

As skipper, I get in amidships, saddled with the passed-to-me oars.

Then Andrew steps aboard, gingerly, and settles himself in the stern of the boat.

Sven goes for'ard; but before sitting down he takes out a handkerchief, placing it carefully on the thwart, presumably to protect the seat of his rather smart shorts (but how he reconciles this square-headed form of fastidiousness, with the flight of his earlier fancy, might be the tip of a teasing conundrum if we only had the critical time to pursue it?).

As it is, we leave Jacque alone on the lip of the wall.

Silhouetted by a harbour-side light.

Looking down on proceedings, while chuckling darkly to himself (so he remains a perceptive old fox).

Now inflatable dinghies are useful bits of apparatus - when not in use, and deflated, they can be stuffed into a small locker - and when *in* use, lightly loaded, they are easy enough to row.

But an overloaded inflatable is an animal with a character of its own

The beast sits low in the water, sagged in the middle, particularly if an out-of-balance punt is burdened by a heavyweight crew.

Any sort of a breeze also makes its presence felt, and there is now a modest but significant nor'easterly blowing down the harbour.

This means I must row in a crab-like manner, across the breeze, angled towards the parent vessel, making due allowance for leeway, otherwise it's possible to miss the objective and end up downwind, with an even harder task in prospect. But this isn't a difficult passage to make.

A short pull on the blades, and we're soon approaching the yacht.

Coming alongside is also easy enough; a few deft strokes on the oars and we're there.

The next decision concerns who is going to be first to move from the dinghy, stepping up, and handily cocking a leg over the lifelines, to gain the safety offered by the deck of the parent vessel.

But Andrew seems to have made up his own North of the Border mind, without sensibly waiting for the punt to be held securely against the hull of the boat, while he makes this critical move, and he's now *standing* in the dinghy, hand outstretched, making a grab for the lifelines.

Not the best way to board a vessel with a comparatively high freeboard, from a volatile sort of punt and, of course, the inevitable happens.

The outstretched hand misses what's been grasped for.

The inflatable moves marginally off from the yacht.

Andrew remains briefly suspended ....

Then falls with a splash in the drink.

Sven is laughing fit to bust (what Andrew is saying is lost in the splash) when he does resurface, it centres rudely about one of his bodily functions, while from a distance comes the sound of an equally rude Francophone hoot.

A jolly enough scenario (if you're not the idiot in the water).

There's also a twist in the offing, because while we've all been highly amused, apart from possibly Andrew, the inflatable has drifted slightly away from the yacht, and is now being influenced by a gust of wind that's rippling in and out of what was previously a moderate puff of a breeze (in racing parlance, a little black'un. [9]

Not much of a squall; it doesn't really earn the title.

Yet here again, the ill-nature built into the beast we're embarked in is revealed by the way the inflatable is now being blown, silently, and slowly, yet nevertheless decisively, further away from the boat. Not far, only a few feet, nevertheless far enough to put the yacht out of tangible reach of what remains of the short-handed crew in the dinghy.

In the meantime, Andrew, having had just about enough of a swim, is trying to get aboard the yacht, but is finding the vessel's freeboard presents something of a problem. Try as he might, even at full arms-stretch from his and her waterline, he can only *just* get the tips of his fingers over the toe-rail, prior to hoisting himself out of the wet stuff.

No laughing matter (although Sven, of course, is still in gigglin' stitches).

However, don't middle-aged, perhaps out of condition, rather sedate gentlemen, deserve at least *some* degree of sympathy? After all, this may develop into something which could turn out to be rather more than just the arse-tipping end of a piss-whistled evening. So the sensible thing now is - we should row back and pick poor Andrew up.

But this turns out to be something easier planned than accomplished, because amongst the laughter and the kerfuffle, it seems one of the oars has been displaced, and is no longer in the punt.

Have you ever tried to row an inflatable with just the one blade?

Or, for that matter, learnt how easy it is to let go an oar, in the middle of a darkish sort of an otherwise hilarious night, when laughing at some other poor devil's misfortune?

In these circumstances, even if you were stone cold sober, there's a degree of difficulty involved; because while circles are easy, *progress* is not, unless, quite simply, you can call on a Celt to serve as your cox while he's also employed as a one-handed crew for your coracle. [10] And this is not a skill that's easily acquired - you may have to be born *into*, to be able to escape *from*, this type of one-oared deprivation.

Meanwhile, yet another little black'un has taken further part in proceedings, and not to put too fine a point on it, we are now further away from the boat than we were a minute ago, and still moving in the wrong direction. So it's a question now, not of strategy, but of tactics (the strategy was blown, perhaps the moment we entered the pub?), so it seems sensible - not to try and recover the short distance back to the boat, a just about impossible task anyway - but somehow manoeuvre, in order to influence the downwind direction we're taking.

And there is, rather fortu . . . fortu'it . . . fortuitushly? (Hell, the same old problem) a rather large trawler just under our lee; so it's only a matter of splashing along, using one oar for rowing, and one hand for paddling, as we drift downwind, soon rubbing alongside the hull of this vessel, shouting back, as we bump past, 'Andrew, don't bother about getting aboard. *Look round for a blade*, we seem to have lost one!'

Now, there *are* people who would take this excellent piece of advice, and act on it, even with alacrity. But unfortunately Andrew isn't one of them.

To give him his due, he does have problems of his own.

He can now be seen, not all that far away, vaguely through the gloom, clinging ape-like to the anchor chain, having presumably run out of puff concerning his own little problem of freeboard - so he obviously needs another, even louder shouted prompt from those of us left in the punt.

'*Andrew*, look out for the oar !'

'*LOOK OUT for the OAR* !'

As these messages are being bellowed back to the dinghy, we're still drifting slowly astern; but an opportunity now presents itself in the shape of an open port in the trawler's hull, which Sven can just manage to reach, even though he's sitting in the forepart of the dinghy. This is quite handy, because now he's got a decent handhold, Sven can stand up, and hopefully get a better view of where our recalcitrant oar is presumably floating in the water. Yet it takes a deal more bellowing to finally persuade Andrew to release his grip on the anchor chain and start casting about for our missing bit of equipment.

In one way, it's fortunate Sven possesses a voice which could be used to understudy a fog horn. In another way, there may be a penalty involved because, perhaps hardly surprisingly, a light has come on in the cabin that's served by the port we're finding so handy, and into this brightly lit circle a head has been thrust.

A bullet-shaped, slant-eyed, darkly-shaven head of a distinctly brown-faced gentleman, who is also pug-nosed and presenting the unmistakable impression of being somewhat miffed.

For some reason, Sven seems taken aback by this development.

Yet who wouldn't be, having disturbed, in the middle of the night, the dream of a kip of the hard working skipper of the fast asleep crew of the trawler. Nevertheless, Sven stands his ground (if you can do that in an out-gunned inflatable) and *stares* back at his opposite number, without even beginning to offer what would, or indeed should amount to a decently worded apology.

Their faces are inches apart, and rather attractively framed by the light of the brightly lit porthole - for all the world presenting something of an oriental/occidental stand-off - even though the whole thing is obviously accidental.

However, Sven seems incapable of getting across the quite reasonable explanation he has at his fingertips, try though he might, in several languages, with what any reasonable person would deem an almost endless amount of repetitive impatience.

This sort of thing can't go on forever.

Indeed, it seems to have gone on long enough, because our oriental gentleman has become irate, has started fiddling with the glass, and the deadlight, is about to slam the whole of the bad tempered lot on the porthole - so Sven must remove his fingers in double-quick time.

But then our shipmate then makes what must be regarded as a tactical error. Instead of accepting the inevitable, after the port has been slammed shut, he sticks his face against the glass, flattens his nose against it, and proceeds to stick his tongue out (too childish for words, really). Yet he must have felt the need, because this has actually been difficult to accomplish, the truth being, that now the port has been shut, there remains only a small ring, a lip of rusty steel to hang on to - but he manages it, and moreover seems inordinately glad he's been able to.

Now, it must be asked, if this schoolboy prank has added presumed Western insult to injured Eastern dignity?

And it may indeed have done so, for in the matter of a moment the trawler's deck lights come on, accompanied by the rumbled start-up of a hefty diesel generator. These lights are not just a glimmer, they are glaring arcs, perhaps half a dozen of them, and we are now on a brightly lit and all too wobbly stage.

Men are appearing on deck, roused from their slumber by Sven's horn of a voice, as well as the call of the Master himself.

And they are built as he is; short but powerful, shaven-headed, beetle-browed, the sort of spear-carrying, loyal followers who are prepared to slog across inhospitable foothills, to lay siege, even storm any ill-tempered pique their Captain plans assault on.

They are not actually *carrying* spears (if they were, they would look silly, because they're only dressed in their underpants) but they are muttering together, starting to giggle, which is always a bad sign when a group of disturbed Koreans, or Bow Bell cockneys [11] for that matter are being encouraged to indulge what may turn out to be one of their cruder forms of unrestricted licence.

And then, at this juncture, there's a hail from the quay.

Jacque has been standing on the jetty, not far away, probably within sound, if not within sight of the action. With the aid of the floodlights he can see what's going on, while on the other hand, we can't see him, because we're on the seaward side of the trawler. Unfortunately, he's too far away to be anything other than an indistinct collection of heavily accented words, nevertheless, whatever he's saying probably relates to the trawler because, on looking up from the inflatable to the height of the vessel's bulwark, it seems the crew members are looking down on the dinghy and fiddling about with their Y-fronts.

So we're now faced with a row of five, rather short, muscular, and almost naked gentlemen, who seem intent on getting ....

What in the Name of God are they doing?

They're actually getting their dongs out, or whatever people who hail from well the other side of Suez call their dicks, when they judge the word cock to be just the one unacceptable step beyond what the truth now presently calls for.

The upshot (actually, the impending down-shot) of this development being, this crew of comedians are about to collectively - not pee over the dinghy - but piss in the punt. A totally different scale of endearment, prompting Sven to burst out with an exclamation (perhaps one of the very few sentences he's ever delivered which doesn't kick-off with his trademarked Swedish gambit). But instead of *Jah*, all he has time for is *Hey* and the rest of the sentence is lost in the mind boggling breadth of the broadside.

He may not be the prime target, but he's directly in the firing line, and cops it down his shirt, over his shorts, over his legs, over his sandals, because while this crew of cretins may not amount to much as marksmen, this trawler is wind-rode, providing no breeze-assist regarding range.

But for scatter, it's a different matter, enabling the five big bladdered buffoons to get off a cascading curtain of fire.

Sven can hardly believe it - yet how many microseconds do you need to respond to this sort of treatment?

We are shouting insults, while pushing off as best we can from the side of the trawler, hoping to escape the deluge.

I have the benefit of the one remaining oar, to use as a fending-off pole. Sven has to use his hands, so he's still vulnerable, well within range, and gets a most unchristian sort of a christening, splattered all over the vulnerable back of his neck.

While this special sort of confrontation (confirmation?) has been going on, Andrew's been casting about for the missing oar.

And seems to have found it, because here he comes, wallowing along, but anyway bringing the paddle, which he shoves over the side of the dinghy, while taking care to keep well away from the trawler (so he must be au fait with developments). Nevertheless, the brave fellow does what he can to help, by swimming alongside the punt while at the same time towing us away from the cascade, which in any case is all but over (the sort of in-use ammunition being, thankfully enough, not in unlimited supply).

Making the most of the lull in procedings, Sven is stripping off his shirt.

Getting out of his shorts.

Pulling off his sandals.

Down to his underpants, he flops over the side of the dinghy, using the rollover backwards technique most of us employ when scuba diving from an inflatable, which raises a ragged cheer from the trawlermen who evidently see this final act of our pissed upon withdrawal as some sort of an achievement of their very own devising (yet doesn't this merely show that disparity of cultural background does occasionally give rise to differing standards of barely credible behaviour?).

Whatever; their bit of fun is over anyway, because now I have both oars I'm once more in command (?) of the boat.

A quick pull takes us beyond range, outside the bright circle cast by the trawler's floodlights.

A welcome breathing space, that Andrew uses to heave himself aboard the dinghy, where he lies, panting, after the effort involved in his swim, which again, one must suppose, leads to the conclusion that too much of the sauce is not really conducive to maintaining the level of fitness which may be needed when involved in hair raising (for Sven, hair splattering) antics of this reprehensible sort.

To be fair, Sven is in better physical shape than Andrew.

In fact, he's a strong swimmer, now employing a bold freestyle which keeps his head partially submerged, only allowing a sideways, open mouthed gulp every third or fourth stroke to enable a replenishment of air.

This is all very well, but he's swimming blindly downwind, towards the jetty, certainly, but not towards the steps where we originally boarded the dinghy. This is a natural mistake, probably brought about by the fact that he's not all that worried where he's swimming *to* - more concerned with what he's swimming *from* - with the added bonus that he now has the benefit of a refreshing, a genuine getting rid of the pee sort of plunge which he was in no doubt at all that he needed.

Not wishing to lose sight of Sven (and despite a sliver of moon, it *is* a dark night) I'm following in his wake, with this row being easy enough.

It takes the punt well clear of the trawler, and offers an unobstructed view of the jetty, where Jacque can be seen, walking along, while at the same time gesticulating as well as shouting a barely distinguishable message.

'Atención; *atención!*' (or words to that effect).

Although not much of a linguist, I'm vaguely aware this bit of French shorthand may be the idiomatic equivalent of the well known Germanic word *achtung,* but how this all too brief communication relates to our present situation, I'm not, at the moment, all that clear in my mind; yet Jacque is persisting.

'Atención, Sven; atención. *Stop, mon ami.* Stop. **STOP** ! You are swimming towards a fil'thee part of ze 'arbour.'

The trouble is, with the sort of stroke Sven's employing, it's not easy to pick up messages of any sort, as most of the time he has both lugs flooded with water, so there's nothing we can do to warn him that he's about to swim into whatever happens to be lurking about in the corner he's now heading for.

True enough, he's swimming towards the jetty; and now we're a little closer, it does seem there's another set of steps located roughly where he's bound for. Yet the overriding factor involved with this sort of square-headed lack of perception is - his ill-chosen course is downwind, and rather a lot of other stuff has preceded him in this dubious direction.

Assorted junk, that's collected in a smelly cul-de-sac.

A disgusting bay (apropos Jacque's well-meant advice) formed by '*a turn in ze 'arbour wall,*' and into this crappy little corner, clumps of seaweed have been quietly accumulating, with other floating debris.

Bits of planks.

Broken hatch boards.

Plastic bottles, glass bottles.

Plastic bags, discarded dunnage.

The not so occasional knotted-off condom.

All sorts of nautical knick-knacks, brought and then held together with a generous slurp of goo, made up of the filthier sort of froth, that's composed partly of spilt diesel fuel and a threatening layer of waste oil.

The sort of stuff which should have been changed long before some lazy mechanic eventually decided it was way past the time he should, at last, have got somewhat reluctantly round to it.

Not a salubrious spot, so no wonder Jacque is trying to raise the alarm.

But Sven is still swimming obliviously towards it.

It's only when he feels, on the forward over-arm reach of his freestyle, the odd bit of timber coming into contact with his fingers he realizes there may be something wrong. And even then, he ploughs on for a few more strokes, before he *knows* he's made a mistake.

But the damage has been done.

He's right in amongst the plastic, the planks, and the soft stuff.

Literally, because while most vessels are supposedly equipped with holding tanks, they are not all that meticulous about using them, and God knows what could be knocking about in this particular part of the harbour, the most appalling sorts of floating turds being found revoltingly amongst them.

It's about this time that I, and I think also Andrew (because he's just let out a heartfelt groan) become aware we are about to be brought, perhaps not without a degree of rough justice, to the reluctant conclusion that the night's excess may be about to catch up with us.

Sven is obviously in need of assistance, so what we have to do now is make a real, even if it is a despairing effort to paddle the inflatable into the corner that he's bobbing about in. The lad apparently having been brought to a halt, not only by the goo, but also, one might suspect, by a perhaps unhealthy degree of fatalism, as it seems he's not making much of an effort to escape from his unbearably sticky predicament.

He's obviously at something of a loss, so Andrew offers him a few words of encouragement.

'Wha'hay' (he says) ' Wha'hay.' (12)

Now I have always assumed this sort of a *Wha'hay*, goes along with the well known phrase *Scots Wha'hay wi' Wallace Led*, but perhaps I've been wrong about that, because what I think Andrew's offering is some sort of a well-meant morale booster to Sven, who certainly appears to need it. The poor chap seems positively discouraged. Unable to make any decisive move, which means I will have to paddle the punt down into the middle of the goo that I had, quite honestly, been hoping to avoid.

This is not the most generous of thoughts, but the manoeuvre, in the murk, and well in amongst the worst of the muck, does at least enable Andrew to reach out a supportive hand, in order that Sven has some assistance when coming aboard over the stern of the dinghy.

The situation now is - we have one man rowing, upwind, and hopefully away from further catastrophe.

Andrew is helping Sven, who comes aboard with a heave of slippery ease, while displaying the slimy gleam of an oil-slickened porpoise. Nevertheless, they are now both crouched safely (safely?) in the stern of the inflatable.

This is certainly an improvement.

However, it's also a poor arrangement because, dammit, the weight distribution's all wrong (for one rash moment, the thought does occur that one of them should move for'ard), but then again, with our present run of accident-prone luck, perhaps this otherwise simple rearrangement should be postponed, just for a while (one can't have everything, can one?).

I'm now pulling manfully away, close to the harbour wall, proceeding alongside it, where Jacque can be seen silhouetted against the gleam of the dockside lights. These columns are arranged at regular intervals, perhaps forty or fifty metres apart, providing useful pools of light, also dark shadows which gloom off into the blacker parts of the jetty. As I row along, we pass into, and then out of these various patches of illumination, and as we're now leaving the lamp that threw its bleak and dispassionate beam on Sven's particular cauldron, both he and Andrew are back-lit, with their forms appearing as little more than dark shadows against the loom of the first of the harbour-side lamps. But as progress is made, we move into an area where the next of the jetty lights is predominant, and both Sven and Andrew are visible.

It's not a pretty sight.

Andrew is fully dressed, but soaked to the skin.

His filthy clothes are sticking to his body in an unbecoming way.

He's been rubbing his oil-covered hands over the front of his shirt, in a misguided attempt to remove some of the goo he picked up when helping Sven aboard the boat.

Nevertheless, he's still recognisable as our erstwhile Scot who, while no longer Bonny, does come across as a man who has escaped, perhaps not entirely unscathed, from an awkward situation.

Sven, on the other hand, presents a desolate picture.

Clad only in his underpants, which are no longer clean, he sits hunched on the stern of the inflatable, giving the impression he's no longer able or interested in defending himself, even if his life depended on it. For him, it would seem, the bell *has* tolled - not just for the end of the round, but to mark the end of the contest.

And who can blame him?

He's covered from head to foot in a gleam of diesel fuel.

The yellowish tint darkens significantly on the upper part of his body, while from his shoulders, around his neck, in and out of his ears, to the top of what was previously his rather attractive head of fine blond hair, he's plastered with the most disgusting crap imaginable.

Dark streaks, of what is probably waste oil.

Brown streaks, of what could be almost anything - is more than likely stuff which would have been far better left in the holding tank - and some of this gunge has worked into his eyes, which are screwed up with discomfort.

A man obviously in a state of shock.

Traumatised, emotionally drained, static in every department.

He's also muttering, *fy fan - fy fan - fy fan.'*

Now, what this Swedish phrase translates as, I'm not altogether sure. It could be the sort of pronouncement a man makes when he has suffered an indignity, of the sort which left him convinced that Fate has dealt him a cruel blow, and the scale of the event indicates that only a Supernatural Presence could have been involved in the malevolent extent of it.

There's not much you can do in these circumstances, short of a glance heavenward, in the hope a Benevolent Being has the time to intercede on your behalf (but as we all know, this sort of Divine Intervention can't always be relied on) so Andrew is doing what he can to comfort our stricken shipmate, this action being well intentioned, but perhaps not entirely successful.

Even though he's had the sensible idea that the worst of the goo should be removed from Sven's head and shoulders, short of attempting to scrape the stuff off using his bare hands, he doesn't know how to tackle the problem. Casting about for some sort of an instrument, he's lit on the pile of clothing which lies in the bottom of the boat, and with perhaps insufficient hindsight, has begun mopping Sven's muck-covered head with the same man's previously discarded shirt, and at first the job goes well enough.

Then the patient becomes restless.

Fidgeting about, trying to prevent Andrew carrying on.

'Hold still, Man. I'm doin' ma'best, and it's a definite improvement.'

But there's a wild look in Sven's eyes, which are flashing, still amazingly white, from an otherwise blackened face - which may be an indication that he's making at least some sort of recovery.

Previously, he seemed incapable of any sort of movement, but as he now mutters 'Jah' followed by an indeterminate mumble, it seems he could be on the mend, which up until this moment has been the matter of at least some degree of doubt.

There's only so much the body and the imaginative mind can take, and it seems that Sven has just about taken it, so in the circumstances - to display an adverse reaction to what is obviously a well meant attempt at a clean up does show maybe the partial recovery of his faculties, even if amounting to little more than a hint of the discrimination which was triggered by the unpleasant recollection of why he disposed of his foul smelling shirt in the first place.

While this minor, but still significant, rehabilitation has been in progress (and isn't recovery of short-term memory nothing less than a godsend?) I've been rowing away, forced to take short pulling strokes with the oars, partly because the inflatable is grossly overloaded and hard to row, but also because the whole experience has got to me - wrapped its sticky arms about my grubby physical condition - adversely affected *my* just about pissed upon persona.

What this means on the purely practical plane is - I'm running short of puff.

Without Jacque's verbal encouragement, which he's delivering while walking along the jetty, in order to keep up with the slowly moving punt, I would be hard pressed to row back to the original set of steps (those slippery bits of concrete-faced contrivance) where we all embarked, not much more than a debilitating, and for at least one of us, a demoralizing half hour since.

However, this thought does provide it's own particular, even if it is a rather peculiar incentive, because *The Steps* have now become a *target* (keep going, keep rowing, all will be well in the end). The sort of bizarre self-deception only a man who has been over-long at the sauce, far too long from his bunk, and is now close to some sort of physical and mental limit, could possibly aspire to. So when we *do* reach the steps, I feel a genuine sense of relief (what's in the past, is in the past) the rose-tinted present consists of getting Andrew and Sven ashore, sound and safe (safe and sound?) but in any case, you can see what I'm presently getting at.

That we have actually made it.

Arrived at the jetty, where a slight but sullen surge absent mindedly reminds anyone interested in the reach of the ocean's swell that a certain amount of care is needed when moving from an inflatable, to, and then up, a slippery flight of steps.

Andrew is first out, stepping gingerly; indeed, with even more care than he previously exercised. Making damned sure he's got a'holt of the handrail where he waits, good fellow, while Sven steps cautiously ashore.

Sven follows Andrew, to gain the safety of the jetty.

Jacque is waiting at the top of the steps, standing under a harbour-side lamp, arms akimbo.

He's smiling; at least, I think he's smiling. He is actually too far away for me to be absolutely sure, because I have prudently remained in the punt. But from where I am, although disadvantaged by having to look up into the light, it seems, while he's glad to see us, he's also trying to keep a straight face.

Due to a perhaps understandable oversight, Sven has left his discarded clothing in the dinghy, but when I shout up to remind him, it's Andrew who comes down to recover the soggy bundle. And the first thing he does is rinse them out, in rather more than a cursory manner, washer-woman style, while kneeling on the jetty steps (so he obviously has recent events somewhere other than merely in the back of his mind).

While this sensible bit of laundry's been going on, Sven has reached the top of the steps, and now he's done so, Jacque is examining him - starts walking round him, in an exploratory manner.

He's obviously more than somewhat taken aback, by the extent of the skin-dripping diesel. The oil-blackened, crap-covered, foul-smelling, man-like apparition that's answering to the name of square-headed Carlson, previously a shining example of all we expected from clean living Sweden.

Who could possibly believe it?

'Mon Dieu: it is worse, even than I thought.'

And having expressed his opinion, Jacque falls silent; but stands back to get, so it would seem, an even better view, having offered what some of us might think is less than the degree of sympathy Sven may expect he's entitled to.

However, Sven says nothing.

What can he possibly say?

But it's only the matter of a moment before I hear Jacque doing what he can to encourage our casualty. He's talking about getting him back to his apartment, in double-quick time, where he has plenty of *'hot wa'taire; detergent, nail brushes, lots of medication. And when did you 'ave your last jab, mon ami, for zose nastee leettle tetanus infections?'* - so he's still seeing things as he always unerringly sees them, while Andrew is also running true to form.

Now he's safely ashore, his mind is once more focused on the main issue.

'Are you coming back to Jacque's place, Val? I reckon we deserve a really thumping nightcap.'

Good God: have I heard him correctly?

Are we going to Jacque's place, for anything approaching a madcap?

I hardly have the strength, let alone the sense, to say nothing of the lack of sensibility to row my punt *half-way* back to my boat; while for the other doubtful half of this now vital journey, I will have to rely on the fitful puff of an unreliable breeze, which I'm not even sure is going to be blowing anywhere near my unreliable sense of wandering direction. Put another way - even if I manage the distance, I may not manage the course.

Plagued by the doubt, it does seem best to turn down Andrew's invitation; not that it matters a hoot, because there are other mumbled messages of *'O.K., we'll see you later.'* which just about matches my own *'I'll catch you in the morning.'* although which came first, and who said what to me, and what I then replied could well be the matter of yet another circular debate.

Not that anyone's got the time for it, because The Three Caballeros are moving along the jetty, while I row back in what I hope is the direction of my boat. My thoughts firmly centred on a badly needed pee, a desperately needed bath (this will be in the cockpit, with a bar of soap and a bucket) regardless of the long looked forward to bliss of getting my alarmingly reeled about head down.

However, as I row, I experience a twinge of conscience, amounting to real concern (is Sven going to be all right?). After all, it's not every day of the week that you can jump from *any* sort of frying pan into *this* particular fire, and I'm wondering what effect this escapade may be having on my new-found shipmate, who has turned out a crackerjack companion; so while pulling on the oars, I'm looking back at the jetty.

They're still in sight, but our square-headed hero is a little ahead of his two companions.

He seems to be skipping along, bollock naked, prancing towards the next of the harbour-side lights, and when he gets there, and is well illuminated, he's throwing up his arms in what could be interpreted as an undignified manner. One could almost say, with a degree of immodest acclamation.

He's also attempting a clumsy pirouette.

Can this be so?

Has anyone *ever* seen what amounts to a *brazen* pirouette?

Whether or not it is teetering?

Then, from across the water, comes the faint echo of laughter, accompanied by a very Scottish *Wha'hay*, as well as a laudatory Francophone hoot (I think Jacque may even be clapping).

So I rest my case

but not my oars
which now seem lighter
considerably lighter
in a weird sort of weigh
than they've ever felt before.

CHAPTER TWO: PAGE NOTES

---

(1) Page 31. Line 13 ...... *'may not have defended the bridge .... but have at least crossed one'.*

A reference to one of the poems of **Thomas Babington MACAULAY**, (*Lays of Ancient Rome*) which has been included in the perhaps tongue-in-cheek hope that the provision of an adequate role-model (Horatius) will go at least some way towards ensuring the seaman doesn't run away with the idea that, because he's completed a single-handed passage (no matter of what duration) he's accomplished anything of real significance.

The poem was written in India, the author having decided to dramatise four episodes from early Roman history and present the events in ballad form. The whole of the encounter, which centres around the defence of a narrow bridge by larger-than-life characters, runs to seventy stanzas, every one of which contains eight or more carefully constructed but occasionally over-laboured lines. If there is a lesson to be drawn from the work, it is of prodigious scholarship deployed in praise of patriotic fervour; brilliantly, even if bloodily, coloured by the comradeship displayed by gallant men at arms.

Macaulay was born at Rothley Temple, near Leicester, on October 25th 1800. From his earliest years he displayed a precocious talent, his mother claiming *'he could read almost as soon as he could speak, and write almost as soon as he could read'.* After private schooling he entered Trinity College, Cambridge, where he was only moderately successful, yet he was elected a Fellow of Trinity in 1824. He read law, and was later called to the bar, but never practised, being far more interested in politics and literature, where he soon made a name for himself with a series of articles, particularly a brilliant essay on Milton which was published in the Edinburgh Review in August 1825. His talent brought patronage; he was made a Commissioner in Bankruptcy in 1828 and eased into Parliament in 1830. Three years later he accepted a seat on the Supreme Council of India, and during his 5 years of service there left as a monument to his ability the Indian Penal Code, and also the Code of Criminal Procedure. On his return to the United Kingdom he became M.P. for Edinburgh, and was appointed Secretary for War. He served as Paymaster of the Forces from 1846, and was raised to the peerage in 1857. Yet Macaulay's major work is his *History of England*. The first instalment appeared in 1848, and then further volumes on a regular basis until the fifth, incomplete book some ten years later; but the task remained unfinished as Macaulay died in 1859, claiming he had left untouched seven-eighths of the work he actually contemplated.

(2) Page 32. Line 15 .... *'Jack Tar's bar'.*

The *'Jack Tars'* in this instance are ordinary seamen who, in the days of sail, revealed their calling by their rolling gait, and also by the traces of tar that were difficult to remove from their hands and clothing.

(3) Page 33. Line 22 ………. *'Bacchanalian scene'*.

A reference to *Bacchus*, the Roman god of wine and fertility; identical to the Greek god *Dionysus*. In Rome the festivals called bacchanalia became progressively objectionable until, in 186 B.C., they were forbidden by law. These celebrations were called *Dionysia* in Greece, and also marked by the consumption of large quantities of wine and other licentious goings-on. Bacchus is associated with the Egyptian god *Osiris*, who was perhaps not quite such a bad hat.

(4) Page 35. Line 13 ………. *'a tribute from no less an actor than Gielgud'*.

A reference to the English actor **(Arthur) John GIELGUD** who was born in London in 1904. He made his debut in 1921 at the Old Vic Theatre, and was recognised as an outstanding talent - perhaps the most influential actor of his generation.

He directed several Shakespearean Memorial Theatre productions after establishing his reputation as Hamlet (1929) and later moved into films, amongst them the role of Disraeli in *The Prime Minister* ((1940). He won an Oscar for his role in *Arthur* (1970); his last film being *Prospero's Books* in 1991. He was knighted in 1953, and in 1985 received the Laurence Olivier Award for his service to the stage.

The London Globe Theatre was renamed after him in 1994.

His books include an autobiography, *An Actor in his Time* (1979); *Backward Glances* (1989); and *Notes from the Gods* (1994). He died in the year 2000.

(5) Page 42. Line 29 ……….*'trip to the Gardens'*.

Referring to the *Tivoli Gardens,* in the city of Copenhagen, founded in 1843 by the Danish architect **Georg CARTENSEN**; now offering a variety of entertainment, from roller-coasters and theme rides for children, to beer gardens and restaurants for their parents. It's also possible to attend symphony concerts, enjoy pantomime theatre, or just feast your eye and your nose on some of the 100,000 flowers that bloom during the holiday season.

(6) Page 44. Line 3 ………. *'Gonzalo Rodriguez'*.

A master winemaker who gained experience in several premier locations, but is now responsible for the output of *Castillo Labastida,* the bodega situated in the north of the country, in the province of La Rioja, which is named after the river Oja and associated with the best known wine producing district in Spain. Although bounded by the Pyrenees to the north and the Sierra de la Demanda to the south west, the region of Rioja is not protected from the vagaries of climate; but the Labastida is an excellent example of how a master craftsman can produce fine wine in the face of occasional adversity. The *Vinicola de Labastida* is a cooperative, founded in 1965, with over 160 members, all of whom are located in Ripja Alavesa, having the sort of well-established vineyards which in favourable years are able to compete with the very best bodegas.

(7) Page 45. Line 33 .... *'five-card brag'*.

The card game is a form of poker, popular amongst those customers of waterfront bars who require something more demanding than pontoon, but have decided against seven-card stud.

(8) Page 59. Line 33 .... *'on the travail to (or was it from?) Damascus'*.

The occasion of the Apostle Paul's vision of Christ (*on* the road to Damascus) which marked his conversion to a faith other than that of a Pharisee; henceforth he became totally committed to the spread of Christianity throughout the Roman Empire, with his theological teaching exerting a profound influence in the Western world.

(9) Page 62. Line 19 .... *'little black'un'*.

The term is small-boat slang for a squall that ripples and darkens the surface of what otherwise remains a placid stretch of water. The initial effect is local, not much more than a puff, far from a genuine squall, but quite often these little black'uns precede an alteration in the wind pattern which shouldn't be taken lightly.
   In coastal conditions (in addition to the passage of a weather front) the configuration of the land, the formation of a bay, the receding extent of an estuary, the height of a prominent headland, can all affect the breeze enough to influence the outcome of a yacht race - if the competing helmsmen are quick enough to take advantage of the distortions, which often provide a useful weight of wind, and a shift, which has within it freeing capabilities. *Freeing* in the sense that it enables either the sheets to be eased, and thus increase the speed of the vessel on that particular course; or otherwise remain close-hauled, but able to lay the racing mark in prospect without having to waste time tacking.

(10) Page 63. Line 9 .... *'one-handed crew for your coracle'*.

Reference to an ancient boat, remarked on in Celtic waters after Caesar's second invasion of Britain (56 B.C.) but dating long before that significant event. Similar vessels are still used on Welsh rivers (principally the Teify) for netting salmon and sea trout, fished for under licence by locals who construct the craft from split wattle and tarred canvas (previously animal skin). These boats are difficult to control; as might be expected, because a coracle is round, extremely light (but not fragile) and small enough to be carried by one man who, when embarked on the sometimes fast flowing river, must manoeuvre the craft by the use of just one paddle.

(11) Page 65. Line 19 .... *'disturbed Koreans, or Bow Bell cockneys for that matter'*.

The Korean people chart their history back for more than 2,000 years and they are fine upstanding folk, industrious, and remarkably talented. The expression *'disturbed Koreans'* refers to the fact that the crew of the trawler had their watch-below disturbed, so they can hardly be blamed for being annoyed.

From the 17th century onward, the expression *'cockney'* was used to describe those Londoners born within the sound of the bells of the church of *St. Mary-le-Bow.*

These particular citizens came to be recognised by their peculiarities of speech (London, working class, and proud of it) complete with distinctive accent and clever rhyming slang.

(12) Page 69. Line 11.......... *'Wha'hay'* .... *he says* .... *'Wha'hay.'*

The carelessly quoted opening line of a Robert Burns poem, which reads:

> *Scots, wha ha'e wi Wallace bled* (Scots who have with Wallace bled)
> *Scots, wham Bruce has often led* (Scots whom Bruce has often led)
> *welcome to your gory bed*
> *or glorious victory*

And five more stanzas, with this absentminded presentation perhaps requiring an explanation for those people who are not familiar with the national bard of Scotland.

The 'poem' is in fact a song, entitled *Bruce at Bannockburn,* written by Burns in 1793 to commemorate the famous Scottish victory over Edward 2nd in 1314, when the English king was attempting to relieve the garrison at Stirling. The tune used to carry this ode was traditionally *Hey, tuttie taitie* and legend has it the poet's eyes brimmed with tears whenever he heard the opening notes of the melody carried on a hautboy (earlier name for an oboe).

Robert BURNS: born at Alloway, Aryshire, January 25, 1759, the son of a farmer who followed his father's footsteps for some years, then in a succession of perhaps less than successful endeavours, not all of which were concerned with the land. In 1789 he became an excise man, but found the work uncongenial; however, his unhappiness was due, so we are perhaps maliciously informed, partly to his own imprudence.

He had many love affairs, amongst them Mary Campbell; but he married Jean Armour in 1786.

His poetry appealed to his contemporaries because of its disarming simplicity, in marked contrast to the florid style otherwise representative of the age. The shorter poems carry an element of musical lilt, while others, such as *Holy Willie's Prayer* are masterpieces of satire. He could also be amazingly productive, writing *Tam O'Shanter* (1790) within the space of a few hours.

But for his songs alone he is worth his place in the annals of his country.

The first publication of his work, in 1786, was a literary event of importance, and from that date Burns has been the subject of an immense literature.

He died at Dumfries, on July 21, 1796; only 37 years old, but not without having enlivened our own age, as surely as his own.

MOVING ON WEST

IT seems to me, the man who first used the phrase *'the morning after the night before'*, probably stumbled across it immediately on waking to the blur of a well deserved hangover. To hit this wail of a cliché, so well and truly on any sort of a throbbing ache of a head, requires a view of the world that's likely to be present after an over-long night in a pub. And this unpalatable fact is well emphasised if you happen to be living aboard a poorly ventilated boat. In these circumstances, when you do wake up, particularly if the temperature is in the upper eighties, the atmosphere in the cabin is unbearably oppressive, little short of stifling.

Having opened one eye, which takes an inordinate, not to say ridiculous amount of effort to accomplish, the immediate impression is; everything seems far too hot for any sort of comfort.

Much too close for any sort of focus.

This may be a surreal sort of a problem, because the boat, or the cabin, can't have changed shape overnight. Nevertheless, it's a disturbing reminder of the distorted and out of focus images which plagued the previous night's tottered about indulgence, that are hung over now as a reluctant sort of retina - with the only hope of improvement being, get out of your bunk, struggle to your feet and, with what you would have to admit is genuine reluctance, stick your head out of the companionway hatch.

An incautious act, which turns out to be the second mistake of the day, prompting as it does the drunk's very own but usually silent lament, because aren't we always convinced, that the day that now dawns, would be far better served by the night before last?

However, this hope is beyond reach - nobody can skip the result of a tramped-about night on the tiles - and the reality is, and not only on this particular day, the sun will have already climbed over the foreshortened height of the yardarm.

It could be midday, and there's hardly a cloud in the sky, judging from the eye-piercing reflections that glint from every dancing wavelet, which all seem to be moving relentlessly in one dazzling direction.

Even when you avert your gaze, and look into the cockpit, all that greets you there is the evidence of last night's rude excess - a pile of dirty clothing.

The bucket is also nestling, untidily, on the afterdeck, complete with a half-used bar of soap and a cast-off smelly towel.

Climbing gingerly out of the cabin, and into the cockpit, it's possible to see the dinghy.

Dangling from the end of her painter.

Plastered with a filthy scum of oil.

So perhaps the first job, after what we hope is not going to turn out to be a trembled cup of coffee, is start on the task of cleaning up the punt.

This involves buckets of hot fresh water, which take an age to heat on the boat's primitive equipment, but it's worth waiting for, because the combination of hot water and a generous slurp of detergent just about does the job, providing it's combined with a genuine application of elbow grease.

However, this chore, which requires both physical and, perhaps more importantly, mental application, does provide a bonus, because work of this nature, conducted under the glare of a tropical sun, raises a sweat that would pass muster in a Turkish bath, which would probably have turned out to be cheaper, you may think, than the expense you've already been put to.

This churlish appraisal can't hide the fact that the stuff which is plastered over the dinghy is mostly on the outboard side of the inflated tubes. But there's also a crystalline sheen, over parts of the boat, that would provide an observant urologist as well as a reticent seaman with a fruitful line of research. This being yet another thought to push to the back of your mind, as you slave away, trying to bring order out of chaos, which is not made easier to bear by the knowledge that not all the pain has been self-inflicted.

So midday drifts, as well as being worked into the now beginning to ease headache of the blistering afternoon. And it's only a matter of a little more time, another cup of coffee, and a taste of cardboard sandwich before the thought finally surfaces, concerning when to organise the next, hopefully more sensible trip ashore - which you swear to God will not be allowed to run off the rails in the way last night's escapade was allowed to.

Absolutely not.

There are things, now, that need attention, with the filling of the fresh-water containers at the top of the list.

Then comes refurbishment of the ship's general stores, together with a trip to the Yacht Club, to sign the visitor's book and keep *out* of the bar, as well as indulge in a badly needed shower. In other words, a sensible reappraisal of what should have been done yesterday, so when a figure is observed, perhaps not all that clearly, standing at the top of the jetty steps, shouting what seems to be an encouraging message, the reaction, albeit reluctantly, is to wave back and not retreat below into your still hung-over shell.

It turns out to be Andrew, who asks, when I've boarded the punt and rowed over to within easy hail, if I've brought my laundry ashore (now there's a sensible fellow). Even if it does mean a pull back to the boat, to stuff into a kitbag the amazing amount of gear that's become grubby to the point of being obnoxious, and has reached this nose wrinkling stage within the relatively short space of the seventeen-day passage that terminated at this reprehensible spot. Yet it's nice to meet up with my old mate again; a thought which demonstrates how a few beers can knock the rough edges off a budding friendship in double quick time, and go on to foster the illusion you've known this guy for ages. Maybe even long enough to trust him with your laundry, and that wouldn't necessarily be the case in some other ports you've been into. He also helps bring the inflatable ashore, which we stow, with the oars, behind the back of the same shed where we were lucky enough to find her yesterday (an euphemism for this morning) but we're both well aware of that.

'How do *you* feel?'

'Ach, a bit rough about the edges, I'll have to admit. But it was a good night, wasn't it?'

There's no need to answer this rhetorical question, yet it's not to be ignored, because it raises the nagging little doubt that he may not be feeling quite as bad as you are. There's also the implication he thought it all worth-while, with these straws in the wind being a reliable indication of what may be just around the corner, if you're daft enough to lose control of this particularly sensitive tiller.

'What happened to Sven?'

'We went to Jacque's place; it took an age to scrub the crap off him.'

'Did he catch his plane?'

'Aye, and Jacque arranged a call at the hospital along the way.'

That's a relief.

It's all very well being up to your neck in the soft stuff, one helluva joke for everyone concerned; but the next move should be straight to the Doc and roll your sleeve up for a large shot of broad-spectrum antibiotic.

'What's Jacque doing today?'

'He's back in his office, probably wondering how many crew members will fail to turn up for duty.'

That leaves Andrew.

He's a nice enough guy, but I've known him all of nine hours, and here he is, turned up at the jetty, obviously intent on carrying the how d'you do a step further; maybe wanting to develop it in his own particular way.

Is this a peek at incipient paranoia?

I hope not.

It may be the jaundiced look that's apt to colour your attitude when you're still slagged off with the booze. Nevertheless there are still things and places to explore, hopefully without getting slushed to the gills again while you're doing it, or giving the impression of being the sort of long-nosed, sticky beaked prat who can't rest until he's explored the ins and outs of everybody's backside.

'Is there a laundrette in town?'

'Yes; but I've got an apartment in one of the hotels, the staff there'll fix it up.'

So it goes; what could turn out to be a reasonable relationship - without the accent on relationship.

But what's he doing in Lanzarote?

And what, for that matter, am I doing here, living aboard a small boat that's recently pulled into the harbour, and is soon about to pull out again.

However, you don't ask yourself these questions just because you've met someone in a waterfront bar, even if you happen to meet again later; if you do, you're not heading for *incipient* anything - you've got it, and the prognosis isn't encouraging.

My own experience being, that a free-wheeling attitude to strangers gathers its own momentum amongst people who sail about in small boats. It may be, somewhere along the line, and the line would be drawn well before this passage was undertaken, or even contemplated, there's been a tendency towards introspection which sticks out like a childishly sucked thumb in some budding ocean wanderers.

Yet after you've spent a week, or maybe a month or more alone, in what turned out to be something less than your previously imagined splendid isolation, when you *do* make port, and get yourself ashore, if you were shy, surly, or just plain awkward before you started, the likelihood is, you have at least given the gregarious side of your nature a chance to find, maybe even fight its way to the surface, and this could be the well buried reason that tempted you afloat in the first place.

But if this is going through your mind, when you're standing on the jetty, having rowed ashore with your bag of dirty laundry, then - the men in the white coats are on their way.

However, there's no gainsaying the fact that, hail fellow well met or not, some people *are* inclined to come on just a bit too strong, and it's apt to raise at least some questions in the mind of the person who thinks he's about to be leaned on.

But I don't think this is the case with Andrew.

The attractive proposition is - *he's got a car* - and would I like a look around the island?

Too good an offer to turn down.

And it's not only the wheels that come in handy, because dropping across someone who knows the place is also a significant advantage.

In these circumstances, even if you had to tramp about with holes in your boots and an empty rucksack, it would be unforgivable to move on without making some sort of an attempt to explore this fascinating place, with the proviso that, for someone wandering around in a small boat, *all* islands fall into this catch-all of a category. So we're soon rattling about the hinterland in a jeep, with Andrew driving.

The fact that the old vehicle doesn't possess a top, hard or otherwise, doesn't matter a hoot on Lanzarote. And it soon becomes apparent that the place has a barefaced charm of its own, as the track sweeps across a dusty tableland, the *Meseta de el Risco,* then skirts the cone of *Monte Corona,* two thousand sweltering feet from the valley floor. The whole of the blistering island composed of lava flow and pumice, as grey deserts fall off brown cliffs that plunge recklessly to blue seas, flecked with white breakers sweating rainbow driven spray from the surge of an encircling ocean.

So you could say, that parts of this island are apt to catch the eye.

Included in the list are weathered buildings which started life as impoverished casa de labranzas, but they've found their real niche, and now provide a glass of wine and a well served comida to cross-roaded travellers, lounged under the shade of flowered pergolas, arrived on the equivalent of draught-laden donkeys.

Then, before returning to Arrecife, a visit to the *Institute Manrique* [1] to learn a little more of this artist's life and work, some items having been previously admired on the drive round the island; including, particularly, a three-dimensional pastiche. An intricate contrivance which tickles a seaman's fancy by offering what appears to be the boss and battered remains of one chipped blade of a ship's three-bladed propeller. The barrel of a bilge pump which must have proved inadequate to keep even the smallest vessel afloat. And a battered binnacle, rescued from yet another shipwreck, that the Court of Enquiry found was caused by the compass being somewhat less than adequately protected.

Put thoughtfully together, the whole is so much more than merely the sum of its derelict parts. Much in the way that Lanzarote is more than a pile of arid cinders, because this volcanic place and its people, together with Manrique's unerring eye as an artist, undoubtedly are, in their own dramatic and provocative fashion, taken one with another, *absolutely stunning.*

So Andrew's well pleased with our little excursion, which took the whole of the later part of the afternoon, as well as on to a darkening evening, leaving us tiredly ensconced in a smart restaurant, overlooking the emerging lights of a soon to be twinkling harbour.

Enjoying a beer, which I paid for; because I've been careful, throughout the jaunt, to keep more than just my bare financial end up.

'You liked the island?'

'Nothing less than amazing; and thanks once again for the trip.'

'Going to stay long?'

'No: I'll be on my way tomorrow.'

'Where are you bound?'

'I'll be moving on west.'

'Calling at Tenerife?'

It's a good question, with the answer being I'm not exactly sure where I'm going to call. There are half a dozen places which could be on the agenda. Probably not Fuerteventura, the next island in line. But Gran Canaria sounds attractive - who hasn't heard of Las Palmas? Why not call there?

'The reason I ask is; I happen to have a house at Tenerife. As a matter of fact, I live there, and I was wondering, if there was any chance?'

And well he might.

There are lots of reasons for sailing alone, and if I looked hard enough I could probably find a few now. It might seem invidious, but I'm extremely cautious about taking on crew, because in *every* circumstance, for good or ill, the people aboard alter the whole character of a voyage. And when you think about it, they're bound to.

It's also worth bearing in mind that the strategic small-boat harbours of this world, the ports of departure for ocean passages, are littered with vessels which have come to grief; not brought about by the difficulties involved with the sailing, or even lack of finance; but by crew problems. The plain truth being, that to be cooped up with someone in a small boat involves its own hazards, most of which, while they may seem too trivial to mention before the voyage begins, become impossible to live with well before the agonizing trip is even halfway screamingly over.

So how does Andrew fit into the scheme of things?

Not very well.

He's fond of a drop, and I have a rule: no booze during a passage.

He smokes, while I can't stand the stuff myself, and I don't see why I should put up with such a stupid, not to say disgusting habit.

Yet what do you do?

You buy the guy another beer (that's what you do) and while enjoying your meal, which now seems slightly less appetizing than previously, try and find out a little more about him.

He's fifty, if he's a day: he *smokes* (but why keep on about it). And he's just ordered a cigar, which he obviously intends to fire-up while he enjoys a glass of port, after he's finished, or maybe even before he's finished his carelessly-eaten cheese and scattered about bits of biscuit, which just happens to be another of those hardly worth mentioning - nevertheless what I rate as being *far* too close to the sort of bad mannered table habits which irritate the hell out of me.

The other side of a different sort of coin is, Andrew's married, and he tells me his wife is waiting for him in the house on Tenerife. They have two children, girls, one of whom is over in the 'States at Columbia University, while the other is back-packing about Australia.

It all sounds normal enough.

And it *is* only a few days sail to Tenerife.

The sort of little more than coastal passage, where it could prove beneficial to have another person aboard. There are also plenty of small harbours along the way, any one of which may prove handy as a bolt hole if it turns out to be needed.

'When can you get away?'

'Whenever I like, my work here has reached the stage where I could leave tomorrow morning.' (got it all worked out, hasn't he?). So the next thing to find out is, what seagoing experience he's got. A question that's not all that important, yet might as well be asked.

'I've mucked about in boats, and done quite a bit of sailing.'

Now hurrah to that; and with this reply, it may seem reasonable to assume he's the man for the job.

However, there's just one crucial word too many involved in the answer; because those of us who haven't forgotten how to holystone a deck are also aware that, *'quite a bit of sailing'* may be another of those naïve inversions, where the misplaced nuance of a word is apt to turn the whole of the inexperienced thing on its head. While the real old dog, whose family name is *Dana* [2] (who you haven't got to ask, anyway) turns the question aside, with the smiling admission that he has done a bit. Then then closes the door, because for him and his salt there's seldom much of a call for quite a bit of sailing.

This may seem like the splitting of hairs, the rustle of straw in the wind, or just the sigh of unused breeze in the riggin'. And in any case, there are other things which influence your decision, regarding the web-foot or otherwise of the person who now seems to want little more than just a bit of a sail.

And perhaps we should leave it at that.

Because where does all this backing and filling leave our prospective relations with Andrew?

On an even keel, that's where it leaves it, because he doesn't know any more about me than I know about him which doesn't amount to a lot. The sort of classic situation where, if you don't nip the thing in the bud, it blossoms all over the port, regardless of the blasted cigar, to the point where it's too late to turn the clock back without offering real offence.

So we're now deciding who is going to do what tomorrow morning, with Andrew responsible for purchasing stores (strict admonitions not to buy too much), while I'll bring the punt alongside at nine-thirty sharp, in order that we can ferry the stuff back to the boat.

What an evening.

What a couple of days!

It's a relief for the skipper to say 'see you tomorrow' and get back aboard, because the morning comes quickly enough. As another fine day, without anything resembling the hangover of the night before last, which is just as well, as Lanzarote seems to be turning out to be another of those damned but interesting places where one thing leads to another.

Andrew's on time: nine-thirty, at the top of the jetty steps, having marshalled what seems a mountain of gear.

A pile of kit that includes a dirigible of a suitcase, and its younger brother; both of which would fit well enough in the hold of a 747, but will be somewhat harder to stow aboard an already overcrowded thirty eight-foot cutter, where the accent is necessarily placed on a five letter word spelt s.p.a.c.e.

Along with Andrew's domestic chattels are two specimen cases, equipped with a series of drawers, protruding handles, and very sharp corners. They also require somewhere to live, regardless that the contents are no longer with us, but are still making claims on the five letter word, and an expletive, with one fewer letter than that.

He also has a shoulder bag, of the type a third world airline may be persuaded to allow through as cabin luggage. That the owner then finds won't fit under his seat, or in the overhead lockers that run the length of the aircraft. And we haven't finished yet.

The grub takes up four bulging plastic bags, so we will hardly be short of food, or booze, because two more bags have been doubled-up, one plastic skin slipped within another, making sure there's no doubt they're up to the job of supporting the weight of who knows how many bottles of wine, which Andrew assures me is his own stock, and nothing to do with the boat.

There are still more softly clinking items, also under Andrew's wing, which have been discreetly wrapped in tissue paper. And yet another container; the sort of upmarket, tastefully decorated cardboard tube that purveyors of the better class of whisky use to attract their customers' intriguingly drawn attention.

My own modest contribution to this pile of gear consists of eighteen, empty, two-gallon, plastic, fresh water jugs, ferried ashore in the dinghy, which now have to be rinsed out and filled. A job Andrew agrees to undertake, while I hump the second-class stuff down the steps, and start to load some of it into the dinghy.

While this work is in progress, Jacque turns up, with another plastic shopping bag, containing a selection of fruit and two sticks of fresh bread, which are handed over after he's cast an amused eye at the gear piled on the jetty, with the smiling remark to Andrew, and a sly little wink to me.

'Here you ar' mon ami, a leetle present, just in case you run short of any-zing on your *long* journey to Tenerife.'

He's also taken the trouble to visit the Harbour Master's office, get a weather report, and file an Intention of Passage Certificate, or whatever they call that sensible precaution in this easy-going part of the world.

So, amongst the mountains of gear, we're preparing to leave.

Andrew, with Jacque's help, has filled the water containers, and we're engaged on the task of carrying them down the jetty steps, then ferrying everything out to the boat. The job takes the best part of an hour, with the suitcases being the really awkward items. The procedure being, to hold the dinghy alongside the parent vessel while Andrew makes the transfer, then I pass his baggage up, so he can get hold of the handles and lift the kit safely aboard.

Piled on the afterdeck, the stuff doesn't look any smaller than it previously did on the jetty. But it's got to go somewhere, and we might as well start on the task, with Andrew lowering the gear down, through the companionway hatch, while I'm below deciding where to put it.

His personal gear can go for'ard, in the sail locker, well cushioned, as it happens, by the bags of sails themselves. The grub, mostly tinned stuff, doesn't present a problem - there are lockers under the pilot berths which offer plenty of scope.

It's when we come to the booze that a little more thought is needed.

This difficulty raising its head when Andrew, who has cleared the afterdeck and passed the last of the plastic shopping bags below, climbs down and joins me in the saloon. He's a large man, and the term saloon is open to misinterpretation in this context. The boat may be thirty-eight feet long, but the hull is narrow, with drawn-out ends that are noticeably short of headroom. Even in the saloon, which is all of six feet wide between the pilot berths, it's impossible to stand upright; unless under the plastic dome (a viewing bubble) which enables a sometimes reluctant crew to keep a reasonable lookout in a turbulent seaway without actually getting his head wet.

After all the hard work, Andrew has perched himself on one of the saloon settees, taking a well-earned breather. But to call this piece of plywood a 'settee', is pushing it a bit, because it's not upholstered furniture in the accepted sense of the phrase. Merely the top of a narrow locker, equipped with a strip of canvas-covered rubber, kept in place by a batten of timber, narrow enough to cut into the thighs of anyone rash enough to assume that he, or she, has at last found somewhere to settle their butts.

Spartan, is the word that springs to mind, and this is usually confirmed by the apprehensive look which sometimes drifts into the eyes of unsuspecting strangers, strayed aboard this simple vessel, Andrew not excluded.

'Where shall I put the wine?'

There's nothing remotely resembling a wine locker to be found aboard the hooker. The small amount of booze normally carried usually gets stuffed into odd corners, more often than not ending up, wrapped in cold weather clothing; which is, after all, nothing less than the rational, well-cushioned, bottle-saving solution.

'Don't you have a fridge, or an icebox? I've brought a few bottles of white.'

'I'm afraid not.'(and while I'm passing on this information) I'm also wondering if I've remembered to tell him I don't normally drink, when working, as against living aboard the boat.

It's well into the forenoon, and the cabin's becoming stuffy, even with the companionway hatch wide open and the for'ard hatch propped up. And this lack of a cooling draft may be quite significant - a real straw, but not in the real wind. Nevertheless, it is an indication of how much of a sailing breeze might be found on deck, so after we've stowed the bottles and the other fragiles, it's time to get out of the cabin and start thinking about the task that lies ahead.

The vessel is swinging round a hook that's located, broadly speaking, in the southern part of the harbour.

We only have the benefit of a light air, and what there is, hails from a nor'easterly direction. This means we will have to weigh anchor and sail close-hauled until we can tack and clear the harbour entrance.

There's nothing difficult about this manoeuvre, particularly when there's a crew aboard the boat. In these circumstances, the deck work falls to one person, while the actual conduct of the sailing - getting the vessel to pay off correctly - will be the province of the unencumbered other. A simple exercise, provided there's enough breeze to keep the wheels in motion.

'It looks as if, Val; we'll ha' to motor out.' (indeed we might, if we had an engine).

'By the way, Andrew; you've obviously told your wife we'll be sailing down the coast. Did you happen to mention our likely time of arrival?'

The upshot of this minor contretemps is - Andrew rows ashore in the dinghy to 'phone from a dockside booth, while I get the sail-ties off the mainsail.

And when this task has been completed, start getting the big genoa on deck; hauling the sail, in its bag, from the locker, up through the for'ard hatch, and then on with the job of snapping the piston hanks along the outer forestay. While I'm about the task, I can see Andrew rowing back to the boat, and he's soon alongside.

'Did you get through to her?'

'No, she must be out: but I did get hold of Jacque, he'll pass the message on.'

So we're just about organized.

The delay has got to be laid at my door, as I have been somewhat less than frank in my dealings with Andrew. I should have told him the vessel doesn't have an engine. To pretend that it slipped my mind is to offer a degree of speciousness which does little more than bugger the beggar's belief.

How does Andrew take it?

With a broad grin.

So we're now sitting in the cockpit, grinning at each other, while deciding on the next move.

The dinghy must be got on board, deflated, and stuffed down the for'ard hatch, on top of Andrew's cases.

The mainsail and genoa are ready to set, so the question now is - shall we take lunch before we make sail?

Or shall we get on with the job, and then grab a bite in the cockpit after we've cleared the harbour?

Obviously, we get on with the job.

We are not aboard this hooker as pressed men, [3] the name of the game is enjoyment, and there's a great deal of pleasure to be gained by sailing your vessel about.

Because there's not much wind available, the big genoa is an absolute necessity. This area of canvas, the largest fore-and-aft sail carried aboard the boat is set on the outer forestay, with the luff running from the tack, right to the top of the mast, while the foot of the sail sweeps across the foredeck, outside the standing-rigging. A single-part genoa sheet leads from the clew to a turning block, situated well aft, and then forward again to a powerfully geared winch. The canvas (a super-strong synthetic cloth) is of the lightest possible weight that's been found to stand up to the stresses involved in the setting of the sail, without losing its essential shape, which has been carefully designed to do no more, nor much less, than bend a bit of wind.

It's all just as simple as that.

Andrew is up for'ard, recovering the anchor; not too hard a task, as there's not much length of chain involved and the hook breaks out easily enough. The mainsail and the genoa are both up, not yet drawing, so as soon as Andrew has the anchor weighed, I intend to get the vessel to pay off on starboard tack, gathering way in order to sail up the harbour until we're in a position to go about and make another board, which will take us clear of the mole and out beyond the breakwater.

So it's still just as simple as that.

But there is a moment of truth approaching, because in order to get the vessel footing correctly, I need some help from the crew.

'Back the genoa, please, Andrew. I want to get away on starboard.'

I'm now watching my foredeck hand rather carefully - not simply wondering if he knows port from starboard - but conscious that, should we pay off on the incorrect tack, we will be heading in the wrong direction, about to bungle into a group of trawlers and other small craft which clutter that part of the harbour.

'**Back the Genny**, Andrew.' (a sharp command) while shades of *quite a bit of sailing* pop in and out of the mind.

This challenge raises another broad grin from our Scottish hero, while he grabs the genoa and holds part of the sail outboard - on the correct side (blowing her off) bringing the breeze over the starboard bow. Then as soon as we're heading in the right direction, Andrew feeds the sail around the inner forestay in order that I can haul on the genoa sheet - just enough, to prevent the unbecoming rattle of uselessly flapping canvas.

Not sheeting in so hard that the bow continues to blow off.

Merely *shaping* the sail in order to get the essential bit of a draw which will move the vessel forward, gaining steerage way, because without this positive movement . . .

'What shall I do with the chain, Val?'

'How dirty is it: any mud?'

'Aye, it could do with a bucket or two.'

While Andrew tidies the foredeck, we're beginning to foot to the light nor'easterly breeze, not attempting to pinch her to windward, just close-reaching. Taking advantage of the puffs, to pick enough way to see her through the patches, using the weight of the vessel - the two grey tons of lead which hang as the fin of the keel; so with the hull, we now have four long tons of engineless boat ghosting silently along.

Unless you count the sound of the brush and the splash of the bucket that Andrew is using to scoop and then chuck, sluicing great dollops of deck-wetting 'oggin over the mud-covered anchor and chain.

Aren't some of us easily pleased?

Just because the tiller feels as light as an *f* in a feather, while I'm sitting down to leeward, looking at the genoa, watching for the tell-tale flutter which indicates an unhelpful wind shift, and having eased her through the setback, feeling the surge in the hull, levered through the length of the tiller as a freeing puff strains the bellying canvas.

Sailing?

What a simple, yet enduring pleasure.

'Shall I leave the pick hangin' over the roller, Val? Or do you want it all below?'

'If you come aft, Andrew, I'll tend to it; then we'll tack, and you can take her out of the harbour.' (another large grin from the crew).

As we change places, and wait for another puff. The puff that'll make sure we have enough boat speed to see us through the eye of the wind, such as it presently is.

Andrew at the tiller, smiling, with one eye on the luff, while the other scans the jetty, looking for Jacque (the best bit of his day so far). And the day ain't over yet, because Jacque *is* standing on the jetty, so Andrew sails her within easy hail, but says nothing - studiously ignoring his friend.

'Looking good, mes amis.' (and Jacque is laughing) as he shouts his over the water greeting.

'Au revoir, Andrew: see you again in two weeks, eh?'

Andrew is sailing the boat.

Andrew is sailing the boat!

Wow!

Andrew **is** sailing the boat.

And as with all such events, the time comes to acknowledge the fact, so I'm at the sharp end, ready to haul the bulk of the genoa clear of the inner forestay.

'Lee . . . Ho.' . . . (a rather Scottish lee-ho, yet it's a grand Lee-Ho for Awe' That).

The helm's down, the sheet's free, the crew's hauling like mad, pulling through the genoa.

Andrew is smiling. The audience applauds (not *all* that ironically), the breeze shows up on the other bow, and we've tacked.

Sailing away from the jetty.

Heading for the outer mole, well upwind of the breakwater.

Leaving barely the trace of a wake. At least, not one you can see, as Andrew turns, and then waves; one, slow, overhead movement of an outstretched, oh-so-seaman-like arm (any more and he'd spoil the effect).

I think I can hear Jacque laughing, as Andrew keeps her footing away from the jetty.

Mainsail and genoa drawing nicely.

The boat picking up speed as we clear the breakwater and feel the benefit of a clean sea breeze, as the swell lifts and then lowers the hull, lifts and then lowers the hull, lifts and then lowers the hull while a freeing puff heels the vessel. A timely and rhythmic reminder that the anchor and chain are still cluttering the foredeck, when they should be below, out of harm's way (the result of acting the goat in the harbour).

'How far is it to Tenerife, Val?'

I have absolutely no idea (I thought he might know that). So after the anchor work, it seems we should have a look at the passage chart; initially British Admiralty Chart No 1870, which only takes us as far as Gran Canaria, but it's enough for the moment.

We should be steering a bit west of south, nothing more precise than that.

If we lay this course, it means the breeze will be brought well round, ending up fine on the port quarter, and as it's little more than a light air we'll have to take in the genoa and set our biggest spinnaker. A rarely-used sail that's been in the locker long enough, it might even be discoloured in places.

'Run her off a little, Andrew; I want to hand the genoa and clear the foredeck; you can latch-in the self-steering gear.' (a bit of a pause, then).

'I'm afraid I don't know how to do it; I haven't been shipmates with one of these gadgets before.'

But it's worth using the gear, because we'll have an extra hand available to set the big balloon.

Aboard this vessel, *setting the big balloon* involves a pair of spinnaker poles and their heel lifts; two topping lifts; two guys and two braces; as well as the spinnaker sheets, together with two endlessly rove inhauls and outhauls, complete with *their* blocks. The sort of mad cat's cradle someone who usually sails by himself contrives, over a head-scratching period of time, to solve the problem posed by a double-headed rig where, because the inner forestay limits the swing of a conventional spinnaker pole, a double-pole arrangement provides a convenient answer to a nice little nautical problem (one man, attempting to gybe a large spinnaker) with far too much wind in the sail and a dangerous lurch to the seaway.

So what happened to beautiful simplicity?

It's all been led back to the cockpit, where Andrew and I are now sitting, enjoying the sight - steering the vessel while playing with a diaphanous bubble that's attached to the truck by a halyard which allows the kite to fly, but not float, or float, but not fly, free from the top of the mast.

This topping, often titillating, sometime tease of a sail billows, fills, falls, and then billows again to the varying puff of a breath of an air, A brilliant, if delicately balanced bauble that's bright blue, with scarlet rays radiating from the yellow eye of its brightly-centred sun.

(don't jump to conclusions) this isn't a radially-cut sail.

This lovely piece of nonsense is this big and balloon light because, in a boat without an engine, it's sometimes essential to keep way on the vessel in the lightest of following airs, which could turn into a - being set ashore, sort of a situation - where the vessel *must* be kept moving, else all is in jeopardy, and that includes the crew of the about to be shipwrecked disaster.

'That's quite a sail, Val.'

Indeed it is.

It's also time for lunch; well past noon, on a blisteringly hot day, running before a zephyr of a breeze, bound for . . .

Who cares where?

So it really *is* time for lunch.

'What's easy to get, Andrew, of the grub you brought aboard this morning?'

'There's a nicely-cooked chicken; Jacque's bread rolls; some excellent cheese; plenty of butter; several good bottles of white to choose from; a fine heart of celery.'

Sounds great: he may even be able to cater, if you discard the related problems, and this means the butter, which will have melted into a barely recognisable blob (also, what am I going to tell him about the ship's standing orders, regarding the use of booze aboard the vessel?).

We are sitting in the cockpit of a small boat, sailing from one fair isle to another. The trip, short though it will probably be, should turn out to be an enjoyable, even if modest additional step in Andrew's seafaring experience. Regarding the booze; it seems a pity to restrict his anticipated enjoyment, with what he may see as the application of a draconian rule, particularly when, up to this minute, he knows nothing at all about it.

And there's the rub.

What I should have done, when we were discussing the passage, is casually mention the fact that I don't drink when aboard the boat - and left it at that. He would then have been presented with a fait accompli which would have been hard to ignore. The only response available now, short of an argument, is to smilingly accept (or decline the prospect) and keep on filling his glass.

That's as maybe.

I didn't tell him when I had the chance, so I'm now left with a rather tricky decision.

It's all very well enjoying a liquid lunch, when you are safe and sound ashore. But when you're afloat, dependent, quite possibly, on a degree of awareness which doesn't fit all that well with other people's idea of watch-keeping . . .

'Where do you keep the corkscrew, Val? There's a bottle of Chardonnay that'll go very well with the chicken.'

Caught by the short and curly.

Bowled.

By a degree of ebullience that's hard to deflect (in a small boat, where are you going to deflect it *to*?). So it looks as if we *are* going to open the wine. And of course it does go well with the chicken, even though it's mullingly warm in the glass, with the meal providing, and the crew enjoying a picnic in the cockpit, while the vessel ghosts along under the spell of her brilliantly-coloured spinnaker with the sail playing its own particular part in proceedings by harnessing every puff of vagrant air that's hobo but honest enough to wander carelessly over to crisp up the contours of our capricious but capable kite.

'Do you want some more cheese, Val?' (not really; as a matter of fact I'm becoming vaguely interested in the course we're *not* steering).

As usual, we've pigged-out on the grub; but if we're sensible, we should avoid doing the same with the booze.

'How far *is* it to Tenerife?'

Back to the chart; not as it *should* be examined, sensibly laid out on the chart table - just scrambled about in the cockpit, where greasy fingers leave smudgy imprints on the well-ruled margins of an otherwise pristine publication.

But roughly speaking.

Haphazardly measured, it's about two hundred miles to Tenerife.

It sounds a decent hop, yet it's actually little more than a coastal passage, as most of the time we'll be well within sight of the shore, firstly running along the eastern coast of Fuerteventura, then altering course to make Gran Canaria, with this waypoint being about one hundred and thirty miles from where we are now.

Time to set watches.

Normally, when sailing alone, I try to get some sleep during the day, under the reasonable presumption that other vessels, on their lawful business about the world's oceans, keep a seamanlike lookout - at least in the direction they're heading.

But that fond hope has been dented on several occasions, and I now proceed on the assumption that *all* powered vessels, particularly two hundred thousand-ton supertankers, creaming along at speeds in excess of fifteen knots - all craft of this sort, suffer from the *Mary Celeste* syndrome, [4] which means, that if boarded, these vessels would be found devoid of wing of the bridge watch keeping crew. Apart from the ship's cat; the role model mog, [5] bred and born in Cheshire who, when supposedly on mouse-watching duty, is caught fast asleep in the pantry (a cautionary tale, which highlights the problems posed by our own unseamanlike procedure).

'We have to set watches, Andrew: do you fancy doing four on, and four off; or six on and six off?' (but I don't want him to vote for the second of those options), so it's a nice little question, and not only for him.

'I'm not bothered, Val.' (that's in reply, I sincerely hope, to the enquiry concerning the *duration* of the watches). 'Do you want a drop more wine?'

'Not just now, Andrew; thank's all the same. I've just about had it. Regarding the watches: shall we take four on and four off?'

'Suits me.'

So we're slipping into a seagoing routine.

Running before the same capricious air.

Having to steer the boat, because there's not enough wind passing the self-steering vane to keep the vessel on course.

This isn't an imposition. It just means the big spinnaker is so effective we're almost keeping up with the breeze, with the helmsman having something to do. A useful development, because there's nothing worse than lounging about in the cockpit of a small boat without a nautical focus.

In such idle-Jack circumstances, there are slumbrous forces at work. As the vessel moves to the loll of the swell, the hand that's not tending the tiller, cradles the face of the deep, finding the sigh of the following air 'mounts to no more than the languorous lilt of a lullaby.

So it comes as no surprise to see Andrew is fast asleep.

Stretched out on the leeward side of the cockpit.

His straw hat pushed down, shading his eyes and the lower part of his face. The back of his head awkwardly supported by the bridge-deck bulkhead (so he's guaranteed to wake with an alarmingly stiff neck).

While over on the starboard quarter Lanzarote is slipping quietly astern. And fine on the other quarter there are several vessels, four or five miles distant, one of them on a parallel course to our own, overtaking at a bow-waved rate of knots.

We are six miles off shore.

Sailing before a moderate puff of an air.

Rolling quietly about in a hinderable lop.

Making significant progress, because we have the benefit of an easily driven hull, and that super, super-light spinnaker.

However, we should keep our wits about us because, although the specialist sail is doing a marvellous job, we are not all that manoeuvrable when under this sort of restrictive downwind rig. If we had to alter course and take avoiding action, we only have the option of a point or two either side of an almost dead run, which is the course we're presently steering.

'Andrew.'

But he really is zizzed-out.

'And . . . drew.' . . . (more in hope than anger) 'will you take the helm for a moment; I want to go below and get the binoculars.'

And not only the binoculars; it really is time to get on top of the job.

We are making about two knots and an onion (which is, for some totally obscure reason, the way some of the greyer of the grey old dogs used to describe a fraction of a knot). And on top of this, which I still find charming, as a notifiable degree of imprecision, we probably have a half-knot of favourable current under the hull. So taking one guess-estimate with another, we will probably be within a few miles of Puerto del Castillo by two o'clock in the morning, as this small boat harbour is about thirty five miles further along the track.

'**Andrew**, come on mate, *Wakey, Wakey*; it's your trick. I've got things to do below.' So although we've only been at sea for the latter part of the afternoon, spilling on to the evening, you begin to wonder how sharp the crew is going to be throughout the coming night, particularly during the early hours of the morning. The dismal graveyard watch, which follows midnight's long-yawned hour.

'Come on, Andrew; you've got to get up!'

'Coming, Val, coming . . . Hell, I've got a stiff neck.' (and he does look a bit ragged, particularly about the eyes).

But long years in and about the tropics have inured Andrew to the blistering effects of the climate. A pair of shorts, with a short-sleeved shirt and open-toed sandals are his normal everyday rig, so his forearms, hands, knees, legs and insteps are a wind-beaten, sun-surfeited brown. However, like many Scots, he's sandy haired, with facial pigmentation which doesn't augur well for sunburn resistance from the neck up, so sensibly enough, he invariably wears a straw hat.

This is the self-same hat he let slip, to shade his face, when settled to his afternoon snooze in the cockpit. But called to duty, he's pushed this bit of protective clothing slightly up his forehead and is now peering from under the brim of his hat with the sleepy-eyed look of a turtle.

Yawning, and then (slowly, but hopefully) 'I could certainly use a cup of coffee.'

'O.K., if you take the helm, I'll slip below and start the primus.'

'And while you're down there Val,' (rather quicker, now) 'would you mind having a look in my holdall? There's a bottle of Scotch there somewhere. I could just about do with a dram. There's also a small tin of panatellas.'

(Difficult, isn't it?) but there's precious little I can do about it now, those particular cats are out of their respective bags. There really is no alternative to rummaging about in Andrew's holdall, and finding the bottle of Scotch is easy enough (as a matter of fact, there are several snugged away there).

'What do you want in it?'

'Oh' . . . (he's probably just remembered we haven't got a fridge) . . . 'it doesn't matter, a drop of water will do.'

While I stay below, it's Andrew's trick at the helm.

And he's making quite a good job of it. Totally at ease (now he's got his fist round a glass and the bottle handy) he's dealing with the tiller in an experienced manner. Not sawing at it; just easing the boat down the track. Hardly bothering to look at the compass; and this is a good sign, because he's steering by the feel of the breeze on his neck.

'Aren't you going to join me, Val?'

'No thanks Andrew; I'm going to stay below and get my head down. If you're in doubt about some other vessel, give me a shout, in plenty of time, so we'll be able to do something about it. O.K.?' (if only it was as easy as that).

The truth is, I'm somewhat nervously on edge, with the prospect of actually getting some sleep way down the list of probabilities.

From where I'm lying, stretched comfortably but rather tiredly out, feet for'ard, occupying the starboard pilot berth, I'm able to hear everything that's going on, both above and below deck, because aboard this small boat, as in every other, there's no escape from the assortment of creaks and what often seem to be groans as the vessel rolls to the lift of the swell, together with the tug of your sheets, and *her* halyards.

And this is fine; what it amounts to is a proper division of labour.

Highlighting the fact that, when you're alone in a boat, you get to know, and then, later, as you learn, come to appreciate the sort of informative nautical chitchat which has superimposed on it a host of other shipboard, and now just as importantly, *someone else's* ship-born, but distinctively water-borne noises (and there's nothing exaggerated, or fanciful, about this hard-earned but useful facility).

For a seaman, it's all part of the job. Creating an understanding, which may, in some circumstances, be involved with the priceless gift of survival as you develop the ability to interpret what to a newcomer may seem little more than the irritating squeak of a sheave (while you, the other half of the seafaring contract) know - not only what rope has been led through that particular block, but why it isn't asleep. And if this does nothing else, doesn't it illustrate just how close you can get to the vessel? Down below, surrounded by a host of these nautical whisperings, padded footfalls scuff the deckhead as a rush of cutless-toothed pirates (mayhem imagined) only a few inches from the soles of those trampling feet.

And I can tell, that Andrew just stood in the cockpit, has stepped over the coaming, to stand on the sidedeck, where I hope he's taken a sensible hold of the backstay (maybe a minor point, but a major transgression if, as I'm sure is now the case, he pees overboard).

And here's another thing.

It will soon be getting dark; yet the little matter of safety harness hasn't even been mentioned. Admittedly, running before a tropical air may not pose the sort of problem raised when sailing close-hauled to a deck-swept northerly gale.

But we're under a spinnaker; if anyone fell overboard, there would be one hell of a scramble to get the big balloon down and on deck. And even then, a headsail may have to be hoisted before it would be possible to beat back and pick the man up, if indeed you could find him. So there's plenty to think about. It can even get to the stage where you have to sing out.

'Everything all right, Andrew?'

But all this gets is the age-old response.

And what is it worth?

When you stick your head out of the hatch (and who could resist the temptation?) the lower limb of the red-setting sun is about to dip behind the island of Fuerteventura.

The sea calm.

The swell slight.

The breeze following.

But there's a steamer, hull down, showing fine on the weather quarter, while Andrew is sitting in the aft'part of the cockpit, lounged over the tiller. By the screwed-up look to his eyes he should be using sunglasses, nevertheless, he looks happy, even carefree.

'Marvellous evening, Val.' (and not only that; time to change watches).

Andrew has done his trick at the helm, so it's my turn on deck. But before I climb out of the companionway hatch, I mustn't forget the bucket.

Not just, *any old bucket.*

This is the rare, plastic bucket that has been sought, chosen, and purchased, because it has a particularly strong handle. And this useful piece of kit has been equipped with a lanyard, long and strong enough to enable the container to be dipped over the rail and then recovered, full of water, *with the handle remaining intact.*

A *very* useful bucket.

The bucket I always use while standing safely in the cockpit ....

Not perched on the sidedeck, piddling over the lifelines, with the doubtful security of no more of a hand to the ship than the crook of an arm round a backstay (this may seem a small point) but it's attention to detail, the sort of detail that makes for safety aboard.

'Aren't you going to join me in a tot, Val?'

'Not just now, thanks, Andrew. I'll stick to coffee for the moment.'

So rearranged in the cockpit, I've taken over the tiller, and now have the opportunity of casting a skipper's eye about the boat.

The nor'easterly breeze has picked up.

Improved to a moderate air, it's filling the spinnaker, with the occasional puff bulging the pot-bellied bag of that nevertheless beautiful balloon, while the island we are sailing past is on the starboard beam. A somewhat menacing, even if fascinating outlook, because the setting sun, dipping behind the landmass, has darkened the foreshore - merged the cliff with the seascape - with the scene providing little more than the usual shaded evening's view from a small boat, making a coastal passage (so how blasé can you get?).

Nevertheless, it does contain at least one significant nautical hint, because if we want to keep well offshore, we will have to bring the breeze out on the port quarter.

This means a sail change.

Handing the big balloon, and setting in its place a radial-cut spinnaker which will allow us to reach across the breeze, slanting our course from the shore.

So while Andrew goes below to sort out and then pass up the new sail, I must latch-in the self-steering gear, prior to going for'ard to set about the work on deck.

'What do you want me to do, Val?'

'It's O.K., Andrew. I'll manage here; you stay below and rustle up some grub.' (this may seem competent, but it's a dubious move).

It would be easier, and safer, if we both worked on the sail change.

A balloon spinnaker can be something of a handful for one man.

A carelessly cast off halyard, and it's all too easy to drop the whole bag of tricks in the drink.

However, sailing makes all sorts of demands, even if there's help to be had from the crew - one of them being the necessity of feeling, maybe even demonstrating you're in control of the vessel - so I'm on the foredeck, getting on with my perhaps larger than life task, bent on displaying my big-headed half of the programme.

'I can't find a frying pan.' (Andrew, searching in the galley) 'Where do you keep it?'

'I'm afraid we haven't got one.'

'No frying pan?'

'How am I going to cook the bacon?'

I've just let go the spinnaker halyard.

The big balloon's been deflated, has left the top of the mast, it's on the way down. If I'm not careful, the foot of the sail will dip in the 'oggin, and I'll have a hell of a job to get it back on board.

'Vaa . . . aal; if you haven't got a frying pan, what can I use instead?'

The foot of the spinnaker has fallen further than I thought it would, it's in the water, so I've grasped what remains of the business-end of the halyard with my teeth, with most of the strain being taken by the one remaining turn round the cleat. But as a result of this old dodge, I'm able to use both hands - hauling away like mad in a desperate attempt to gather what looks like an acre and a half of canvas, weighed down with what feels like a ton and a half of ocean.

'Vaa . . . aal.'

'Aand-rew.' (there seems to be some sort of meeting of minds here).

Yet it's not easy to sing-out, hampered as I am with a mouthful of rope. But I must speak up, while keeping my mouth shut, because the foot of the sail is dragging further under the water . . . *and if I let go the halyard !*

'Aan . . .'roo, Gimeean'andmate.' (with this near-ventriloquist's bleat prompting the other half of the crew to stick his head out of the for'ard hatch).

'Come on, you silly 'ugger .... get out andgivemeean'and.'

And he does.

Popping up on deck as quick as any Jack-in-the-Box, to get hold of, and then sweat-up the standing part of the halyard, providing, and not in any way incidentally, welcome relief for my teeth.

So up comes the big balloon, rescued from a goodbye dip in the deep, as we drag the sail back on deck.

'What took you so long?'

'I was looking for a frying pan.'

'We haven't got one.'

'I know that now.' (with a broad grin). 'Do you want me to give you a hand?' (with an even bigger grin) 'To hoist the reaching spinnaker?'

So although we've only been shipmates for a few hours, we're getting to know each other quite well. As a matter of fact, I now feel certain I can teach him a thing or two about cooking.

We're sailing along, reaching comfortably enough under the newly hoisted flatter-cut sail, with the breeze brought far enough on the quarter to ensure we keep well offshore. After the ups and downs of the just-escaped trauma, it seems reasonable to assume the evening meal should be a jointly produced event, the more so because Andrew still doesn't appear reconciled to the fact that the vessel apparently lacks a skillet and boasts just the one saucepan.

'What can you do, Val; with only one pot?'

To be absolutely truthful, there are two saucepans on board, *and* a well stowed frying pan. I keep the second saucepan in strategic reserve (one never knows when the Old Man may call in his own, does one?) but as I regard this as necessary nautical caution, I feel justified in slipping in the odd boastful remark, usually when dining extravagantly ashore, to the effect that I've been living out of just the single battered receptacle for several irresponsible years.

And not only living *out* of it.

On one well-remembered occasion, I was also sick *into* it. But perhaps that little drama should be left unrecorded, at least for the time being.

'Did you get any carrots, Andrew, amongst the stores you carried aboard this morning?'

'As a matter of fact, I did.'

'Any onions?'

'Yes, and a few peppers.'

Great: so we're sitting in the cockpit, peeling and dicing onions. Topping and tailing, scraping and slicing carrots. Gutting peppers (how else can you describe this job?). Otherwise getting on with the work involved with the preparation of the evening meal.

'What have you done with the bacon?'

'It's still in the bag.'

'O.K., here's what we do. You stay on deck. I'll go below and fire-up the primus.' (this is sensible enough). I've just made a complete balls of getting the spinnaker down. So isn't there leeway to make contritely up?

In any case, I quite like cooking, particularly when we're sailing over smooth seas and the lull of a slumbering ocean.

Retired to the galley, I soon have the primus roaring. The blue-tinged flame reflects handily off the deckhead, and I can just about see, in the bottom of the battered old saucepan, strips of pink Danish bacon sizzling away in a green slither of Spanish olive oil. As soon as the meat is sufficiently rendered, I'll be tipping in a tin of chopped Bulgarian tomatoes, together with the diced Egyptian onion. The carrots come from Texas (the country of origin is stamped on the plastic bag). The peppers are local produce, probably from Tenerife. There's a decent selection of dried herbs on board, so a pinch of English rosemary is heading for the pot.

'Andrew: how are you on garlic?' (this is bellowed the length of the saloon, and hopefully up through the companionway hatch).

'What's that, Val?' (But it's too late; two large cloves of garlic, country of origin unknown, have been crushed and scattered in the stew).

Why hang about?

It's hot below deck.

The pasta, all the way from Italy, will take ten or twelve sweaty minutes to cook. As soon as I've checked the seasoning, made sure there's no need to add more water, given everything a final taste and a stir, most of the cooking time can be spent refreshingly on deck.

'How's the cook doin?' (Andrew, in an expansive mood, lounged in the cockpit, enjoying the grip and the grin of his evening's grog).

'Aren't you going to join me, Val?'

It's very tempting.

The cockpit of a small boat is a companionable place, particularly when there's just enough breeze abaft the beam to keep the old tub slipping handily along.

'Do you want a glass of whisky, Val?'

I'm not sure if I do.

It may sound strange, but my own little world is just about complete, because right now - I'm focused on a meal, that's cooking in a pot, balanced on a stove, which is floating past an island. However, what I'm *really* concerned about, is whether the ship's small but rather old stock of Parmesan cheese has succumbed to the damp conditions, and I won't be able to shake it out of its handy little container. If that's the case, we may have to make do with mousetrap - not an imposition, it tastes great - just as grated Cheddar should as we sup our evening meal out of battered tin mugs, using bent spoons, while enjoying the last of the ripped-off chunks of Jacque's thoughtfully provided French bread.

'What about running lights, Val?'

(So who's focused now?).

And I would have to agree I've been reluctant to discuss with Andrew the limitations imposed by the vessel's lack of an engine, because sailing, even drifting, as opposed to motoring about the world's oceans may be enjoyable. But there are other people about - at this minute I can see four other vessels. One on the port bow, showing open masthead lights and a green sidelight (this steamer is bound north) passing ahead and inshore of our present position, well clear of our track.

However, there's another vessel, fine on the starboard bow, showing masthead lights almost in line and a red sidelight.

'How's your night vision, Andrew?'

'Quite good; I think.'

But is it good enough?

A small, but significant proportion of the general population are to some extent colour blind - *and if you can't tell red from green* !

Nevertheless, it's a fine night, and we're getting along famously.

Since departing Arrecife, we've notched up thirty-five very useful miles on the ship's log - that puts us somewhere off Puerto del Rosario. In another hour or two we'll be picking up Point Lantailla light house, and this useful stab in the dark will provide a reasonably accurate position, enabling us to haul away for the next significant way-station, Punto de Morro Jable.

'Are you going to turn-in, Andrew?'

But before resolving this little problem, we must alter course, because while we've been lounging about in the cockpit, the steamer showing a red sidelight has remained on a constant bearing, which means we're on a collision course.

Nothing to get worried about - the vessel is still a distance off. Nevertheless, she's bearing down on our cockleshell, and we've got to do something about it.

Let go the main boom preventer. [6]

Unlatch the self-steering gear.

Shove the helm upwind.

Flip the main (the breeze has been brought round the stern of the vessel, and the mainsail's been gybed) so we can now set up the new boom preventer, harden-in the mainsheet, and that's the mainsail secured.

What about the spinnaker?

It's almost as easy: the twin-pole rig has solved the problem.

Fiddle about with the guys and braces, muck about with the inhauls and outhauls, swing the whole bag of tricks from one bow to the other, reset the sheets on the poles.

'That was easy enough, Val.'

(Was it?).

Andrew has remained seated in the forepart of the cockpit, still with a glass of whisky in his hand, while this cocksure display of sail handling has been performed in what I hope is not a theatrical manner (and what a barefaced lie this is). But I hope the point's been made.

'Shouldn't we be displaying running lights, Val?'

(I knew he'd come back to it, because it's something that has to be addressed).

We're sailing through a dark night, not showing a trace of a light; unless you count the finger-tipped glow as Andrew sucks on yet another panatella.

The atmosphere is as clear as a bell, apart from the irritating drift of smoke which wreaths from the end of the weed. But as we're not alone on the ocean, aren't we obliged, by Law, to draw their attention to our cockle-shelled position?

'I am a bit surprised, Val; that you don't carry navigation lights.'

And he has every right to be concerned.

Nevertheless, there was a time, and not all that long ago, when it was legal for a smallish class of vessel to explore the oceans of this world without so much as the glimmer of a light. Provided that, *on the near approach of another vessel,* the appropriate lights *were* lit and correctly hung in the rigging.

However, those hoary old rules have long since been overtaken by events, particularly the up to date International Regulations for the Prevention of Collision at Sea; so, *right now*, we are undoubtedly breaking the Law.

'Are you sure you won't join me in a nightcap, Val? I think I'll have just one more tot before I turn in.'

Our one and only defence is - we are merely a threat to ourselves, as a smallish sort of vessel, run down by a largish sort of steamer, would leave no more than a superficial scratch on the overhanging threat of a bulbous type of bow.

And incidentally, in the fateful wake of that now avoided steamer, have you ever come close to being swamped? Trying to rekindle, and then keep a guttering flame alight, in a quaintly-described hurricane lamp? While battling the challenging environment provided by a midnight threatened north Atlantic gale?

Yet that's all as maybe.

Tonight we enjoy a following breeze. As far as our ship-to-ship safety is concerned, the major alteration of course we made a minute ago has solved our immediate problem. The vessel which posed the threat has passed clear ahead, so we can return to our original course, moving on west, and far enough offshore to be well clear of local traffic.

Plain sailing: if only Andrew would turn in.

But instead of getting his head down, he's hanging about in the cockpit, and there's little I can do about it, short of employing the straight down the middle, one in the eye, type of irascibility most of us try to avoid.

'Why the hell don't you get you're head down, Andrew; your next trick will come round soon enough.' But all this gets is a self-indulgent chuckle, because Andrew is totally relaxed. And who wouldn't be? Comfortably afloat on the day's intake of gorgeous amber liquid.

So we spend three-quarters of an hour gossiping about Rangers Football Club. What a grand place Glasgow is. How pleased he is with his daughter's progress in the 'States. How amused he is by his other daughter's antics in Australia. Some, quite detailed talk of his previous sailing experience. The splendours of Princes Street, Edinburgh. His friendship with Jacque. When he first met Sven. His job - which leads comfortably into an exposition of the mating habits of a particularly rare type of long-horned stickle-backed beetle which has recently been entered on the endangered species list because its habitat has been severely reduced by the careless introduction of a hitherto unsuspected species-dominant competitor which itself is not thought to be doing all that well in its otherwise endless battle for survival.

And a great deal more (with one significant omission); nevertheless, it's *fascinating* stuff, even though the charming monologue is all too regularly interspersed with - 'Are you *sure* you won't join me in a nightcap Val?'

But the evening has long gone.

It may even have gone on longer than that, as in my scheme of things we should be well into the fair division of the long night's watches.

Yet here we are, making a thorough-going balls of the job.

Because we haven't stuck to our original intention !

If I wanted to be awkward about it, I could reasonably claim we haven't stuck to our previous agreement. And this is enough to *get him on a Charge,* because every minute Andrew spends on deck, when he should be below, means yet more slippage being added to the abandoned wreckage of our watch-and-watch arrangement. So when he *does* come round to the opinion, that the time *may* have come to turn-in, it's approaching midnight.

The very time he's supposed to be taking over the watch.

Great Scott: the best we can hope for now, before he *finally* decides the time *has* come to go below, is he doesn't splatter the side-deck, because it seems that Andrew still hasn't got the scientific hang of where to stand and fill, or how to aim and chuck that same old plastic bucket.

Midnight.

A relieved sort of midnight.

Not for the skipper, who has found it hard to retain a sense of proportion, to set against the variable depths of his somewhat battered sense of humour.

This is not a critical view of Andrew, who is turning out to be an excellent companion.

It's merely a reflection of how beautiful it can be, while ghosting quietly along with nothing more intrusive than the chuckle of the bow wave. All by yourself, in the drowsy middle of a night, which sails a shade of layered cloud to hide a curl of silver moon just to drift serenely by with Andrew fast asleep below.

But regardless of the disposition of the crew, we are eight miles offshore, roughly twelve miles or thereabouts from Lantailla lighthouse, and we should be able to (indeed, I can *just* about see the flicker of the beacon).

This lantern is charted as nearly six hundred feet above sea level, but the range of the light is listed as only twenty-one nautical miles, so there may be something other than 20/20 vision reducing its practical utility.

Not to worry, the visibility is clear enough.

Yet why do otherwise sensible authorities locate their expensively installed facilities so high up their sometimes mist-enshrouded mountains?

However, this is a minor problem, with the simplistic solution being: don't build a lighthouse on the top of a towering cliff.

In any case, we are well offshore, in over 500 fathoms of water, sailing past an island which has no dangerous off-lying reef.

There are also one or two other bankable items that might be thought to favour our ultimate chance of survival.

Three-quarters of the way up our gently swaying mast there's an expensively purchased, permanently rigged radar reflector, the vessel's major concession to the march of nautical progress. [7]

And just inside the companionway hatch, there are two battery-operated torches that are powerful enough, if well directed, to give another attentive watchkeeper his own attention-getting stab in the dark.

And these items of equipment are always handy - like us, they not only have their essential part to play, they've been provided with their own well constructed niche, so no matter how dire the emergency, when you reach out in the pitch black drama of a night, what you need comes reassuringly to hand. Much in the way that I look to the solace of the tiller, in order to settle down to what will probably turn out to be an eight-hour trick at the helm.

I'm not daunted by the prospect, because when you *know* what lies before you, it's so much easier to pace yourself for the expected length of the task.

An hour may trickle by, but the sleepy watch-keeper is buoyed by the knowledge that progress is being made. Lantailla light house showing up clearly as a group flash 2 + 1 every 18 seconds, letting us know that it's only another twenty miles to Punta de Morro Jable, the southernmost point of the island.

Then five more hours of watchkeeping, with the head beginning to droop a little, brought about by the slog of this hard-grafted stint, but it's amazing how dawn offers the rejuvenating prospect of the warmth of a brand new day.

A resurgence of energy, leading to a little more breeze, which tends to haul to the nor'ard as the sun begins its effortless climb. A glorious reminder, that the relative flame is stationary and it's the tired eye which has drooped, almost to the point where it would now *prefer* to be deceived.

The usual sleepy start to another tropic day, if you happen to have been up all night, doing your best to keep awake and maintain a safety-conscious lookout.

In these latitudes, and in these circumstances, an even-money bet would be, that as the forenoon advances we will have the benefit of a bit more weight in the wind. So if I want an undisturbed watch below, we should make a sensible reduction in sail, sooner rather than later - hand the spinnaker, set a headsail - while padding about on the foredeck, which I hope *will* disturb the watchbelow.

'Morning Andrew.' (a greeting which prompts the crew to stick his head out of the companionway hatch).

'Why didn't you call me before, Val?'

'It's O.K. I've been cat-napping in the cockpit. There's hardly any shipping about. But I am looking forward to getting my head down.'

'Shall I make breakfast?' (why not?). But as I know where everything is, I may as well go below and give him a hand.

'Have you got any quick-cooking oats in the galley stores, Val?' (what else would he ask for?).

While the porridge is brewing on the primus, I might as well explain the ins and outs of the old-fashioned hand-pumped seawater toilet, which is located in the open-plan forecastle, only a few feet from where we're sitting.

This *is* a small boat.

Afloat on a rapidly shrinking world.

A world which has, as its vanishing point, a thing that used to be called *privacy*. But right now, I'm tired to the point where I couldn't care less, and not only about breakfast, because all I want, after my Mornin' George, is a stretch of blessed shut-eye.

'Don't you want any porridge, Val?'

Not really; but I'm reluctant to tell Andrew, while standing in the companionway hatch, explaining the reduction in sail, how far it is to Gran Canaria, what course to steer; why I hope, indeed think, he should buckle on his safety harness.

'And whatever you do, Andrew, *please* call me if there's any serious shipping about.' (this amounting to a series of assurances and reassurances) sought and given from both sides of the responsible and irresponsible divide, because what's coming to the fore here is the change of attitude that's been brought about by Andrew's presence on board.

When sailing alone, it's possible to get your head down, and be happy to pop up at regular intervals; perhaps not maintaining a guaranteed 100% lookout, yet resigned to the fact that, should you come unstuck, you only have yourself to blame for the impending catastrophe. However, a mildly amusing double-edged sword seems to have made an appearance, because I would now be distinctly unhappy if we were involved in a collision when Andrew had charge of the deck. And while this may seem to amount to a half-arsed reversal of the previously held idiosyncratic position, there comes a point when, even if you may unfairly harbour a doubt concerning your crew's ability to maintain a seamanlike lookout, you eventually get to the state where you *have* to get your head down.

This may have been presented in a convoluted manner, but it's blindingly obvious to anyone who has been up and about for over twenty-four hours, labouring under a debilitating workload that includes a straight through the night watch keeping spell in the cockpit.

In these heavy-lidded circumstances, sleep becomes the name of the game.

Whacked out in the pilot berth.

Gone to the world.

Enjoying the best of . . .

Relieved of . . .

'**Val.**' (Hell's Bells: it seems I've only been zizzed for five galloping minutes, and here comes a call).

'Vaa . . . aal.'

'What is it?'

'I thought you might like to see.' (I certainly would) jumped up from my bunk, standing in the companionway hatch, because not far away on our starboard quarter steams an overtaking vessel.

The largest ocean-going behemoth I've ever seen in the whole of my seafaring life. A Cruise Ship, giving the impression of being over a quarter of a mile long.

Twice as tall as Nelson's Column.

Certainly as big as two Hilton-sized hotels which have been cunningly Conradded-up in their endlessly extended tourist-touting fashion. [8]

And not only that; this leviathan is bearing down, cleaving the blue of the briny in a white-frothed roll of the deep, while giving two short, very low-register, basso profundo toots, that together amount to the smallest of all possible tittles on her massively impressive tattle.

'What do those two half-blasts on her siren mean, Val?'

It means, in polite seafaring parlance - *maintain your course and speed. I'm altering my course to port* - (coming on down to see us) with her overhanging bow swinging imperiously in our inquisitive direction. Bearing regally down on our vulnerable cockleshell, while we sail before a breeze which allows no more than three inescapable knots on top of our laughable onion. So it's only the matter of a smart move from the companionway, to the cockpit, before she's going to be near enough for an exchange of nautical pleasantries.

This is much too good to miss.

'Where are the binoculars, Andrew?' (not that we need them).

Andrew certainly doesn't. He's well-ensconced in the after part of the cockpit, indulging in his now well-practised . . . **ever** so slow, **ever** so experienced, . . . **oh so nautical** wave.

'What do you think of that lot, Andrew?'

Quite a lot, it seems, because no sooner he's waved his imperial greeting, he's toasting the passing assembly, raising his glass in a typically Scottish salute.

Gaining an appreciative ripple of applause from passengers who line the promenade, as a gaily decked-out mob, passing within coin-tossing distance, who give the undoubted impression of being able to appreciate a good thing, even if they're only fleetingly able to see it.

But the thrill doesn't last long.

She steams on - leaving our small vessel bobbing about in her wash, until all we can hear, after the parade has moved (not sailed) majestically past, is the sibilant hiss of millions of bubbles in the turbulent froth of her wake.

'Where do you think she's bound, Val?'

It seems she doesn't have to make much of an alteration of course to get back on her original heading - so she isn't bound for Las Palmas, or Santa

Cruz de Tenerife. She's lined up to pass south of Gran Canaria, and could be going anywhere, with the rest of her expansive day stretching out invitingly before her, very much as we have.

'What do you fancy for lunch, Val?'

Can it be lunch time?

When Andrew called me, I thought I'd been asleep for only a minute or two; yet if it *is* lunch time, I must have had the benefit of a four-hour caulk.

In any case, it's time for another watchkeeping stint. But before I take over the deck, I'll have to go below and get some clothes, as it's far too hot to set a naked bum on any sort of a blistering seat.

'Can you make do with beans, Val? And a can of beer?'

I suppose we must make do with what comes frugally to hand.

In this regard, I'm not put out by the fact that we've just been visited, and left astern, by what amounts to a Five Star International Hotel, which is fully mobile, seemingly upmarket, yet actually providing very good value for money. On offer there, in any one of her three air-conditioned restaurants, are menus that display more than a touch of Escoffier, [9] and a fair-minded person would concede that the superb wine lists which compliment those menus would be sufficient to ensure a shoregoing establishment, of similar style, would gain an honourable mention in the appropriate edition of Michelin. [10] Should customer expectations have been raised, but not entirely satisfied, there are desert trolleys aboard the vessel that positively groan under the weight of their diet-destroying disasters. Nevertheless, after finishing their six-course luncheon, her lucky passengers will be able to rest assured, safe in their surfeited knowledge that they will enjoy the attention of rows of white-coated stewards, who will politely enquire if they would prefer their coffee and liqueur to be served on deck, *'under the awning Sir?'*

'Or the quiet side of the sun lounge Madam?'

So how does this compare with sitting in the cockpit of your own small boat? Clad in a ragged pair of shorts and a battered straw hat. Looking forward to sharing the best Mr Heinz [11] has to offer, provided by your fellow crewmember who is below deck, searching for, but so far failing to find, the ship's one and only can opener.

No contest: because I'm absolutely sure he will sooner or later find it.

And I am also watching - enjoying in an idle manner - how well our small vessel is dealing with the lift of the moderate swell, and the wetting slap of a crest, both brought playfully about by the weight of the quartering breeze, as we sail through a raft of jetsam that's half a bobbing mile long and, in places, all of a stinking foot deep. The obnoxious trail of garbage that's just been dumped on behalf of a thousand passengers by the seven hundred members of the hard-working crew of the well polished pride of the sun seeking fleet.

'Don't worry too much about it, Val; most of it's bio-degradable.'

A lot of it probably is, and there's no doubt a golden goose can be expected to lay a large and very expensive egg, while producing and then leaving, thankfully astern, an amazing amount of her own disgusting effluent.

Yet, you do wonder, if there just maybe a better way of sorting out one blessed thing from another?

We are rather more than half way between Fuertaventura and Gran Canaria. The afternoon has drifted on, and I can see the hazed outline of the distant island, perhaps twenty miles on our starboard bow. The boat's making about four knots, up or down our still delightful onion, so as we have another seventy miles to run before we can expect to make a close-aboard landfall, our time of arrival off Tenerife is beginning to look like ...'

'Andrew, where exactly is your house situated?'

It seems it's on the southern shore, west of Punta Montana Roja, a villa, set back, enjoying its own private access to the beach.

This sounds like an open roadstead; but if the breeze holds nor'easterly there should be a reasonable amount of shelter available there.

So it's nice to know where you're going, and have a rough idea of when you'll get there, even if you're not absolutely sure what it's going to be like when you do eventually arrive.

The other big plus to this less than tightly buttoned down equation is the knowledge that Andrew has now settled in, and quite amazingly well, to the watch-and-watch arrangement. To put it in perspective as well as in a nutshell, the penny has dropped to the extent that for his last watch he turned up precisely on time, did his stint on deck, and promptly got his head down. So, come midnight, it's nice to find we're well to the south and also to the west of Punta de Maspalomas, Andrew having kept the vessel, as agreed, ten or more sensible miles offshore during the time he's been in charge of events. This tactic being required because there's a shelf, running out further along the shore, with depths which may be thought to encourage local fishing activity.

When I've settled in the cockpit, and picked up my night vision (which

I've been surprised to discover isn't any better than Andrew's) I can make out Maspalomas lighthouse, flashing its endlessly repetitive message; another group flash 1 + 2 every 13 seconds, with a range of nineteen miles.

This means that from where we are now, we have another forty miles to make good before we reach the last of our passage-points, Punta Montana Roja.

The breeze is holding up well, and as it's still abaft the beam we're able to reach just before, rather than across it, at something approaching our most comfortable boat speed. But as my four-hour watch on deck proceeds, there's an imperceptible, yet real enough wind shift.

She backs half a point; roughly five and a half degrees when it's transposed to the compass course we were previously able to manage, so together with the necessity of making absolutely sure we don't drift down to the leeward of Montana Roja, this means we will have to harden sheets, and what a difference this makes.

Previously, with the wind just abaft the beam, we were able to lope along, barely wetting the sidedeck. But now we've hauled a little to the nor'ard, and brought the apparent wind for'ard of the beam, there's the occasional scutter of spray as the old boat rises to the swell, and shoulders away the tops of the crests that have been formed by the increasing weight of the breeze.

But this is good sailing.

When you sit in the for'ard part of the cockpit, to take advantage of the shelter offered by the companionway bulkhead, the spray does little more than patter about the oilskin which protects the back of your neck. And when you turn your head to windward, to keep a weather-eye lifted, the dollops of 'oggin which strike your face and trickle from your forehead to drip off the end of your nose - those dollops - are salty, and warm to the tip of your tongue.

The tropics, where sailing is easy, and a four-hour trick is a breeze.

'Andrew.' (in this small boat, the watch keeping call needs to be little more than a murmur, offered over, not even down the companionway hatch).

'Andrew; time to change watch.' (and a few minutes later). 'Andrew.' (not a moan, just friendly reminder).

'O.K. Val, I'm on my way. What's the weather like?'

'You'll need your oilskins; but it's a fine night.'

'How are we doing?'

'Pretty well, perhaps less than twenty miles off. I've hauled her up a little, just to make sure we make the headland with something to spare.'

'Can you see the light?'

'There isn't a lighthouse on the point.'

'I know; but there's an aero-beacon a mile or so inland, it usually shows up quite well.' (so at least one of us knows what he's doing).

After I've made Andrew a cup of coffee, yacked with him while he's drinking it, poured him another (all this done while *he's* in the cockpit, and I'm standing in the shelter of the companionway hatch) it's easy to turn in.

And just as easy, some time later, while still in my bunk and fast asleep, to know he's confident enough of our position to ease sheets and start the run in to the shore.

This knowledge hasn't just arrived, or been gained as the result of a Neptune-like sense of perception, or an intuitive link between fast asleep skipper and crew.

The rhythm of our small boat's stride has been changed.

So I'm awake; and not only awake, I'm aware the celestial page has had a massive finger laid upon it.

'Val; you'd better come up and have a look at this.'

When I stick my head out of the hatch, Andrew is no more than a dark shape, silhouetted against the start of the tropical day. But with every passing second our world is changing colour.

A grey dawn has merged the ocean with the cloud base.

'Just look at the bottoms of those clouds.' (once they were grey).

Now they are pink.

'Haven't you noticed, Val, how that sort of puff-ball cloud quite often seems to .... ' (no: they *were* pink), while those that float over the eastern horizon have deepened to the stronger-drawn red of the day.

Those directly over the boat *are* still pink, while at the same time, away to the westward, the grey-lagged clouds are *still* as grey - as grey as ever they were. *Were* as grey as ever they were - because *they* are now pink, sprayed with a careless burst of colour from the sun that has yet to make an entry over the eastern rim of the world.

' Just look at the island.'

'How high is Teide?'

'The central peak is twelve thousand feet above sea level.'

A volcano, wrapped in a swirl of scudding cloud, but the bellies of those clouds are turning pink, with a wash of surplus colour spilling

117

brown, beige, green fissures tumbled down the mountain.

'Have you been to the summit, Andrew?'

'Many times. Pico de Teide is a wonderful place. An exceptional place, if you're lucky enough to catch the sunrise.'

(while here we are)

Stuck in our little coracle.

However, I'm reasonably sure Andrew is aware, as I am, that it's not so much a matter of what you're looking *at*, or even where you're standing; more to the point is what you're looking *through* . . .

At the turn of the new-found day, which now hasn't got a peep of grey or pink about it, as white clouds sail over a blue sea while the red sun pops a bright rim over the heave of the eastern horizon, just as the softly-fingered but still majestic lens brings the island into so much better focus that it now seems we're closer than we thought.

'Is that Montana Roya fine on the starboard bow?'

'Yes, the airport's a few miles inland of the point.'

'Where's your house?'

'Further along the coast.'

'What's the foreshore like? Can we anchor off?'

'It slopes away rather quickly, but I think we'll be O.K.'

And we've still got time for breakfast. Three hardboiled eggs, eaten as apples dipped in salt; followed by a real apple, a couple of slices of crisp bread, and a bite of fine Caerphilly. [12]

'Coffee?'

(why not?).

We can lounge about in the cockpit, because as we approach the coast, we're running into the shelter offered by the rise of the island itself. Beam-reaching to the nor'easterly breeze while we enjoy the lee of the land (so all we have to do, as we close the shore, is plan the work on deck).

From Andrew's earlier reply (he *thinks* we'll be O.K.) he may not be absolutely sure of the safety of the anchorage, even though it's located directly in front of his house. This is hardly surprising, because most of his sailing (he told me, the night he *didn't* get his head down) has been done in charter boats and dinghies, so as we ease sheets and approach the end of the passage, we'd better start thinking about digging the lead line out of the locker, then hauling an anchor and chain on deck, prior to making what will have to be a cautious approach.

'What sort of a bottom is there, Andrew? Say in four fathoms, in front of your place?'

'To be honest, Val; I'm not sure.' (so we *will* be taking soundings).

Slowing the old boat down, spilling wind out of both the mainsail and the headsail, in order to have time enough to heave the old-fashioned lead.

A satisfying pastime.

As the line runs through the palm of your hand, the rip of the wet-fingered rope arcs with a splash in the 'oggin with the sort of exploratory plop that only the chains can achieve. [13]

'Leadsman, what have you there?'

(translates as)

'How deep is it Val?'

I haven't armed the lead, but a few more casts give some assurance.

I can feel a patch of soft mud running a quarter of a mile out from, and along the line of the shore.

If we pick our spot carefully, we will be able to anchor, not too far away, but still far enough off the beach to avoid the danger of being set ashore by the sort of fickle turn of events the cautious seaman should always keep somewhere in the accessible part of his mind.

This is good advice, because although we've arrived at Andrew's place, on further examination, from an old dog's point of view, it isn't all that welcoming.

Yet it's a pretty enough spot.

There are trees and flowering shrubs in the background, running down to a jumbly sort of a cliff.

It's not really much of a cliff.

More a bit of a bluff, perhaps twenty feet high, and this untidy shelf falls to a strip of dark sand, not more than forty paces wide.

The overall impression is - the foreshore's cramped. In adverse conditions, the beach could be swept, right to the base of the cliff.

'How often do you get a southerly wind here, Andrew?'

'Very rarely; we do get onshore sea breezes, but I've never seen any dangerous surf.'

That's as maybe.

The immediate trouble is, a few more casts of the lead have revealed the bottom falls away so rapidly that a stone's throw out from the beach finds four fathoms. And another stone sent skittering over the water would give soundings which are too deep to set an anchor - in a boat without a windlass - where the amount of chain would be difficult to recover by hand. So there's the need here for even more caution, which means we should be thinking about hauling another lot of chain and a second anchor out of the fo'castle locker (a real pain in the old bosun's butt).

Nevertheless, better than standing on the beach, looking at your vessel, with a sense of utter disbelief (the recognition of a nautical come-uppance) because the offshore breeze, having freshened, has allowed the boat to tug at just her one anchor - dragging the solitary pick *off* the rocky shelf - into deeper water, until the insecure bag of tricks is suspended, anchor, chain and all, from the bow of your about to drift away boat.

With this in mind, we must make a running moor.

Positioning the vessel upwind.

Dropping the first anchor, then sailing parallel with the shore. Paying out chain until we've reached the spot where we intend to drop the second hook. And when this sensible bit of gear has been set, hauling back on the original scope of chain, until the boat's lying midway between her two securely-placed pieces.

'That was quite a lot of work, Val.'

Yep.

And worth it, because we have doubled our security regarding dragging an anchor offshore.

Eliminated the possibility of swinging round one solitary contrivance that's been placed much too close to the beach. So close, a fickle current, combined with an unfortunate wind shift, could start the vessel sailing round her anchor, with distressing results, because in these careless circumstances you are left, either standing on the beach, looking seaward, and feeling no end of a fool; or swimming out to your boat, attempting the dangerous task of trying to board a wandering vessel caught in a tumble of surf.

Yet it's hard to believe there will be waves of any sort breaking on this particular beach.

The breeze is blowing off the land.

The sea is calm.

There may arrive, occasionally, an unannounced surge that runs playfully along the sun-drenched length of the coast.

But there's no line of breakers.

This favoured part of the volcanic island being lapped, apparently, not by an ocean

.... merely by a pond.

CHAPTER THREE: PAGE NOTES

(1) Page 85. Line 37 .... *'the Institute* **Manrique**'.

The organisation that commemorates and bears the name of the Spanish artist and architect, born on the island of Lanzarote on April 24, 1919. His ability soon became apparent, and he was able to organise an exhibition of his own work in Arrecife in 1942. In 1945 he received a scholarship to attend the *San Fernando School of Fine Art*, Madrid, and studied there until 1950. Early experiments with non-figurative painting led to his co-founding the *Fernando Fe Gallery*, and then his first exhibition of abstract painting at the *Clan Gallery*, Madrid, in 1954. For the next ten years he exhibited widely in such places as Havana, Paris, Basle, Munich, Rio de Janeiro, Buenos Aires, Montevideo, Lima, Santiago de Chile, Valparaiso and Bogota. In 1965 he moved to America, living and working there for the next three years, successfully exhibiting work at the *Catherine Viviano Gallery*, New York. In 1968 he moved back to Lanzarote and began the constructional stage of his house *Taro de Tahiche*, while at the same time installing his sculpture *Fecundity* in the museum he established in the centre of the island, both works being, in their respective ways, intended as a tribute to the local peasant farmers.

The artist was perhaps out of his age in proposals for integrating art in nature, and his architectural work stands out from that of his Spanish contemporaries. Throughout his life Manrique received Prizes, Gold Medals, and many International Awards, with some of his work in the diverse fields of fine art, sculpture, and architecture being on display throughout the island of Lanzarote.

He was killed in an automobile accident, 1992.

(2) Page 88. Line 9 .... *'whose family name was Dana'*.

Richard Henry DANA was born in 1815, in Cambridge, Massachusetts, and so was a native-born American; but he died in England in 1882.

Poor eyesight curtailed his Harvard education, so for the sake of his health he decided to spend time at sea, signing as an ordinary seaman on a voyage from the East coast of the United States, to California, around Cape Horn. He then spent a hard seafaring year on the Pacific coast, before returning to Boston, evidently in an improved physical condition because he was able to complete his education at Harvard Law School. Admitted to the Bar in 1840 he soon published *Two Years Before The Mast*. The book made him famous, as it was not only an exposé of the harsh conditions prevailing at the time, but it had a style and quality about it which may have owed something to his father (also Richard Henry Dana) who had gained a reputation as a journalist and also as a poet. *Two Years Before The Mast* was followed by *The Seaman's Friend* (published in the U.K. as *The Seaman's Manual*) which set out to explain to the seafaring community what their rights, as well as their duties were. This volume also enjoyed a degree of success, but another book, *To Cuba and Back*, failed to make an impact.

Dana hoped for a political career, and his support for the under-privileged as well as outright opposition to the slave trade brought him further public acclaim, and he was appointed ambassador designate to Great Britain. But opposition from the Senate (that charnel house of reputations) forced him to withdraw from the appointment, and it was probably this setback (the accusation of a lack of probity) which prompted his departure from the 'States and the four declining years he spent in England.

Two further works were published, both posthumously, *Speeches in Stirring Times* (1910) and *An Autobiographical Sketch* as late as 1953.

(3) Page 92. Line 23 ....'*not aboard this hooker as pressed men'*.

It's worth recalling that not so long ago there were indeed 'pressed men', particularly in Nelson's day (1758-1805) when a significant proportion of the crews serving in the Royal Navy were not volunteers earning their living in the profession of their choice, but were representative of those seamen who had been dragooned into the fleet by a system which was almost as repugnant to those who had to administer the law, as it was to those who were unfortunate enough to have fallen foul of it. The legal foundation for this type of enforcement dated back to an *Act of Mary Tudor* (1556) and then of *Elizabeth 1st* (1563) which was put on a permanent basis during the reign of *Charles 1st* (Act of 1631) but over the years the legislation was further developed and some exemptions established. An *Act of Queen Anne* (1703) disbarred the *impressment* of apprentices below the age of 18, and then men of 55 years of age and more were protected by an Act passed in 1774. However, by that date the pressure exerted by the chronic shortage of experienced crews had brought about the type of savage usage exemplified by the term 'Press Gangs', which were sometimes groups of ruffians who earned a dubious living operating a hijacking system which swept men off the street and homeward bound merchant ships (illegally, in both instances) to serve an indeterminate period afloat in the 'service' of the realm. But the system was complicated, and modified by the usage of the age, so we would be unwise to judge cause and effect by modern social standards. There was, for instance, movement from the ranks of those who had been 'pressed' to augment the number of the volunteers. This being the case because the latter were eligible for bounty, while the pressed men were not, with the beneficial upward movement facilitated by the all too common act of desertion .... and then immediate re-entry into the ranks, with the men bold enough to make the move often staying to become professional seamen, the like of whom enabled the Fleet to maintain its position throughout the days of British naval supremacy.

Probably the best book dealing with seafaring life in the 18th century, and which is quoted here, is **Dr N.A.M. ROGERS** *The Wooden World, an Anatomy of the Georgian Navy*, first published by William Collins in 1986; this deals in a scholarly way with service afloat, and is recommended reading for those interested in the problems of the age.

Horatio, Viscount NELSON, K.B., Vice Admiral of the White (1758-1805) is generally recognised as the most renowned of British seamen. He entered the navy when he was 12 years of age and served with distinction until (1787) he was forced, partly by ill-health, to spend some time in retirement. He rejoined in 1793 and spent his remaining years in the service of the realm, gaining (amongst others) victories at the battle of Cape St Vincent, the battle of the Nile, and the battle of Trafalgar; in the process losing an eye while commanding the Naval Brigade at Calvi, Corsica; and his right arm during an engagement off Santa Cruz.

Nelson's entry in the **Dictionary of National Biography** awards him every accolade. A man of immense strength of character; leadership qualities without equal, combined with a degree of compassion which was rare in the harsh environment found in the navy of his day.

(4) Page 98. Line 14 ………. 'the *Mary Celeste syndrome'*.

On November 7th 1872 a vessel sailed from New York, bound for Genoa, but the passage was never completed and the circumstances surrounding the voyage now form the basis for one of the oft-repeated yarns which decorate the annals of the sea.

The ship had been built in Nova Scotia (1861) and when launched had been given the name *Amazon*, which some of the superstitious longshoremen at the time considered to be tempting fate, as the title began, supposedly inappropriately, with the first letter of the alphabet. On her maiden voyage her Master was taken ill, died, and was buried at sea; this tragic event prompting a change of ownership, and a name-change for the vessel, which was henceforward known as the *Mary Celeste*. At the time, these three inauspicious happenings (the poor first choice of name, the death of the Master, and then the change of name) caused those same longshoremen to declare the vessel carried a jinx, with bad luck attached to her until the end of her seafaring days.

This prophecy seemed to have been fulfilled when the vessel was found abandoned 590 miles west of Gibraltar, some 5 weeks after she had departed New York, bound for a Mediterranean port. When the derelict was boarded she appeared to be in seagoing order; she was sound, well-rigged, and well provisioned; nevertheless her crew, amounting to seven seamen, the captain, his wife, and their two year old daughter - the entire ship's company had disappeared. No entirely satisfactory explanation has been put forward to explain this mysterious event, which has been enlarged over the years to include uneaten meals on the saloon table, half-drunk cups of still warm coffee, and signs of blood-stained violence which were presumed to indicate foul play of one desperate sort or another.

But the case of the Mary Celeste isn't in need of embellishment.

When boarded by the mate of the Nova Scotian brigantine *Dei Gratia* (Captain Morehouse) on December 5th 1872, the plain truth is, the ship's boat was missing, and the for'ard hatch was open, perhaps for the good reason that her Master thought the vessel in imminent danger of either fire, or explosion (possibly both) because she was subsequently found to be carrying crude alcohol, in barrels, nine of which were empty, having leaked, presumably into the vessel's bilge. The silver lining to the *Mary Celeste* affair was shared by Captain Morehouse and the crew of the *Dei Gratia* who collectively pocketed a salvage award of £1,700 for the safe delivery of the vessel to the port of Gibraltar, where the brig was sold, and later resumed trading, still registered as the *Mary Celeste*. She was later wrecked, near Miragoane, Haiti (Jan 3rd 1885) on a clear day and in a calm sea, the reef being marked on the chart and obviously breaking. None of the crew of seven men were lost, and the suspicion remains she was set ashore deliberately.

By far the best account of the mystery, directly quoted here, is contained in the *Directory of Disasters at Sea during the age of Steam* (1824-1962) by **Charles HOCKING**, FLA (formerly Librarian of Acton, Middlesex, England).

(5) Page 98. Line 16 ………. *the role-model Mog'*.

A reference to Lewis Carroll's *Alice in Wonderland* where the principle character (Alice) is told by The Duchess that a Cheshire cat (the role-model Mog) 'always grins like that'
Lewis CARROLL (1832-1898) the pen name of **Charles Lutwidge DODGSON** writer and mathematician who delighted in the company of children and wrote, in addition to *Alice in Wonderland; ….. Sylvie and Bruno, ….. Sylvie and Bruno Concluded,* and *The Hunting of the Snark.*

(6) Page 107. Line 16 ………. *'the main boom preventer'*.

Standard equipment aboard a small boat that is being sailed short-handed (or indeed aboard any well-managed vessel). The 'preventer' describes a tackle (usually a handy-billy) which is rigged from the boom to a convenient spot on the side deck, and when this purchase is set up it prevents the boom swaying (perhaps taking charge in a seaway). A person alone is well advised to have two preventers, permanently rove, so that when the vessel is tacked it's only the matter of a moment before the boom is once more well secured.

A *'handy-billy'* is seafaring slang for a portable rope purchase, having one block fitted with a single sheave, while the other block has two …. so that when the single-sheaved block is attached to the boom and the hauling part is led aft from the other block, the tackle offers a mechanical advantage to the power 3; while if the tackle is reversed (the double-sheaved block being the moving part) the mechanical advantage is increased, to the power 4.

(7) Page 110. Line 23 ………. *'major concession to the march of nautical progress'*.

There are several other concessions. The vessel is equipped with a life-raft, which is kept well within its service date. There's an EPIRB (emergency radio beacon) handily stowed on the afterdeck, while in the cabin, looking rather out of place on the bulkhead, there's a VHF transmitter. This gadget is a hangover from the boat's previous racing days, and is due to be sold as soon as possible, regardless of the price, because as the vessel doesn't have an engine and the 12 volt lead/acid accumulator has seen better days (no longer holds its charge, even if it *could* be charged) the 30 mile radio range supposedly offered by the VHF transmitter is no more than a mirage.

Additional emergency equipment includes, daylight smoke signalling flares, hand held flares for use at night, together with a standard pack of parachute flares stored in their purpose-made watertight container.

(8) Page 113. Line 5 ...... *'Conradded-up in their endlessly extended tourist touting fashion'.*

A reference to the hotel chain that the American entrepreneur **Conrad HILTON** built over a period of some twenty years, eventually establishing a global enterprise. His son 'Nicky' married the British-born Hollywood film star Elizabeth Taylor - the first of her eight husbands, if account is taken that she married the Welsh actor, Richard Burton twice.

Miss Taylor became a Dame of the British Empire, a well-deserved honour, bestowed on her by Queen Elizabeth 2nd, on May 19th 2000.

(9) Page 114. Line 18 .... *'more than a touch of Escoffier'.*

Auguste ESCOFFIER: master chef, born in Villeneuve-Loubet, France, about 1847.

He made his way in the profession of his choice not only because of his culinary skills, but because he displayed formidable organisational ability, which enabled him to obtain employment with the Russian aristocracy, and then further advancement as *chef de cuisine* with the general staff of the Rhine Army during the Franco-Prussian war of 1871. After the armistice, he furthered his career at the Grand Hotel at Monte Carlo, before being head-hunted (in modern usage) by the internationally renowned hotelier César Ritz, who persuaded him to come to London, in order to provide the *haute cuisine* that was required to advance the establishments in which he (Ritz) had a pecuniary interest.

Amongst his many contributions to the (in more ways than one) well-being of his customers, he invented the *Pêche Melba* and *tournedos Rossini*. The first as an accolade to the Prima donna, **Dame Nellie Melba** (the professional name of the opera singer Helen Armstrong, who was born in Melbourne, Australia) while the other celebrated the famous Italian composer.

Escoffier also wrote the *Guide Culinaire* (1903) and *Ma Cuisine*, published in 1934. He died in 1935.

(10) Page 114 Line 22 .... *'Michelin.'*

The first guide was published, in France, by Andre Michelin in 1900, with the intention of providing the general public with a list of garages, reasonably priced hotels, and other information which would prove useful for a motorist touring that country.

It proved an immediate success, and since that date, no doubt because of specialized development in the field of top-end catering (haute cuisine) it has gone on to become one of the most influential (perhaps *the* most influential) guide book relevant to the restaurant business.

The geographical scope of publication was expanded over the years and it now covers not only France, but Germany the Netherlands, Belgium, Luxembourg, Spain, Italy, Portugal, Switzerland, the United Kingdom, and the Republic of Ireland, together with most of the developed world.

There have been disputes, from time to time, as is inevitable when a claimed independent judgement is being made regarding the quality of the food and the style of service being provided - the sort of information which is bound to influence the success or otherwise of ventures which have been built up over the years by people who have devoted thier professional lives to satisfying the needs of wealthy clientele. But broadly speaking it now seems generally agreed that the Michelin 'star' system does offer the customer a reasonably reliable method of assessing what is on offer in a particular establishment - one star indicating *'very good cuisine* (in its category). A two star rating represents *'excellent cuisine, worth a detour'*and a three star rating (a rare honour) *'exceptional cuisine, worth a special journey.'*

(11) Page 114 Line 33........... *'Mr Heinz.'*

This business was founded by Mr Henry John Heinz, in Sharpsburg, PA, USA, in the year 1869. It is perhaps best known, world wide, for its ketchup (colloquially known in Europe as 'tomato sauce'). From modest beginnings, the company now employs 32,500 people, has total assets of over 9 billion US dollars, with a yearly revenue of 10 billion US, and an operating income of 1.5 billion. By any standards, a substantial player in the global culinary field, regardless of the fact that it is, in practical (snobbish?) terms, at perhaps the other end of the spectrum when compared to the clientele who are guided by Michelin (see above).

(12) Page 118. Line 23 .... *'fine Caerphilly'.*

A distinctive type of cheese, named after the market town located 7 miles North of the Welsh capital (Cardiff).

(13) Page 119. Line 8 .... *'that only the chains can achieve'.*

The *chains* mentioned here is the platform a seaman stood on when taking a sounding. It was usually a small grating hinged from the vessel's side, let down when required, allowing the leadsman to lean outside the hull of the vessel, and high enough above the waterline to make a swinging cast of the lead easier to accomplish. A swinging over-arm cast being necessary in a vessel making way through the water in order to get the lead far enough for'ard, so that it had time enough to sink and reach bottom when the leadsman was vertically over the point of the sounding.

The *lead* was just what it sounds like. A lump of that metal, fashioned into a round or sometimes hexagonal shape about 14 inches long and 3 or 4 inches in diameter, with the size varied to suit the circumstances pertaining at the time. The bottom of the contrivance was hollowed out to form a receptacle into which tallow was loaded (*arming* the lead) in order that, when hauled to the surface (after the sounding) it could give some indication of the type of seabed over which the vessel was passing at the time (typically: sand, gravel, mud, etc.).

The line was usually a piece of soft-laid hemp, no thicker than required for comfortable handling, twenty fathoms in length and marked in the traditional manner, with enough spare end to accommodate the freeboard of the vessel. The *bitter* end of the line was *always* made fast, so there was no possibility of the leadsman (perhaps a raw, just-aboard-ship snotty-nosed midshipman) being placed in the embarrassing position of having to reply, when asked what he had found:

'. . . *I'm sorry, Sir. I've just dropped the whole lot overboard.*'

The 'snotty-nosed midshipman' mentioned above is a sideways glance at the term *snottie;* naval slang for a midshipman, supposedly derived from their habit of wiping their noses on the sleeves of their jackets. Legend having it that the three buttons worn on their cuffs were put there to prevent them indulging in this reprehensible practice. New midshipman entries were called *warts,* and the Lieutenant who supervised the half-deck was colloquially known as the *snottie nurse.*

The lead line was marked as follows:

@ 2 fathoms, leather with two 'ends'.
@ 3   "   leather, with three ends.
@ 5   "   white calico.
@ 7   "   red bunting.
@ 10   "   flat leather with a hole in it.
@ 13   "   thick blue serge.

@ 15   "   white calico.
@ 17   "   red bunting.
@ 20   "   cord with two knots.
@ 25   "   cord with one knot.
@ 30   "   cord with three knots.
@ 35   "   cord with one knot.
@ 40   "   cord with four knots . . . etc.,

In use, the significant depths were know as *marks,* so the leadsman finding the piece of thick blue serge at water-level, would sing out ...'*by* **the mark,** *thirteen.*' But if the depth were thirteen and a half fathoms, the call would be ...'**And a half,** *thirteen.*' while for thirteen and three quarter fathoms *a quarter **less** fourteen.*' The intervals between the marks were know as *deeps,* so if the leadsman found six fathoms, he would then call '**Deep,** *six.*'

It will hardly have escaped the reader's notice that this is all archaic stuff, long overtaken by events, with electronic sounders now found aboard every sensible (?) vessel - yet there is still a great deal of pleasure to be found when taking a cast:

the rip of the wet fingered rope
which arcs with a splash in the 'oggin
with the sort of exploratory plop
that only the chains can achieve

is a real event

not without its own emotive quality

STEPPING BRIEFLY ASHORE

'Not a bad little anchorage, Val.'

WELL, the beach looks attractive enough, the weather certainly doesn't present a threat, and now we've taken the precaution of limiting the vessel's swing, by laying out good ground tackle, we're not in any danger of being set ashore. But to judge this place as being 'not a bad little anchorage', says as much about my shipmate as it does about the absence of shelter on offer in this scarcely indented bay. From my admittedly prejudiced viewpoint, which is influenced by the fact that I'm the one who owns the boat, we're lying in an open roadstead, but perhaps we shouldn't be too fussy about it, as we have arrived here with a definite purpose in view.

'Whereabouts is your place, Andrew?'

'Our house is set back from the foreshore; we've got a bit of land between us and the beach.' (so it sounds, and is, a very nice location).

Viewed from the cockpit of the boat, the strip of sand may seem narrow, yet it's inviting, partly because the sea is so calm the line of the strand has a disarming look of permanence about it. And this air of tranquillity allows the seaman's eye to wander up the beach, where the bluff rolls back in a tumble of scattered boulders.

The outline of this debris is softened by a background of brilliantly flowering shrubs (looks like bougainvillaea) [1] which ease the eye still further, and to cap it all, a series of tropical palms march away from the foreshore waving green fronds from strongly fingered crests.

There *is* a breeze, but we're under the lee, and while the tops of the palms are moving, there's very little wind on deck. For those of us acting-out our parts as loungers (leaning over the boom, admiring the view) it's a sun-scorched tropical scene.

'What about a cup of tea, Andrew; or maybe even a tot?'

To tell the truth, I'm hoping for something a bit stronger than tea, as we've now completed the coastal passage, and a celebratory drink surely wouldn't come amiss, so I'm getting on with the job of stuffing the light-weight genoa into its bag, folding the mainsail over the boom, then taking the trouble to rig its tatty old cover (to shut out the rot-making ultraviolet) while I'm expecting Andrew to take up what I think is the better part of the hint.

However, he remains in the cockpit, evidently fascinated by his own private bit of beach, until it seems pride of possession can only take you so far, and we've reached the point where we'll have to do something about it.

'What's the plan, Andrew?'

But the face he turns in my direction is pensive, and quite frankly, I just can't fathom it out. My own inclination, which I'm sure is somewhere near the seamanlike norm, is - get ashore as soon as we can. Given a free hand, and not being bashful about it, I'm thinking of stripping off and enjoying a swim, all that's holding me back is the little matter of protocol.

'Shall we eat before we hit the beach, Andrew? Or shall we get the dinghy out now?' (but this suggestion isn't well received).

'Hold on, Val; we should think this thing out. I don't suppose they know we've arrived, and if we *both* march in . . .'

That's true enough, every married man knows that.

'Why don't you go ashore and see how the land lies. I'll pump the dinghy up, while you get your gear together.'

It gives some indication of how slowly he's moving, if note is taken that I've completed my part of the bargain, and it's a sweat-raising job, well before Andrew's got half his kit on deck. And I'm the one who organises the transfer to the punt and then handles the oars during the short pull up to the beach. This is easy enough, and we have no trouble landing, with my shipmate struggling through the soft sand, carrying his portmanteau, a cabin bag slung over a shoulder, and the sharp-cornered specimen case tucked awkwardly under his arm.

'Shall I give you a hand?'

'It's O.K., Val. I'm going to dump this stuff at the top,' (he's puffing a bit; can't be all that fit) 'then I'll walk to the house. I'll be back as soon as I can.'

So while Andrew's off ashore, hopefully meeting his missus, I can return to the boat and organise a sluice in the cockpit.

We've been afloat a few days, but this is the first real shower, and it delivers its usual lift to the boy, who also has time to look in the mirror and note he needs a beard trim.

Ablutions accomplished, I feel more than ready to row ashore again, when Andrew reappears on the foreshore, having been away not much more than an hour, and presumably fixed whatever marital fences he may or may not have found to be in need of repair. However, instead of coming down to help me with the dinghy, he's content to survey the scene, while I row the punt ashore and shoulder the inflatable up the beach, well out of the reach of the tide. Nevertheless there has been a useful development, because by the time I've carried the inflatable up to the bluff, I can see, hammered into a fissure in the rock ledge, an old iron ring (so someone else, who intended to look after their expensive bits of equipment, has been using this section of beach).

That leaves the oars, which may as well be taken further out of harm's way, to the top of the bluff, and it's now only a matter of asking my shipmate how he got on with his better half.

'Everything O.K., Andrew?'

'She seemed surprised to see me, even though she's been expecting our arrival.' (a comment on our married state, which has the ring of truth drawn engagingly about it?).

'She's also smartened you up a bit.' (with this snide remark raising a rueful smile from Andrew, who *has* been smartened up, and by rather more than just a little bit), because here we have a man amazingly transformed - from an easy-going yachtie, to a well turned out, super sartorial model of late Colonial spruce.

His ragged old shorts and faded cotton shirt have been discarded; all that remains of the seagoing rig is a reasonably smart straw hat. But everything else he's wearing is well upmarket of that.

The shorts have been replaced by spotless white trews, made of expensive cotton duck, with these trousers being of the sort which hold their very smart crease and are not ever supposed to bag, even slightly at the knees.

In place of the faded cotton shirt, is a regimental style tunic top, of the same white duck, with the usual show of externally sewn, button down type of distinctly military pockets.

This jacket doesn't actually *have* epaulettes - if it did, they would be of the sort that had been carefully designed to set off a badge of rank which couldn't possibly turn out to be anything less than thoroughly distinguished. And his spotless white shoes are to the same amazingly high standard.

Taking one smart thing with another, and standing as I am, bareheaded, barelegged, and barefoot on a boulder-strewn beach, I reckon he may be slightly overdressed.

However, my judgement's probably been influenced by the length of

131

time I've been living and lounging, and occasionally roughing it aboard my old boat. And because I now feel somewhat underdressed myself, even though I'm quite proud of my set of clean, somewhat threadbare shirt and shorts, which I've always been convinced went rather well with my cheap and cheerful, really inexpensive, plastic reef-walker sandals. Yet strangely enough, as we walk through the grove of trees and flowering shrubs which effectively screen Andrew's house from the beach, it's the well dressed but unusually silent man who appears to be the one who is nervously on edge.

'Anyway,' (he eventually says, totally out of the blue) 'it's coming on time for lunch.' (this is nothing less than a self-evident remark) as the noonday sun is blazing overhead, and we haven't had anything to eat, or drink, since the seven o'clock breakfast of this rather unusual morning.

'Can you manage a kedgeree?' (right now I feel I can manage just about anything that's set before me) but I'm completely at a loss regarding Andrew's display of edgy behaviour, and this is quite apart from his rig.

While these questionable asides are being passed, mostly unspoken, from one old shipmate to another, we are walking away from the beach, through the trees and shrubs, past what looks like an old potting shed, towards a very nice house. A beautifully proportioned Spanish style villa, boasting white stuccoed walls, a red-tiled roof, and shaded verandahs that offer access to a paved courtyard, which turns out to be a sun-drenched area having as its centrepiece a circular garden, providing a well tended riot of brilliantly flowering shrubs - not all of which are bougainvillaea, because there's an unmistakable waft of perfume in the air.

The perfect setting for an extensive, eye-catching dwelling, just the right size to unashamedly convey to the visitor and provide for the fortunate owner the style and standard of living all of us so much admire, and few of us ever achieve

'What an attractive property, Andrew.' (a laudatory remark that seems to have escaped my shipmate, so it might be worth repeating).

'This really is a marvellous house, Andrew: how long have you lived here?'

'I wonder where she is.' (says my erstwhile, previously well mannered shipmate).

'Ah, there you are my dear. I'd like you to meet Mr Howells, who was good enough to provide me with what turned out to be an amusing little passage, all the way from Lanzarote.'

Now, I would have to concede my immediate impression of Andrew's house, and Andrew's wife, may have been influenced by my old mate's slight, yet it seems to me - significant change of style (or have I missed something here?).

I haven't known my shipmate long (two days afloat, and two days before that, a total of less than a week) but it has allowed me to form what I assumed to be a sensible appreciation of the man, and at least some of his everyday works. Yet this supposedly well-balanced judgement is apparently in danger of coming apart at the seams.

And what do I know about Mary?

The first impression conveyed by Andrew's wife is - she's stepped straight out of a *Homes & Gardens* magazine - with all this implies in the way of English charm, even if the recognisable type is sometimes equipped with an aloof-enough exterior.

This cool aura is only partly dispelled as we walk through the garden and then into her house, which reflects the style of living some women achieve with no more of a discernable effort than by merely being there.

There are bowls of tastefully arranged flowers, which are meant to complement, not dominate, the décor.

The furniture is not only beautiful, but comfortable, as well as being of an age, weight and quality that's had bestowed on it a depth of patina which couldn't possibly have arrived by any other recognisable route (it's been in her family for ages). Everything fits, including Mary, so well into place, that a person describing this establishment should be careful how he does so, because to go overboard would expose the observer to the charge he views the whole thing from the down-beat end of what could be judged a snooty social spectrum. Even so, I may have been wrong about Mary, because she isn't turning out to be snooty in the normal use of the phrase. If I *had* to describe her behaviour, I would say she seems on the withdrawn side of welcoming, yet who can fault her for that?

By the time these surreptitious little glances have been scattered hither and thither, and other no doubt false impressions filed away as the basis for further confusion, we have moved along, Mary leading the way, out of the spacious hallway into a dining area, a room having a refectory table with five places set for luncheon.

The impression here is of gleaming silverware, bowls of flowers, snow-white napkins, cut-glass tumblers, but not a Paris goblet - a decorated layout arranged about the centrepiece of solid silver cruets. A sure indication that somebody has spent time and effort about the presentation of this most attractive table; yet Andrew's wife will persist in fussing over it, moving a knife here, rearranging a fork there, until this finicky display and lack of conversation is thankfully relieved by the less demanding tone of a softly ringing bell.

A telephone, which has a distinctly Spanish edge to it. A call to an instrument that makes its presence felt - not by an insistent *burp, burp*, but by a much slower, and lower toned *zzzuuurrrr* intended not to disturb a siesta, yet it still gets Mary's attention and launched into a stream of voluble Spanish.

'Aquien habla? Puede coger el telefono? Hay alguien herido? Muy bien, por favor digale al Padre Anthony que lo siento mucho, si, luego.'

Of course, not having the language is something of a handicap, but as there's no possibility of eavesdropping it does provide the opportunity of another look at the room.

It's just as well-proportioned as it appeared to be when we entered it. A high ceiling, cool white walls, forming the backdrop for several large, probably ancestral oil paintings. A quarry-tiled floor that's seen service enough to show appreciable wear, particularly in a doorway which obviously leads to the kitchen. On either side of the doorway are sideboards, carrying silver-topped dishes, some of which are bains-marie of one electric sort or another. There's a glass jug of what looks like orange juice, another jug which seems to contain lemon and barley water. Conspicuously absent is anything resembling an alcoholic drink, and this is somewhat surprising, when I recall the way in which Andrew has displayed an astonishing ability to support Scotland's premier industry, almost single-handed, throughout the whole of the time that I've known him. But Mary's still rattling away on the telephone.

'Esta bien, no hay problema, ya acordaremos vernos en otra occasion, que espero sea pronto.'

Not knowing what's going on, I'm free to set off on perambulations, and soon arrive at the end of the dining room, which has a staircase leading off it, giving access to a landing and another flight of stairs to the second floor of the house.

Looking up from the bottom step, the stranger's eye is drawn to a stained-glass window, which illuminates the landing with the diffused glow a leaded-light provides, and also gives a hint of how the owners of this house may view the rest of the world - perhaps even the whole of Creation, because the subject of the stained-glass is nothing less than the

Last Supper, (2) a powerful image, which I suppose most of us associate with the New Testament and acts of reverent worship.

This is all very well, and of course very much better than that.

But I'm gripped by the thought that to actually pass this icon, every day, effectively shoulder to shoulder when you're on your way to breakfast, which could be corn flakes, maybe a boiled egg, possibly a badly needed cup of coffee (this is not just a nudge - more of an arm-twisting start to the day?). However, now I've had my eyes at least partly opened, I can see there are other straws in the ecclesiastical breeze which seems to be circulating about this intriguing establishment.

Leaving the staircase astern, and arrived at the corner of the room, I've come across a sideboard, and note that the top of this piece of furniture has been covered with a lace runner, and on this runner stands a photograph, while just above the photograph, hanging on the wall, is a crucifix.

The print is of a young man in his late teens.

He could be nudging twenty, and a guaranteed chip off Andrew's old block, yet what I find intriguing is the alignment of his image, with the crucifix, which is not set high on the wall, but immediately behind the picture.

'Would you like something to drink, Val?' (this coming as an absent-minded surprise) because while I've been speculating about other people's lives, and wondering what Mary's rattling on about, I've almost forgotten that Andrew is part of this learning curve of a scene. But here he comes, bearing a jug, and a tumbler, containing a few cubes of ice.

'Orange juice, Val? Or perhaps you'd prefer lemon and barley water?'

So at least I've been right about that.

While this skirmishing is in progress, Mary has finished her telephone conversation.

'A change of plan Andrew; it seems there's been some sort of a traffic accident, nothing serious, but they will be delayed.'

'Are we going to wait for them?'

'No; I've told them it would be better if they came another day.'

So Mary's away to the kitchen, while Andrew explains briefly, even if off-handedly, in a backhanded way, that the guests who are not coming were church dignitaries of one exalted sort or another (intriguing, but I'll have to be satisfied with this partial explanation) because a lady of the competent housekeeper type is sailing close-hauled into the dining room, with an attractive olive-skinned girl in tow.

This youngster is so shy she can barely raise her eyes from the floor; but she's under the wing of someone who is well in charge of events, and in the matter of a moment the unwanted luncheon places have been cleared away, leaving the table looking unbalanced, as the three remaining places are grouped at one end. Nevertheless, the meal's about to be served, with Andrew indicating where I should sit. Then another straw sways, and in rather more than just the breath of the ecclesiastical breeze.

Mary's back from the kitchen, but instead of Andrew taking head of table, his wife assumes the role, and she also says grace.

'Benedice, Domine, nos et haec tua dona quae de bonitate tua sumpturi sumus. Amen.' (then sits down; almost too quickly for me to be able to push her chair forward as she does so) because for someone of my rough and ready nautical background, I'm now on my very best behaviour.

Not that I feel *too* badly out of place. It's merely - there seems to be something here which doesn't quite fit?

'It was very kind of you to give my husband a lift home, Mister Howells. Was he at all helpful during the passage?'

'As a matter of fact he,' (but before I've got time to reply, Mary's off again).

'Will you be staying long? '

Even if I knew, it seems I would have difficulty getting the information across, because Mary's holding the floor, giving pointed orders to the shy young girl; slightly more consideration to the Spanish galleon who is getting luncheon under way, serving iced gazpacho.

'What part of the world are you from, Mr Howells?' (while I'm telling her) we're helping ourselves to a series of side dishes, one of which contains hard-boiled eggs.

'Can I pass you the salt, Mary?'

'How long have you been sailing, Mr Howells?' (followed by a series of questions) which I do my best to answer, while I'm busy with other bowls of goodies.

'Andrew's told me you're married, Mr Howells: have you any children?'

'Yes, two; now.'

'How old are they?'

'Early twenties.'

And this isn't the end of it.

We have only just got our feet under the table, barely unfolded our napkins, when she sounds off with, 'I can hardly believe your wife approves of your sailing escapades.' (which I think, at this early stage in proceedings is a dubious remark) at the very least, it carries an edge to it which I find challenging.

However, the soup is delicious, and when we've finished the course, the shy young lass clears table, while the fully rigged ship serves the kedgeree, which turns out to be a whole lot better than Andrew gave it credit for. The only fly in the rice is Mary, who is giving a series of orders to her husband.

'After luncheon, Andrew; I'd like you to find out how Father Anthony got on.'

'Yes m'Dear, I will.'

'And when you're on the telephone, make sure you ... '

So the meal proceeds, punctuated with crisp instructions, and several provocative remarks.

Then two enlivening events occur.

The desert turns out to be nothing less than a triumph; a Coupe Jacques, served in a tall glass flute crammed from its belly-bulging bottom up with sliced peaches, mixed fruit blobbed with maraschino cherries, ice cream hiding teasing chips of dark chocolate, all topped off with a generous whip of real cream, studded with blanched almonds and drenched in Melba sauce.

Then Mary asks yet another question.

'Are you a communicant, Mister Howells?'

Well, first and foremost, I'm a guest, who now has a succulent cherry poised on the pointed end of a very narrow spoon - so perhaps I should do what I can to suppress a wry smile and concentrate on this particular fruit. And having achieved the balancing act, dart what amounts to a sharp-enough glance at Andrew - who seems intent on other business.

Not that it makes much difference, because Mary's pressing ahead, determined to establish *she's* in command, that it's her turn, and it's going to remain her turn well into the foreseeable future.

'As a matter of fact, Mr Howells, we are very fortunate here; we have an excellent relationship with our local church, even though we're relatively new to the island.' (from where I'm sitting) it's tempting to wonder how long she *has* been on the island.

But idle thoughts are not much good in situations of this sort. It's obvious there isn't much point in offering anything in the way of a good-natured reply to Mary's crashing monologue, because it's just about impossible to get a polite word in edgeways, even though, as a good little boy, I do try.

'Where were you living, Mrs McNeil, before you ....' (but she's determined to press on, particularly about 'The Church') while at the same time keeping her other chosen subject well to the ear-bashing fore.

'Do you always make a point of sailing alone, Mr Howells?' (followed much too quickly by) 'don't you find it all just too boring for words?'

Now, most of us know there's a short answer to this sort of question, particularly when there's more than a suspicion that the point that's been given to it hasn't been sharpened by accident - rather by design.

Then again, conversational gambits are diverse, and they occasionally make use of an overly boisterous, sometimes dubious remark, of the men-only, locker room type of joke, when the person addressed receives a gratuitous insult - and then feels free to reply in similar vein.

Yet again, at the other end of what might be seen as a sexist-leaning spectrum, there's a particular type of chatterbox who can be genuinely amusing - if she's pretty, and you've been attracted by the spark of wicked humour in the glint of her twinkling eye, no matter how cattily she's been obliged to draw your teased attention to it.

However, these extenuating circumstances don't apply to Mrs McNeil.

And further on even than that, my irritation is not just concerned with her choice of words, or subject matter, but because she isn't carrying on a conversation in the accepted sense of the term; she's conducting a monologue, shaped to her own steam-rollering end, and preached from her own unassailable pulpit.

And even that isn't the end of it, because she's deliberately talking down to both Andrew and myself, and while he may be prepared to put up with it, the game has reached the point where it's in danger of becoming tiresome. But before I chance my arm, perhaps I'd better call to mind what my old school master told me, all those years ago.

He used to say, and he literally drummed it into me, there were two things a gentleman never mentions when he has the privilege of being able to place his feet anywhere near someone else's table, particularly when there are ladies present. The first thing to avoid being *Religion*, while the second bit of advice concerned what he always discreetly referred to, in his old-fashioned way as - the *private parts* of either unmentionable gender (not that it's likely to happen here, if only because I'm not included in the conversation). It's Andrew's wife who is breaking the golden rule, and she's warming to her task, developing a theme which can be described as evangelical, in the combative sense of the term.

'I can never understand, can you, Mister Howells, how we put up with the way the ungodly have the nerve to come to church, in order to be able to march up the aisle to that wonderful theme from Lohengrin. And then return to their own dismissive little world expecting to be accompanied by the Wedding March from Mendelssohn's Midsummer Night's Dream.'

So it's now come to the stage where I'm sitting a few feet from Mary McNeil, being subjected to a pompous drone, and I'm beginning to wonder how it's all going to end.

At the same time, unlikely though it may be, if she only knew it, she's preaching to the converted (because I actually agree in a cautious way with at least some of the themes she's developing). But that doesn't make it the less embarrassing, to the point where I have to slide a glance in Andrew's direction, to see if there's anything on offer there.

Now I've finished my ice cream, I have time to take more notice of Mary, not so much *what* she's saying - but how she's actually saying it.

She's still preaching (it seems we're stuck with that) and if anything she's become even more self-righteous (the ungodly are still getting it in the neck) so here we have a lady who's on a crusade, maybe intent on a charge.

And who is going to stop her?

Ordinarily, I would sit back in my chair and enjoy the rhetorical fireworks. However, there's a development which may alter the course of this embarrassing encounter, because while Andrew's wife is on her high horse, there's been a change of pace - a trot sat down to a canter - and she's not merely talking *down* to me, or even talking *to* me, she's actually talking *at* me, as she **gallops** by, and I'm not sure she's going to be satisfied, even with this dig in the tenderest part of the ribs.

'You see, Mister Howells.'

Now: people who open a sentence with '*you see,*' all too often go on to make an assertion of the '*I've no doubt at all*' variety, and have every intention of pressing on to flatten whoever is foolish enough to stick his head over the unprotected part of the parapet.

'You see, Mister Howells; in your part of the world, in West Wales, there have been so many unfortunate developments as far as the Church is concerned.'

It may indeed be true.

But if we're talking about particular locations, we're getting closer to home. Much closer to home; so close, I think I may know rather more of what's going on there than does Mrs Mary McNeil, so if I'm going to get my foot in the door, this may be the time to attempt it. However, my polite, deferential (certainly a mistake) yet quite reasonable ....

'Well, Mrs McNeil, I take note of what you're saying; but the situation is complicated by the relationship between the Church in Wales and the different denominations of Chapels. In this regard, one could say we have, throughout the Principality, almost a proliferation of places of worship.'

But, this truthful and not altogether gormless response merely gains an admonition.

'That just begs the question, Mister Howells. There's absolutely no doubt at all,' (and on she goes), blathering away, making it almost impossible to put forward an alternative view. And I do actually have one, easy enough to set out.

Old habits die hard.

The mindset drummed into me by my old schoolmaster has left an indelible mark.

I feel uncomfortable when caught up in thickets of this sort.

Spelt out in words of I don't care how many syllables, I'm reluctant to cross swords with Mary McNeil. Not because I don't want to talk religion, or *can't* talk religion - but because I'm absolutely convinced I **shouldn't** be talking religion.

That's a breeze which has an unfortunate habit of backing. And I would be well advised to remember I arrived here by boat, have just stepped briefly ashore, and shouldn't allow myself to be tempted into an argument (seaman, know your place, as well as keep a weather-eye lifted), because if, by some bemused turn of events, my old seagoing mates were present as flies on the proverbial wall, the group who could be roughly but affectionately described as *the bums,* would be in danger of bustin' a gut. While the other half, although marginally better behaved, would be heading for the nearest door, hiding their smiles in their napkins.

And I could hardly blame them.

I've only been involved with Andrew's wife for thirty tedious minutes, yet it's long enough to get fed up with her pompous monologue, and she's still at it, has moved on to what has probably been her principle, but so far shielded objective. Because the substantial bee now buzzing about in her less than tightly tied bonnet is, broadly speaking, uncompromising fundamentalism - specifically, how the fragmentation of the Church since the Reformation has led inexorably to a lowering of tone.

A deterioration in standards (not Mrs McNeil's) because, as with most Fundamentalists - she is right, and *you* are **WRONG** - with Andrew displaying the sort of cringe which leads to the conclusion he's long since played the cur to this dogmatic lesson; that he has no intention of making an effort to divert the deluge of assertive opinion which is just about flooding the table; so it looks as if it's going to be up to the boy, if I can get her attention.

'Mrs McNeil.' (followed by quite a long wait). 'Mrs McNeil,' (she does eventually stop talking) 'we do indeed have a lot of denominations in Wales. Let's see, quite apart from the Anglicans, we have Baptists, Methodists, Calvinists, Wesleyans, Seventh Day Adventists and no doubt several more I can't bring immediately to mind - we even have Primitive Methodists: are you familiar with them?' (this is quite unfair) it is, actually, a nasty-minded trap being prepared for you know who.

'Primitive Methodists, Mister Howells? I've never heard of that funny little sect. Where do they fit into God's grand scheme of things?'

'Oh, they're the sort, Mrs McNeil, of whom the old saw says the eligible members of the congregation go to chapel with their bibles in one hand, and their cocks in the other. [3] And that isn't the end of it Mrs McNeil, they also say the female half of the congregation are genuinely glad the others have taken the trouble to chance it.'

There's a slight pause here (to be absolutely honest, it's quite a long pause) but it's not being wasted, because during it I'm getting a certain amount of pleasure by sliding a smirk of a glance at both my host and my hostess. This is no doubt a childish pastime, and probably no good will come of it, but it's irresistible, because Andrew's face is a picture.

He's wide awake now, no doubt about that, and attempting the difficult task of darting a warning signal in my direction, while at the same time sending a silent, yet placatory message to his wife.

He's also put the spoon with which he was eating his ice cream carelessly down on his side plate, and the resulting tinkle could be interpreted, not so much as lack of precision - but because he's just this minute dropped it.

His wife is made of sterner stuff.

Although it takes time for the insult to sink in (maybe all of two-tenth's of a blood-raising second) when the penny drops, there's no doubt that here we have a prim lady who *was* on a high horse (side-saddle, of course)

141

but, having been insulted, is now very angry indeed.

I would also have to admit that the scale of her reaction is proving more pronounced than anticipated; indeed, it may even be cause for concern.

I'm only two feet from her, and can see a vein throbbing at her temple (not the one she feels has just been desecrated) but above her right ear, near the line of her coiffure, which she wears as a severely combed, tightly pinned, back of the neck drawn-out bun.

The impression given, in a perverse way, is quite attractive.

Her pale forehead, flashing eyes, taut nostrils, the throbbing tick at her temple.

The way in which she's narrowing and pulling back her lips, prior to delivering what I have no doubt will amount to a stinging rebuke.

Yet while the storm clouds are gathering (Force 6, nudging 7) not on the Beaufort Scale (we're talking Richter here) something else is happening.

A moment ago, fractionally prior to the time-ticking scale of the blood-rushing second, Mrs McNeil was a poised, even if over-assertive woman who was so sure of her ground she thought few people worth a second glance, much less worth listening to.

That's probably pitching it a bit too far, but it's the sort of judgement you arrive at, if you have been talked-down to for so long, you've been driven to use words - not as a means of communication, but as weapons, with which to wound, possibly bludgeon your opponent, even if she is your hostess, into what you hope is submission. And this isn't difficult, if you're ruthless enough to put the whole of your rough seaman's steel toe-capped boot in.

The trouble is, we are apt to underestimate the scale of the injury which is bound to be involved, and when you see the collateral damage, a reaction takes place (so I'm not feeling all that proud of myself) while waiting for the retaliatory broadside I'm sure is on the way.

But Mary McNeil has yet to say anything, as time continues to tick remorselessly by, for at least one more embarrassing second.

'Are you alright, My Dear?' (this is Andrew, voicing his concern, feeling his way towards pouring oil on troubled waters, and not without reason).

His wife is drawing back from the table, not moving her chair, just edging her bum, then straightening her back (winding up, I assume, before she pitches a bean-ball at me); yet she's still not *saying* anything, and it's beginning to look as if she may not even get round to it.

Her face, which was previously pale, has now become flushed, a narrowing frown is drawing her blackly arched eyebrows closer than ever to the bridge of her aquiline nose. Nevertheless, as well as her affronted *stare,* it seems she is at last about to say something; yet *still* doesn't seem able to say it, as her face and her features are falling apart, and for one dreadful moment I'm beginning to wonder if she's about to suffer a seizure (and this remark, by the way, is not anywhere near as trite as it sounds).

I'm *genuinely* relieved when she says, 'Andrew.'

'Yes, my Dear.'

'Andrew.' (hesitantly; requiring an effort to get the word out), 'will you say Grace; I just can't manage it. I have this terrible migraine.' while pushing her chair back from the table, dragging the wooden legs of this substantial piece of furniture over the tiled floor, with the movement producing a distinctive rasp of sound, which comes astonishingly close to a collective expression of regret.

As we all get up, and wait, until Andrew gathers himself (he needs this second, to collect his thoughts) then stands behind his chair and recites the prayer 'Agimus tibi gratias, Omnipotens Deus, pro donis tuis [(4)] per Jesum Christum, Dominum nostrum - Amen.'

Word perfect; not that it's difficult, nevertheless it shows he's part of the household, and this is borne out by his wife's next remark. 'Will you help me, my Dear?'

It's worth noting, there have been two role-reversals (*Andrew* has said Grace, and his wife is calling *him,* m'dear) and in a way, it's touching.

But this is an admission which says as much about me as it does about them, as I now feel totally inadequate - succumbed to a feeling of guilt, reduced to standing behind my chair, wanting to offer help, but waiting for something to happen, as we move from the table with Andrew shepherding his wife towards the flight of stairs.

'Come along, Mary,' (helping her, one tread at a time), 'come along m'dear,' (gaining the breathing space of the landing), 'you really must lie down,' (while encouraging her), 'I'll get your tablets,' (past the stained-glass window), 'then I'm going to call the doctor.'

'No: don't do that Andrew. I'll be perfectly all right.'

As they negotiate the second part of the landing and pass the *Last Supper,* all I can hear is a murmur of what could be a low-keyed argument.

Doors shutting.

Andrew talking to someone, I think on the telephone (I can't hear what he's saying) then, while I'm standing idly about, at the foot of the staircase (feeling about as useful as a spare pork chop at a Jewish festival) the housekeeper comes into the room, bearing a tray supporting a steaming filter of coffee, cups, saucers, spoons; and a bowl of dark brown sugar, which she sets out on the refectory table. She does seem surprised to find I'm the only person present, but gives me a nice smile as she retires to the kitchen, leaving me to help myself to what I recognise as a badly needed stimulant. The coffee's hot, and strong enough to need a little sugar, all of which I'm grateful for, as apart from anything else, it gives me something to do.

Perhaps there *is* something worse than waiting for your host to reappear, after you have just enjoyed the dubious pleasure of gratuitously insulting his wife (but I can't bring it to mind at the moment).

You can of course tap your spoon against the rim of your coffee cup, and if I hadn't given up smoking all of eighteen years ago, I would be tempted to light a cigarette. But there's no alternative to exercising patience, even if this commodity is in its usual short supply.

In unfortunate situations of this sort, you have to put up with another door being closed. An act which doesn't shut out the half-strangled gurgle of an old-fashioned Spanish lavatory about its no doubt indelicate business.

More footsteps, padding along a corridor, and yet another door being shut.

All of which builds a degree of suspense, which leads to another sip of coffee, and the somewhat less than idle speculation as to how the whole of this sorry mess is going to eventually pan out.

However, help is at hand, and from an unexpected quarter.

Andrew has reappeared on the landing, but no longer dolled up in his ambassadorial suit.

He's changed out of that smart, amazingly sharp, but stuffy rig, and now wears khaki shorts and a short-sleeved shirt of the sort that sports a floral design which would stand out amazingly well in a fairground. He's smiling (or is this the deceptive smile) more a grimace really, some people employ when they are about to embark on what may turn out to be unpleasant business?

Only time will tell.

And the moment has arrived, because Andrew has come down the stairs, is walking towards me with a purposeful step.

So am I about to get, albeit once removed, my marching orders from Mary?

My host is standing alongside the refectory table, about to say something, which could turn out to be any one of a dozen sorts of rebuke; but what he actually says is 'What's the coffee like, Val?'

This remark may seem out of context, and my reaction to it is not quite on the scale of the drunken riots that engulfed the streets of London when the British government announced they'd just received telegraphic news of the long-awaited Relief of Mafeking; [5] nevertheless, I'm quietly encouraged, as well as relieved by the turn of events, and when Andrew decides not to take coffee, but opt for, as he says, 'something just a wee bit stronger than that.' I'm sure we've turned another corner of one significant sort or another.

Having expressed his preference, my old shipmate is moving towards the kitchen, leaving me nursing a half-drunk cup of coffee.

I can hear him talking to the Spanish galleon, and he soon reappears bearing a jug of ice cubes.

'I think we should go out to the garden, Val; will you bring a couple of glasses?'

This doesn't present a problem, there's a whole array of cut glass, heavy bottomed tumblers decorating the sideboard, quality Waterford stuff [6] stacked alongside the bains-marie.

However, I feel guilty about jumping ship without leaving some sort of word with the crew.

'Before we go, Andrew, would you mind passing my compliments to your housekeeper? The meal was delicious, and I wouldn't like her to think it hasn't been appreciated.'

'Why don't you tell her yourself, she speaks good English.' (this with a wicked smile).

So I'm now wondering, if his Spanish staff have picked up the embarrassing knowledge that some Welsh chapel-goers have been known to display ambitions which have been closely linked with the extent, perhaps even the length of their previously mentioned short-arm'd pretensions. [7] This is only a fleeting thought, not something that should be endlessly pursued, because when I stick my head into the kitchen, both the fully-rigged ship and her accompanying frigate are hard at work, cleaning up after the meal. They have their backs to the dining room door, so I can see how much broader one is, than the other (a much beamier, fuller bottomed vessel) but they both turn round, as I get their attention with the usual ploy.

'Err, excuse me.'

'Señor?'

'I'd just like to say how much I enjoyed the meal, particularly the Coupe Jacques. I thought it was a masterpiece.' (this seems to have been understood, as it earns two very nice smiles) so I have tried, and my conscience is clear, at least as far as the Coupe Jacques is concerned.

Andrew has left the kitchen.

He's standing alongside the sideboard, with the jug of ice cubes in one hand; with the other he's picking up what remains of the orange juice, then off he goes, with a good natured, 'don't forget the glasses,' as he leaves the dining room, passes through the vestibule and goes out through the front door of the house with me in his wake.

It's an amazing transition. Inside the house, it's been cool (for one significant moment, it's been cooler even than that), but outside the house, my embarrassing brush with Andrew's wife has been left thankfully astern; wafted away by the afternoon's breeze, which is whispering its own lazy way about the white-washed walls of the villa. A breeze that's tattling its own little tale; reminding the leaves of the trees to clip the red sloping eaves; of the trace of perfume, which drifts (can it be from the dry potentilla?).

So it's tempting to linger awhile. Enjoying the move from Mary's presence; breathing in the heavy air, while wondering which of the flowering shrubs are providing this fragrant oasis. But I won't be able to indulge this fancy, because Andrew is marching along.

Striding down the path leading to the beach.

He's still in sight, but making a detour, moving off the path, walking towards the small shed I noticed when we first stepped ashore.

This is a quaint, lopsided old building.

To call it a potting shed may be doing it a disservice; yet to call it a 'summer house' implies a grander structure - a term which shouldn't be applied to a ramshackle hut that's showing its age, bleached by years of exposure to the wrinkling glare of the sun.

This all too casual little castle is built of cedar, and has the dried-out, but durable, russet-toned look of that particular timber. It's not very big, with a shingled roof made of the same material. It does have a window, but now I'm nearer, I can see the panes have been covered by layers of dust, and the disused look is shaded still further by traces of cobwebs, hanging inside the brown layered oblongs of glass.

Andrew has arrived at this retreat (he's juggling his two glass jugs, and seems to be pointing at the door) but what he's actually doing is freeing, and then introducing, with some difficulty, his index finger into the hole that gives access to the wooden, internal latchkey.

I haven't seen one of these old-fashioned gadgets for years. But now I've joined Andrew, and he's got the door open, I can see into the building, and it's dustily obvious the contents of one person's potting shed, bears an astonishing resemblance to another person's potting shed the whole of the garden world over.

There's the usual array of agricultural tools; a spade, two forks, several Dutch hoes, with most of these implements hanging on nails that have been hammered into the studding.

The major items cluttered about are - a petrol-driven lawnmower that started, then stopped seeing better days all of six years ago. And an equally rusty old wheelbarrow, with a pneumatic tyre that's as flat as a tit on a witch (but nothing at all, at all, at all to do with Mary). There's also a rough table, and this is handy enough as it provides a place on which Andrew can set the two glass jugs.

Now he's got his hands free, my old shipmate is rummaging about in the pockets of his khaki shorts, soon coming up with a key, this bit of equipment apparently being needed to unlock the lid and gain access to a wooden chest which stands in a corner of the shed. An intriguing item, partly obscured by junk (looks like empty gunny sacks) that may or may not have been deliberately draped over it; nevertheless, whether it's been camouflaged or not, there are several folding chairs stacked on this battered old box.

'Would you mind taking these outside, Val.' (he means two of the director chairs).

'Set them up somewhere in the shade; then I'll fix you a drink.'

'What would you like?'

I'm looking over his shoulder at the contents of the chest, and at first glance it seems to contain little more than the pile of empty sacks. But Andrew's rummaging around, and soon comes up with something I'm almost sure I've seen before (it's a bottle) wrapped in tissue paper, and there are several other similarly packaged items.

'Fancy a drop of vodka and orange?' (sounds reasonable, after all, he's taken the trouble to bring the juice and ice cubes), 'or perhaps you'd prefer a vegetable mix? I've also got tomato juice; carrot and celery; the complete V8; all sorts of stuff.'

Indeed he has.

Apart from the half-dozen discreetly wrapped bottles, which he probably purchased when we were in Lanzarote (when I think back on it, didn't he bring them aboard the boat there?), besides this illicit shipment, which seems intended to boost his 'let's slip a sly one in sort of supply', there's a barefaced bottle of Scotch, more tinned juices, a long tube of nesting plastic tumblers, a packet of swizzle sticks, a box of panatellas, a tin of waterproof matches; and hanging from its own length of twine, secured to a staple hammered into the lid of the chest, one of those gadgets you need to punch a three-cornered hole in a can.

So it's quite an array.

A well-equipped cocktail cabinet, tucked away in this old potting shed, offering endless possibilities, maybe not all of which are connected with the booze he's got stashed in the box.

'What do you want, Val?'

'I think I'll have,' (I was going to say a Bloody Mary; but I've changed horses in mid-smile).

'Do you mind if I have a drop of Scotch?'

'Not at all; have what you like. What do you want with it?'

'On the rocks will do fine.' (this decision prompted by the fact that, or so I would perhaps unreasonably claim, I've just about had a bellyful of orange juice).

I reckon I can do with a decent drink.

Partly because there have been so many ups and downs to this particular day, I've got to the stage where I'm not only glad we've left the house, I feel we've *escaped* to the beguiling waft of the garden. This may not reflect too well on my behaviour, but what's happened, has happened, and here we are, my old shipmate and I, lounged in two folding chairs, looking at each other.

He's got his fist around, and has already taken an appreciative swallow from a plastic container (the Waterford glass I carried out having, presumably, been judged too squat and too small) so he's using a tumbler that's full to the brim with a few ice cubes, a lot of vodka, and just a suspicion of orange juice.

He now gets up, and goes into the potting shed, to emerge with a folding table, the box of panatellas, and the tin of matches. Then goes back once more into the building, which seems to be equipped with all the facilities anyone may ever need from a 'let's both get potted shed' to re-emerge, carrying his plastic tumbler and displaying a well-satisfied smile, as he's obviously just freshened his drink.

And he's still not out of ideas.

He's put his Smirnoff & Smirnoff, laced with a drop of the same stuff, down on the folding table. Then back he goes into Aladdin's Cave (Pandora's Box?) to come out with two more director-chairs, one of which he gives me, then proceeds to unfold the chair he's retained for himself.

So he's now lounged, with his feet up, striking a waterproof match, while sucking expertly on a slender panatella, and I can't say I'm worried because I'm upwind, and the haze is drifting away from where I'm sitting; nevertheless, I am beginning to wonder, how old Andrew ...

'Not a bad sort of day, Val?' (this said in an expansive manner) between puffs of light blue smoke, while looking skyward, finishing up with another puff on his panatella and a wave at the tropical palms.

Now, it *is* a nice day; with this appreciative comment prompted by the fact that Andrew's not the only one who's enjoying a tot.

And he's not mean either, as I have my fist around what's left of a generous three-fingers of an excellent malt [8] (so we're both playing the same sort of game) even if he's in a different league. Nevertheless, I can't say I feel comfortable about the way this thing is developing. There is, after all, the small matter of Andrew's wife, who is presumably lying in a darkened room, waiting for the doctor.

Then there's the cause of her malaise in the first place.

Taking one sad thing with another, and even after yet another sip at the malt, there does seem to be a certain amount of happy-go-lucky, bugger-everybody carelessness, of the *to hell with it all* sort, associated with my companion's behaviour; yet it's a difficult subject to broach.

'Err, Andrew. I really must apologise for the smart-arsed remark I made when we were having lunch.' (a fair-enough start?).

'It obviously upset Mary no end, and I'm sorry about that.' (which seems like a good place to stop), but as I'm not getting any help from Andrew, I have to press on.

'I didn't intend to give that degree of offence you know. It was the sort of rude comment which just pops out now and then.' (to be honest, I'm finding this an uphill task) and I've reached the stage where I think it's time he threw me a line; but short of a decent response, I'll have to carry on helping myself.

'Does Mary often suffer from migraine?' (hell's bells, he's *still* not saying anything) just looking at me in a glum sort of way.

'Do you think we should go back indoors, to see if she's alright?'

'No, no; there's no need to go back to the house. I've told Cara to let me know when the doctor turns up.' (I thought that might get a reply).

And it's turning out to be more than a marginal improvement, because my old mate is getting himself back into gear.

The glaze to his eyes, and the bloom to his cheeks - those telltale signs produced by the over-large tot, which together amount to the habitual drinkers re-launched feeling, and look, after a day off the booze - that surge has got down to his socks, and it might be fair to assume he's feeling better, as he now seems to be winding-up to say something relevant. But he's saying it in a resigned way, as if the information is being dragged out of him; that he's being forced to discuss something, when he would prefer to remain silent.

'As a matter of fact, Val,' (but very reluctantly), 'I should have told you some time ago, when we were aboard the boat; that Mary and I, we're going through a difficult time.'

'In what way, Andrew?'

'You may recall the night I didn't turn in; when we spent some time exchanging views.' (he means when he was gossiping away, for hour after endless hour).

'Do you remember? I told you that Mary and I have two daughters? But what I should have gone on to tell you is - we also had a son.'

'So?' (there's a long wait) but he eventually comes out with it.

'Well, unfortunately, he died, about three months ago. Actually, it was three months and eight days ago.'

It's still a nice day.

The sun's as bright as ever.

The breeze still wafts the palms.

The smoke from Andrew's panatella is still drifting as a blue wisp, from the end of what I recently thought was an over-long cigar.

And he's still got his fist around the drink which I know, now, may have been over-diluted with orange juice (but apart from that, I'm having difficulty in thinking of something to say).

The place has become rather quiet; so quiet, there's nothing else for it; it's got to be back to basics.

'I really am sorry to hear that, Andrew.' (the usual cliché).

But what can I say, having been caught off balance by the speed, as well as the manner in which Andrew has changed the colour and shape of his hat (not that he's wearing one, because he left the house bareheaded) but this being the case, he's devoid of shelter, even though giving the unmistakable impression of being badly in need of it.

Only a moment ago, we were enjoying a drink - two saucy lads, celebrating an escape from the disturbing consequences of my bad manners. But we're now experiencing something that's already turned out to be more than just a change of manner. And there's no way of avoiding the rest of it, because Andrew's perched on the edge of his chair, engaged as his own grief-relating oracle.

'The trouble is Val; the circumstances were so tragic; it was all so unnecessary.' (it might have been avoidable then), but it's inescapable now.

'What happened?'

'It was one of those drug-related tragedies, of the sort you read about in the papers, then assume it's never going to happen to you.'

'That sounds, awful.'

'It was, and not only *was* - it still *is.* And it's not getting any better, because Mary's reacted in a distressing way.'

'What do you mean?'

'She's got it into her head it was some sort of a judgement; and worse on than that, it was a judgement we brought on ourselves.'

'That's hard to believe.' (in fact, I don't believe it) particularly if he's putting it to me in her terms.

'Where did it happen?'

'He was away at Edinburgh University; then we had a call from the police to tell us that David was, dead.' (this, with a significant pause).

` 'And I have to tell you Val; Mary was, and is, absolutely devastated.'

'I can understand that Andrew.'

And I don't need anyone to tell me that my old shipmate is also close to his own emotional shipwreck.

He's picked up his plastic tumbler, holding it at eye-level, while giving his drink a defiant *glare,* as if the solution to the problem might be found floating about in the booze (so who's to say that it isn't?). And while he's about this held-aloft soul searching, he's taking a pull at his cigar, but the damned thing's gone out, so he throws the useless weed on the grass, then goes through the motion of grinding the dead end out with the screwed down heel of his sandal.

I can see all sorts of difficulties looming here, and to be honest, I'm glad I still have a good swallow of malt swilling about in my crystal.

And when that's gone, I feel I could do with another reassuring drop.

'I say, Andrew; do you mind if I have a spot more Scotch?'

This may look like a cack-handed cook failing to lift a whistlin' kettle that's been left far too long on the blistering hob of a cherry-red alcohol stove (or words to that effect). Yet this may not be as daft as it sounds, because it's not very often, when you ask for another drink, you get what amounts to a relieved look from your host, as Andrew goes into the old potting shed, and comes out with two bottles - one for himself, and one for me - from which he pours another generous measure of Scotch.

He sits himself back in his chair, then leans forward, fixing me with what he probably thinks is a piercing look, having adopted the earnest, elbows-on-knees approach most of us assume when about to make a pronouncement that we think will be of some significance.

But he's taking his time about it, which allows me to wonder - why old Andrew didn't get around to telling me about his son before.

Before what?

Well - there have been plenty of opportunities

For instance, if I'd known about the bereavement, my attitude to Mary would certainly have been different (to the point where I would have been bold enough to ask about the placing of a crucifix?).

And why weren't there any photographs of their two remaining daughters? Wasn't there plenty of room, on what I can look back on now as that rather significant sideboard?

This whirl of speculation taking place in the moment that Andrew is using to settle himself in his chair, and take another sip at his Smirnoff, which is probably just as well, because my old mate seems about to tell me something that I hope is going to move this thing along.

However, what he comes up with is, 'You know, Val; I've come to the conclusion, you probably have to experience this sort of thing at first hand, before you can appreciate the way it effects your personal relationships.'

I suppose you could say that; but from where I'm sitting, it sounds the sort of gem which may raise a bit of a smile - not only because I can see the banana skin that's been skidded on - but because Andrew isn't the only person present who decided to keep the cards reasonably close to his chest. Yet this bit of obtuse information will have to be chewed over for a while, because I can see (out of the corner of my real, not my retrospective eye) that someone has come out of the house, and is walking towards our old potting shed. This turning out to be the Spanish galleon, waving what looks like a tea towel, while at the same time firing off a stream of Spanish, with the word *medico* conveying what I assume is the significant part of the message.

'It looks as if the doctor's arrived, Andrew.'

'Yes.' (this brief reply being uttered without much enthusiasm) which may sound callous, but it isn't far removed from my own reaction to the news that at least one of us should go back to the house.

Andrew, of course, must go.

I'm not too keen myself.

The whole thing seems fraught with difficulties, some of which would surely be better dealt with at a later date.

Another convenient cop-out?

Yes: but not entirely, because I don't have to look very far for a reasonable excuse.

'I know, I should come back with you Andrew, to make my number with Mary.'(funny how we don't like using the simple word *apologise,* isn't it?). 'I'm concerned about the boat; we've been away some time, and I'm never happy leaving her swinging round a hook in an open roadstead, without anyone on board.' (and this should sound convincing, because it's near enough the truth).

Nevertheless, while it may be near enough the truth, it isn't anywhere near the solution to the problem.

Andrew has got up from his chair.

He's holding his drink in his hand, contemplating the contents of the plastic tumbler which is still half-full of vodka, and what he reluctantly introduced into the tincture in the first place - so being a reflective sort of a bloke, who has just consumed two large tots of very strong malt, I'm wondering if my old mate is going to take another kick at the world, before he limps disconsolately back to what he expects will be another unwelcoming wail, emanating from the walls of his (or maybe it's *her* villa?).

But what he actually does is - take another look at his Smirnoff (not even the suspicion of a sip from the snifter), and when he's got the stuff swirling nicely around, he fires the lot into the bushes, with the booze describing a graceful parabola as it shoots from the plastic tumbler, over what looks like a not-yet-flowering Mimosa, [9] to fall with not enough of a splash to embellish what may appear a theatrical act of renunciation.

As I've been enjoying my single malt (indeed, I don't know how I would have managed without it) I find Andrew's extravagant act slightly embarrassing, partly because I have one or two bits of information I would like to pass on to my old shipmate, before he goes back to his house.

153

In this regard, I may not have much time at my disposal, because he's poised, presumably trying to decide whether to leave me as monarch of all I survey, which does of course include the shadow capable of being cast by what remains of the in-use bottle of Scotch.

Not that he's worried about me helping myself (and of that, I'm absolutely sure; we've been shipmates long enough to scotch that mean little thought).

So it seems he's trying to decide, whether to leave the potting shed open, or collect the table and chairs and stack the lot inside (tidy up, that untidy part of his life) before going back to see how his wife is getting on with the doctor.

'Don't worry about this stuff Andrew; I'll put it away, if you want a private word with the medic.' (which seems a reasonable suggestion) yet it's actually a mistake, because Andrew has taken the opportunity offered and is about to start walking towards the house.

'Oh, by the way, Andrew; I do have to get back to the boat you know, so I may have to catch you later; but before you go, there is something I would like to mention - it concerns.' (but the opportunity is slipping away) and in a manner I suppose I should have anticipated, because the Spanish galleon has reappeared, and there's more tea towel waving in a style, and a torrent of Spanish in a tone, which could leave a stranger in some doubt as to who is employee and who is employer; however, there's no doubt about the degree of urgency involved.

'I'll have to go, Val; if you move down the coast this evening, give me a ring, then we'll get together as soon as we can.' (so he knows I'm thinking of moving on, which is some consolation), but it still leaves me nursing another, private message, because my old mate, who I suppose I've been getting to know a little better, almost hour by hour, as this day has slipped on by, is not far away, in geographical terms.

But five feet and walking is too far to launch the thought that's been uppermost in my mind ever since Andrew came out with his poorly polished, yet still well-enough cut little gem - to the effect that we have to experience bereavement at first hand, before we're in a position to appreciate the trauma that's involved in the grief-inducing process.

That's plausible enough (even if it's not precisely what he said) but life being what it is, and having taken another appreciative sip of the balm that's been arrived at as a consequence of the amazingly productive bubble 'tween the barley, the peat, and the burn, I'm of the opinion there are few people around who have *never* faced bereavement, in one devastating form or another, even though, when *you* are facing bereavement, this disarming truth is apt to be overlooked - much in the way that Mary has not only been devastated by the loss of her son - she can't understand why it was allowed to happen to her.

And further on than that, she's not willing to concede it *should* have happened to her - has been casting around for a reason, which is about the time Andrew was confirmed in his alcoholic opinion that he's being used as some sort of an all-too-convenient Sally.

Yet this bit of drunken speculation is so much idle chatter, because Andrew is out of convenient earshot, and you can't raise your voice to gain a person's attention, while at the same time conveying the message that you too have lost a son; buried now, out of sight, in a quiet country churchyard, [10] who always comes to mind when someone makes a telling remark to the effect that ...

'You should have first hand experience.' (I forget how Andrew got round to innocently phrasing the rest of it).

The old potting shed's still there, as brown and ragged as ever.

The smoke from the peat drifts over the malt, under the smouldering eyes of the Smirnoff.

And the director chairs are probably expecting someone to make a stage-frightened dash from the scene.

But as I've already had my prompt from the wings, I'm getting on with the job of folding the props.

Taking the half-empty bottles back to the shed.

Checking the tops, then placing them carefully in the old seaman's chest.

Andrew's empty tumbler is easily dealt with (I've found a black rubbish bag, handily placed in a corner of the dusty old shed).

The Waterford crystal presents a problem because, courtesy of my host's generous elbow, the glass I've been using is still half-full of malt; so in the circumstances (a half-cut seaman, in charge of a beautifully cut, half-full container of whisky) I think I'd better decant the booze into a plastic tumbler.

And I can tell you, straight up, now I've taken another sip of the malt, it doesn't taste as good out of plastic as it did out of the Irishman's success with the crystal.

There's also the box of cigars, and the tin of matches to stow away, and when that's done, it's only the small table to fold up, carry inside, and place on top of the chest.

I can't do that until I've found a spot for the jugs Andrew carried down from the house.

This still leaves two Waterford glasses to place, very carefully, on the up-turned top of the table (because doesn't it pay to be extra careful with really nice stuff, particularly after you've had what's turned out to be a longish sip at the sauce?).

So after I've done my bob-a-job task, my Boy Scouting good deed for the day, I'm about ready to move on.

Closing the door to the potting shed - having to insert my finger in the old-fashioned hole, and lift the old-fashioned latchkey, before closing the old-fashioned door of the old-fashioned shed.

To wander on back to the boat.

Ignoring the whispering palms.

Past the blooming bougainvillaea, with my fist around a plastic tumbler which isn't quite so full of malt as it was a minute ago (and for one greedy moment) the thought does occur, that Andrew wouldn't mind if I had just one more spot.

Yet enough's enough.

It's only the matter of a few more steps and I'll be able to see my old boat.

And there she is.

Floating quietly away - though still very much at anchor - reassuring her returning owner, who doesn't have much difficulty remembering where he put the blades.

Then when I've shouldered them, and negotiated the boulder-strewn bluff which leads on down to the black-sanded beach, spend a well-satisfied moment looking at the way - to my eye - lovely old boat, is supported so peacefully by the breadth of a blue-shimmered ocean.

Being struck by the *astonishing* simplicity of that inanimate object, before coming to the nothing less than *guilty* conclusion, that I can't understand *how* I could *possibly* forget to ease the pressure out of the inflatable.

To make allowance, as I *invariably* do, for the drum-tightened tube that *always* occurs when a well pumped up punt is left leaning *far* too long against a tumbled down break of sun boiling boulders.

An inflatable, that's been brought to the expansive point where an expensive report has only just been narrowly avoided.

All brought about by stupidly forgetting the power of the midday sun.

So the first thing to do, after parking my plastic of malt in the shelter of a big-shouldered boulder, is valve-off the tautened old tubes - which let out a rather nice *hisss*.

Then carry the boat down to the warm water's edge, and once she's afloat, walk back up the beach (finding the sand's damned hot, compared to the comparative cool of the shallows) to pick up the blades and the booze.

It's quite a short row back to the boat, with the plastic tumbler carefully placed, and kept upright, between my two barefooted feet, with that plastic mug and its contents having pride of place, only a few oar-strokes later by being 'piped' first aboard.

Then it's the turn of the skipper.

And I must say how marvellous it is to be back aboard.

Able to look back at the beach - and have a badly needed pee over the side, while scanning the foreshore for Andrew - because as things have turned out, I think it may be in everyone's interest (when did I claim to be free of deceit?) if I moved our old tub a bit further offshore, which does mean a bit of pulling and puffing, because there are two lots of chain and two heavy anchors to recover.

Indeed, without a windlass, doing the work by hand, you have to ease a lot more of the second, to have the slightest hope of recovering even a foot of the first.

Apart from this nice little Neptunian enigma, and the dead easy task of setting the mainsail, it's only the matter of twenty sweat-dripping minutes, of very hard work, before we're headed offshore.

Drifting away from the beach, before a light nor'easterly air.

The skipper lounged in the cockpit, while enjoying all that's left of the tot; then popping below to get the trusty old notebook, in order that we'll have some sort of record of this particular departure.

The waving palms.

The blooming bougainvillaea.

The black bouldered bluff.

The murmuring strand.

The waft of perfume.

(all the usual, nostalgic old stuff).

And while I'm below, I may as well pick up a stub of pencil, because now I come to reflect on it, I don't think I filled in the book when approaching this anchorage, so I'd better jot something down - now we're drifting away from it.

Let's see.

The last compass course steered *has* been entered, together with the wind speed, weather conditions, and other little nautical niceties.

This means it's only a matter of recording what we actually did when we arrived at this particular spot, which is easy enough.

'Ten o'clock of the forenoon, anchored off Andrew's place, lying to a running moor, in four fathoms, over a rocky bit of a shelf.'

All very well, just as far as it goes.

However, I generally add a personal note or two (there's a special, rather cramped place in the book, under the heading *'remarks'*) and after a sloppy sort of a suck at my gnawed at skipper's pencil, I might as well finish off the entry, just a couple of in-filling words, really, to the effect that we ...

had lunch ashore.

CHAPTER FOUR: PAGE NOTES

(1) Page 129. Line 22 ………. *'looks like bougainvillaea'*.

Nyctaginaceae: genus of woody-stemmed, scrambling type of climber, which grows profusely in the tropics.

The plant was named *Bougainvillaea* after **Louis Antoine de BOUGAINVILLE** (1729-1811). During his early years in Paris this distinguished French citizen studied law and then mathematics, making a significant contribution to the development of integral, as opposed to differential calculus, with the work being recognised by his appointment to the British Royal Society when he was serving as secretary to the French Embassy in London.

He also enjoyed a successful military career, even though involved in inauspicious circumstances when serving with Montcalm during the unsuccessful defence of French Canada. He was then sent to found a colony on the Falkland Islands, which were later transferred to Spain. He joined the French Navy in 1763, and between 1766 and 1769 organised and led the first French circumnavigation of the globe. The voyage, in command of the ships *La Boudeuse* and *L'Etoile,* brought him world acclaim, not only because of the adventurous nature of the undertaking, but by reason of the detailed scientific record he made of his findings. It was during this period he earned the distinction of having his very own flower, and the honour of attaching his name to the largest of the Solomon Islands.

In the American War of Independence (1775), with France involved as an ally of those who were opposed to continuing British dominion, he commanded several ships of the line. But on his return to France he rejoined the army and rose to the rank of field marshal, while later being reappointed vice-admiral in 1791. Towards the end of his days this amazingly talented man returned to his earlier scientific interest, having been Soldier, Sailor, Senator, Count of the Empire and holder of the Legion d'Honour (Grand Cross) and, surely, those of us in any way connected with the sea should take our hats off, as a mark of respect, every time we notice bougainvillaea.

(2) Page 135. Line 1 ………. *'the Last Supper'*.

Referring to the meal shared by Jesus Christ with His disciples on the eve of His crucifixion. The expression later being applied to the consecrated elements absorbed into the usage of the Roman Catholic Church in the sacrifice of the Mass.

At the Reformation, the break-away church adopted the term *Holy Communion*, while other Protestant churches (usually known as the 'high church' end of the Anglican communion) and the Catholic Church itself now encompass the 'giving of thanks' in the Eucharist.

Jewish teaching recognises the Last Supper as a paschal meal (pertaining to the Passover) historically associated with the slaying of a lamb, this ceremonial act later devolved to portray Jesus Christ as 'the Lamb of God' in the New Testament.

Passover: the name of a Jewish feast, now held on the evening of the fourteenth day of the 'first' month of Nisan, instituted by Moses to commemorate the passing over (otherwised described as 'the sparing') of the Hebrew dwellings, on which the blood of a sacrificial lamb had been sprinkled during the trauma of the exodus from Egypt. This was linked (along with the slaying of the lamb) with a seven day festival of unleavened bread, and this two-fold feast was observed until the destruction of Jerusalem in the year A.D. 70.

(3) Page 141. Line 20 .... *'with their bibles in one hand, and their cocks in the other'*.

At first sight this is a contentious, vulgar, and near enough blasphemous remark which has been used in a particularly nasty way, with the delivery timed to provoke maximum offence. The sort of rude gambit that has, as its only possible justification, its use as a riposte of last resort to Mary McNeil's continued over-assertive stance. And if that's all there was to it, there's not much more to be said.

But there *is* rather more to it than that, because phrases of this sort don't pop into the lexicon at the drop of anybody's hat; they are usually too forceful, and apt, to have been coined at the spur of any spiteful moment, so it's worth looking more closely to see where and how this rough little jibe first fell into its all-too-common usage.

In this case ... *with their bibles in one hand, and their cocks in the other* is a literal translation of the Welsh ... *gyda'i ei beibl mewn un llaw a'u cala yn y llall* and this provides a significant clue as to the origin of the phrase. It dates back at least to the turn of the 19th century; a time when the various Welsh nonconformist movements were experiencing something of a religious revival. They were certainly a force to be reckoned with in those long-gone days, when they enjoyed the support of the majority of the rural population. In those circumstances, with the chapels providing the hub of congregational worship, and a focal point for social intercourse, it was natural for the younger members of the congregation to attend with what was known colloquially as *the main chance* well to the fore, of perhaps not only their enthusiastic minds. This being a reference to the opportunities offered young people in the way of developing friendships, which led to engagements, and proposals of marriage, right up to the altar steps, if there were any in use at the time. But while this may go some way towards explaining the old-fashioned meaning hidden within the phrase, it doesn't ameliorate the difficulty experienced, perhaps by most of us, when what we hold to be sacred is aligned too closely with what we may still pruriently judge as profane.

Put another way:

> *however the Celtic argument rumbles*
> *and raises, perhaps, more than one little wink*
> *this sort of thing will no doubt remain*
> *too close to the supposedly finer bred bone*
> *of people like Mary McNeil*

(4) Page 143. Line 16 .... *'agimus tibi gratias, Omnipotens Deus, pro donis tuis'*.

It would seem Andrew is familiar with the prayer, as he didn't display any difficulty when called on by his wife, so he intoned 'grace after a meal'.

> *agimus tibi gratias, Omnipotens Deus, pro donis tuis*
> *per Jesum Christum, Dominum nostrum . . . Amen.*
>
> *accept for thyself, Almighty God, thanks for thy gifts*
> *through Jesus Christ our Lord.*

while Mrs McNeil had spoken 'grace before a meal'.

> *Benedice, Domine, nos et haec tua dona quae de*
> *bonitate tua sumpturi sumus . . . Amen.*
>
> *bless, O Lord, us and these thy gifts which by thy goodness*
> *we are about to eat.*

The term *Amen* being used after both prayers in order to emphasise acceptance, as the final word of belief. These two Latin graces are those normally used by the *Inns of Court,* particularly *Gray's Inn,* so perhaps her choice of grace gives some indication of Mary McNeil's professional background.

The **INNS of COURT** are 'voluntary' societies with the power to call law students to the English bar. There are four such organisations, dating back to Queen Elizabeth 1st., with the London premises located in the angle formed by Holburn and Gray's Inn road. The original Elizabethan structure was badly damaged during World War 2, but parts of the lower walls survived and the restoration, after the war, under the supervision of *Sir Edward Maufe* (1883-1974) recreated the hall as nearly as possible in its original form. The gardens associated with the societies were laid out by *Francis Bacon* (1561-1626) while the name comes from the fact that the land belonged to *Lord Gray de Wilton* who had a house there at the time. This dwelling being acquired in 1733 by the **Honourable Society of Gray's Inn** which has since been associated with the practice of the law. The sign of the inn is a griffin:

> *which occasionally seems to be grinning.*

(5) Page 145. Line 6 .... *'Relief of Mafeking'*.

The town of Mafikeng (*Mafeking*) is situated in the Cape Province of South Africa, about 189 miles west of Johannesburgh, and seves as a local station on what was the main Cape to Zimbabwe *(Rhodesia)* railway line.

During the Boer War (1899-1902) the town (pop. 2,000) was defended by a group of civilian volunteers, and a small British garrison under the command of Colonel R.S.S.Baden-Powell. Surrounded by the Boer army and not all that well supplied with either food or ammunition, the settlement was under siege from October 13, 1899, to May 17, 1900, and came close to surrender on several occasions. It became something of a cause célèbre, particularly to the British public, with the Relief of Mafeking resulting in much clamour and the establishment of *Mafeking Night* to record what was generally accepted as a significant feat of arms.

This event and the war generally being reported back to London by, amongst others, a youthful war correspondent working for the Morning Post, who happened to be W.L.S.Churchill Esq..

(Sir) **Winston Leonard Spencer CHURCHILL** (1874-1965) English statesman; historian (*The World Crisis;* 4 volumes, 1923-1929), (*The Second World War;* 6 volumes, 1948-1954), (*History of the English Speaking People;* 4 volumes, 1956-1959). Biographer of *Marlborough* (4 volumes, 1923-1929). Union card-carrying bricklayer. Amateur painter. Member of the U.K. parliament who served as Under Secretary of the Colonies (1905). President of the Board of Trade (1908). Home Secretary (1910). First Lord of the Admiralty during World War 1; and then, after time spent in the political wilderness between the two world wars, and almost as a footnote to his illustrious career (but *what* a footnote) as British Prime Minister during World War Two.

His despatches from South Africa are some of his earliest published work, but it is perhaps ironic that he, as a staunch supporter of Empire, was covering a campaign which reputedly had as one of its significant outcomes the recognisable high-watermark and conceptual decline of British imperialism, and ultimately the encouragement of other colonies to demand and gain independence from the crown. Another thing of note being, that one of the devastating outcomes of the Boer War was the quite disgraceful treatment meted out to Dutch women and children, who were herded into concentration camps and left to perish; perhaps by neglect (but possibly design).

Robert Stephenson Smyth BADEN-POWELL (1857-1941) forged his early career in the British army, serving in India and Afghanistan, then in the Ashanti Wars and the South African conflict which became known as the Matabele Campaign. He afterwards became Head of Constabulary in South Africa; and later, Inspector General of cavalry in England. Founded the Boy Scouts in 1908; was knighted for his service to the crown in 1909, and made a Baron in 1929.

(6) Page 145. Line 18 ....'*quality Waterford stuff*'.

Although fragments of glass have been found in Ireland dating back to the early Iron Age, the rare pieces that have survived are associated with objects of greater intrinsic value, with the 8th century *Tara Brooch* being a beautiful example of the use of glass in this secondary role. It was not until much later, into the second millennium AD that the necessary skills were acquired by Irish craftsmen, who were licensed to set up glass producing workshops by those Venetians who were not only the masters, but also the de facto controllers of the trade.

The earliest surviving account of this developing business mentions a *Mister George Longe* who opened premises near Dungarven in 1590, and a separate establishment located at Ballynagerah, in the south of County Waterford in 1618. It wasn't until 1700 that *George Ravenscroft* of London, improved the product by the introduction of a heavier, more durable type of flint (crystal) glass, that the modern Irish manufacturing base became established. This trade flourished until an Act of the English parliament in 1746 forbade the export of any glass from Ireland. A prime example of restrictive and thus irritating colonial legislation, which limited the development of this Celtic industry for almost forty years. It wasn't until the 1780s that further progress was made, when *George* and *William Penrose* established their own successful manufacturing business in Waterford in 1783. However, the Act of Union in 1801 led to more political meddling, particularly the imposition of crippling excise duties, and by the time of the Great Exhibition (1851) in London, the Irish and Waterford Crystal industry had been priced out of the market and effectively eliminated.

This remained the sorry state of affairs until the 1940s when members of **The Old Waterford Society** put on a special exhibition of early Waterford glass, and this revival led to the establishment of a small factory at Ballytruckle on the outskirts of Waterford Town in 1947. From that date, the craft and art of glass blowing has flourished, and the enlarged business of Waterford Wedgwood now employs over 500 people, producing premium quality crystal generally accepted as being amongst the finest in the world.

(7) Page 145. Line 31 .... *'short-arm'd pretensions '*.

In case there are innocents abroad, it may be necessary to explain that *'short-arm'* is the slang term for penis. Hence the term 'short-arm inspections' which in days gone by, some members of a crew were subjected to, prior to the ship's doctor filling in the vessel's official 'Bill of Health'. To explain a little further: a short-arm inspection became necessary if there was doubt concerning the honesty of answer, members of a crew gave to questions that related to their freedom (or otherwise) from sexually transmitted disease. This has little to do with Waterford Glass, or a Coupe Jacques for that matter; and only an oblique relevance to the congregational displays referred to in item (3).

(8) Page 149. Line 15 .... *'an excellent malt'*.

The earliest written account of Scotch whisky occurs in a statement contained in the Exchequer Rolls of Scotland (1494), to the effect that *eight bolls of malt were delivered to Friar John Cor, wherewith to make aqua vitae*. But there's no doubt the spirit was distilled in Scotland long before that date, with the name evolving through the Gaelic phrase *uisge beatha* (water of life), to the present day (Anglicised) *whisky*, spelt in Ireland and the USA with an additional *'e'* as whiskey.

There are two distinct methods of distillation, which result in their own specialised products. The oldest being malt whisky, with the other being the relatively modern development now marketed as various blends (one of the finest examples being **Chivas Regal**) with some 100 distilleries contributing to the production of many hundreds of different commercial brands. The malts are produced by a batch, but nevertheless complicated, process that involves the traditional pot still, while the grain whiskies, making up by far the largest proportion of the blends, derive from a continuous process made possible by the invention of the Coffey Still, which takes its name from *Aeneas Coffey* and dates back to 1831. The corn for the malt is exclusively barley, with the ears being malted by immersion in water from the burn. After the initial sprouting on the floor of the malt house, the process of germination is arrested by drying in kilns, which are recognisable today by the distinctive pagoda-shaped chimneys characteristic of almost every Scottish distillery. The kilns were traditionally fired by peat, with the smoke from the fuel allowed to drift though the wire mesh floors of the loft to impart the *peat reek;* the distinctive aroma which contributes to the nature of the whisky itself. But this is only the initial stage of an ongoing and involved manufacturing process, and anyone interested in the way the Highland Scot has combined craft with art to produce a spirit smooth enough to satisfy the Gods, could do no better than contact the **Scotch Whisky Association**, at 20 Atholl Crescent, Edinburgh. EH3 8FH. Telephone: 0131-2222-9235. Fax: 0131-2222-9200; e-mail: pa@swa.org.uk

Grain whisky for the blends is made from wheat or maize which is first cooked under pressure, in order to break down the contained starches into fermentable sugars, with the process being as complicated in its own way as the production of malt; perhaps even more so, because the resultant product has to duplicate, year by year, exactly the same quality and style of drink the customer has come to expect.

The term *single malt* refers merely (merely!) to the fact this particular whisky is the product of one distillery. There are of course single grain whiskies, but they are rarely marketed under this heading as they go to make up the blends which are required to keep the still-expanding market well supplied with Scotland's, and reputedly the world's, most rewarding tipple.

(9) Page 153. Line 33 .... *'not yet flowering Mimosa'*.

This 'Mimosa' is really blue-leaved Acacia *(Acacia cyanophylla);* in this species, what seem to be leaves are really flattened leaf stems, brought about by the scarcity of water, which perhaps gives some indication of the dryness of the location.

(10) Page 155. Line 15 .... *'quiet country churchyard'*.

Christopher David Howells, the author's son, is buried at Bethel Baptist Chapel, Loveston, in the County of Pembroke.

MEETING LIKE-MINDED PEOPLE

THE retreat from Andrew's anchorage may not have been prompted by the best of intentions, but isn't difficult to make, with a light nor'easterly blowing off the land, and the benefit of a calm sea looking enticingly blue, as only the briny can when shimmering under a blistering tropical sun, there's plenty of searoom down to leeward, so it's just a question of letting the old boat drift downwind for a while, and when well offshore, heave-to. A manoeuvre easy enough in a cutter, because it involves little more than sheeting in the mainsail, setting a small staysail with its clew hauled out to windward, lashing the tiller (helm down), and there we are.

The vessel is still heading away from the land, but put conveniently to sleep. Leaning against the weight of the breeze and the lift and loll of the swell, yet not going anywhere, which is convenient enough, because this salty old dodge has restricted the rhythmic rolling which would have occurred if we'd just taken the sails down and lain under a lazy bare pole.

And there are other advantages, if you happen to be in a contemplative mood. As we're hove-to, there's very little noise, just the unused sigh of a breeze that's been put out of a job and has nothing better to do than whistle about in the rigging, providing time enough to consider the next move, which can't avoid being influenced by the ongoing effects of Andrew's generous elbow.

A glass or two of wine at luncheon would have been civilized enough (if it had been available at the time), yet even the light end of a bottle of Scotch can be a heavy item to carry, if it's been consumed in emotional circumstances. So a snooze is indicated, which may seem a doubtful decision, as the next port of call is little more than six hours down the track. But as it's well into the later part of the afternoon, and we are only twenty-eight degrees north of the equator, it'll be black dark in an hour or so.

Put another way, and spelt out for the benefit of a sleepy seaman - you don't require a pocket calculator to reach the conclusion that, if we let draw too soon, we are going to arrive just after midnight, which may not be the best part of the day to pick out a berth, and slide quietly into it without disturbing the brethren.

It's bunk time, but before drifting to sleep, the lazy half of the crew does spend some time (all of 15 seconds) trying to decide if it would be better to rig the paraffin lamp now. Get dear old Nightingale [1] out of the locker, oiled and fired-up, and swinging in the rigging, while the owner puts up with the marginal waste of fuel. Or turn in for a bit of a zizz, and rely on an in-built sense of self-preservation to wake up not long after the sun has set, while there's still a bit of twilight about, and *then* rig the steamer warning signal.

The sort of weighty debate which does seem to have been marginalized when you wake, and find it's approaching midnight, struggling out of your bunk to see if there's shipping about, and being quickly drawn to the rueful conclusion that we've been lucky.

There *is* a ship, not far away; passing inshore certainly, but a vessel that may have presented a threat to a small boat devoid of a riding light and any sort of watchkeeping crew.

Could there be a better nudge to take on the graveyard watch?

Prompting the crew to settle in the cockpit, determined to keep awake and finding, almost immediately, even though we're in the tropics, it's cool enough for a sweater and something to keep the extremities warm (a ground-down brew of the beans, sugared and held in a cupped hand) while casting what you hope is a seamanlike eye about the boat.

Coming to the conclusion, that while I've been sleeping we've been set away to the west'ard; nothing unusual in these waters, nevertheless it has put us further offshore, so the island is now a distance off, which means there's going to be more close-hauled work than had been planned for.

It's nothing to worry about.

The nor'easterly breeze is still sighing away, begging, as usual, to be allowed to do something useful; so it's only the matter of easing the staysail sheet - lettin' 'er draw, and we've got the old tub pointing in the right direction; sailing towards what looks like a collection of pinpricks, apart from the flash of the light that marks the headland we're bound for.

It's not the sort of thing that's jotted down in a boat's log, yet it's worth recording that beating, single-handed, up towards a landfall offers a challenge which soon disperses the comfortable illusion that you've been here and done it all before, because as you make your close-hauled way to windward, the rhythms associated with being offshore are dictated by the weight of the breeze and the state of the sea and the swell.

An accommodating lurch, as a cooler puff passes over the vessel.

An air that's just rolled down the twelve-thousand foot slope of a slumbering volcano, then bumped into an influential outcrop, which might be out of sight, but still dominates the scene by imparting enough of a twist to these diverting black'uns to heel the vessel.

Dipping the toerail, as she swans easily over the swell, yet can't be expected to do much more than duck before the slap of a crest comes aboard as more than just the threat of head wetting spray. But it's all playful stuff, even if it does attract your sleepy-eyed attention by hitting you, nearly always with some degree of surprise, smack in the rueful part of your salt spattered face.

And it's no use complaining.

These little puffs are just what the doctor ordered, as each time she heels there's a significant increase in boat speed, and often a freeing element as well, which the attentive vane picks up immediately, quicker even than all but the very best of human helmsmen - because aren't most of us softies more interested in keeping our heads down, and dry, than in following every blessed wind shift?

So here we are, just before dawn, making board upon board towards the shore - quite content to let the self-steering gear show how much better it is, than we are at it.

This may seem lazy, to the point of being casual

It doesn't matter - because we're making progress.

A mile or more on each heeled leg, port tack being the major in this particular instance; then going about to make yet another board; working upwind, with each close-hauled fetch bringing us nearer the shore, which is still a mile or two to wind'ard, picked out now by what look like harbour lights, roadside lamps, the occasional crawl-along vehicle.

Who knows what sort of energetic folk are already up and about, at this unearthly hour of an about-to-break tropical morning?

The people you can bank on are the inshore fishermen.

And here they come, as a succession of bobbing lights, some showing red sidelights as they leave the harbour entrance and turn away to the nor'ard. Then a smaller southern-going bunch, showing green lights as they putt-putt-putt-putt-putt away in the opposite direction.

I can hear their single-cylinder diesels, propelling their wooden vessels out and about with (now they're passing out of sight - but up to wind'ard) the additional whiff of a ripe enough niff to add to the thump of the last of their burbling presence.

This is fortunate - means the harbour will be less crowded when we get there - because when manoeuvring about the entrance, prior to making our final approach, just about the last thing we want to be mixed up with is a bunch of inshore fishermen, streaming out while baiting-up, and not expecting anyone to loom out of the shadow of their predatory morning.

There's also another consideration.

As we're approaching the entrance, the breeze is becoming fitful.

Understandably enough, because we are well under the lee of the land, and hindered by the high-rise buildings which have sprouted, as ever, up and around the town. So the combination of a faltering breeze and an unhelpful wind shift, and not much room to do anything about it, could mean fun and games before we're safely tied up somewhere.

Time to get the fenders out.

Make sure the hook's ready to run.

Have plenty of warp handy (all the usual, approaching the solid state stuff).

It's also time to take over the helm, because while the gear's cute enough, in these tricky conditions there's nothing like having the skipper's hand on the tiller - designated Officer-in-Charge - the really responsible lad, who comes quickly to the reluctant conclusion we haven't got enough of the white stuff up.

There's got to be a quick sail change.

Hand the staysail, and set a light genoa that'll bend a bit more of the fitful breeze, in order that, when we *do* have the benefit of a puff, we'll be able to make best possible use of it.

Gaining enough boat speed to see her through the next flat patch, of which there seems to be plenty about right now.

This is an attractive scenario - a previously tired seaman (because he's been up since midnight) who is now enjoying what could be fairly described as a meaningful lift, as he's engaged on the fascinating task of getting his boat into harbour, and safely berthed, without bumping into too many embarrassing objects while he's patiently engaged in doing it.

The sail change has helped, but there's an associated problem because, while the genoa offers a larger area of canvas, it's more difficult to tack - it has to be pulled around, outside the inner forestay - which is easy enough, yet a task that does take a few precious seconds, before the bulk of the sail's been hauled through and sheeted in, to draw on the freshly taken up board.

However, if you are halfway towards being a cagey old dog, this is a satisfying job - coaxing your vessel towards the harbour entrance, with barely enough dockside light to see what's what.

Where everything's located.

How much room there is between the berths.

What's the best tack to be on when entering the basin.

This is a yacht harbour, that used to be, perhaps could still be nostalgically described as a fishing village; but now the visiting wealth is tied up stern to the quay, economically stashed, the harbour master intent on crowding 'em in, while at the same time giving everyone board-walked access to the accommodating jetty.

The glossy white hulls.

The stainless steel hardware.

The purposeful masts.

The tip, and repetitive tap of poorly sweated-up halyards (to this seaman's critical ear, an irriating sound).

But this isn't the time or the place to idle about, because - blow me down, we've just sailed into another ruddy flat patch, with only just enough way on the bewildered old tub to turn her round and trickle her out of the harbour.

A bit of a pain in the butt.

Yet a lot better than drifting towards a gaggle of boats without a clear notion of where you're going, or even if you know where you're going, being unable to get there.

Blundering, into a twilighted cat's cradle of other people's warps and chains, with the impending disaster brought about because I haven't been patient enough.

Wanted to get on with it, but have just made a *complete* balls of it, and must make another approach.

Work up a bit more boat speed.

Sneak up, even tighter against the harbour wall.

Taking the calculated risk that, while we'll be sailing into a wind shadow, when we come out of it, we'll be somewhere near the right place and have time to pick out an empty berth (always provided there is one) and edge on in towards it.

Dropping the hook in just the right spot, so we can swing to the pick.

Head upwind.

Ease out chain, and warp on down to the jetty.

This isn't as easy as it looks - for starters, we should have a few more fenders out - but it's too late now for anything other than keeping her slipping along, under the harbour wall, for a few more feet, and then, if we're lucky (and there *is* an empty berth, amongst a group of yachts which seem well enough matched), they're about the same size as our old hooker.

When you're engaged on this task, there's not much room to bother about anything other than the job in hand, which comes well supplied with challenges. However, now the hook's down, and we're swinging round it, another more leisurely look about this yacht harbour confirms the original impression.

With a bit more daylight about, it's possible to see there are fifty or more vessels here, all tied up stern to the quay, and the empty berth that seems tailor-made is not far away; yet manoeuvring into the space may not be easy, because there's not enough breeze to overcome the weight of chain we've got hanging from our bow, down to what I hope is our well-embedded ground tackle - so paying out chain isn't going to help.

There are several seamanlike courses of action which can be taken in situations of this sort.

By far the best is - make a decent harbour-job stow of the canvas, and when you've got your small vessel looking reasonably shipshape, go below, fire up the primus, and wait for the billy to boil.

This may seem a touch on the blasé side, but when you've become used to wandering about without an auxiliary motor, you get into the habit of looking at things from an altered perspective.

For instance; when you are trying to berth in a crowded marina, and contemplate joining the crac'ach, [2] you wait - for some observant soul to throw you a line - or if anyone happens to appear on the jetty, give 'em a hail, and see how good you are with your own monkey-fisted version of Davy Jones' lariat.

And if neither of these things happen?

Enjoy your tea (Earl Grey, with a slice of lemon) just the thing to ease taut nerves, that have been wound up during the ghosted entrance; the walk-on accomplished without anything in the way of a mechanical prompt, or more than a glimmer of footlights to illuminate the now folded, but well-feathered wings of this nautical stage.

Not that the place is a hive of activity.

There's time for a second cup of tea, before a tousled head emerges from the for'ard hatch of the boat adjacent to the empty berth that seems purpose-made for our old tub. And even then, it pays to take it easy (give this guy, whoever he is, time to notice there's an arrival anchored in the basin); however, he's not looking in our direction - he's intent on what he thought was his unobserved start to the day.

Have you noticed, when braving an early morning in this type of determinedly upmarket marina, during the beguiling interlude when most people are awake, but few people have surfaced, how even a well-aimed tinkle sounds like a torrent gushed over a cliff?

The sort of stream that reverberates from one end of the place to the other, while leaving the fascinating circle of bubbles (what used to be you) but has now moved on, from one personal realm, to bobble about on another.

Now he's made himself comfortable, and has become aware of, and recorded our presence, by way of an unabashed smile, it's obvious he isn't a guy at all, but a young lad who is probably in his late 'teens and very well made for his age.

He also seems to know a thing or two about boating, certainly enough to understand the age-old message implied when someone displays the bitter-end of a rope, so it's only the matter of a moment before he's leaning over the pulpit of his boat, getting ready to catch, while I'm preparing the flight of the monkey.

And when this bit of unsung coloratura has been successfully accomplished (with what I hope isn't *too* much of a flourish) he's hauling away, while I'm easing chain, so the cutter's snugged into place; then it's only the matter of arranging the fenders, coiling the spare ends of warps, and it's time for introductions.

The young man turns out to be David Hutchinson, an Australian, crewing aboard his father's boat.

This vessel is about fifty two feet overall, rigged as a ketch; a well shaped craft, beamy enough to offer a centre-cockpit layout and an owner's cabin aft. She is perhaps a little on the old-fashioned side (because she's timber built), but this aspect is more than balanced when you look at her rigging, and note the three different types of radio antennae.

A radar installation.

And the sort of mini-dome used to protect a gyro-controlled satellite communication dish, with this kit being serviced by a taffrail-mounted wind generator and an array of solar panels of which *NASA* would be proud.

The other vessel we're lying alongside is smaller than the ketch, modern in style, with a more than adequate amount of freeboard. She's rigged as a sloop, also has a centre-cockpit, and boasts a transom ladder which leads down to a marlin board, [3] so when she's anchored in those delightful bays she's undoubtedly designed for, her crew won't have difficulty climbing back on board after enjoying their invigorating splash in the salt.

There's nobody about on either of these vessels (although I did see a questioning face appear in a porthole, when we were elbowing our way into the berth). Now we're moored, all's quiet, with my Australian helper about to head back to the welcoming arms of his cart; but not before he tells me there are 'blutions on the jetty, and the harbour master's office opens pretty early, then closes for an after-lunch siesta, which is anyway par for the course in this laidback part of the world.

Regardless of the minor difficulties, this isn't a bad time of day to pull into this sort of port. As Johnny-just-arrived you've got time to stretch your legs, before there's anyone about, able to cast an inquisitive eye over craft that have assembled here, prior to setting off on the trade wind passage that'll take them over the pond.

Strolling along the jetty, towards the deeper, seaward end of the basin, in a pair of shorts and a battered straw hat, with my clean kit and toilet gear slung over my shoulder - slopping happily along in my come-to-Jesus sandals - the vessels get bigger, with a seaman's eye drawn to a large yacht, rejoicing in the name *Malachi* (I suppose her figuratively speaking port of registry would be *Jerusalem*) but the vessel herself sailing, conveniently enough, under the Panamanian flag.

She's a schooner - not a Bluenose; [4] the modern development which provides her owner with the thrill of displaying the image of what he's always had in the back of his mind. And now he can afford eighty-five gorgeous feet of it, he and his fourth wife use the vessel as a penthouse which they move from place to glittering place, with Monte for the Grand Prix, Cannes for the films, and a Caribbean interlude regularly attended.

The rest of the jet-setting year hinges on what happens to be the smart thing of the moment, or indeed in prospect, with the next extravaganza being pencilled-in, a berth booked, and guests already invited.

Right now, four of the paid hands - about half the crew - are scrubbing the teak deck, so when the owner and his companion surface, during the not always early part of the lounged-about forenoon, the view from the poop will be as near pristine as elbow grease can get it. And all apparently achieved with barely a glance at the clock.

Yet this is mere bagatelle compared to the vessel that lies at the ultimate end of the marina, separated from the commercial dock by a knuckle in the breakwater.

It would be pushing it a bit to describe this craft as a yacht, because her corporate size precludes her being categorized as such. She's not tied up stern to the quay, but lying along the length of the mole, in order that she can make use of a traditional gangway, and reserve enough room on the jetty to give the contract-hired stretch limousines plenty of space to park.

If I had to speculate about this particular vessel (and isn't this half the fun of bumming about on the jetty?), I would say she was built in Italy, by a yard specializing in high speed naval craft, but the business has moved into the lucrative field where their superlative standards of workmanship command the premium some people are willing to pay for a *super yacht*. The sort of vessel which provides the stage they use to negotiate their share enhancing deals (so mere money, as a saved or salaried item - apart from the staggering fees, and the tuck away of the amazingly generous stock option doesn't come into it here).

The layout of the yacht's superstructure has been dictated by the need to provide an uncluttered pad on the after part of the vessel, making sure that the helicopter has a clear approach when flut-flut-fluttering down to her flat as a pancake type perch (because you can't say *'coming in to land'*, can you, when describing this type of manoeuvre?).

The name of this super yacht is *Palatia*, but it's a brickbat seldom used, as she's known to the cognoscenti as *Corporate Raider,* with her Port of Unwritten Registry being one of the high-sided fjords off Wall St.

The vessel is huge - yet she's comparatively light; built of aluminium, with gas turbines in the engine room that provide enough grunt to power a World War 2 destroyer.

However, I must say there may be a downside to this type of extravagant trinket, because the last time I climbed the gangway of an almost identical vessel, I was met at the top by a steward who, although immaculately dressed, did seem to have a significant bulge under what I thought at the time could have been his paramilitary armpit. This visit being prompted by an out of the blue invitation from another, perhaps not quite such a high profile, but certainly more dangerous group, who were reportedly not concerned with making money - they had solved that problem, even if the grubby nature of the product depended on getting it laundered.

Who knows?

Here I am, standing on this jetty, admiring these magnificent yachts, while wondering where the municipal authorities have located the communal baths impecunious yachties so much appreciate when we pull into this sort of port.

Walking back along the jetty, it's nice to see the crew have finished hosing down *Malachi*, and are about the task of adjusting the afterdeck awning, with a cheery wave to me (confirmation that, although I've only been here twenty admiring minutes, I'm well on my way towards becoming part of this upmarket scene); noting, that while the vessels get smaller towards the shallower end of the basin, there's plenty left to attract the inquisitive eye of a stranger.

The quality, as well as the variety of craft on display, is so much part of the charm.

A good example being several Uncle Sams, which just must be from the board of Sparkman & Stephens, [5] because these vessels delight the seaman's eye with the lift of their graceful sheer, allied to the strength of their seagoing ends - so what more can any old dog ask for?

There are dozens of yachts here, designed by all sorts of people, and built in places as far apart as one end of the world to the other. Its just a question of pressing on towards the showers, with a twinge of trepidation, because occasionally, as a hangover from the days when this place was still a fishing village, and had not been upgraded to an ultra-smart marina, the ablution block offered an unflushed experience which should have been avoided if it was at all costs possible to do so.

That was years ago, and the place is now equipped with the very latest machinery, which is almost indestructible, and difficult to block, with the tiled sides of this gleaming facility high enough to deter all but the most determined of aerosol artistes, who have the cruder sorts, but not their genuinely amusing graffiti, power-washed off the walls, almost as soon as the quick-drying paint has been sprayed with a lopsided grin from the irreverent squirt of its clandestine can.

So after a good natured smile of a shower, it's only a matter of trundling on to the harbour master's office, to report our arrival, and make sure the apparently empty slot we've occupied really *is* available, because there's not much to equal the embarrassment of being thrown out of a berth, after you've just elbowed your way into it. And it's nice to be able to walk back to your own boat, knowing you're a paid-up part of the scene, even if it is one that has several straws in the wind in it, if you're a pernickety type of a bloke.

Part of the problem - actually, it's not really much of a problem, merely a reflection on the sort of self-indulgent nitpicking some of us resort to when, early on a sun shining morning, we take a critical look at another person's boat, as we stroll along a jetty that has tied up to it, a display of yachts, some of which are smart enough to make our old hooker look like an agricultural implement.

However, there is a flip side to this little gibe, because while the tap of an early morning halyard may be the sort of evocative sound which engages a transient listener; to have to put up with the endless tap, tap, tap - tap; tap, tap - tap - tap; tap, tap, tap, of a synthetic rope against the sounding board of a drum that's forty feet long (even if the owner is convinced it's a mast, it's a mast, it's a mast), can be a bit wearing, if you happen to be the poor sod who's tied up just out of sight of it.

Then there's the way some of these vessels *are* tied up.

All this gorgeous hardware.

The stainless steel fittings.

The square-set gratings.

The laid teak decks.

The mahogany seats.

The 2-speed self-tailing winches.

Then you come across a cow hitch, that's not been *carelessly* cast on a cleat, because this would imply the clot who threw the bight the wrong way over the bollard *knew* how to correctly hitch up the craft.

There again, one must suppose beauty really is in the eye of the beholder.

Much in the way that the variety of national ensigns on display enliven the craft they embellish, with another fly on the hoists being - in the good old days, 'colours' would be made (ensigns and other significant bunting hoisted at eight o'clock in the morning, from March 25 to September 20 inclusive, and then at 9 a.m. for the rest of the calendar year). Yet it seems this is a custom now largely ignored, even by well-intentioned seafarers, who seem happy enough to let sunsets come and sunsets go without laying a hand on a halyard.

This may be no more than a grumpy acceptance that things don't always change for the better. And the feeling is enhanced when one of the power boats - a sports fisherman, 42 feet overall, with twin 400 hp Cats and a fly-bridge set off with a beautifully balanced bimini, [6] starts a diesel generator, which may indeed be quiet and well enough insulated for those people presently on board *that* particular boat. But for the neighbours, the combination of a burbling transom, coupled with the drift of obnoxious exhaust, doesn't do much for breakfast when the breeze is blowing from a nauseous direction.

I could spend hours sticky-beaking my way around this marina, recognising that the people and vessels assembled here are part of a group who can be fairly described as the 'yachtie community'; because many of these craft are owned by like-minded people who long ago decided they'd had enough of it all, and decided to set off on the cruise of their dreams, with the Australian yacht we're berthed alongside being a handy example of the type, if her name is anything to go by.

She has *Out from Under* emblazoned across her transom, as well as her port of registry, which turns out to be the New South Wales collection of villages most peple recognise as the magnificent city of Sydney

While I'm admiring the craft, her crew are surfacing, with someone who just must be David's father sticking his head out of the aft-cabin hatch, and he's followed by my old heaving line pal, so I'm already halfway towards getting to know them.

'Do you mind if I come aboard?' (this being the gambit necessary because I haven't rigged my own gangway to the jetty), and can't regain access to my boat without walking over their side deck.

'Help yourself, Mate.' (so aboard we go) to meet the skipper, who turns out to be Richard Hutchinson.

A Sydney Sider, I'll bet you a quid, who comes close to being an archetypal 'Strayne. He's above average height, and directly spoken to the point where the typical Pom from the old country would judge him to be, perhaps not always easy to deal with. Nevertheless, if you know the type, you also know that beneath the abrasive exterior, the guy's unlikely to be quite as rude as he sounds.

'Could you use a cup of coffee?'

'I certainly could.'

'Yeah, he will have a cup, Sue.' (this remark dropped down the companionway hatch), presumably to the person who's below deck, waiting, perhaps not all that patiently for it.

So below we go, leaving young David to get on with the job of hosing the deck, while I'm introduced to Richard's better half (Suzanne, always known as Sue) and then - coming as a genuine surprise, to two young girls, who turn out to be the proverbial peas in a pod.

I don't know why bumping into identical twins is apt to give me a turn, but it always does, and these lasses are no exception to the rule.

They are about thirteen years of age, brunettes, with hazel eyes, wearing faded blue shorts, shirts, and the sort of freshly engaged smile any old dog would appreciate. Their mother is also decked out in cotton sail cloth, as indeed is Richard - so this Swiss family Robinson (transposed to the Oz family Hutchinson) have adopted the sun-bleached look which suits those Breton fishermen, who may be a dying breed - yet didn't pass this way without making their own special mark on the international fashion industry.

Now I'm below, it's also possible to appreciate the size of this vessel.

She may be only fifty and a few feet overall, but her beam, freeboard, and centre cockpit layout have provided enough room for a spacious saloon. And an aft cabin (which I haven't yet seen) that must provide tiptop accommodation, partly because the donk is bulkheaded off from the rest of the boat and located directly under the cockpit.

Taking one well thought out thing with another, this design provides the degree of privacy that's essential if a married couple set off to cruise the world, accompanied by their teenage son and two young girls (Zoe and Zee) who maybe thirteen years of age just now, but are going to develop into a bit of a handful long before everyone knows that they're bound to.

The vessel has an air of spaciousness, and the charm so many wooden craft possess, apparently because of the nature of the material (this may sound a biased opinion, but it's none the less true), particularly when the craftsmen who put the boat together take care to finish the timber to *its* advantage. As they certainly have done here, bevelling and fluting the beams, so that the arched, dark red, richly burnished pieces of hardwood terminate in carved hanging knees, which compliment the joint between the beams and their matching frames - so for anyone interested in boats, it's only a matter of asking the obvious question.

'What's she built of?'

'She's planked in Huon Pine, [7] copper fastened, on sawn oak frames, lead keel, with bronze bolts throughout.'

'How on earth did you get hold of the pine?'

'It took several years, rescuing the odd tree here and there, until we'd built up enough to go to the mill. Then it was just the matter of another three years air-drying the timber.'

'How long for the actual building?'

'Another year and a half.'

'Did you build her yourself?'

'No: I'm an anthropologist. Sue's a nutritionist; while the timber was being selected we were working in Papua New Guinea. We know more about the sexual habits of the highland tribes and the macabre aspects of Kuru [8] than we do about the noble art of boat building.' (that's as maybe)

177

they certainly know how a vessel should be *used* to best advantage.

The Hutchinsons have been afloat for four years, setting off to spend a year in the Pacific, some of it in Tahiti, where Sue got the family to improve their French. From the Pacific they meandered through the Indian Ocean, later making their blistering way up the Red Sea, to spend a season in the Med, another in Europe, and having got their bank balance somewhere near the black, are now waiting out the end of the hurricane season before making the trade wind passage across the pond, to spend Christmas in Barbados.

While I've been learning about the Hutchinsons, young David's been busy on deck, and he must have finished the scrub, because here he comes, making his way down the companionway to present the picture of a strongly built, well muscled, golden skinned, barefoot, tousle haired eighteen year old, dressed in what were recently stylish and no doubt expensively purchased jeans.

However, the tight fitting pants have been cut off at the knees, with the right leg left longer than the left (to not only prompt a smile) but provide the ragged-arsed look that's been carefully enhanced by a deliberate rent in the seat of what has now become by far his favourite garment - so as the young blood knows he's correctly attired, he displays an air of cool expectancy.

'Who's cookin' today, Mum?'

A stranger may reasonably assume this is his way of establishing the fact that he's starving, as usual - can't wait until he's got his feet under the saloon table, and started on what he knows is going to be a substantial Australian breakfast. And this *is* a significant part of the message.

But young David doesn't really have to ask 'who's cooking today,' because aboard this vessel, there's a rule which makes sure the person who does the cooking, is not the person who deals with the dishes, with everyone in the family knowing exactly who does what, and when, merely by reference to the roster that the boss (and guess who this turns out to be) makes sure is pinned to the ship's notice board, and kept well to the fore of everyone's mind.

' Will you join us for breakfast, Val?'

'That's kind of you, Sue; I'd like another cup of coffee, and if there's a bowl of cereal handy.' (so we're spreading ourselves around).

Zoe is cook of the day, with her father second-stringing.

The girls don't drink coffee, or tea, so Zee, designated steward, is setting out breakfast - a selection of juices, cereal, muesli, milk, and plenty of fruit to choose from. The exception to the possibly vegetarian rule is that David is waiting, perhaps not all that patiently, for his first light snack of the day, with this hors d'oeuvre amounting to three lamb chops, a piece of steak, two fried eggs, a sausage ('only *one* measly sausage, Zoe?'), and a well turned out flapjack of separately fried bubble and squeak. There's also a special request, for a piece of fried bread - 'if there's any fat left in the pan.'

I'm impressed, and not only by the size of David's breakfast (because who, apart from Sue, could fault it?), but also by the way this family is organised, particularly the easy-going relationship which exists between parents and crew.

Part of the surprise stems from my original off-the-cuff assessment of Richard, because when I heard him say, 'help yourself *Mate*,' I thought he may fit into the smelly little pigeonhole, labelled *Ocker*, with all this entails in the way of the extravagant banter sometimes put forward as humour in the up-side-down part of the world. But now I've had time to take a leisurely look, over the breakfast table, *at* Richard, it's obvious he's a well mannered light year away from being a loud mouthed pot-bellied Ock, even though he's on stage as a genuine Australian roo.

It was noticeable, when helping with the cooking, he took care to play second fiddle to his daughter. In this significant relationship *she* - the thirteen year old - was allowed to be high-hatted chef, while her father was plate-passing scullion. But now we've finished breakfast, Richard has replaced his skipper's hat, and from the outset it's obvious he's immensely proud of his yacht.

'I designed her myself, but took care to have the lines, scantlings, ballast ratio, sail area, metacentric analysis [9] and so on, checked by a professional team.'

'Who did you choose?'

'Van de Stadt.'

'The Dutch company?'

'Yes, I wanted people with wide experience, and thought they filled the bill.'

'Why did you choose to build in timber?'

'I just love the stuff; but more than that, I wanted a traditional long keeled heavy displacement vessel, with the accent on sea-kindliness; speed was a secondary consideration.'

'So you were happy with a ketch?'

'Yes, we don't do much windward work, and the second stick is handy to hang stuff on.'

By 'stuff' he means the antennae I noticed as I came aboard the boat, (the 'stick' is the mizzen mast), and now Richard's showing me around, it's obvious his other love is equipment, with all this means in the way of the gadgetry currently available.

There are thirteen electronic devices of one sophisticated sort or another aboard this traditional vessel; VHF transmitter, SSB transmitter, SW communications receiver; a separate ham radio outfit, radar set, weather facsimile, satellite 'phone, global positioning system and plotter; compact disk and tape deck player with broadcast reception, recording facility. And to finalize the list (for the time being) an emergency beacon (EPIRB) stowed conveniently on deck.

This equipment isn't just scattered about, a great deal of care has been lavished on the way it's been fitted in, with the CD hooked up to stereo speakers which have been strategically placed in the saloon.

In the chart room, the different items of equipment have been provided with their own joiner-built teak lockers, with carved foldaway fronts, so the two echo sounders (one paper print-out, the other visual-audio with a relay to the cockpit) share bulkhead space with a complete set of computerised instrumentation, which not only measures, but pronounces on absolutely everything - apart from, perhaps, the chance effect of one of Paddy's re-curving hurricanes. [(10)]

'Who does the navigating?'

'We take turns; the various ocean passages as well as the coastal sections are portioned out; sometimes we draw lots, if it's a particularly attractive trip.'

'You mean *everyone* has a turn; that Zoe and Zee sometimes act the part of navigators?'

'No: they don't *act the part* at all; when it's their turn, they *are* the responsible navigators.'

Touché (and let that be a lesson to you, Howells) because it's beginning to dawn on me that *Out From Under* could turn out to be an unusual yacht, crewed by unusual people.

Richard has shepherded me out of the chart room, and is leading the way towards the galley, located in the port alleyway between the saloon and the aft cabin. However, to describe this place as merely a galley is misleading, as it's not just MacDonald's, it's the domestic heart of the boat.

Beside the obligatory stove (LP gas, with six hobs and a capacious oven) there's a huge fridge, a monster chest freezer, a large washing machine, a tumble drier, a commercial dishwasher, an ice-making machine that could take care of the needs of a busy petrol station forecourt, together with the usual array of small gadgets (mixers, slicers and so on) that normally grace a well equipped shore-side establishment.

'Great Scott, Richard: how do you *service* all this stuff?'

'You mean the power requirements?'

'Yes: but apart from the power, what about the consumption of fresh water?'

'We've got a desalinating plant, for use at sea, and when we're in a marina, we use the shore supply.'

'That still leaves the electrical requirement.'

'No problem: all the equipment has had the original high-voltage machinery replaced, with either 12 or 24 volt motors.'

'Even then - *a tumble drier* - aboard what is, after all, not a very large yacht?'

'When we were planning this cruise, Sue made one thing crystal clear. She wasn't going to become a second-class citizen, struggling along with little more than camping equipment, while trying to maintain the living standards we've become accustomed to. And I must say, I agreed with her entirely; so we got our heads together, and not only worked out *who* is going to do what, but *how* we were going to do it.'

'O. K., but what about the power needed for a tumble drier? In any case: why *bother* with a tumble drier. In the tropics it shouldn't take long to dry a whole line full of washing.' (dependent, of course, on where you are), and, perhaps just as importantly, the season of the year.

'That's just it; we don't want *our* yacht to look like a rundown gypsy encampment. As for the tumble drier - we've installed an under-sole hot air heating system needed when cruising higher latitudes; but there's a bypass which diverts the hot air through the drier when the gadget's in use, then back over the heat exchanger before it's recycled around the hull if the boat's being centrally heated.' And this is the beginning of an eye-opening tour, which soon reveals it's not only in the domestic department that *Out From Under* is worth a second look.

The machinery has been bulk-headed off from the accommodation. The whole area is fully insulated, with the vessel's generating set being provided with a special box, set up in the engine room, with this twice-isolated and insulated compartment floating on rubber mounts and ventilated independently. 'There's also a special exhaust system.'

'What's so special about it?

'I'll show you when we go back on deck. But before we do that, I'd like you to see the rest of the boat.'

So it's on with the conducted tour, for'ard of the saloon this time, where Zoe and Zee have their separate, tiered bunk accommodation; while David also has his own cabin, which I half expected to find in a disreputable state ('teenage young bloods being what they are?'). Yet what actually greets the eye is an apple pie outfit - of an unusual sort, because David has been allocated sufficient space to allow his patch to be panelled off, with the for'ard portion fitted out as a studio, complete with easel and the usual work areas, which are amazingly tidy when compared with the portrait of the artist as a young man, or the talented lad who sets determinedly off to squander his gifts, while dismaying his friends, on his bulbous-nosed way to the dogs. [11]

'This is certainly interesting, Richard; having a *studio* aboard a boat is most unusual. Isn't it a bit niffy at times?'

'Well, sometimes it is; but we feel it's worth putting up with the occasional waft of turpentine, which can happen *'when he doesn't keep the door shut.'* (this aimed at the young man in question) yet delivered with a good-natured smile.

'What's he working on now?'

'Well: what *are* you working on, David?' (and I like the way the father steps aside) and passes the question to the person it should have been addressed to in the first place.

'For a start, I'm into watercolours; so don't believe all that guff about turpentine wafting about. I'm on a set of drawings which illustrate some of the flora found on Tenerife.'

'Anything I can look at?'

'Of course; the finished items have been filed away in the chart room.'

So back we go, and now we're on our way aft, I can see that a map of the world - all of four feet high, and six feet long - has been positioned on the for'ard side of the saloon bulkhead (well out of sight of visitors), and the vessel's track, amounting to three-quarters of a circumnavigation, has been superimposed on the chart. The mainmast has also been enhanced, with the alloy stick (previously, hardly a thing of beauty) sheathed in teak, and these boards have been carved, Hindu style, complete with explicit erotica.

'Who decorated the mast?'

'I wish I'd done it.' (David, with a saucy smile). When we spent time in the Maldives, anchored off one of the smaller islands, Dad got to know a family of woodcarvers. They did the whole job in not much more than a month; they also did the hanging knees in the saloon, and the locker fronts.'

I think I'm beginning to get a bit of a drift here, because having passed through the saloon, on our way back to the chart room, there's nothing much in the way of purchased memorabilia on display. Apart from a few personally dived-for shells - the usual Cruise Ship trinkets are absent, so it seems what's going on aboard the good ship *Out From Under* represents, at the very least, a refreshing change of outlook.

The finished drawings David mentioned when we were in his studio, turn out to be substantial albums which have been given pride of place in the chart room, displacing the portfolios of charts well equipped yachts carry in the series of shallow drawers specifically designed for that purpose.

The parts of the world the Oz family Hutchinson are bound *for*, are covered by detailed charts of those areas.

But where this engaging family has *been*, the charts are no longer required, and these drawers carry a record of what has happened along the way, set out in a series of paintings, with some of the early illustrations utilizing poster paint, with later work favouring watercolour.

These magnificent journals date to the period before the boat was launched, to the very special day when the keel was laid, and they provide a fascinating account of day by day occurrences, together with the changes which take place as some people age, while others approach maturity.

The twins, Zoe and Zee, were not much more than nine years old when the decision was taken to up sticks and have a good old-fashioned look at how the other half functions; and the artist has captured an elfin look, which perhaps isn't always representative of a degree of childish innocence.

'Are these original drawings?'

'Do you mean - did I do them?'

'Not exactly: I know you did them. But you must have been pretty young when the twins were only nine years of age.'

'I was seventeen, going on eighteen.'

'That's young, to turn out work of this quality. Have you worked them over?'

'Yes, as a matter of fact I have.' (and this is said with the trace of a rueful smile).

'Did you keep the originals?'

'In the beginning I didn't, and I regret that now. But after about a year, I realized I wasn't only mucking about with a record of Zoe and Zee.'

It's a perceptive and far reaching remark, because David's portraits have developed - from not much more than colour washed pencil sketches of the twins when they were nine years of age - to delicate watercolours of girls reaching puberty, displaying the look of fillies who have already glanced twice at the notion they have nothing whatever to lose.

And there's lots more to see, because David's work extends well beyond a perceptive record of his sisters growing up. His father has been cleverly transformed; from an earnest, pince-nez'd academic - to the skipper of a vessel which has cruised the reef, visited islands, weathered gales, anchored off, then rowed ashore to wander those delightful strands.

Yet, while his father has changed, David's mother appears - not grown younger with the passing of the years - but as someone who is now so much more accessible to the artist, who just happens to be her son.

From David's sea-broadened outlook, this gal (she's forty; but she's a good looking forty-something, even if she is his mother) was born on a Queensland station, [12] so it's not surprising she rides well, handles a rifle, and knows how to kill and butcher a beast.

She won her place at Sydney University by persevering her out-backed way through the State-provided correspondence course, and while at Uni met and, after graduating, married Richard Hutchinson. Since they've had the boat (after years of joint professional endeavour), she's taken to the life of a wandering seafarer, and is now familiar with the ins and swings of celestial navigation.

When and how to reef.

How long you've got when diving to 30 metres; and how many stops you need from fifty. [13]

She also plays a good hand of bridge, understands cricket, is worth her place in mixed doubles, and doesn't *always* take the twins' part when they're throwing a deafening, patch-defending tantrum (what more *could* anyone ask for?).

She's also an excellent cook.

While this glance at David and rather more than his watercolours has been going on, his Dad has kept his mouth shut; but hasn't been able to hide the look of pride, which comes at least partly from the knowledge that the decision he and his wife took years ago has turned out so well. In contrast to the forbidding gloom of his friends, some of whom were quick to point out what they were sure would be the unacceptable price of putting two promising careers on hold - 'just to cruise about in a yacht'.

'Let's go back on deck. I particularly want to show you the exhaust system we've rigged for the generator.'

'Is the generator running now?'

'Can't you tell?'

'When we were in the chart room, I noticed one of the meters was indicating a hefty charge - certainly more than you'd get from solar panels, even backed up by a wind generator.'

'Well, as a matter of fact, the diesel generator *is* running.' (and this is delivered with a smile of genuine pleasure).

'There is a give-away, you know.'

'What is it?'

'I can just about hear the cooling water piddling into the 'oggin.'

A remark which delights the skipper of *Out From Under*, who spent months working out how to satisfy the power requirements of the appliances they've got on board, without at the same time ruining the dream that tempted them afloat in the first place.

And his solution to the problem is worth a second look.

What he's done, after putting the auxiliary donk into a vibration-damped chest in the engine room, is arrange for the exhaust of that unit to be taken to the truck of the mizzen mast, while at the same time using the stick as a fresh air intake for the fans which keep everything cool. This means the mast is larger section than usual, because it carries three separate systems.

(1) stainless steel pipe for the engine exhaust.

(2) cooling air *inlet* duct.

(3) hot air *outlet* duct - with the baffled discharge and louvered entry points being ...

(a) mast head.

(b) just above the crosstrees.

(c) six feet below masthead.

This neat arrangement not only keeping the internal exhaust pipe cool, but moving the noise, which normally burbles irritatingly out of deck-level engine room vents, to a place where only the gulls can complain.

'Where are the fans?'

'There are three, located in the engine room.'

'Why have *three* fans?'

'The whole system is geared to the ambient temperature, and also the power output of the auxiliary. The harder it works, the hotter it gets, and if it's 100 degrees in the shade on deck - you need a lot of air movement to keep everything under control.'

'What about the length of the exhaust pipe?'

'One of the fans takes care of it. It's actually a blown exhaust system which provides negative back-pressure at the manifold. We've also made provision to sweep the length of the pipe, but so far there's been very little accumulation of soot.'

'What about the weight involved?'

'It doesn't matter. We've also got in-mast mainsail reefing, as well as roller-reefing headsails. It's all been taken into consideration when the beam, draft, and ballast ratio of the boat was being decided.'

'Who decided to mount the radar on a self-levelling cradle, so it scans horizontally, even when she's hard on the wind?'

But this comes close to being a damn fool question, because it's obvious that while Richard may be an anthropologist by profession, he does have other interests.

All the sheet winches are electrically operated and self-tailing.

The twin masthead high-cut jibs (doubling as running sails and separately stayed) have their roller reefing systems electrically driven.

The staysail also reefs to the touch of a watertight switch.

The mainsail furls inside the mast, while the mizzen rolls into the boom (the mast being full of the afore-mentioned exhaust pipe and ducting).

'Great Scott, Richard: what if anything goes wrong?'

'It already has: we had a bad night in the middle of the Indian Ocean. It was blowing hard, as usual, and we were well reefed; then along came a terrific squall, really high wind speeds, with horizontal rain and all sorts of thunder and lightning. It was quite an event, because just at the wrong moment, the autohelm got tricked by an awkward wave, and we broached. [14] In the confusion, the clew outhaul wasn't cast off correctly, when we were hauling the last part of the mainsail into the mast.'

'What happened?'

'We tore the clew out of the sail, which flapped about like a demented banshee. We were damned lucky not to lose the mast. Since then I've arranged an overload clutch, which activates a klaxon if there's too much strain on the reefing gear.'

'Have you had any trouble with the electric motors?'

'Never: they only run for a few minutes, at most, so they're all sealed units, not ventilated casings. But we did have trouble with the windlass, which used to be electrically driven.'

'What was the matter with that?'

'It was associated with the time it takes to weigh anchor. When cruising the South Pacific, we sometimes wanted to kedge in deep water, maybe 30 fathoms, or more; and found the windlass, even though it was powered by a 24 volt motor, wasn't up to the task of recovering a long length of chain. The sealed unit overheated. On one memorable occasion we burnt the damned thing out, and had to recover the hook by hand. It took hours, and presented all sorts of problems.'

'So what have you done?'

'We've replaced the electric motor, and now have a powerful hydraulic system which is more than capable of heaving away, all day if necessary. The pump for this outfit has a magnetic clutch, so we can draw torque from the generator when it's needed, just at the touch of a button.'

While these learning curves have been looping their way all over the place, we've been strolling along *Out From Under's* side deck, and have now reached the point where her skipper, having extolled the virtues of his own vessel, feels free to cast a critical eye over the boat recently tied up alongside his own yacht. And I would have to admit, my old tub does look a bit (shall we just say, *sparse*?), when compared to (shall we venture, *the real thing*?). Yet that would hardly being fair to our old hooker, because she (and note the use of gender) does have at least some seagoing virtues; simplicity being one of them.

But I'm saved from having to discuss our lack of sophistication (and note the collective use of the pronoun) because, while Richard and I are leaning over the rail of his very smart yacht, looking at my apparently threadbare home, there's a diversion aboard the vessel which forms the significant third leg of our marina grouping.

During the hour or so I've been aboard *Out From Under,* this particular morning has moved on to the middle of its own forenoon, allowing the sun to gain sufficient height to be able to bounce a tropical glare off the reflective water of the marina.

The breeze has also picked up, and is dodging between the bunting flying in the rigging of the dozens of vessels scattered about the basin; so apart from the comings and goings of the occasional dinghy, there's plenty to distract a seaman's eye. Even so, it's difficult to ignore the other vessel we're lying alongside, because this is the smaller, and at first sight, more up to date of the craft we're berthed between.

The name of the yacht is *Bouton de Rose,* and while this seems a bit of a fancy-Dan, there's no doubt about it, because I'm looking at it, stencilled in black lettering on the vessel's quarter-sectioned life rings.

She's flying the French ensign, and is recognisably a mirror-image of the smart craft displayed centre-stage at the International Boat Shows that have become so much part of the global yachtie scene.

For anyone who has wandered through those fascinating halls, there's no doubt this particular *bateau* has been beautifully built by *Beneteau,* with the vessel's modern lines enhanced by the arrival on deck of a lady.

Long legged.

Brown as a berry.

Slim, but curvaceous.

Blonde, mid twenties - the sort of good looking beaut who is well equipped to embellish this sort of good looking boat, even though she's carrying a pile of about to be pegged out laundry (with this old seaman's rheumy eye registering, that the gal's dressed in a briefer than brief sarong). [15]

No matter what she's wearing, she's dealing with the washing and, as usual, what the neighbours string in the rigging, is a useful guide to the collective lifestyle they enjoy.

In the matter of an eye-filling moment, this attractive newcomer has hoisted three white pillow cases; two gaudy cushion covers; eight brief items of lingerie; two polka dot bikinis (faded to the extent they're reminiscent of a bygone age); three beach towels; and last, but surely not least, in amongst the lacy bits, a rather unusual jockstrap.

While these chores are being attended-to, this gal has had her back to us, and the well curved view has provided time enough for Richard to quietly enquire if I speak French. And I've reluctantly confessed to barely enough to make absolutely sure of producing a string of schoolboy howlers, while once again recognising it's too late to do anything about it, apart from making yet another hopeless resolution.

'Bonjour Fifi.' (this is Richard, greeting his neighbour, who still has her gorgeous back and bum to us).

'Bonjour Reesh'ard,' (over her shoulder, to him) 'il fait beau, hein?'

To this old seaman, it seems this could be another of those unfortunate situations where a previous lack of application, and of course aptitude, could once again be about to deliver its regularly occurring come-uppance. But I'm partly saved by Richard, who switches to his Australian drawl, and goes on to tell the gal who was previously his neighbour what little he knows about me, which doesn't amount to a lot.

The change of language doesn't bother Fifi, who has an excellent, if accented, command of English; but she's joined by another lady, and a gentleman, who could be described as flamboyant if you had to look facts in the face.

The two newcomers, and Fifi, are leaning over the coaming of their smart Beneteau, looking down, in perhaps more ways than one, at the quaint little vessel berthed between them and *Out From Under*.

The conversation has reverted to French (despite Richard's good natured attempts to shunt it back into English), and I must say I do feel a teeny bit out of it.

However, this exclusion does have a compensation of sorts tucked away, perhaps introvertedly within it; because I now have time to cast my roast-beefed eye over the crew of *Bouton de Rose* (I was right about Fifi; she is an absolute cracker), and now I've been introduced to the others, I can see there's plenty more to admire.

Pierre is in his forties.

A powerfully built, suave, masculine type, who favours multi-striped Bermudas, of the sort that would have been a matching order for Jacob. [16]

These shorts are topped by a shirt having a collar with a crisp enough cut to let the wearer look cool, even though the temperature is nudging a high humidity eighty.

The front of this shirt is casually open, from Pierre's neck to his waist, revealing a hairy chest draped by a heavy linked chain, embellished with a nugget the size of a walnut, and this icon swings over the dip and wink of his navel.

Pierre has also been blessed with powerful forearms.

Thighs that would suit a professional wrestler, with the sexy ensemble embellished by a debonair grin and the twitch of a raffish moustache.

The third person to grace the deck of *Bouton de Rose* has been introduced as Collette.

She's another of those slim, but well curved ladies, a few years older than Fifi (early to mid-thirties?), but the passage of time has had a perhaps disproportionate effect; because, while her shipmate retains the carefree bloom of youth, and knows it, Collette has reached the age where careful attention to the financial section of *Le Monde* has become of more than passing interest. Nevertheless, she makes a stunning addition to the threesome who, now they've had a look and a bit of a gossip about my old boat, seem to be planning a trip to *la plage,* which I assume is some sort of stroll on the strand.

The Hutchinsons are apparently included in this expedition, and I'm also welcome to come along.

Yet it's all a bit of a tease, because there's no doubt the skipper of *Bouton de Rose* knows very well the crew of *Out From Under* have a schedule to keep to. The mutually agreed part of their round the world ticket. And while they (Pierre, Fifi, and Colette) are cavorting on the beach, the twins will be working their way through a maths tutorial conducted by Sue. David will be discussing with his dad some of the opinions expressed in Kenneth Clark's *Civilisation,* [17] while Richard Hutchinson will be drawing his son's attention to Gombrich's *Art & Illusion,* [18] including the arguments involved with the complexities, together with some of the psychological niceties concerned with what others may see as merely the placing of paint on a canvas (perhaps even of words on a page?).

Could there be a better-timed hint, which allows a simple old seaman to beat a retreat?

So I'm glad, now the crew of *Bouton de Rose* have departed, and I've thanked the Hutchinsons for the breakfast provided, I can make my excuses and slide on back to my boat - with the first job being the provision of my own private gangway to the jetty, despite my neighbour's assurance that they don't in the least mind me walking over their side deck, in order to make the transition from tub to Tenerife.

Rigging my own gangway involves scouting the waterfront, until I've come across a bit of dunnage, [19] long and strong enough to serve as a gangplank. But this is only half the solution, because it's not just a question of slinging the timber from the vessel's stern to the jetty - the old tub's transom is so narrow the wind vane of the self-steering gear has got to be dismantled to make room for the plank, all of which takes time.

Yet it really is worth doing, because, despite Richard's assurance that *'there's absolutely no need to carry out this bit of social engineering,'* anyone who has spent a few days tied up in a marina, knows very well that having someone traipsing over your side deck, at all hours of the day, and probably not too silent night, does provide the sort of abrasive occurrence which is apt to take the shine off good neighbourly relations.

Having done my best to avoid this pitfall, it's time to check on the stores, which reveals we're running short of spuds, carrots *and* sardines.

This means I have to make a trip to the shops, and while ashore, see if there's anything held *poste-restante.*

Then there's the Bank, to cash a small traveller's cheque.

And after these chores have been taken care of, a look round the town, to see how much remains of the village which was previously located in what used to be this tinder-dry neck of the woods.

Even to a casual visitor it's obvious there's been more than just a change of emphasis, because what was previously a tight-knit community has been submerged, in a forest of high rise structures, spread far beyond the waterfront.

Some of these buildings are modern hotels, while others are timeshare apartments with their supposedly advantageous terms set out in estate agents windows in a variety of languages; German, Swedish, French, English, with this cosmopolitan blend confirmed by crowds of visitors who throng the newly-paved boulevards.

Families window-shopping at smart boutiques.

Mums and Dads lounging with their kids at sidewalk cafes, as they take time-out, either on their way to, or from, the palm fringed, sea lapped, table and parasolled, big ball bouncing beach.

And there's a welcome development associated with this holiday scene, because after I've enjoyed what passes for a very late lunch - a salad and *two* expensive icecreams (the spendthrift result of having been to the bank, and a couple of bob in my pocket). Or maybe a case of trying to indulge myself out of an unaccustomed twinge of the glums, [20] (could be a bit of both), I've come across a secondhand bookshop with the usual dog-eared paperbacks and remaindered items scattered about the trays.

This *is* fortunate, because one of the things I'm always short of is reading material, so when you're ostensibly vittlin' ship, in a foreign port, to drop on a bookshop with a selection of English titles really is a godsend. Yet here they are; a pile of *Dick Francis'* horsey thrillers, [21] *Dead Cert, Flying Finish, Blood sport, Rat Race, Slay-Ride,* and half a dozen more of the old best sellers; all the way to *Straight*; and, last of all, *Comeback*, which I haven't read before, but it does make an excellent start with - '*I'm Peter Darwin; everyone asks, so I may as well say at once that no, I'm not related to Charles.*'

The other items which have to be purchased, before I load up with carrots and spuds and wend my way back to my boat are - half a dozen drycell batteries for the transistor radio that, so far, hasn't been used on this particular jaunt, but might come in handy in the weeks which lie ahead.

So I'm down to the gunnels, humping four heavy plastic carrier bags along the jetty, past the ablution block, strolling with as much of a nonchalant air as I can muster (with my arms pulling out of their sockets) along the rows of yachts that are as fascinating as ever - which I haven't got time for now.

Glad to get back to my boat, negotiate the narrow gangplank, dump the stores, and then lounge in the cockpit with more than the trace of a self-satisfied air; which doesn't last long, because I've just realized that while I've got plenty of spuds, carrots, batteries, and books - I've forgotten the blasted sardines.

It's getting on toward evening.

No activity on *Bouton de Rose* (after a hard day on the beach, they're probably having a snooze).

The twins are mucking about on *Out From Under,* and it's not long before they're leaning over the rail of their smart yacht, looking down at the tub.

'Can we come aboard, Val?'

'Of course: but mind how you go; there's quite a big drop from your side deck to my coachroof.' (an irrelevant remark, because they've already jumped, and landed light as feathers).

They've soon explored the deck from one end of the boat to the other, and it's only the matter of a well mannered pause before they get round to popping the inevitable question.

'Can we go below?'

'Sure.'

Off they go, slipping down the hatch like a couple of eels.

Then a face appears (could be Zoe, could be Zee, climbing back up the companionway ladder).

'Aren't you going to show us around?'

'Good Lord no: there's no need.'

'What do you want me to say?'

'This is the primus.'

'Here's where I keep the charts.'

'This is the oil lamp.'

'This is the loo.'

'Here's where I stuff my dirty socks.' (which does achieve a giggle; then I get).

'Don't you like showing people over your boat, Val?' (but before I can dodge this perceptive little arrow, another head pops out of the hatch).

'Where's the engine?' (asked, I think, by Zee).

'Haven't got one.'

'What happens in a flat calm?'

'I wait.' (while wondering if it's Zoe who is asking the question, or if it's Zee who is smiling at me).

This goes on for a while.

The little devils are adept at ringing the changes, first one asking a question, then identikit-sis popping up to ask the same question, as if it hasn't either been asked, or (if it *has* been asked) hasn't been answered.

They eventually tire of the game, ending up as two smiling heads and Siamese-twinned shoulders, sticking out of the hatch at, thankfully, one and the same time.

'So *who* is Zoe?'

'And which one of you is Zee?'

But before either can answer, there's another remark floating in the air.

'You 'ave a ver' interesting leetle boat zaire, Valenteen.'

Fifi: dressed in very short shorts and a diaphanous blouse (no bra) leaning over the lifelines of *Bouton de Rose,* displaying all the charm, and perhaps a little bit more than can be expected of, what this salacious old seaman thinks epitomizes the essence of carefree *Paree.*

'Can I come on board?'

(is there a choice?) so it's only the matter of a short, shorts stretching moment, together with a flash of long thigh, before this brown berried rep from *Bouton de Rose* is gracing the cockpit, and the twins are chattering away in a mixture of French and English, which soon boils down to.

'Can we show Fifi the cabin Val?'

'Of course.' (but I must concede this polite 'of course') isn't quite as spontaneous as the first 'of course', the twins collected when they asked if *they* could come on board.

Nevertheless, below they go, and I can hear the tinkle of girlish laughter, which doesn't bother me at all. But it's interspersed with barely suppressed giggles, which does bother me a bit (what have they found now?) and I'm relieved when this intrusive threesome resurfaces, with Fifi pursing her lips, but laughing with her eyes, and while it's an intriguing combination, it does leave me wondering what this experienced gal has noticed, which I hope the ferreting twins have missed.

'Did you find my Visitor's Book?'

'No: where is it?'

'I keep it in the secure locker. The waterproof hatch is located under the mattress, at the foot of the starboard pilot berth.'

No trouble at all to the twins, who disappear with the enthusiasm of Jack Russell terriers, leaving me with Fifi.

'They're quite something, aren't they?'

'Zey certainleeaar.'

After they've signed the book, with Zoe and Zee proudly adding *The Crew of Out From Under* and carefully dating the entry, Fifi signs *Fifi Leclaire* with an extravagant flourish, including (and at such short notice too) one little tease of an undated kiss; then goes on to say, 'you must come and meet Pierre, Valenteen. I know 'e 'as one or two leetle things 'e would ver'much like to talk to you about.'

And I would have probably 'ave to declare 'zer are one or two leetle things I would ver'much like to talk to 'er about.' But the twins are leading the way, Zee leg-upping Zoe (or is it Zoe leg-upping Zee?) in order to scale Bouton de Rose's high freeboard with the unrestrained whoop of a wooden-walled boarding party.

Followed by Fifi, with another flash of thigh and a stretch to those short shorts that are, now she's got her knee up to her eyebrow-plucked eye-level, in order to be able to place her bare but scarlet nail polished toes on Bouton's stainless steel toe-rail - **those shorts**, are not only brief, they are tight enough in the crotch to bring what would pass for tears in any old seaman's eye.

This gorgeous bit of *bateau* (the vessel *Bouton de Rose*) is modern in appearance, and very well thought out.

Access to the accommodation is via a companionway which doesn't offer the encumbrance of a washboard, but a walk-through to the half-dozen teak, rubber-faced steps that lead down to the saloon.

The layout is open plan, so when you stand at the foot of the steps, you can see from one end of the boat to the other.

There's very little old-fashioned spun yarn seamanship on display (where every finger's a marlin spike and every thumb is a fid), but there are compensations, because in place of the smell of tar and oakum, there's a waft of perfume, which is perhaps more reminiscent of a boudoir, than your average seagoing yacht.

The other thing of note is - there are lots of mirrors about. And bowls of flowers, so together with the ultra-modern decor (a design that presents a large, semicircular leather upholstered settee, complete with a set of matching, scarlet coloured, sea-island cotton cushions), this click of an image, conveys the heady impression that what's on offer is more than just a boat, could be on par with a penthouse.

For some reason, the twins seem reluctant to enter this - what I suppose is, to them, exotic world, but have remained on deck.

Corner-eyed by Sue, who is sitting out of the sun in *Out From Under's* well-canopied cockpit, apparently reading, yet only separated from her offspring by the beam of my old tub (all of nine eavesdropping feet) which is, as careful parents know, almost out of shepherding range.

I can't hear every word, because I've just stepped down into Bouton's spacious saloon, but the upshot is, the boss wants Zoe and Zee back on board *Out From Under* in double quick time, and no arguments please, if they expect her to shorten the dresses they've said they want to wear tonight (as a mere man, and recalling two bean-stalking girls) I would have expected the dresses would have to be lengthened, not shortened.

But I have other things to deal with, because now I'm below deck in *Bouton de Rose*, Fifi's about to introduce me to the rest of her crew.

Pierre isn't in the saloon.

Collette is seated at an escritoire.

The lady has obviously been working on a sheaf of papers, which she's gathering up and stowing in an expensive-looking briefcase. This attractive woman is taller than Fifi (five 9, maybe five 10?) but is equally well-proportioned. She's also dressed in white shirt and white shorts, but in her case, the shorts aren't quite as short as Fifi's, and while her blouse is every bit as diaphanous, I would have to say I'm relieved, yet somehow disappointed (confusing, isn't it?) to see that she *is* wearing a bra.

She's greeting me in perfect English, obviously bilingual, able to switch languages without even a moment's hesitation.

'How nice of you to visit us, Valentine. Pierre is having a shower, he'll be out to greet you very soon, in the meantime, can we get you a drink?'

Everything's to hand.

The saloon table has concealed within it a well-stocked drinks cabinet.

'Scotch?'

'Gin?'

'A glass of wine perhaps?'

'Orange juice?'

I opt for the Scotch - ask for a thin one, while Fifi is mixing something for herself and Collette.

'Cheers !'

It's quite an auspicious occasion.

Although I've wandered about a bit - sailed a variety of yachts - this is the first time I've found myself aboard a vessel where I have the feeling that I could be - out of my depth.

It might be a man's world (*hold on, lad*: when the chips are *carefully* counted, I don't think it's *ever* been *just* a man's world), but the balance of probabilities here is - it's the gals who are calling the shots.

How do I know?

The aura of the boat is different.

It's difficult to put your finger on it (that's a lie, I've already adopted the rheumy old seaman's perennial hope, that it's not going to be *all* that difficult to put your finger on it), but this intriguing situation is now being enlivened by the imminent arrival of Pierre.

The shower-running sound has stopped.

There's movement in the cubicle, which is located aft of the engine compartment.

This essential bit of equipment (the shower, not the donk) has two doors, one to port, one to starboard, offering easy access to and from the vessel's aft cabin, which is, despite its location, the focal point of the boat.

This grand apartment is large, very well appointed, doesn't have a bunk, but offers the largest king-sized bed which can be fitted into a boat that's merely forty-six feet long.

Pierre has finished showering, is stepping into the saloon, with a bath towel wrapped about the lower half of his body.

'Ah, Valentine; they've enticed you aboard, have they. I'm so very pleased to meet you.' (all in faultless English, without any trace of an accent).

'I see the girls have fixed you a drink; but nothing, as yet, for *me*.' (smilingly directed at Fifi) who comes back with a little tongue-out grimace, as she proceeds to fix his tipple, which turns out to be black currant juice and soda.

Pierre is a picture of health.

Head-hugging curls.

Darting blue eyes.

Pencil-thin 'tash.

Flashing white teeth.

Well-muscled shoulders (have I mentioned his barrel-like chest is covered with a dense mat of curly black hair?).

It's worth repeating, because the towel has slipped a bit, and if you think his chest is broad and hairy - you ain't seen nothing yet.

It's only a matter of time before all is revealed, because Pierre, having offered a few more pleasantries, is moving towards the aft cabin, drink in hand, and as he does so, the casually hitched towel falls from body beautiful, to reveal a bum which has tattooed across it the legend, *'if you want it.'* (left buttock), *'why wait?'* (right buttock).

The last time I caught glimpse of this motif was in a back street dive in Cairo, where an Egyptian belly dancer, having filled her own card, was drumming up business for colleagues, who showed their appreciation by keeping her supplied with large boxes of squishy Turkish Delight.

That was years ago, but the lesson hasn't been wasted, because I can't say I'm in any way put out by the sight of Pierre's back end - not even when he bends over, not down, to pick the towel up. And *he* obviously couldn't care less, because he's moving about the cabin, *sans serviette*, presumably looking for something to wear.

The other thing of note is - when you're invited aboard a hooker (absolutely no round about, under the blanket, between the sheets, or any sort of double entendre intended), you have to accept that the people you are meeting can't be expected to alter their lifestyle, just to accommodate what they probably see as either your prejudices ....

Or your limitations.

For those people who are unfamiliar with the yachtie scene, this may seem a risqué sort of a do - yet it's nothing exceptional. If you choose to knock about in a boat, it's a mistake to think you will be able to maintain shore-going standards of privacy.

The average yacht is too small to offer this indulgence (which is perhaps why some people go to sea in the first place), so walking about in the rude is nothing for other people, as visitors, to get hot under the collar about.

A fact not lost on Pierre, who seems to have found what he was looking for, and is pulling on a 'garment' of the sort which caught my eye when Fifi was hanging the washing out, during the earlier part of the day.

I thought that particular jock was a bit odd at the time.

Of course, it's years since I wore a similar device (rugby-playing schooldays), but what we used then, to keep the essentials tidy and out of harm's way, only bears a passing resemblance to the kit Pierre is slipping into; with the principle difference being - our old-fashioned jocks were intended to maintain the status quo, while Pierre's nifty little number has a hole (silk embroidered round the edges) that's *just* large enough to allow

197

his appendage to weave about, *outside* the purse designed to offer protection to the wrinkled skin of his scrotum.

Quite frankly, I would have thought this sort of lash-up more trouble than it's worth (must be uncomfortable to wear). But Pierre seems happy enough, because having tucked himself in, and winkled his cock out, he's stretching the elasticised straps of the jock - pulling them off the cheeks of his arse - letting them back with a *thwack*.

'Can I freshen your drink, Valentine?'

'I beg your pardon?'

'Would you like a drop more Scotch?' (this is Collette, who has caught me, I would have to concede, just out of what some people may judge as rudely-centred focus), but when I've shifted my attention back to the Scotch, and sensibly refused a second drink, the other crew members of *Bouton de Rose* are turning out to be an interesting pairing.

Fifi *is* a dish, of the type we yachties recognise as the sort who not only allows, but saucily *encourages* those luscious second helpings.

However, of the two gals, it's Collette who fascinates the perhaps harder bitten seaman.

She's very well rigged, and tautly set up.

A type which must be admired, and then, if you're sensible, given sufficient sea room, because when you look at her dispassionately, she's in some ways more attractive than Fifi. Yet if you wanted to take it to the point of defamation, it's possible to infer, that while she's a class act, she may leave a claw mark occasionally.

To the unsophisticated seaman, the situation aboard *Bouton de Rose* appears complicated, to the point where I'm beginning to wonder who is wearing the pants.

Who is paying the piper?

Is it Pierre, who doesn't appear to be short of a bob?

Or is it Collette, who may be running her own agenda (using Pierre as a stake-out). And if she is, does that leave someone, somewhere, spread-eagled between a jackal and a jackass?

Is this how Fifi fits in the frame?

Was she invited aboard as prey - then turned out to be the answer to a prayer?

The sort of exotic bird who has a foot in both camps, and enjoys playing the tongue-tootled tunes very few people can play on a flute.

All this is, of course, not only pure - but quite disgraceful speculation.

I've only been aboard *Bouton de Rose* fifteen intriguing minutes, and it isn't time enough to form a sensible appraisal of how things are organised aboard this fascinating vessel. If I'm not careful, I could find myself overtaken by even wilder conjecture, so it's probably time to steer the conversation along a mildly exploratory path.

It's not all that easy to do.

Pierre has joined us in the saloon, smelling of aftershave (I don't know much about this either - it could be an upmarket version of *Brut*). And he's dolled up in toreador pants, the equivalent of pony club stretch jodhpurs, which terminate just below the knee in order to show the finely-turned calf of his well-muscled leg.

His dazzling white shirt is open to his just below navel, but the embroidered front catches the eye, and compliments the way in which the shirt tucks into a garment embellished by a snakeskin belt, having a silver filigree buckle (a *large* silver filigree buckle), which has been fashioned into an indecent representation of what an insatiable satyr *really* shouldn't be doing with a *far* too compliant nymph.

'Will you be staying in port long, Valentine?' (this is Collette, who has been watching me, damn me if she ain't, with an amused expression writ large about her all but flawless features).

'Err, I'm not sure; there are a couple of places I'd like to visit. I'm really here to wait out the hurricane season, before setting off across the pond.'

'Where are you bound?'

'Barbados: I fancy spending Christmas and the New Year there. And you?'

So it goes.

After the initial splash into this whirl of a pool, and my attempt to keep my seafaring end up, it's obvious there's far more to Pierre and his crew than the wrong-headed glance of a biased impression, because this smart Beneteau isn't set up as a tawdry, down at heel bordello - she's very well appointed.

When Pierre vacated the shower compartment, I caught sight of a gleaming white bidet with a glint of gold-plated taps.

And I can see, out of the corner of a somewhat amused eye, there's a full-length mirror above the king-sized bed, securely fixed to the deckhead.

Nevertheless, I might do well to remember that I'm aboard a yacht, and whatever the impression I've formed of the crew - one of them owns the vessel, has skippered her to this jump-off port, and they seem set to continue the voyage, regardless that I've been mesmerized by Pierre's antics, Fifi's diaphanous blouse, and Collette's beautifully cool, but also calculating gaze.

However, there's more to *Bouton de Rose* than an intriguing sexual circus.

I'm relieved to see there's a well-stocked library, which offers more shelf space than usually found aboard your average yachtie's yacht; and the books carry a hint of needs which extend well beyond the seductive feel of a sheet.

Aboard this vessel, de Beauvoir rubs shoulders with Baudelaire, while Jean Paul has retained his place on the shelf.

There's also a selection of the French equivalent of the *Mariner's Library* with Bardiaux, Colas, Moitessier, Bernicot, Gau, Plisson, Auboiroux, Garnet, Gerbault, and Tabarly, [22] all well presented and prominently displayed (if not chronologically arranged).

'You have a good library here, Pierre; most intriguing. I see the marine end of it is devoted almost exclusively to seamen who have made single-handed circumnavigations; with the notable exception of Tabarly.'

'You know them?'

'Most of them; in translation, of course. Alain Gerbault's first book [23] was one of the seafaring yarns I read as a schoolboy (it was published in English as *The Fight of the Firecrest*). I can't remember the exact year of his transatlantic crossing - it was probably mid 1920s.'

'I think eet was nine-teen twen-tee three.' (this is Fifi, to whom, I would have thought, nineteen twenty anything would be something which relates almost to another planet).

But I'm wrong about that, because Fifi knows all about Gerbault's seafaring exploits, and his status as a tennis player, particularly where he fits into the history of a game which has produced its fair share of idols, who have been joined - perhaps not by the likes of Cash (who frowned at the thought that he might), but by Agassi, who smilingly knows that he can - all of which tickles Collette.

'So you like tennis, Valentine?'

And I must agree that I do - mixed doubles preferred. And I would also have to admit I can't resist name dropping, as and when it suits me, so it's only a matter of time before I've steered the conversation back to Tabarly.

'You knew him, then?'

'Yes; I sailed against him a couple of times.'

'What happened?'

'He won.'

A remark which delights the crew of the French yacht *Bouton de Rouge*. The saloon resounds to the sound of Gallic laughter (all well intentioned, of course). When it dies away, I have the opportunity of explaining that of all the people I would choose to lose *to* - Eric is miles ahead of the fleet.

Then Pierre comes back with - 'if you knew Tabarly, you probably knew Chichester.' [24] (and I have to say that I did). 'How did you get on with him?'

'Very well, with Francis.' (admired him for his courage, and determination to succeed). 'But, like most other yachties at the time, I found it difficult to get just the right amount of the nautical knight, without having rather too large a helping of his lady wife, who was inclined to take the lofty view of what she all too easily saw, from her giddy elevation, as other people's failings.'

This does raise a laugh, but there's not quite the same degree of spontaneity, and if someone wanted to spend a microsecond analysing the difference in response, I suppose you would start with niceties of speech. Those inflections which are not always accessible to people who have to learn a language (as against those who have absorbed one), and then move on to the way his compatriots, and seamen generally, so much admired Tabarly; and having looked that fact squarely in the face, wonder why Francis is not held in such universal acclaim (as perhaps his supporters think he should be).

Nevertheless, having something in common does provide a social lubricant (the days of nationalism are numbered, if only we can lay jingoism to rest?) and the time spent aboard *Bouton de Rose* is turning out a gas.

Fifi knows about tennis.

Pierre goes on about sailing.

And Collette?

Is looking at me with a smoothly reflective expression, through a haze of hazel eyes, while at the same time playing with a propelling pencil (pulling it through her fingers), and when she's pulled it through, pulling it back again (which may not sound much of a deal). But she's pressing the button at the end of the pencil, so the lead pops out, and then - when she's slipped it through those caressing fingertips once more, thumbing the button (so the lead pops back in the pencil again). And this absent minded use of a crayon, solid gold Parker though it may be, is on the brink of driving me well on the way to the funny farm.

Time goes by (I'm riding it out).

It seems Pierre is a mining engineer, with an inventive turn of mind. He left the corporation he was working for, and set up his own business. Then sold the business back to the corporation, while at the same time negotiating a consultancy arrangement which has given him the best of both worlds.

Collette is a writer who contributes regularly to glossy Women's Magazines, of the sort that can be confidently described as feminist, in the *avant-garde* use of the term.

Fifi is a graduate of the French equivalent of The Royal Academy of Dramatic Art, has done television work, not quite so much legit. She's between jobs, and boy friends, so decided to spend a month or two aboard *Bouton de Rose,* just to keep her hand in.

All standard yachtie stuff.

And I'm getting on well with the crew of *Bouton de Rose,* partly due to the fact that nobody's smoking, nobody's drinking, and the conversation bounces along with barely a pause for breath; so when someone suggests going ashore for a meal, it seems the natural thing to do.

'Why don't we make it a partee?' (this is Fifi, who knows the twins are in line for a treat).

'If we ask Suzanne nice-lee, maybe zey'll all come along.'

The next twenty minutes are spent debating where we should eat.

I don't know what's on offer, but my unspoken concern is - it shouldn't be outrageously expensive. I've known French meals that started at nine, saw out midnight, and when the bill came, at 2 in the starry eye of the morning, everyone said the food was *exceptionnel,* the champagne *delicieux,* and the outrageous bill - merely a trifle.

But it seems Pierre knows just the right restaurant. 'Not the sort of *touriste*-touting bistro, my dear Valentine, which caters for the *vulgaire* hoi-polloi; eh?'

However, Fifi and Collette put forward the view that, although it might be quite a good place to eat, it isn't the best place to dance; so (having accepted the fact that it *is* going to be outrageously expensive) my concern now is, what am I going to wear?

This does have a smile in it.

Here I am, a wander-about yachtie, and I'm wondering what to wear?

Most of my sailing mates would be bustin' a gut, if there was even an inkling that this preen of a thought had crossed my mind (but they haven't spent the evening aboard *Bouton de Rose,* have they?). So while Pierre and his crew are getting their act together, I'm digging into my clothes locker, hoping to come up with something which, even if it is creased in all the wrong places, and no more than slightly mildewed, will at least allow a reasonable strut of the stuff.

About an hour later, and it could be more (the ladies, all five of them, have been dressing). Eventually, we're walking the length of the jetty, on our way to bright lights, while presenting what must be close to a show-stopping sight.

Pierre is leading the way, arm in arm up Broadway.

He's centre-stage (of course) and has Fifi hung on his left, with Collette hung on his right.

The twins are at each end of the line, skipping along hand in hand with whoever is next to Zoe (or it could be next to Zee) while us mere mortals, Suzanne, Richard, young David, and a rather tall, gangling old fellow, who isn't quite as well dressed as his companions, bringing up the rear, which isn't a bad place to be.

Pierre is sporting a white rig-out (I'm tempted to call it a zoot suit) [25] but I'm concerned the use of this term will reveal the old-fashioned mindset I have to contend with. But whatever the modern equivalent of this particular rig, the effect is nothing less than splendid, even though, by other people's standards, it's probably on the deplorable side of outrageous.

If you can take your eyes off Pierre (and this depends on sexual orientation, as much as the tight-arsed cut of his pants) it's intriguing to note that Fifi and Collette are identically dressed.

Here again, if I was foolish enough to express an opinion, it would reveal how little I know about French couture.

But whatever the reason for this peas in a pod approach, the result is worth the effort; because it seems to me, as someone who is struggling to avoid being judged a gauche old voyeur, they are wearing the out for an evening equivalent of the little black cocktail dress.

Garments which depend on the art of understatement.

That's to say, they are designed to be alluringly tailored, seductively fitted, expensively purchased, and reach; not necessarily in that order, bewitchingly down to the knee.

The twins, having pestered their mother, have had their gingham dresses shortened, and are now skipping along in what could be described as bum-freezers (if it wasn't such a balmy night).

These pert youngsters form the perfect foil for the chorus line now high-stepping along the jetty, past the rows of stern-to yachts, some having crews who indulge in wolf whistles, and the occasional catcall, probably directed at Pierre (from the shallower end of the basin).

Nevertheless, the crew rally round.

Collette sticks her nose in the air, while at the same time pushing her chest out (Fifi doesn't need to). Either way, it's a bit of a let down when we've negotiated the jetty and entered the brightly lit part of the town.

The *'Otel Splon'deed'* I assume we're making for, is further away than I thought, and turns out to be - not a hotel at all, but one of those high-rise structures I was inclined to look down on when exploring this area earlier in the day.

Neither the building itself, nor the entrance seems all that impressive. But the foyer is patrolled by a uniformed attendant, and after he's greeted Pierre (too effusively, in my opinion) this flunkey touches a button, and we're ushered across reception, to lifts which serve what's turning out to be a somewhat deceptive establishment.

We can't get into the set-apart elevator, until Pierre has slipped a plastic card in the appropriate slot, and after that hurdle has been negotiated, the guard dog (who doubles as the flunkey) growls into a wall-mounted microphone.

The door slides open.

We enter, and are on our way to a rooftop supper club, where the entrée is money in serious amounts, allied to the approval of the other members, who may not be the sort of fish who are all that keen on increasing the size of the pool.

No matter, we're in.

Pierre is in his element, being greeted by the *maître-d'hôtel,* who has obviously been forewarned of our arrival.

Fortunately, the table we're being ushered to is not only well-positioned, but round; so there's none of the indecisive shuffling which sometimes takes place when order of precedence is allowed to raise its sometimes embarrassing head.

Not that it matters in this instance, because Pierre knows exactly where he wants to sit, and has chosen the dominant position (looking across the table into the uncluttered centre of the room). So it's only a matter of everyone taking the chair he's suggesting, and that little problem is solved.

He has Fifi on his left, and Susanne on his right.

I'm next to Fifi, and have Zoe (I think) on my left.

Then comes David, with Collette on his left, followed by Richard, then

Zee, and back to Susanne again.

Not a bad arrangement for nine people, everyone seems to have someone; in any case, the table isn't all that big and it's easy to talk across, as well as to your neighbour.

Now everyone's settled, the menus turn out to be leather-bound and an inch thick.

Nothing's priced, so it's only a matter of deciding what you want, then holding your fire until you see the whites of the maître'd's eyes (the rough old Anglo-Saxon technique).

But this is a French occasion, and a certain amount of discussion is necessary before the order can be placed. This involves an assessment of the beef, lamb, pork, chicken, duck, turkey, game, fish, snails, prawns, lobster, and pâté.

A choice of five salads, three soups, several madly exotic dishes (crocodile, moose, ostrich) with this bewildering inventory exhaustively debated in a mixture of French and English, until everyone's decided what they want, or don't want, which turns out a hodge of a podge selection.

Nevertheless, this is only halfway along the track, because when the wine list arrives - a medieval, also leather-bound, hand-tooled manuscript which takes delight in illuminating what's boastfully on offer - allowing Pierre to carry out an assessment of the pros and cons of half-a-dozen vineyards and vintages; from a barely-drinkable bottle of poor wine, priced at the outrageous equivalent of thirty pounds Sterling; to a selection of the finest Champagne that, if I was asked to express an opinion, on a value for money basis, I should say would be best left to someone with a more discerning palate than I've had time to develop.

The range of food on offer seems impressive, but in the rustic little corner of the hill'd and valley'd world where I am proud to hail from, we peasants would judge this sort of menu to be just a little *too* extensive, and indicative, not so much of class - as ostentatious lack of it. The whole thing having more to do with the depth of the freezer than the culinary skill of the chef. And I suppose this is what Fifi and Collette were concerned with earlier, when they expressed their reservations.

Yet Pierre seems happy enough.

He's caught the head waiter's eye, and in the matter of a moment this important gentleman is attending table, together with his second-in-command, who is pencil and note book poised to take our finally arrived at selections.

Taking into consideration the complexities of the situation, it might be fair to assume the waiter would be allowed to sort it out, in his own time, person-by-person, until the order has been understood and then committed to paper.

However, that underestimates Pierre, who proceeds to discuss the finer points of the menu with the maître'd in a mixture of French, Spanish, Italian and English, together with a list of suggested improvements he hopes will be passed to the chef.

Having muddied the waters, Pierre reels off the whole of the complicated order, item perfect, and correctly personalised - 'Madame will have this, Mademoiselle will have that.' - at breathtaking speed, to the pencil-poised second-in-command who is doing his best to take it all down.

Even if this was *all* Pierre got up to, it would be very much more than enough. But our virtuoso, instead of sticking to the job in hand, is catching the eye of people he apparently knows very well, prominent amongst them being Mr Leonard J. Fincklestein, the Third, with a wave of his hand, and 'how *are* you, Lennie?' (the owner of *Malachi*) who is nicely tabled with (Pierre winks it privately round our group) someone who is definitely *not* his fourth wife.

Only after this divertimento has been delivered, does he go back to placing the order; until he notices someone else to comment on, not always charitably, or to the amusement of the waiter who, to give him his due, is doing his best to keep his temper. But has now reached the stage where he's considering dropping his pencil in order to pick up a knife.

While Pierre's been making the most of his opportunity, and infuriating the staff, other guests are arriving - of a special sort apparently, because they are not being hovered-over by the maître d'hôtel, but welcomed by people who give the appearance of being involved with the upper echelons of management.

The group being flattered by an elaborate greeting, are entering the restaurant preceded by a broad shouldered gentleman, sporting a red bow tie, immaculately creased pants, black patent-leather shoes, a white dinner jacket, and a watchful pair of eyes.

This gorilla (who doesn't actually *have* a receding forehead) walks straight past the management, to take up a position in an alcove, a little to one side of the general arrangement of tables and chairs; nevertheless, it does give the occupant the double-edged advantage of having his back to the wall, and a commanding view of the room.

I don't know much about this type of security.

I just assume, in a simple sort of way, there *are* people about who need this level of protection, which if it does nothing else, is inclined to unsettle the rest of the guests.

It takes the arrival of our vintage champagne (*Pol-Roget, Sir Winston Churchill*) [(26)] 'just an apéritif, my dear fellow, a modest apéritif,' before we've settled back in our chairs, and resumed what passes for normal conversation amongst a group of yachties, at least one of whom is beginning to feel - this just might be the night to go determinedly out on the town. Being further encouraged in this belief by the arrival of a group of musicians, who are now taking their places on a dais adjacent to the dance floor.

After they've sorted themselves out, this band kicks off with the sort of low-key number a combo strums when the night's young - the wine has arrived, but not had time to displace those silly inhibitions.

It's not long before the first bold sprite takes to the floor, and surprisingly enough, it isn't Pierre, but a Latin-looking type from the recently arrived party, who have also settled in, and drawn attention to themselves by the way their women are dressed.

If not to kill - at least draw blood - would be a fair description, because it's obvious even to a dude who's normally dressed in a duffle, that a great deal of time and effort, to say nothing of money, has been lavished on ladies who are mincing about in high-heeled sandals, arse-tight dresses with floor-sweeping hems, swooping necklines, tucked up tits, piled-up hair (not all of it their own), diamond-studded broaches (not even a *tiny* little tiara?). But I suppose you have to draw the line somewhere, although whether this piece of sound advice has filtered through to Pierre might be a matter of doubt.

Our Leader, having quaffed a glass of champagne, and got halfway down another, is preparing to join the people who are straying towards the dance floor, but before he enters the fray, he takes off his coat (gives it to a passing waiter, who doesn't seem all that pleased, as he's already got his hands full), nevertheless, it allows Pierre increased freedom of movement, and the opportunity of competing on what I suppose he sees as approaching equal terms.

Having taken his coat off, he's down to his zoot pants, and a shirt that offers batwing sleeves, tapering to buttoned wrists, on one of which a bracelet peeps - golden, just below the cuff.

His zoots are worth a second look, because they are not equipped with your common-or-garden zipped or button flies, but the split falls beloved of the County Set, who have their 'britches' built for 'em by the old retainer of a tailor (he does all the Master's work; is proud of the Hunt-buttoned waistcoats, as well as his pride and joy - an occasional side-saddle skirt).

Not a bad start. Yet there's more to come, because Pierre's pants are tight, and high cut, to the point where support is necessary for the embroidered edge of trousers that terminate well above his waist, so Pierre has selected a pair of braces of the sort that, if they were worn *outside* a pink coat, [27] you wouldn't even know they were there.

If it wasn't for the bolstering effect of the wine, I suppose those members of our party who are basically retiring violets (and I often find myself struggling to extricate myself from the tacky fringe of this inhibited group) might be feeling slightly perturbed - not by the way things are developing, but by the looming necessity of asking someone to dance.

The trouble is (straight up) I'm the sort of clumsy old hoss who is always casting a shoe, and have become adept at postponing the moment when, out of misguided politeness, I *have* to pop the question.

So I'm relieved when Pierre asks Collette out on the floor; Richard invites his wife. David blushes (I can't think why), then follows Fifi's gorgeous amble, which leaves me with the twins, who are looking in my direction, then decide discretion is by far the better part of valour and skip off to dance with each other.

The band are into the sort of tune that, now I'm still glued to my chair, it seems all too easy to follow.

A dance number, which Pierre is using to propel Collette around the edge of the floor, partly because it gives him the opportunity of passing the odd remark to people who still have their bums on their seats. But the sly comments he's dropping are not intended as the sort of bricks which other people can build on - but as a means of attracting attention.

Something Collette isn't concerned with, because she's one of those rare birds who inhabit the world peopled by the glamorous image of Rogers, [28] whilst I, lucky fellow, in my own little set-aside island, have just landed the toe-tapping part of Astaire. [29]

Richard and Sue are gyrating, with the asexual assurance of a couple who have lived together for twenty well-bedded years.

Pierre and Collette are an eye-catching pair - she's sexy, rhythmic, gorgeous, and beautifully understated - while he's peacocking proud and displays it.

David is the picture of tousle-haired youth, paired with a professional dancer, who could, if she wanted to, make him look a proper Charlie. But she's far too nice for that, and is content to let him have his head, until it's time to up the ante (couldn't *possibly* be satisfied with being *anybody's* aunty) and decides to audition the role of Salome. [30]

The twins, on the other hand, who have sometimes invoked a tomboy'd response, are now on the floor as long-legged and cheeky gazelles. Their dresses end at the tuck of their bums, and they're flipping their pony-tailed hair from shoulder to skinny-framed shoulder, as they respond to the tip and tap of a bongo.

And if that's all they were doing, it could be left right there as a display of adolescent high jinks. But these lasses are *identical* twins, and they present the image of what Zee is doing, Zoe is doing.

What Zoe is doing, Zee is doing.

As Zoe raises an arm, Zee is raising an arm.

When Zoe is tapping a foot, Zee is tapping a foot.

So I'm looking at youngsters who are dancing a few feet apart. Apart from the fact that they are one (or is it *two* of the same person?) who are theatrically joined by their genes.

I have to abandon this intriguing image when the head waiter arrives,, with a gang of supporting minions, who start fussing over cutlery, glasses, fingerbowls, napkins, and the rest of the bits and pieces which are indispensable for the elaborate grub that's now on its way from the kitchen. The sort of round the table activity which drops the hint to the dancers - that it's time to stop cavorting and rejoin the sitting-out folk.

Not that I've been *all* that backward in coming forward, because while they've been enjoying the dancing, I've been able to indulge in a slurp or two of the old 'Rojay', which is undoubtedly a very fine wine. The trouble is, the steward is the sort of assiduous type who persists in anticipating demand (the quicker you drink, the faster it flows) so there's no such thing as an empty glass, which is all very well, but could lead to complications if I'm going to stay sober and safely parked on the inhibited part of the shelf.

Meanwhile, Sue and Richard have got the message, and are on their way back to our table, followed by David and Fifi; then Zoe and Zee, so it's only Pierre and his partner who are holding up proceedings.

Not that Pierre gives a damn, because now he's got the floor to himself, he's persuaded the band to try out a tango, and he and Collette are parading about - while the soup is getting cold.

Actually, Pierre isn't having soup, he's having oysters, which he insisted be brought to the table *in*, and not *on* their shells; so there are now a dozen or more of these unsuspecting bivalves, supported on a shallow bowl of crushed ice - waiting (probably hoping, fools that they are) for something decisive to happen.

The band are also happy they've got a live one.

They're keeping on and on with the tango, and Pierre is so engrossed with his over-sways, back-drops, and closed-promenades, it takes a message from the maître'd to bring this extravagant parade to a halt (an irritated glance to the leader of the combo that conveys the professional message - *enough already, get this idiot off the floor, we've got work to do*), so Pierre is obliged to return, smiling, blissfully triumphant to the table; which allows me to play the gentleman with Collette, by pulling out her chair, then push it in again, when she's got her gorgeous bum correctly positioned above the receptive curve of her seat.

The grub is now the centre of attention.

Perhaps not before time, and it turns out to be well on its way to a triumph.

Pierre has excelled himself in the choice of wines. Those having soup will be offered a tot of Sanlucar de Barrameda, Manzanilla (not a bad choice for a salty old yachtie), while those in line for smoked salmon will enjoy a Pouilly-Fumé, Baron de Ladoucette.

Collette is having partridge, and the bird will be enhanced by a fine example of Penfold's Grange Hermitage (possibly Pierre's bow of acknowledgement in Richard's Barossa Valley direction?); while Fifi and Susanne will be able to sip a chardonnay, from Cloudy Bay, as they daintily toy with a sole.

It would be hard to criticise this selection, unless you know more about wine than Pierre apparently does, and possess the knowledge he's delighted to share with the steward. The intimate exchange of ideas that's intended to be, and indeed is, loud enough to include everyone else in the room.

These two lads are undoubtedly made for each other.

Bottles arrive, and are theatrically displayed on the crook of a jacketed arm, in order that our commissar of a connoisseur can examine the label.

Take note of the year.

Look at the foil.

Follow the screw.

Appraise the cork.

Sniff the end, and wait - for a snifter of the precious liquid to be tipped and then offered (Pierre thankfully centre-stage again), so he can look high through the glass, give it a twirl, see how it hangs, examine the tint, approach with the nose, brush with the lips, savour the taste, rotate with the tongue, suck in his cheeks.

Look hard at the steward.

And then, nod - his *very* casual approval.

What *I'm* waiting for, is the moment when Pierre announces himself dissatisfied, and condemns a wine out of hand.

But that debacle doesn't occur.

The chances of an absolute dud being brought to *this* table are on the distant side of remote, so the whole thing goes with a swing, with Pierre knifing bivalves, sipping wine and slipping oysters into the wide-lipped smile of his mouth as he twitches his pencil-thin 'tache at his guests.

He's also rolling weird-looking eyes at the twins - acting up the image of the risqué old coot - who comes close to being the sort of dirty old man inexperienced young girls would be well advised to avoid.

Pierre is wasting his time.

Zoe and Zee have tramped more reef pools, speared more parrot fish, and sampled them, still twitching, than Pierre has had amorous ladies for breakfast. The idea that he can somehow give these girls the frights just by gulpin' oysters has got 'em both in stitches. It's also worth recalling that outside the door of their cabin, carved on *Out From Under's* teak-sheathed mast, there's a display of Hindu erotica which is explicit enough to leave nothing to the flutter of any shy little lid.

My own part in proceedings is about as low-key as I can make it.

I'm enjoying the grub. The salmon (supposedly Spey) [31] was good, very good, and I'm on my way through a saddle of Swedish roe deer - not the whole damned saddle, even though it *is* small - but far more than is going to be good for me. A bit of a beast, so tender, it could easily be carved with a spoon, with each morsel enhanced by a sip of a wine that Penfold's have labelled the best they made, in a year as good as ever it gets. So what more *could* anyone ask for?

I wish to hell I could dance.

When the meal has progressed to the point where decisions have to be taken, both Collette and Fifi opt for fruit, but only if they can be sure of having a Chateau d'Yquem as a special treat to go with it.

I'm going to sample the Stilton because, greedy old dog that I am, there's a vintage Port on offer, and even if it *is* the most expensive wine in the list, Pierre's going to order it, come what may, so it's only a matter of waiting my turn before this drop of old and crusty will bring a very fine meal to a close.

The band, who have been strumming along to little purpose while we've been trenchering away, are now reasserting their presence, and couples from other tables are beginning to drift their way to the floor.

Amongst our group, the end of the meal has run into the sands of small talk, so Pierre has assumed part of his job includes encouraging his guests to dance.

He's leading the way with the twins, got David partnering Collette. Richard escorting Fifi - which leaves me, trying *not* to catch Susanne Hutchinson's eye who, nice lady that she is, deserves better than having a clumsy old seaman trample all over her corns.

However, when everyone else is hoofin' - wouldn't it be rude *not* to ask Susanne to dance?

There seems no way out of this dilemma, with the only thing in its favour being, that the band are playing an easy-going trifle, which is a blessing (now I'm partnering Sue) as it enables me to shuffle about, trying to disguise the fact that my sense of rhythm is about as reliable as a hundred to one shot on a racecourse; and I'm the sort of awkward clot who's not *absolutely* certain which foot to put hesitatingly in front of the other.

But there *are* people around who can dance.

The Latin-looking type, who kicked off proceedings earlier in the evening, is giving Pierre something to think about.

So peacocking P is stepping up a gear.

Performing in a manner some people would judge as being much too near the knuckle.

A fact not lost on Sue, who is keeping an eye on her daughters, while at the same time trying to suppress a frown whenever we pass close enough to her husband to take note of how he's getting on with Fifi.

Sue and I have reached the stage where conversation has come at least partly to my rescue.

Although we are apparently dancing, what we're actually doing is discussing the merits of the type of roller-reefing gear they have aboard *Out From Under*. After we've explored this avenue, Sue is kind enough to go into the detail of the stores they've shipped, how much water they carry, with this leading easily enough into a discussion of the type of freshwater-making kit they've got on board.

Taking one desalinating thing with another, I can *just* about keep my end up. But what Sue thinks of me as a *dancing* partner ....

It's only a matter of time - although it does seem to spin out a bit, before I've done my duty with Sue, and find myself paired with the twins, who turn out to be - not quite as forgiving as mother.

Apart from the fact they can dance like Dervishes, [32] they also have an uncanny ability of being able to mimic whoever happens to be in their critical sights (this is *me* right now), so my wooden-legged shuffle is being parodied.

Not by one relentless tease, but by two young gals who are (shall we abandon all hope of putting it politely?) and agree they're taking the piss out of me - in a ladylike way of course - yet it amounts to the same in the end.

But a grey old dog, even though he's stricken with rheumatics, can only stand a limited amount of this Taking the Mick, and I'm determined to put up a better performance (maybe what the twins set out to promote in the first place?) so I'm now winding-up to put on a show of my own.

Helped by the band, who have broken into a quick-fire number which has encouraged me to throw caution to the wind - show these youngsters that even bone-creaking oldies have a trick or two up our sleeves - mine being (as I'm tall and gangling) a whirling about, first this way, then that.

Stomping here; stamping there.

An arm up; an arm down.

A knee up; a knee down.

A leg in; a leg out.

Dancing?

Only in a manner of speaking.

Far better described as an uncoordinated attempt to illustrate that I'm not really a creaking old wooden top - but a real live kid from Kalamazoo.

It can't last.

This startling impression of a demented stick insect presents problems.

It's only a matter of time, before I either wreck a hamstring or slip and fall flat on my arse, with the balance of probabilities favouring the latter, and sooner rather than later.

Either way, it's bound to be embarrassing.

I'm saved by the band, coming to the end of the tune I'm trying to 'dance' *to.* The combo taking a well-earned breather, with the twins leading me, as a breathless old fogey, from the floor, back to our table, where the rest of our party are assembling.

'You seem to be enjoying yourself, Valentine.' (this is Collette, giving me an amused once-over, with those hazel eyes of hers), as cool as you like, with the saving grace of a saucy twitch of a smile as she pops the question.

'Can anyone join in the fun?'

I must admit this is a development I hadn't anticipated.

If I'd thought about it, I would have assumed my mad fandango would have put her (the super sophisticate) off.

Then again, as an old dog, I have absolutely no idea how Collette marks her card. Perhaps she *likes* the idea of an outrageous swing in the woods?

There's also the possibility that her remark, *'can anyone join in the fun?'* is the sort of back-handed comment which comes close to being a put-down.

There's only one way to find out; so, bolstered by another slurp of the fine Ro'jay, I'm asking her out on the floor.

She can certainly dance.

She's tall.

Slender.

Beautifully proportioned.

Possesses a sense of rhythm which wouldn't be out of place in Rio at carnival time - yet is not in any way flamboyant.

How does she do it?

Everything is understated.

The little black dress, is a loosely fitted, demurely down to the knee cocktail dress. A complete reversal of the skin-tight, deck-sweeping drapes the Latin-looking types are cavorting sweatily about in. My partner (get that, *my* partner) not only looks cool - she *is* cool, and her hazel eyes are smiling, as she sees she's got the upper hand, and has me comfortably cooped in the palm of it.

'You can dance quite nicely, when you try, Valentine.'

(*say nothing, Howells*)

Smile? Of course - but I reckon the best ploy here is keep my mouth shut. Try to take advantage of the fact that I've abandoned the demented stick insect approach, for something which tries to reflect Collette's rhythmic shuffle - so I'm swaying back and fore, barely moving my feet, hoping the probability of tripping over them has at least been partly taken care of, and measuring one experimental thing with another, I reckon I'm making progress.

Then our Leader sticks his nose in.

While Collette and I have been (eyeing each other up, is as good a tag as any) Pierre has been whirling around with Fifi, while at the same time trying to remain the centre of attention (a tough go - even for Pierre).

Nevertheless, here he comes.

Heading in our direction.

Walking across the dance floor, with the gorgeous creature trailing in his wake.

'Ah, Valentine, my dear chap. Do you mind if I talk to Collette for a moment? Perhaps we can make it an *excuse me,* and you can dance with Fifi for a while'

I can't say I'm pleased; several of the small problems which apparently lay between me and who knows what, seem to have been reduced in complexity.

Having made progress, I'm reluctant to have to go through the process again. However, now Pierre has manoeuvred me aside (elbowed me aside would be a fairer description) it seems I must ask Fifi to dance.

And I would have to concede that finding myself back at square one, even with someone as attractive as Fifi, is not the best way of approaching the task of escorting a dancer who could embellish the chorus of yet another remake of the Hollywood version of the world famous Folies-Bergère. [33] (Or, put another way), that I'm further than ever from knowing what to do with my feet, and having to partner an obvious pro is turning out to be - just like throwing another inhibiting prawn on my all too embarrassing barbie.

Part of the problem lies in the way Fifi is dancing (beautifully, of course).

The trouble is, she's not made the slightest concession to my lack of aptitude.

She hasn't accepted the fact that all I have to offer is a stiff-legged hoppity-hop.

Trundling round a lopsided maypole in an agricultural manner.

An obvious candidate for professional advice, which it seems I'm about to get, because Fifi is closing the gap, coming closer, to whisper in my ear.

'My dear Valenteen, you must relax; you are much too tense. All wound up, and twang-ing, like an ovaire-tightened 'arp string.'

Who could argue with that?

Not that I want to, because as well as voicing her concern, my partner has stopped dancing - is coming alongside, putting an arm over my shoulder.

'What we must do Cherie - is get ourselves togezaire.'

Sounds O.K. to me.

And now she's taking the trouble to demonstrate what's needed, it doesn't seem all that difficult.

Since she's shown me *where* to put my feet, the whole thing has altered perspective. And encouraged by the feel of her hip moving seductively against mine, I'm beginning to get the hang of this dancin' lark, which does seem to have one or two compensations tucked away within it.

However, while I'm enjoying this development, our Leader is striding into frame.

'Ah, Valentine; I see Fifi's taken you in hand.' (poor choice of phrase).

'I'm afraid I must break up the session. I've had my tête-à-tête with Collette and I'm back to claim my partner.'

Is he indeed.

I've known the skipper of *Bouton de Rouge* for the best part of a day, and he's irritated me at fairly regular intervals. Not to put too fine a point on it, Pierre has got up my nose once too often, and I reckon this as good a time as any to bring the big-headed bugger up with a snagged round turn, with or without the 2 half-hitches. [34]

'I beg your pardon, Pierre; did I hear you correctly? Are you giving me, or attempting to give me, the old heave-ho?'

'Of course not, my dear fellow; merely claiming my own.'

'Claiming your own? Since when were you empowered to *claim your own*?'

'It's just a figure of speech old chap.'

'Just a figure of speech is it?'

'Well here's another figure of speech, Pierre. If you don't haul off and give me plenty of sea room, the chances are I'm going to knock you down, roll you over, and stamp on your balls.'

'Have I made myself clear?'

I reckon I have, because there's the unmistakeable light of panic in Pierre's eyes.

Only momentarily - but long enough to let me know the point's been taken. Yet to give him his due, he comes back with.

'Hell-oh!.' (drawled, as flashy English middle-class), [35] an imitation of a supercilious accent.

'Has our old dog found a bone he's prepared to growl over?'

Which isn't too bad a comeback, from someone who's just been hit in the face with a brick.

While this little spat's been going on - and I really can't understand how it all blew up so quickly (if you'll excuse the lie), Fifi has been standing quietly aside, obviously enjoying the locking of horns.

She's also a gal who has a sense of humour, because she comes out with.

'Boys, *boys.*' (modulated with a delightful giggle).

'What is all ze fuss about?'

'Don't worr-ee; zere is going to be plentee for ev'er'ee'wonne.'

Another dodgy choice of phrase?

I suppose it depends on where you're standing (or on how self-righteous you feel at the moment). But it's as well to bear in mind that leopards can't be expected to change their spots; indeed, depending on which direction you're heading, there are some leopards you may not *want* to change their spots.

However, a late night supper club is not the best of venues to embark on a debate regarding the merits or otherwise on the set-up that prevails aboard the good ship *Bouton de Rose.*

Whether her crew are moral, immoral, or amoral is their own affair.

More to the point is - they're undoubtedly fun to be with.

The evening meanders on in its own uproarious way.

Now I have some idea of the rudiments, regardless that I'm a country mile from mastering the niceties, I'm visiting the dance floor with the abandon of an enthusiastic convert.

Cavorting with Collette.

Frolicking with Fifi.

Spinning around with Sue (after she's agreed, no doubt unwisely, to try out the twists and turns of a tango), with only the problem presented by Zoe and Zee left largely unresolved.

This being the case, because while the ladies are prepared to make allowances, the twins are falling about in stitches if I make a particularly hopeless job when partnering either of them; which may, I suppose, provide some sort of a clue regarding the way the *mature* of the species have learnt how to manage their men.

But the pièce de résistance is Fifi.

Have I mentioned she's a stunner?

A bit shorter than Collette (what's an inch or two between friends?).

That she's a professional dancer?

Has blonde hair.

Blue eyes.

Wears a seductive dress, sports gold ear clips.

Has a gorgeous pair of unrestricted up-fronts.

Is wicked enough to boot.

The sort of vamp who dishes out the treatment; working the lad over, until what we'll politely call - *the steam* - is past the point of rising.

Coming close, to whisper.

'How am I doing? - *big boy* !'

There should be a law against it.

There is.

Unbridled use of the pelvis, in a public place, could get her an overnight stay in the slammer, in some of the less indulgent places in an otherwise salubrious world.

It's Sue Hutchinson who rings the curtain down (looks at her watch) and notes it's twenty past two in the morning.

Richard agrees it's time to go home.

David seems reluctant (he's dancing with Fifi).

I'm about on my knees with fatigue.

The twins put up a rearguard action, but are quelled by the threat of extra algebra when they come on parade, in four and a half hours, *from now*, as their mother forcefully informs them.

This leaves the crew of *Bouton de Rose,* for whom, perhaps, the other half of the night has yet to heave into view - so they're quite prepared to trundle on back to their boat.

Pierre pays the piper - pretentiously beckons the steward, and when l'addition arrives, doesn't even bother to look at the bill, merely flips his card on the salver.

Richard Hutchinson and I dig deep enough to leave a handsome tip, which we place on the tray when the waiter returns with the card (that's certainly been loaded anyway).

By common consent we turn down the suggestion of a limo, to walk slowly back to the boats.

Through the quiet town.

Smiling, at the sound of a good-natured curse, emanating from an unlit alleyway, followed by a burst of high pitched laughter.

A car door slamming.

An engine revving, as the vehicle is driven off into the enveloping night.

There's no moon.

The harbour lights are on, illuminating the breakwater, highlighting the yachts tied up stern-to the quay, so we can cast an eye over them as we walk towards *Out From Under,* and I'm able to see my own boat, snugged comfortably between her and *Bouton de Rose.*

Pierre does suggest a nightcap, but everyone knows it's time to get our collective heads down.

So after goodnights here and goodnights there, I'm down below.

Peeling off my kit.

Chucking it carelessly on the pilot berth.

Rolling into my bunk, absolutely done to the world.

It must be about half an hour later.

I'm fast asleep, then awake, because I know someone has just stepped aboard the tub.

For a moment I let it pass.

Then an inquisitive itch gets the better of me, and I can't resist getting out of my bunk and sticking my head out of the hatch.

There's a figure on the foredeck; David, about to step aboard *Bouton de Rose.*

And there's a figure on that vessel's foredeck; Fifi, half-in and half-out of the for'ard hatch.

The gal doesn't have a stich on, but makes no attempt to make room for David, so he must squeeze past her, and it's a small hatch, on his way below.

Ain't she a caution?

ain't there no limit to the on-going boldness of youth?

219

CHAPTER FIVE: PAGE NOTES

---

(1) Page 166. Line 3 .... *'dear old Nightingale'*.

A slang reference to an oil lamp, hung in the rigging at night as a steamer-warning signal.

Florence NIGHTINGALE was born on May 12th, 1820, in Florence, and named after the city, but she grew up in England where her parents owned and enjoyed homes in London, Derbyshire, and Hampshire. She was educated during her early years by her father, who taught her not only Latin and Greek, but also French, German, and Italian, and she used this educational base to study history, philosophy, and mathematics. Despite obvious gifts, she found social life unsatisfactory, and was soon casting about for a means of escape from what she saw as over-restrictive parental control. But it was not until 1850 she gained sufficient freedom to spend time in Germany, where she studied nursing, and coincidentally found the avenue that allowed her freedom to develop her own distinctive personality.

Soon after returning to Britain she was appointed superintendent of a small private hospital, which she immediately set about reorganising; so successfully, that her managerial talents became widely recognised. On the outbreak of the Crimean War (1854-1856) she was asked by the government to take a party of nurses to Turkey, where she found the barrack hospitals totally inadequate for the task they were supposed to undertake; and moreover, that the senior medical staff were hostile to someone they viewed as an amateur (when they were confronted by perhaps the most determinedly professional person they would ever encounter during the whole of *their* professional lives), with the outcome being that Miss Nightingale - appalled by the fleas, rats, lice, cockroaches, unwashed bedding, and hopelessly managed facilities, rose to the occasion, with her first official purchase being 200 scrubbing brushes and a vast supply of soap.

It was during this period Florence earned the tribute *'the Lady with the Lamp'*. A reference to her habit of patrolling the hospital wards at night, doing what she could to succour those soldiers who knew, only too well, that she and her staff were directly responsible for bringing the death rate down from over 40% of the hospital intake, to less than 10%. And even those poor souls were able to die with at least some degree of dignity, with the result that the enlisted men loved her unreservedly, for care that extended well beyond the normal call of duty.

Anyone interested in this amazing lady (the first woman to be awarded the accolade OM) but who was not without her own difficult facets of character, should read *Cecil Woodham-Smith's* **Florence Nightingale, 1820-1910**; published in 1950 and reprinted in 1983. This may not be the definitive biography, but it is well written and tackles the subject in a refreshingly modern manner.

End-piece: it's very unlikely Miss Nightingale would ever have been called *Florence*. She was known by her family name by everyone, up to and including the commanders in the field, one of whom was Lord Scarlett, leading the successful Heavy Brigade, while Lord Raglan had overall command, and this included trying to explain the debacle afterwards known as ***The Charge of the Light Brigade,*** when over half those taking part were slaughtered by the well-positioned Russian guns that strafed the killing field renowned as Balaclava.

(2) Page 170. Line 22 ………. *'joining the crac'ach'.*

The word crac'ach is colloquial Welsh - approximating to the term 'nobs', used in the context of - 'where the nobs hang out' (usually without any sexual innuendo whatever). San Francisco's, Nob Hill would be the American social, if not geographical equivalent.

(3) Page 171. Line 38 ………. *'Marlin board'.*

The name given to a board fitted to the transom of power boats that are used primarily for sports fishing, with the object of providing a platform that the crew can stand on, 'outside' the vessel, when they are engaged on the task of either tagging or boating the billfish which they spend their time pursuing. This name is also occasionally applied to a similar board, fitted to the transom of sailing craft, but in this instance the platform is used as a convenient halfway house between the vessel and the deep blue sea (a nice place to lounge on, with your feet in the salt and an ice cold G & T in prospect).

(4) Page 172. Line 22 ………. *'Bluenose'.*

The term is a nickname for a person bred and born in Nova Scotia and is perhaps indicative of the harsh climate found in that part of the world. But the name was deliberately chosen for a very special schooner; this vessel was built by Nova Scotians to compete in the International Schooner Race, an event which came into being as a result of rivalry between the seafaring traditions found along the eastern seaboard of North America. The schooner *Bluenose* was designed by **William J. ROUE;** built in Lunenburg in 1921, and generally recognised as a superlative vessel, never beaten in a fairly organised boat-for-boat event.

(5) Page 174. Line 11 …. *'several Uncle Sams' (from the board of Sparkman & Stephens).*

When a seaman walks along a marina jetty (in this context, *any* marina jetty) it's only a matter of time before his eye is drawn to a yacht displaying the lines, layout, and rig which obviously means business, yet carries the graceful air most of us strive for, but not all of us achieve. And while this may sound a high-falutin' approach, to what seems to the uninitiated as 'just another vessel', to a grey old dog, it illustrates that yachting is a sport concerned with style, as well as substance. And that the people who understand this adage, are the ones who get the most from their boats and leave their indelible mark on the fleet.

The firm of *Sparkman & Stephens* was founded in the late 1920s when a partnership was formed between yacht broker **Drake SPARKMAN** and **Olin STEVENS**; a young yacht designer who was then engaged on the not altogether simple task of pulling himself up by his own boot straps. Shortly afterwards (and while he was still heaving away) Olin's father, Rod, Sr., and then his brother, Rod, Jr., joined the business, which ultimately came to dominate the international yachting scene, up to the middle 1970s.

The early years, although hard, were also encouraging, with the break through coming in 1929, after the Wall St crash, when Olin Stephens produced a set of lines which required 28,000 dollars of what remained of his father's venture capital, to turn into a vessel, built at *Minnefords Yard*, City Island, New York, where she was launched as (what some people thought at the time) a lightly built, narrow gutted yawl. But not long after, tied up as ***Dorade***, one of the most significant vessels ever to grace a slipway. During her shakedown season, this yacht, sailed by the *Stephens & Friends* team won her class in the 1930 **Bermuda Race.** In 1931, with the same crew she won the **transatlantic Race** (taking line honours by a two day margin). She then went on to win that season's **Fastnet Race**; won the Fastnet again in 1933, and on her return trip across the pond, easily broke the record for what was, for her, just another 3,000 mile ocean going hop.

Anyone interested in the history of Sparkman & Stephens should get hold of a copy of *The Best of the Best*, by **Francis KINNEY** and **Russell BOURNE**, published in the 'States by W.W.Norton in 1996. There is also a great deal of information in *Classic Boat* (issue 127, January '99) which features an article by Dan Houston talking to Olin Stephens (still going strong at 90 years of age) reminiscing on the firm which turned out over 2,000 superlative designs in over 70 innovative years. There is also Olin Stephens' fascinating autobiography, **All This and Sailing Too,** which can be obtained from the Mystic Seaport Bookstore, 47, Greenmanville Avenue, Mystic, CT 06355, USA. Tel: 800-331-2665 Fax: 860-572-5324.

(6) Page 175. Line 33 ………. *'beautifully balanced bimini'*.

The type of sun awning, usually an elegant design, sometimes of canvas, but now often composed of a glassfibre 'roof', supported on a highly polished stainless steel structure, deriving its name from the Bahamian island where the local vessels and later sports fishing boats adopted this useful device.

(7) Page 177. Line 27 ………. *'planked in Huon pine'*.

Not everyone may be familiar with *Dacrydium franklinii*, also known as Macquarie Pine, which is now difficult to come by. This amazing timber is light, white, durable, fragrant, easily wrought, stable, and insect resistant (so what more could a craftsman ask for?). But the few remaining trees of this magnificent species are being swept away by clear-felling loggers, in their drive for what they see as little more than the raw material they need to keep the woodchip mills in business.

A useful book in this field (which has been directly quoted here) is *A Glossary of Wood*, by **Thomas CORKHILL**, M.I.Struct.E, F.B.I.C.C. first published by Stobart Davies Ltd, London, in 1979.

(8) Page 177. Line 39 .... *'Kuru'*.

A neurological condition, typified by degeneration of the brain, found in the natives of New Guinea; thought to be brought about by the now outlawed custom of cannibalism (the brains of the victims of tribal conflict being a particularly prized delicacy) of interest because similar circumstances led to the spread of BSE (Bovine Spongiform Encephalopathy) in cattle, which in turn is involved in the spread of variant Creuzfeldt-Jacob disease.

(9) Page 179. Line 28 .... *'metacentric analysis'*.

A reference to the theory put forward by Engineer Rear-Admiral Alfred Turner RN who devised a mathematical approach to the problems involved with the behaviour of model yachts (his absorbing hobby) that are necessarily dependent on inbuilt directional stability to maintain a steady course, regardless of their angle of heel and the absence of a crew. This work was developed by Dr. **T. Harrison BUTLER** (1871-1945) who, although by profession an ophthalmic surgeon, was also an Honorary Member of the Institute of Naval Architects and made a name for himself by the quality of his designs, which were at the time usually long-keeled, round-bilged, and of relatively heavy displacement. The insight behind metacentric analysis is - the behaviour of a vessel can be predicted during the design stage, before the keel has been laid or a frame has been sawn. Vessels having a favourable analysis will enjoy directional stability, while those that are 'unfavourable' will turn out to be the dogs that gripe-up when heeled and are otherwise difficult to manage.

Dr. Butler's book *Cruising Yachts: Design and Performance* published by Robert Ross & Company in 1945 and issued as a 4th edition by Excellent Press in 1995 sets out both the theoretical and practical work involved, with this latest edition having a design supplement, complete with photographs and a biographical sketch of Dr Butler. But perhaps the average yachtie would be well-advised to have a damp cloth and a large brandy and soda handy (with the club steward within call) when contemplating the mathematics. But the proof of the pudding is in the eating. The 'Butler Boats' are still in demand, and still being built, much loved by their owners, who have formed a Harrison Butler Association, with the President being Mrs Joan Jardine-Brown (the good doctor's daughter) who is herself no mean hand with a draughtsman's pencil.

(10) Page 180. Line 23 ………. *'Paddy's hurricane'*.

Seagoing slang for a flat calm; commonly described as a breeze that 'whistles up and down the mast'. In days gone by (perhaps a more robust age) when a sailing vessel was becalmed, a rough old bosun would 'toss the mast off' with tallow and a leery glint to his eye in the expectation that Davy or the Man himself would relent and provide a favourable breeze. In our more decorous age (?) the crew may resort to scratching the mainmast with a fingernail, or just stick a knife in the stick (aka, a mast).

(11) Page 182. Line 15 ………. *'on his bulbous-nosed way to the dogs'*.

This is a follow-on to the previous line that mentions *'portrait of the artist as a young man'*. The title of a book by **James JOYCE** (1882-1941), the Irish writer, born in Dublin and educated at University College there.
   The talented lad who sets determinedly off to squander his gifts on his bulbous-nosed way to the dogs', is an eighteen word oblique requiem for **Dylan THOMAS** (1914-1953) the Anglo-Welsh poet who, although the term is no longer politically correct, can be described in this manner because although born in Wales, and writing from a Welsh background, was content to hold his own in English. To complete the reference, **DT** titled one of his stories, *Portrait of the Artist as a Young Dog*.
   Other work dates back to *Eighteen Poems* (1934); *Twenty Five Poems* (1936), and perhaps his best known work *Under Milk Wood* (1954). There was also an unfinished novel, *Adventures in the Skin Trade* (1955).

(12) Page 184. Line 19 ………. *'Queensland station.'*

The term used to describe a tract of land (& nothing to do with a railway) otherwise known in America as a 'ranch', with the term 'farm' not something that can be realistically applied to an area of land that is measured in hundreds of square miles, rather than the acres or hectares of a European agricultural holding.

(13) Page 184. Line 29………. *'how many stops you need from fifty'*.

Sue Hutchinson not only plays a fair hand of bridge and understands cricket, she accompanies her family when scuba-diving on the reef; well aware of the dangers involved with a too-rapid a return to the surface after spending time below.

(14) Page 186. Line 30 ………. *'broached'*.

As a nautical term (and in this context) it describes the action of a vessel, previously running relatively safely before a gale of wind and high seas, but then forced, by the adverse weather conditions, off course, so that she lies beam-on to the sea, and thus in danger of being swept fore and aft, with all this entails to the safety of vessel and crew.

(15) Page 188. Line 17………. *'dressed in a brief sarong'*.

The garment this lady favours (and favours her) has been incorrectly called a 'sarong'. It would be better described as a pareo, the sort of one-piece item which is worn as a sheath, and because it's tightly fitting has to be shorter than short in order to allow the wearer freedom of movement. The other thing of note is that she hasn't chosen the usual type of Gauguin floral print, but has opted for a geometrical design which shows off her voluptuous figure to far better effect. Not to put too fine a point on it (but why beat about the bush?) no matter what she's wearing, the gal's an absolute dish.

(16) Page 189. Line 19 ……. *'matching order for Jacob'*.

A reference to the 'coat of many colours' reputedly worn by Jacob. A brilliant eye-catching garment well-suited to Pierre's flamboyant personality.

JACOB: Hebrew patrriarch; one of the twin sons of Isaac and Rebecca, the shepherd ancestor of the 12 tribes of Israel. In the Koran he appears as *Ya'qub*, the brother of *Isahaq* (Isaac) and is regarded as a prophet.

Scripture declares that the brothers fought in their mother's womb, disputing who should be first-born, with Ya'qub allowing his sibling precedence in order to spare his mother's anquish.

The Hebrew version of events casts Jacob as a trickster - someone who supplants another.

(17) Page 190. Line 11 ………. *'Kenneth Clark's,* **Civilisation***'*.

Sir Kenneth (Mackenzie) CLARK (1903-1983), educated at Winchester and Trinity College, Oxford. After leaving university, he worked in Florence and later became an authority on art of the Italian Renaissance.

From 1931 to 1933 he was head of the department of fine art at the Ashmolean Museum; then director of the U.K. National Gallery (1934-1945), and professor of fine art at Oxford University (1946-1950). He was chairman of the U.K. Independent Television Authority (1954-1957).

His study of *Leonardo da Vinci* received world wide acclaim, and provided a counter-balance to the many, relatively populist volumes he published on his subject. His acknowledge stature was further enhanced by the television series, **Civilization**, which he wrote and directed. A work that was acknowledged as a brilliantly presented account of Man's artistic achievement.

He was appointed a life peer in 1969.

Ashmolean Museum: named after the English antiquary *Elias Ashmole* (1617-1692). He presented his collection of rarities (owing a great deal to *John Tradescant*) to Oxford University in 1677, and this acquisitive research forms the nucleus of what is now one of the foremost repositories of its type in the United Kingdom.

John Tradescant: English botanist (1570-1638), one of the earliest collectors of plants and natural history specimens. He was employed as a gardener by *Charles the First* (1600-1649) and later set up his own museum in Lambeth, London. His son John (1608-1662) carried on his father's work, which he then bequeathed to Elias Ashmole.

(18) Page 190. Line 13 ………. *'Gombrich's, Art & Illusion'*.

Sir Ernst GOMBRICH (1909-2001): born in Vienna and studied at the university there; but influenced by the behaviour of Nazi Germany towards the Jewish people, decided to emigrate to Britain, where he obtained a post at the Warburg Institute (1936), later rising to director and a professor of the history of classical artistic tradition (1959-1976).

During the second World War, as an accomplished linguist, he worked for the BBC Monitoring Service, and by way of recognition of the outstanding service he gave to his adoptive country, he received his knighthood (surely not before time) in 1972.

He published *The Story of Art* in 1950, and then *Art and Illusion* in 1960. The work presented a major advance in the study of the psychological aspects of pictorial representation. Two further books were *The Sense of Order* (1979), and *New Light on Old Masters* (1986).

(19) Page 190. Line 26 ……. *'dunnage'*.

In this context, the odds and ends of timber that are normally employed in the safe stowage of cargo aboard merchant vessels. Matting or even brushwood is sometimes used to protect merchandise from harm, by filling in the voids (preventing chafe) between the various items.

Thinner, more useful planks, are used to provide a layered separation between the cargo consigned to different ports, and it is one of these discarded items that's referred to in the text.

(20) Page 191. Line 23 ……. *'an unaccustomed twinge of the glums'*.

There has been a bit of an odd thing here, because when the skipper was bumming around the town (Post Officing, and so on) there's been a twitch of the old lonesome pine, which is rather strange in someone used to sailing by himself. But perhaps it's part of the *'what could have been'* syndrome, prompted by proximity to the seagoing family, happily cruising the world aboard the good ship *Out From Under*.

(21) Page 191. Line 29 …………… *'Dick Francis' horsey thrillers'*.

Richard Stanley FRANCIS (1920 - 2010) born in Surrey, England, but spent some of his early years visiting relations who were farming then in Pembrokeshire. After creating a reputation as an amateur jockey, he turned professional and enjoyed a successful career, but is perhaps best remembered for his unsuccessful Grand National ride in 1956, when aboard the Queen Mother's mount *Devon Loch*. The race was in the bag when, in an almost unprecedented accident, the horse collapsed (fell spread-eagled when barely 50 yards from the post). He retired the next year, despite being encouraged by the Queen Mum, *'don't worry about Devon Loch, Richard; that sort of thing is just the tough part of racing'*.

As it turned out, perhaps his finest years were ahead of him. He became a newspaper correspondent, then began writing 'thrillers' that drew largely and entertainingly on his racing background. His autobiography, *The Sport of Queens* was published in 1957. His many novels blazed a trail that included an Edgar Allan Poe Award, *Come to Grief, (1995);* and continued until, *To the Hilt,* (1996).

(22) Page 200. Line 13……. *'Tabarly'.*

The finest small boat seaman of his generation was born in Nantes, France, on July 24th, 1931, and inherited from his forebears an innate love of the sea which sustained him until, on June 13th 1998, while on passage from Benodet, in Brittany (bound for Fairlie in Scotland, in order to enter his yacht **Pen Duick** in a celebratory *'Fife'* regatta) he was swept overboard, when working to the nor'ard in not much more than a moderate breeze, 35 miles south west of St Anns Head, the landmark which defines the entrance to the West Wales port of Milford Haven.

He lost his life due to an unfortunate combination of circumstances.

The crew of the vessel were perhaps not as experienced as those usually shipped aboard the cutter, so it was the skipper who undertook the sail changes. A strong tide, combined with the breeze, had raised a lump of a sea in the Bristol Channel, and while the mainsail was being reefed the vessel lurched and the boat took charge. The accident occurred when Tabarly was alone on deck, in the middle of the night (0015 hrs French time; water temperature 11 degrees C.) and the crew lost sight of the man in the water; partly because he was not wearing a lifejacket, which would have been equipped with a pin-point light and a helpfully locating whistle. Having searched, but failed to recover their skipper, the crew resorted to flares and rockets, but there were no other vessels in the immdiate vicinity. Also, there was no serviceable radio transmitter on board, and it wasn't until daybreak that the yacht *Longobarda* was sighted, spoken-to, and she alerted the coastguard. Days later a body was hauled aboard a French trawler and identified as being that of the owner of the yacht *Pen Duick.*

Eric Marcel Guy TABARLY was a seaman in the very best Breton tradition. From boyhood he knew where his course lay, and as soon as he was able, he enrolled at the School of Marine Studies at Brest. When qualified, he served in the French Navy until, having won the 2nd single-handed transatlantic race from Plymouth to New York in 1964, in the record time of 27 days, sailing a specially designed and built *Pen Duick 2,* he decided to henceforth concentrate on small boat sailing.

It's worth recalling that for winning this particular race he was presented, as a serving naval officer, with the *immediate* award of the **Legion d'Honneur** by

General Charles de Gaulle. And not long after he had arrived in Newport, Rhode Island (when he had been flown back to France), a significant portion of the population of Paris turned out to provide their conquering hero with a tickertape welcome down the Champs Elysées.

Their faith was not misplaced. In 1967 Tabarly won *all* the main Royal Ocean Racing Club races (*Pen Duick 3*), including the prestige Fastnet Race. In the same year he was first over the line in the Sydney/Hobart race. In 1969 he won the San Fransico/Tokyo single-handed race (*Pen Duick 5*) in 39 days and 16 hours. He won the Los Angeles/Honolulu race (*Pen Duick 4*) in 8 days and 13 hours, beating the old *Ticonderoga* record by one clear day. In 1976 he won his second single-handed transatlantic race, sailing a vessel (*Pen Duick 6*) which would normally put to sea with a 10 man crew. In 1980, he broke *Atlantic's* 1905 transatlantic record by nearly 2 days, as skipper of the yacht *Paul Ricard*.

He announced his retirement from competitive racing in 1993, but was persuaded aboard the 60 ft open mono hull *Aquitaine Innovations,* and in 1997 won the Le Havre/Cartagena inaugural event. All the yachts he was involved with (not all of which he owned) were called *Pen Duick*. But he ended up where he started; with the first, and what he always thought was undoubtedly the best of them.

(23) Page 200. Line 19…….. '*Alain Gerbault's first book'*.

The French aviator, tennis player, sailor, and bon viveur who was prominent during the early 1920s; and at the time was a friend of the great Suzanne Lenglen. At the height of his fame he gave it all away, bought a boat, wandered about a bit, then set off on a single-handed circumnavigation (some people wondered why).

Ms Lenglen on the other hand, took to writing novels.

Suzanne LENGLEN (1899-1939) French tennis player, born in Compiègne; became famous by winning the women's world hard court singles championship in Paris at the age of 15. She was women's champion of France (1919-23), (1925-26), with her Wimbledon championships being: women's singles and doubles (1919-23, 1925), and the mixed doubles (1920, 1922, 1925). She won the singles and doubles gold medals at the 1920 Olympic Games; then became a professional in 1926. Perhaps the greatest tennis player of all time, and she inauugerated, amongst other things, a new fashion in female tennis attire.

(24) Page 201. Line 6………. '*probably knew Chichester'*.

Francis Charles CHICHESTER (1901-1972) English aviator and yachtsman, born in Barnstaple, Devon. He took part in the first solo transatlantic yacht race (1960) sailing his boat *Gipsy Moth* (named after the type of aircraft he used on a previous record-breaking flight). He deservedly won the Atlantic race, and later made a successful solo (one-stop) circumnavigation (1966-67) sailing *Gipsy Moth IV*, being awarded a knighthood on the completion of this voyage.

But one of the things he *didn't* do was inaugurate single-handed transatlantic yacht racing, by suggesting to Blondie Hasler that they *'race across the pond for a half-crown stake'*. This now well-established myth (which is still being promoted by people who should, and probably do, know better) is quite untrue. The race was Hasler's creation, and anyone who doubts this fact should consult Ewan Southby-Tailyour's well-researched biography entitled, *Blondie (ISBN 0 85052 516 0)* where the author sets out the real state of affairs.

Also, the author's re-written (2011 Edition) of *Sailing into Solitude,* (see the website www.valhowells.com) where the myth is effectively demolished.

And then the letter from Lt Commander Mike Richie, and an even more damning letter from Lt Colonel Ewen Southby-Tailyour, to the Secretary of the Royal Western Yacht Club of England sets out the case beyond any possible doubt.

(25) Page 203. Line 16………. *'zoot suit'*.

The type of flamboyant rig favoured by some New Yorkers during the 1950s, bearing a passing resemblance to a tail coat, but with heavily padded shoulders. The pants were high cut and tight enough to provide a show-off garment that was specifically designed to draw attention to the wearer.

(26) Page 207. Line 6 ………. *'Pol-Roget, Sir Winston Churchill'*.

Winston CHURCHILL had been a loyal supporter of this champagne house since 1908. A stance he maintained throughout his years in the political wilderness (between the two World Wars) and not only he, but European royalty and the beau monde generally, raised a glass of a fine Roget to mark the end of the conflict.

After the war, the directors of the firm (principally Madam Odett and Pol-Roget) arranged for Churchill to have a case of champagne, on his birthday, for the rest of his life (an act no doubt much appreciated by the great man). When Churchill died, the Pol-Roget family paid their respects by ordering that all bottles exported to England carry labels with a black edging, and years later (1984) the company launched its tête de cuvee champagne, *'Cuvée Sir Winston Churchill'*, with the intention of restricting its availability to members of the British Royal Family, and (most significantly) Churchill's descendants. However, it now seems that, at a price, it is more widely available, and it is still a very fine wine.

(27) Page 208. Line 10………. *'pink coat'*.

Commonly but incorrectly called a 'scarlet' hunting jacket. The term 'pink' derived from Mr Thomas Pink who was a tailor in London's Mayfair, in the later part of the 18th century. By all accounts he was the best tailor in London, specializing in gentlemen's hunting coats, and such was his reputation, it was considered a mark of discretion as well of affluence if a person could afford a Thomas Pink coat (giving rise to the expression, *in the pink),* still used today to describe someone in fine form, perhaps on top of the world.

(28) Page 208. Line 33.......... *'glamorous image of Rogers'.*

Ginger ROGERS: stage name of the American actress, born Virginia Katherine McMath (1911-1995) who formed a successful Hollywood partnership with Fred Astaire. As a dance team they were unrivalled, and from 1933 onward appeared in a number of films, including *Top Hat* (1935), *Swing Time* (1936), and *Shall We Dance* (1937).

Ms Rogers won an Oscar for her part in the film *Kitty Foyle* (1940) when she appeared as a solo artiste.

(29) Page 208. Line 34.......... *'toe-tapping part of Astaire'.*

Fred ASTAIRE: stage name of the American actor and dancer, born Frederick Austerlitz (1899-1987), who enjoyed a hugely successful career, which began in Vaudeville (appearing with his sister, who later married into the British aristocracy) and then with Ginger Rogers. After this partnership was discontinued, he teamed up with many of the leading actresses of the day, including Judy Garland in *Easter Parade* (1948).

He is generally recognised as being one of, indeed, perhaps *the* finest exponent of 'tap-dancing' routines; although note should be taken of the fact that there were a number of coloured Americans who, at the time, were undoubtedly his equal, but were unable to reap the rewards (humbugged by racial discrimination) to which they were certainly entitled, with **Leonard REED** being what could be descibed as a disgraceful example.

He (Reed) was born in a tent at Lightening Creek, Oklahoma, in 1907. His mother, who was half-black and half-Choctaw Cherokee Indian had been raped by his white father, and on her death, the two-year-old Leonard was raised by his great-grandmother.

When he was eleven years of age he was placed in a foster home, where he was abused by the staff, and no doubt partly as a result of this treatment, he rebelled, became unruly, and seemed headed for a reform school, but was saved by the headmaster of his high school, who generously offered to adopt him if it would save him from a custodial sentence.

Appreciating the opportunity offered, Reed worked part-time selling popcorn at a theatre in Kansas City. He became fascinated by what he saw, and before long (displaying astonishing natural ability) he had joined those who were performing on the stage.

His career prospered, and he became a highly-paid dancer, partly because he was light-skinned and so was able to appear at both black and white venues. However, in 1933, Reed's racial origins became public knowledge and he was forced to abandon white vaudeville (shunted into lower-paid work by the descriminatory practice of the age).

Not for long: he turned to production and choreography, working at the New York, *Cotton Club*, arranging music for artists of the calibre of Duke Ellington, Billie Holiday and Cab Calloway. He went on to manage the Appolo Theatre, in Harlem (a 20 year engagement) during which he developed as a songwriter, bandleader, and comedian. During the 1960s he was involved with record companies and, amongst others, launched the career of Dinah Washington and a host of other artists.

He acted for many years as Joe Louis's manager, arranging the former world heavyweight boxing champion's personal appearances. He also continued to give dancing lessons until well into his nineties.

He recieved a lifetime achievement award (American Music Awards) in the year 2000, and later recieved an honorary arts doctorate from Oklahoma City University.

He died on April 5th 2004.

(30) Page 209. Line 5.......... *'audition the part of Salome'*.

SALOME: the step-daughter of Herod Antipas (22 BC - c.40 AD) who was the son of Herod the Great (c.74 - 4 BC). She can be confidently described as a femme fatale because, prompted by her mother, she asked for, and got, the head of John the Baptist - served up on a platter. Oscar Wilde used her as one of the seminal characters in a play which, although written in French, was first produced on the London stage in 1905.

JOHN the BAPTIST: the prophet who baptised Jesus Christ. He was the son of the priest Zacharias and Elizabeth, the cousin of Mary, the mother of Jesus. Having denounced Herod Antipas for impropriety, he was imprisoned and later executed at the request of Salome, who was prompted by her mother to deploy her sexuality, in a way that perhaps amounted to rather more than the biblical 'tease', which we are led to believe persuaded Herod into acceding to a malevolent request.

(31) Page 211. Line 27.......... *'salmon . . . supposedly Spey'*.

A fish from the Scottish river Spey, which rises in the mountainous country of Inverness, and after flowing through that county and neighbouring Morayshire, enters the Moray Firth at Kingston, betwen the ports of Lossiemouth and Portknockie. The river has an enviable reputation concerning the quality of its stock.

(32) Page 213. Line 6.......... *'dance like Dervishes'*.

The word describes a wandering mendicant in Turkey and Persia.

Throughout Islam a 'dervish' is classed as a monk; while in Arabic-speaking countries the title 'fakir' is used to identify a similar Moslem order, which adopts poverty as one of its religious platforms, while embracing trance-inducing dances (whirling like Dervishes) in an attempt to heighten the mendicants religious experience. Perhaps a good example of how the modern scientific quest (to understand, not only *what* we think - but *how* we think) could have a bearing on some of Man's astonishing behaviour.

(33) Page 215. Line 21.......... *'embellish the chorus at the Folies Bergère'*.

The theatre established in Paris in 1869, which gained a reputation for the supposedly scandalus nature of its performances. The Holywood film industry was attracted to the concept of the *Follies* as a vehicle for its own high-kicking chorus lines, which probably reveal rather more than was on offer during the relatively staid Victorian era (because haven't frilly-knickers long-since bitten the dust?). But both ages display what amounts to a tempting façade; encouraging stage-door Johnnies then, and now, to stand in line, nursing their primed ambitions (eyes and wallets bulging).

(34) Page 216. Line 19.......... *'snagged round turn and two half-hitches'*.

A 'round turn and two half-hitches' is possibly the most common knot in seafaring usage. It is employed, amongst other things, to fasten a rope to a spar, or just about anything else.

When used in conjunction with the lifting of a spar, a complete round turn is cast on the spar, and finished-off with two half-hitches. The rope is then led, via an elevated block, to a secondary object (the drum of a winch) and after several round turns have been taken around the barrel of the winch, and the object lifted, the spare end of the rope is hitched to the standing part, which means, in this context, the piece of rope which leads from the winch to whatever has been hoisted, and then belayed (i.e. the spar).

One of the advantages of the round turn and two half-hitches is that, when the hitches are removed, it is possible ease the rope out (around the winch-drum) and in this way, safely lower the hoisted object down to where it is needed.

A 'snagged round turn' is a different animal.

The rope which leads from the spar has been inadvertently crossed *over* the 'turns' on the winch-drum, with the result that the rope is jammed, and until the weight is eased, it's impossible to lower away.

However, in dealing with Pierre, a snagged round turn, with or without the two half-hitches, is just the thing to keep the big-headed bugger in check.

(35) Page 216. Line 35.......... *'flashy English middle-class, with a supercilious accent'*.

It's worth noting (because it's true) that ninety-nine times out of a hundred, genuinely English upper-class types are far too polite to use a supercilious tone. But of course, this is also true of well-mannered people, of whatever class, anywhere in the world.

EMBARKED ON THE POND

I reckon there are two distinct groups of yachties to be found scattered about the bays and anchorages which indent the coast of Tenerife, and I've been lucky to find myself berthed between *Out From Under* and *Bouton de Rose,* because strolling about a marina doesn't tell you much about the vessels on display - you have to get close to them to find out which end of the fleet they represent - even then, appearances can be deceptive, and it takes time (together with a glass of wine perhaps?) to come to a reasonable judgement.

A significant proportion have journeyed south to escape the European winter, trickling down the Portuguese coast (others out of the Med, during the autumn months) to spend what used to be the off-season (December through to March) lounged in the tropic sun. Then, when they judge the New Year sufficiently advanced, these well feathered types leave the bird-caged islands and migrate once more, to grace the gilded perches provided by the likes of Cannes and Monte Carlo (they should have it so tough).

Then there's another group, who may be equally wealthy, but not quite so determinedly idle, who use Tenerife and the surrounding islands as a staging post - gathering in the marinas and yacht harbours with another end in view.

They plan to leave the eastern seaboard, and head for the Caribbean, two thousand four hundred miles to the west'ard. But those wet and windy miles are all down hill, so even the smallest vessel, competently managed, can make the transition from the Old World to the New. Provide the entry in the vessel's log, which will enable her skipper, years later, lounged before the homestead fire, grog in hand, with adoring youngsters gathered at his slipper'd feet, to spin an old man's tale of oceans crossed, suitably embellished, and carefully avoiding his banker's and his in-laws sad critique, which is all too often concerned with what it all cost, and how that money could have been *so* much better spent.

While I'm pottering about my own boat (wasting my time and my money?) I can see that aboard the good ship *Out From Under,* although

Zoe and Zee's forenoons still revolve around the tutorials insisted on by their conscientious parents, there's an addition to their afternoon curriculum, which manifests itself in attention to shipboard maintenance; supervised by Richard Hutchinson, as skipper of the vessel, but undertaken by young David and the twins, who swarm about the rigging with the confidence of a brace of chattering baboons. Swapping seamanlike comments with each other, as they are hauled aloft by their brother in a bosun's chair, [1] in order to check the masthead fittings and otherwise cast an eye over items that, if they gave way during an ocean passage, would hazard the safety of the vessel.

Having checked the standing rigging, these young, but nevertheless experienced seamen, examine all the running gear - the halyards, lifts, guys, pennants, inhauls and outhauls - the cat's cradle of lines and lanyards the modern yacht requires in order to keep the show on the road.

And when these bits and pieces have been attended to, there's still plenty left for these industrious youngsters to deal with, because amongst a host of other tasks, the canvas must be checked - the spare sails unbagged and examined for signs of chafe - doubtful places in both wardrobes being either replaced, patched, or occasionally discarded.

This is David's responsibility, because Zoe and Zee find the palm and needle work difficult to cope with, as their delicate fingers haven't reached the stage where they can be employed as marlinspikes, and their thumbs are not robust enough to be forced through the lay of a rope, playing the role of a lignum vitae fid. But it's only a matter of time before they will have mastered what they look on now as just another learning curve of a task.

While this busy scene is underway (and it's a non-stop, afternoon to evening job, which goes on for day after sun toiling day) the crew of *Bouton de Rose* are doing what they can to embellish *their* beautiful yacht.

Fifi is working up a tan, with not a pale patch *anywhere*.

Collette is slightly more discreet, but the end result is the same.

Pierre has hired a longshoreman, a tough-as-teak old Spaniard, who arrives every morning just before dawn, and tries not to disturb the crew as he hoses down the deck and polishes the brass.

Having taken care of these substantial items, he slips ashore to do the day's perishable shopping.

Then returns in plenty of time to prepare the midday meal, which he serves in the freshly furbished saloon (another of his little chores) having put an elaborate display of cheese dips and crackers out on the cockpit table - after re-rigging the aftdeck awning, while at the same time making sure the ice bucket is topped up and handily placed in the shade.

There's nothing untoward about this division of (menial ?) labour.

The longshoreman is glad of the job.

Pierre also employs a professional rigger, to take care of *Bouton de Rose* during the lay-up periods, when the vessel is given a thorough refit.

The varnish brought up to scratch.

The hull scrubbed and antifouled.

The diesel serviced - filters, injectors, and all oils changed, in order that when Collette returns from her twice yearly overseas trips, [2] and Pierre has spent his usual month at the 'tables' (he has special entrée to the glittering casinos); [3] when the owners eventually rejoin their yacht, they do so secure in the knowledge she's in tip-top condition and ready to venture to any part of the seven seas that's not too far from home.

So there does seem to be a difference in the manner in which the vessels we're lying between are managed.

But nobody should jump to the conclusion that I look down on the way that Pierre, or Collette, organise the time they spend either ashore or afloat. Because I'm firmly of the opinion that everyone should be allowed to paddle his, or her, canoe in the manner which suits them best. And if it comes down to it, I would have to admit there are one or two decorative items aboard *Bouton de Rose* that I could find a place for, aboard my old tub, should I be so lucky.

Nevertheless, beggars can't be choosers.

I'm grateful for the odd crumb that falls from the rich man's table, even if I have to acknowledge I'm too old to have any chance of making the most of exciting opportunities (young David's fortunate prerogative), and in any case, I have my own work schedule to consider.

The days are ticking by, and now the North Atlantic hurricane season has run its course, [4] the time of departure from Tenerife, coupled with the planned date of arrival at Barbados, has got to be decided, with this being dependent, not only on the day you sail, more on the size of vessel you own.

All this (well, some of it) has been discussed with Sue and Richard Hutchinson, and we've worked out, that if we want to be anchored off Barbados before Christmas, *they* should make their departure not later than the 1st of December; while I should sail well before that date, because they have the larger vessel, and will be putting in daily runs that'll easily exceed anything I'll be able to accomplish.

The other thing exercising our collective minds, is the feasibility or otherwise of climbing *Teide,* before we set off across the pond.

We are all agreed it would be positively criminal to visit Tenerife, and then swan off without getting to the top of a volcano that's twelve thousand feet above sea level - quite a pile of cinders.

Indeed, it's one of the attractions the tourist brochures never fail to mention. In contrast to the fact that all too often there's a layer of cloud swirling round the summit - so even if you were up, there there's not a lot to be seen.

Not to worry, we yachties are a patient lot, and have plenty of things to fill our idle days, until the weather pattern provides the window of opportunity which doesn't come too often.

I'm busy enough, vittlin' ship, with this being just an old-fashioned way of describing the touring of markets for own-brand bargains and date-doubtful items that help the exchequer somewhat. Although how a farmer in, say, the American mid-west can plough, cultivate, sow, and tend a crop of beans, harvest them, see them processed and canned, then transported half-way round the world and displayed on the local supermarket shelf - all for 9 pence Sterling a pop - beats the bejeeber's out of me.

Yet it doesn't stop me buying the stuff.

Tins of cling peaches (400g) for *ten* pence.

Beautiful tomatoes, all the way from Bulgaria, for *eight* pence a 400g tin.

A *kilo* of flour for 12 pence (usually 75 pence or more).

These are crazy prices - even if they are loss leaders - yet all an impecunious yachtie can do is thank his lucky stars, load the trolley, and cart the loot back to his boat.

However, vittlin' ship isn't accomplished by just one trip to the town.

The fresh end of the locker also needs attention.

Spuds keep well, so do onions, and some of the local varieties are mild enough to be eaten as apples, should the spirit move you.

There are plenty of carrots on display. A bit of a doubtful item, as they're O.K. for maybe ten days or so, but after that, especially in a hothouse marine environment, you end up with a bag of rubbery limp dicks which are not much good for a salad.

There's plenty of lettuce about, green peppers, red peppers, beans, apples, oranges, kiwifruit, bananas.

You name it - and there it is.

So how *can* it be - so many hundreds of millions are starving?

In a boat without an engine, the lack of refrigeration *is* a limiting factor.

You can forget about butter and meat (as we all too conveniently and quite disgracefully do, with the world's still starving millions?).

But the pot-bellied grunt [5] is worth his place, and (instead of the groans of empty-bellied anguish) I can smell those smoky rashers sizzling, with three sunny-side-up's swilling round the frypan, on my primus, as that useful item's *hissing*.

While the housekeeping's been going on (and regardless of the fact that we have let our priorities get unforgivably awry) time's been ticking by.

The days roll on.

But there hasn't been the break in the cloud that will enable us to make the dash to the top of Teide, so we've fitted in a few trips to other parts of the island, and in this regard, Pierre has turned up trumps.

He's hired a car, and when the Captain of *Bouton de Rose* isn't scooting about, meeting and entertaining high-powered friends, the rest of us pile in and make use of the liberating wheels.

This includes a memorable trip to the north-eastern corner of the island, to have a look at the old Spanish quarter, which turns out to be its usual charmingly white-washed self.

Cobbled alleyways.

Tiled roofs.

Shaded doorways.

Eye-catching blooms cascading down cast iron balconies.

An elderly Spanish lady (calm, upright) wearing a down to the wrists and ankles, dignified taffeta dress.

A long way (a light year) from the brown-arsed sunbathers lounging in bare-breasted rows on the tourist beaches, which are not all that far from the marina where we are patiently, or impatiently waiting (depends which way you're heading).

The twins have got the job of monitoring the weather - usually hot and sunny, with very little cover over the island - with the exception of Teide which has, day after blistering day, its usual bank of cloud swirling round the mountain.

So it's beginning to look as if we'll have to abandon the excursion, and that's a shame, because twelve thousand feet, *is* twelve thousand feet (actually 3,717 metres) and I reckon, on a clear day, we would have been able to see Gomera, the next in line of the Canaries, which is only about 25 miles away to the west'ard, while La Palma is sixty three miles off in a nor'westerly direction.

Then, quite unexpectedly, we get the nod that tomorrow may be one of the special days when *Pico de Teide* is going to be cloud free.

Just the sort of day to put Plan B into operation.

What we originally decided to do, (Plan A), was use the hired wheels to get us to the point where the cable car takes off for the top of the mountain. But at the last moment (late at night, and after a few drinks) Pierre decides he would much prefer to *climb* Teide, and issues a challenge to the rest of us, which I have a rush of bubbles to the head and almost accept. Then commonsense prevails (prompted by sensible Sue) and what's going to happen now is (Plan B): Richard's going to drive Pierre, Fifi, and David to the hike-off point, at some unearthly hour in the morning.

When he's attended to that little chore, he'll come back, and after the timid types have enjoyed a sensible breakfast, followed by an early lunch, take us to the cable station - and should we be able to get *on* one of the no doubt busy cars, and Pierre and company survive the hike, we can all meet at the top of Teide. Then, after we've surveyed the world, and acknowledged Pierre's mountaineering achievement, retire in triumph to the near-summit restaurant, where Pierre has, thoughtful as ever, booked a hard-to-get table.

That's the plan.

I'm not altogether happy with it, because it does seem to have downgraded some of us to second echelon types (who wants to be classified as a geriatric old prat?). But the more sensible complaint is, I'm sure I would have enjoyed the hike (if I'd been able to make it) as it would have provided an opportunity to view more of the flora, the display of flowers. [6] The astonishing variety of plants, you can't help noticing when strolling round this island.

But who can turn the clock back?

When we've got to the cable car station, and are able to see the extent of twelve thousand foot Teide, I must say I'm relieved it's David, Fifi, and Pierre who are tramping up - what I am sure they will think an *endless* slope, long before they get anywhere near the summit.

Even from the fore-shortening elevation of the swaying cable car, it looks an extraordinary way from the bottom to the top, and a stomach-lurching drop, from the window of the car, to the terrain we're traversing (when it's actually only a few hundred feet) nevertheless, Collette looks relieved when we've made the ascent.

The steel and plastic bubble we're embarked in stops swaying, and she can step out on dry land - very dry land, as the cone of this volcano, as I suppose of many another, is composed of volcanic gunk of one abrasive sort or another, and whatever rain falls, does so mostly on the lower slopes, so this pile of crinkled cinders seldom gets its head wet.

We are all glad to have arrived.

The twins are ecstatic with this scaled-up version of another trip to the masthead, in something more comfortable than a bosun's chair.

Sue has taken the whole thing in her stride, as can be expected of someone who spent years tramping about the head-hunting highlands of the sweating New Guinea rainforests.

And Richard?

The skipper of *Out From Under* is his usual cool and competent self; yet does seem to be harbouring some sort of an amusing thought, because it seems he's unable to keep the give-away gleam of private humour out of his bespectacled eyes.

The mountain is magnificent. [7]

The *sense of elevation,* may sound a pathetic way of putting it, but unless you're in cahoots with, and can hitch a ride on a wedge-tailed eagle, there's nothing quite like being cranked up to a point three thousand, seven hundred and seventeen metres above the valley floor (a bit of an exaggeration, as we're *only* 12 thousand feet above *sea* level).

We're not alone up here. The old cableway (no doubt well maintained) might seem slow, nevertheless, it's delivering scores of people to the top of Teide, some of whom are tourists (trainers, grubby jeans, tatty lightweight anoraks).

There are others, who are obviously locals. Families with mums and dads in their Sunday best; the children dressed in traditional costume.

Little boys in knickerbockers.

Button-eyed girls; shy seven or eight year olds in velvet dresses, set off with lace trimmings and silver buckled shoes (I guess it could be some sort of a religious day out), a local festival of the soul, paying tribute to the magnificence of nature and the munificence of God (or should this be the other way about?).

Since disembarked from the cable car, we've had a bit of a chat about what we should do, because we're still not at the top of Teide (the hoist terminates a hundred foot below the summit), and agree it would be churlish to move on before Pierre, Fifi and David arrive. After all, they will have *slogged* their way up, so it's a question now, of keeping an eye open for our hikers, amid the groups of other people who are also riding Shank's pony. [8]

Richard has brought his binoculars, and is squatting on his haunches, keeping the seat of his pants clean, scanning the path and the groups of hikers who are moving painstakingly towards us. He can't pick out our party immediately, but we've only been waiting about twenty minutes before he indicates they're in sight (quite good timing really).

And now Richard's not only smiling to himself; he has a broad grin spread across his features.

This is a bit of a tease, and I can't help asking him (knowing what he thinks of the skipper of *Bouton de Rose* as a role-model for his children).

'What's so funny Richard?'

'Has Pierre broken a leg?'

But all this gets is another broad grin, and the mean old devil won't let me look through his binoculars (can't blame him for that). I can't stand other people using *my* optics (to the point where I tape the eyepieces to stop them adjusting the focus), so it's a question now of being patient, and waiting for our mountain-slogging mob to arrive.

There's plenty to see while we're waiting.

Teide sweeps down to a vast cauldron (Las Cañadas). Extending outward, there's an encircling ridge, split by ravines that lead down to the sea, but we can't see all of it from where we're standing.

What we can see is breathtaking, grabs the eye with the splendour of it all, allowing David, Fifi, and Pierre to reach our position unannounced; at least, as far as I'm concerned, because I've been totally absorbed with the view.

Now our party *has* arrived, I can see what Richard's been smiling about.

Pierre has dressed for the occasion; (from the soles up), sports a pair of brown leather, highly-polished hobnailed boots. I think I've mentioned before, he possesses a good pair of legs and footballer's knees, so his short thigh-hugging lederhosen and smart knee-length socks are well enough displayed.

Beneath his flecked oatmeal mountaineering jacket (it matches the socks, and his shirt, and has buttons that equate with the boots) is a dark green velvet waistcoat, having another row of colour-matched buttons.

He's got a Tyrolean hat on his head, which has a band of leather that's been cut from the same hide that provided the buttons and boots. And this hat has a feather - all of eighteen inches long, which exactly matches his dark-green velvet waistcoat.

(wait for it: we ain't finished yet - because neither has he)

Pierre's puffing a bit, and he's leaning on an alpenstock - a built for the business, genuine steel-tipped article.

This five-foot staff has been embellished with an engraved silver band, and sports an elaborately carved ram's horn headpiece. On the middle finger of the hand that's grasping the alpenstock, there glints a silver (or could be platinum-set) opal. The biggest dressed and polished stone, of that sort, I've ever seen in the whole of my wandering life.

(don't go away, because I've just noticed another nice touch).

Pierre's knee-length oatmeal socks are kept up by garters, displaying swallow-tail ribbons, Boy Scout style, and these ribbons are just the shade of green which enhances the outfit's carefully worked motif.

Taking one thing with another, I suppose you could say this is an eye-catching get-up, and then go on to admit it comes close to being slightly over the top. But Pierre seems pleased with it, and he's also delighted we've done the decent thing, and not ventured to the summit of Teide without him ....

So he can now lead the way, having got his breath back, marching up the crowded path leading from the cable car terminal to the top of the volcano.

There are other people on this narrow track, and ordinarily I suppose we would have to take our turn, and keep in the slowly-moving file. However, this isn't an ordinary day, and Pierre is playing his part as an out of the ordinary person, because the people in front seem to know something's happening behind in the queue (when they look astern, there's not only a recognisable sense of occasion, but a stepping back). A polite moving aside, which allows our Leader to pass through the hoi polloi and stride majestically to the top of the mountain.

We've been lucky with the weather.

The upper atmosphere is crisp and clear, and when you haul your eye to the west'ard - there's Gomera, so near you might fancy shying a rock at it.

Further away to the nor'west - the outline of La Palma, as a grey smudge merging with a sky that seems quite content with just blu'ing up the background.

There's a light nor'easterly air, puffing a bit stronger now and then, and when you look towards Las Cañadas, there are wisps of freshly-forming cloud obscuring the view. A sure indication there could be a change of weather in the offing. In any case, we can't stay long, because there are lots of people moving up the path, so as soon as Pierre's had his photograph taken ....

Not as popinjay, but patriarch. Moses, leaning on his staff, bare-headed, looking westward, a jewelled hand shading eyes that are searching now for Canaan. [9]

After this little scene's been played out, we do the correct thing, and make room for those kind folk who had generously moved aside for us.

Now we've walked back down the path, we can see the cable car restaurant is bulging at the seams; if Pierre hadn't had the foresight to make a reservation, we would never get in; as it is, we have to wait while he makes his number with the staff. Not all that easy to accomplish in the scrum, but the alpenstock and Tyrolean hat do help, to say nothing of the feather, and we are all glad when it's been sorted out and we're seated at our table.

A drink of some sort seems called for, and Richard and I start asking everyone what they'd like.

Tea?

Coffee?

Lemonade for the twins?

It's all a waste of time, because Pierre has previously ordered champagne.

The bubbly arrives, the pops go off, and our Leader toasts us - very much in the manner Hillary would have employed on Everest, [10] if he'd had more of an audience than just Tensing to register his undoubted sense of achievement.

It's getting on late in the afternoon, and as I don't particularly want to get involved with another of Pierre's machinations, I'm pleased when Richard Hutchinson broaches the subject of departing Tenerife.

'When do you think you'll sail, Val?'

The others are all gassing away.

Pierre has a three-cornered conversation going with Sue and Collette.

Zoe and Zee are playing some sort of game, which involves clenched or open fingers and much fist-banging on the table top (Sue's already told them to tone it down a bit).

David is involved with Fifi, discussing some artistic question or other; yet with it all, it's a well satisfied group of people who are, without exception, delighted with the way the day's turned out.

There's already been talk of an evening ashore, at what has now become Pierre's favourite restaurant, so Richard is surprised when I tell him I'm going to sail as soon as we get back to the marina.

'You mean tonight?'

'It's going to be getting towards dark before we get back, and you've surely got something to do about the boat.'

'No: I'm ready Mate, and this evening seems as good a time as any.'

To be absolutely honest, I'm being a bit awkward. I should have told the others I long ago decided to sail as soon as we've climbed Teide; that I've been quietly making the necessary arrangements.

Visiting the Port Captain's office for a clearance.

Making sure the water jugs are topped up.

Buying yet more sardines.

Keeping an eye open for more marked-down items.

All the important bits and pieces an impecunious old dog attends to, before he sets off on an ocean passage.

When the news of my imminent departure spreads around the group (takes about five seconds flat) there's much um'ing and ah'ing about the advisability of what appears, to them, to be a precipitate departure. Pierre, particularly, seems distinctly put out, and tells me he has planned a farewell party (I don't like to tell him that's another reason for leaving). Anyway, it's not long before we're discussing how we're going to get back to the marina.

The salient point is, we can't all get into the hire-car that's been left parked at the bottom of the mountain.

There is some talk of making two journeys, but this seems unnecessary, because there's a bus service; and if all fails, we could call for a taxi.

The upshot is - Pierre and Collette, together with Sue, Richard, and the twins, will go back in the car; leaving Fifi, David, and myself to make our own arrangements.

Suits me, the strap-hanging ride in the crowded bus is nowhere near a hardship, and Fifi and David are very good company. He's entranced with her; all I've got to do is keep my mouth shut and listen to lovebirds coo (keeps you young, don't it?).

The bus ride doesn't take long, yet by the time we've reached the marina, we're into twilight, and there's another reproach from Pierre, who still thinks I should put off my departure 'at least until tomorrow morning, Val.'

'How are you going to get out of the berth?'

'The wind is blowing from the wrong direction.'

That's true: yet it's the same old breeze which has been blowing, more or less out of the same old quarter, since Adam was a tousle-haired boy, so there's not much point in hoping this evening's air will do anything other than stay anchored in same old nor'easterly quadrant - for the next eon or so.

'And there's another thing, Val; we haven't got our dinghy in the water, so we can't give you a tow - '*can't* you leave it 'til tomorrow morning?'

This is another way of saying he doesn't want to dig his inflatable out of the locker, pump it up, launch it, and rig the outboard; then spend a couple of hours towing an unlit vessel a mile or so offshore, in order to get me well clear of the island.

'No worries, Pierre. I've already fixed a tow; my mate Pedro's going to bring his boat around, just after eight o'clock.'

'When did you arrange that?'

'And who the devil is Pedro?'

'He's the guy you hired to work aboard *Bouton de Rose.'*

'No he's not; that old man's name is Fernando, and I don't think he owns a boathook, let alone a boat.'

'You're way off-beam about your helper, Pierre. His name is Jose Fernando César Sarrionandia, known to his friends as Pedro, partly because he's a fisherman; and he certainly *does* own a boat.'

I can see Pierre's a bit nettled, and I can't say I blame him. Nevertheless I don't feel obliged to keep him informed of who I talk to when he's away from the marina, usually lounged on the beach. As a matter of fact, old Pedro and I, over a cup of coffee, sometimes with a tot in it, have found we've got a few things in common. I've done some fishing (just a bit of crabbing and lobstering). Of the three of his sons who are trawler skippers, two are fishing out of Vigo, while the other, not only skippers, but owns a flag of adoption trawler, now working out of the West Wales port of Milford, which just happens to be my home patch.

However, there's not much point in going into the ins and outs of who you know, and in what regard you hold them. As far as I'm concerned, Sarrionandia and his salt are people who have earned and deserve respect, while ....

Anyway, time's tickin' on, and if I want to get everything shipshape, I'd better get my arse into gear, because there are several things to take care of before leaving the marina.

Sails out of the locker and hanked on; while the running poles I'll be using are far better heeled-up and rigged here, in the shelter of the basin, making sure that when we're clear of the breakwater, it's just a question of topping them and getting the white stuff up.

I've also got to re-rig the self-steering vane, and reset the pendulum blade, which I unshipped when we moored stern to the jetty.

These are not major items, and don't present a problem; neither does saying cheerio to *Out From Under,* because we'll be meeting up again later in Barbados.

What *is* tricky - is taking leave of *Bouton de Rose.*

You can't just up-sticks and slope off with not much more than a kiss my arse of a wave. For one thing, I've become rather fond of Fifi (in a fatherly way, of course). And Collette is very much a person in her own right; even Pierre has saving graces (generous to a fault) so I've been scratching my head to think of something to give - as individual, but similar gifts to three people, all of whom seem well supplied with worldly goods of one delectable sort or another.

After several false starts, I've come up with the idea of giving them something I'm pretty sure they wouldn't have been offered before.

For several years I've been hording a few sperm whale teeth.

These are not the molars the skilful lads of old used for their scrimshaw work, [11] but the much smaller front teeth, about four inches long and a bit less in circumference; even so, they polish up well and I did initially intend to engrave (rather a grand way of describing scratching with a knife point) the name of my boat on these bits of ivory. Then I thought this not inclusive enough, and what I've ended up with are three teeth, with *Teide* etched and inked on 'em, together with the date on which we all got to the top of the cinders.

Best I can do I'm afraid. But they seem pleased with their gifts, while I'm tickled by the fact that they haven't got anything to pass on from their end of the counter. Apart from, of course, Pierre, who presents me with an autographed photograph of himself, professionally executed, and expensively mounted and framed.

Collette gives me her visiting card; also well upmarket, and carrying her smart Montmartre address (or am I wrong about this, and Bohemia ain't what it used to be?).

Fifi - takes a long look at her gift: wants to know where I got it.

Who killed the whale?

Aren't they an endangered species?

Yet seems delighted; gives me a sloppy kiss and the address of her agent.

'You must come an' see me in a show, Valenteen, next time you 'ar in Paris.'

The thought does occur, that it's unlikely I'll see more (or even as much of her) on the stage, than I've already seen of her on the boat; nevertheless, she's a nice kid and I certainly will take 'er up on 'er offaire.

That leaves *Out From Under:* no problem regarding gifts, but apart from a straightforward - 'I'll see you later,' (which Australians also use when they know damned well they're *never* going to see you again), there's something aboard the vessel I want to see before we cast off from the jetty.

This has come about because Fifi can't keep her mouth shut (some idiot might say that she can't keep her legs together either), but that's untrue, as she's actually very selective - even if enthusiastic. But I know David's been working on a portrait, and if I don't see it now, when it's still on the easel, I may not have the chance again.

This means it's a question of going aboard *Out From Under*, yacking away for a while, and then try and manoeuvre David into showing me his work.

It's not all that difficult.

The twins' cabin is up for'ard, opposite David's studio, and I can use the excuse that I want to wish them goodnight.

They're absolutely tuckered out, have been packed off to their bunks early by their mother, so after I've played Uncle, all I've got to say is 'what are you working on now David?' (while looking pointedly at the door to his cabin).

I don't know if he's peeved or pleased - more likely the latter I think, because he's given me a shy smile, as he opens the door and invites me to follow him in.

His easel is centre-stage, and there's work in progress mounted on it.

I can't see what it is, because there's the usual front cloth, and I have to wait until David gives me another tentative smile, and a sizing me up look, before he lifts the cloth and I can see what he's been working on.

It's a portrait of Fifi, developed as a stunning watercolour, much larger than you would expect from the choice of medium.

The composition is slightly oblique, upper torso, nude, with the sitter in the act of putting up her hair.

David's made a marvellous job of dealing with the problems involved with angular elbows; has put the pose to good use, framed the subject's face to excellent effect.

She's beautiful; the raised arms have tautened breasts that didn't need tautening, and her nipples are puckered up and prominent.

She's smiling; challenging the artist, eyes blazing, with that age-old look few of us can resist (David certainly hasn't) and the viewer is left in little doubt, that the artist's brush is not all that's been used to prompt the flood of emotion which is the disturbing feature of this uninhibited portrait.

There's not a lot I can say (who am I to pass comment?), yet I've got to say something.

'It's magnificent, David: are you going to give it to her?'

I don't think the thought has crossed his mind - judging by the startled look he gives me. But he makes a bit of time for himself, by replacing the dust sheet over the work.

'Anyway, David,' (says I, to help him out), 'if you ever decide to sell, please keep me in mind.' (nothing less than a daft remark) because I know damned well he's never going to part with it. And even if he was forced to, I'll never be able to afford it.

The rest of the time spent aboard *Out From Under*, and it's only a few minutes, is taken up by yachtie talk with Richard (when they're going to sail, and so on). Then Sue springs a very nice surprise, by giving me a tupperware box of sandwiches and a stainless steel thermos flask of coffee, knowing I'll not want to be bothered with cooking on this particular evening - and she's going to get the hardware back in Barbados.

Pedro's on time: his boat is one of those small, high-prowed, low on freeboard, wooden-built inshore fishing vessels I noticed when entering this marina (remember the early morning approach?); the diesel thumpers we heard miles away?

I know he's just had his boat re-engined, and instead of the old-fashioned single-cylinder unit, he's got a brand new twin-cylinder Japanese motor which provides twice the power, with half the weight, and a lot less vibration.

And that's not the end of it, because he's also splashed out on a variable-pitch propeller, in order that he can just trickle along, which is handy sometimes in certain trolling conditions.

Taking one thing with another, he's as happy as a kid with a new toy, and not a bit upset that he had to defray the larger than anticipated expense by taking odd jobs about the waterfront, while his boat was being worked on in the shipyard.

There's no question of having to tell Pedro what I want him to do.

After I've let go *Out From Under* and *Bouton de Rose*, he's got a line aboard, hanging off as I pull our old tub for'ard, recovering chain, and weighing anchor.

While I'm about this task, he comes alongside and couples our fender'd craft together, in order that he can keep the two boats under control as I bucket-up and wash down the ground tackle, prior to stowing it below.

We're only a few feet from *B de R* and *O from U*, and there is a bit of light-hearted banter going on, ending with wishes of 'bon voyage,' 'see you in Barbados,' 'don't forget to come to Paree, cherie' (no fear of that); then we're leaving the marina, being towed by - 'that old man,' (makes two of us) and his pride and joy of a shell.

Taking your towed-out departure at night is a doddle of a job.

One minute, you're inside the basin, conscious of jetty lights and shadowed rows of stern-to yachts, with indistinct friends waving and shouting goodbye.

Then you've left the marina, and moved into the channel formed by the outer mole and the shoreline.

In another minute, the yachts are no longer visible, and all you can hear is the rumble of diesel accompanied by the occasional niff of exhaust.

As you get further offshore, you move out of the wind shadow offered by the breakwater.

The breeze picks up a bit (no more niff), and it's time to give Pedro a flash on the lamp, to let him know, that with this weight of an air, we can let go the tow any time we like (but before I do, I'm going to set up the port-hand running pole, and get a headsail hoisted), making sure that after we've slipped the warp, we can jog along under our own steam.

Now he's free, and recovered his line, Pedro's making a sweep out to starboard, in order to come up on our quarter, positioning his vessel close-aboard, so he can hand me a packet - 'from my esposa.' (he *says*), then it's just a question of 'adiós amigo; I'll see you next time round.' [12] and he's sheering-off, turning through nor'ard - tootling his way back towards the harbour entrance.

It's been as near as I can get to a low-key departure.

Just what the doctor ordered.

No pre-embarkation partying.

And after a headache-free glance at the shoreside lights, and a careful look round the rest of the horizon, particularly to the west'ard, it's just a question of setting up the self-steering gear, letting the windvane weathercock, while I line her up on west sou'west. And having done that, latching in the pendulum-servo, in order that Blondie can take charge of the vessel. [13]

I'm not worried by the prospect of a night spent mostly in the cockpit.

It's the sensible thing to do, because there could be serious shipping about, and there's always the prospect of a trawler - not fishing, maybe on passage from - who knows where, to somewhere near the other place.

The other thing to avoid is the island of Gomera, which is about twenty miles off to the west'ard. Then there's Hierro, another forty or fifty miles in the same direction; but if we make good west sou'west, with nothing to starboard, we'll pass clear of both those places.

Sue's sandwiches turn out to be fowl, with a mayonnaise sauce (yum, *really* yum), even if the chook could have done with a little more salt.

The parcel from Pedro contains chocolate (the dark, rich, Belgian stuff), so with the flask of coffee, I've got plenty to chomp on, and it's only the matter of getting a sweater and smock and we'll be very well foddered and rigged.

It's a fine night.

As we move away from the island the breeze is picking up, and it's a question of deciding how much canvas we need - then how we're going to set it.

We're not in a hurry.

It's just into the third week of November, so we should be safe from the big blows.

And there's no hurry about arriving at Barbados (provided we're there well before Christmas), so we've got any amount of time to cover 2,400 miles.

This means that a round 'ton', made good every day, should do the job nicely. But there are several things involved here, and the daily run is only one of them - I'm more concerned with the way we're going to handle the passage.

I've been looking forward to this trip for years.

For those of us concerned with mucking about in boats, it's just about *the* classic occasion.

Plenty of sea room.

Any amount of favourable wind.

An interesting landfall, at the end of what promises to be an exiting downhill sleigh ride.

All the time in the world to enjoy the experience, and the fact that we're in the tropics is another thing in it's favour.

Previously, I've indulged in Atlantic jaunts with and without crew, with and without engines, with and without radio transmitters of one expensive sort or another.

Sailing west.

Sailing east.

With the upshot of my north-about, freeze your balls off experience being, I'm looking forward to a lounge in the sun, while we make this, should be a fall-off-the-log, trade wind transition, from the Old World to the New.

Yet how we handle the tub is important.

Have you ever ridden a horse?

This may sound an odd sort of question, in these particular circumstances. But as a matter of fact, our old nag (and I've owned a few in my time) does have a bit in common with our old tub.

It's all to do with gait.

If you have not only ridden a horse, but know *how* to ride a horse, you're aware there are four cogs in the box, with - not a stick-shift, but a closed-leg up from one rhythm and speed to another.

It's almost the same in a vessel; so what I intend to do, on this long looked forward to passage is - get the boat to *emulate* the rocking horse stride of a thoroughbred mare (when you've squeezed her) and sat to the marvellous lope of a canter.

Now we're further offshore, it's not only the breeze that's picked up.

The sea is building, and in no time at all, with the usual Force 4, sometimes 5, occasionally 6, a'blowin' mornin', noon, and night, it's going to build a bit more, until there's a decent hump of an ocean rolling forever westward.

No worries with that, because I intend to adjust the speed of the vessel to accommodate this substantial heave of a swell.

There are four things to think about.

(1) is the shape of the vessel.

In this regard we have the benefit of a canoe body, a deep fin keel, and light to moderate displacement.

(2) is the weight of the wind, which in turn influences.

(3) the steepness of the following sea, and lastly.

(4) the effectiveness of the self-steering gear, when faced with these conditions.

252

So with these things in mind, what we're going to do now is hoist the second running pole, [14] and set a high-cut sail on the inner forestay.

This bit of canvas is triangular in shape - not a bit like a deck-sweeping staysail. The choice of cut means that with the extra-long pole, trimmed well for'ard, it's possible to 'angle' the sail - squaring it off to a quartering breeze.

The shape of the sail ensures the clew is well above deck level (not going to dip into the 'oggin if the old tub takes to rhythmic rolling).

The other down-wind sail, also high cut, but larger than the 'staysail', is already set on the outer forestay, utilizing the second of the running poles (the pole we set up when Pedro was with us), with the advantage of this down-wind rig being - both sails are hank'd on stays. So, should we need to reduce canvas in a hurry, all we've got to do is let go the halyards and the stuff comes down real neat and tidy-like.

The next thing of note is, these bits of canvas are going to get us to Barbados in time for Christmas.

If all goes well, and there's no reason to doubt it, there'll be no sail changes. All we'll have to do, is juggle about with the guys and braces, while we enjoy our lounge in the sun - as we *lope* along to the west'ard.

And 'lope' *is* the right word, because the amount of sail we're carrying should be sufficient to provide the speed we need, yet not be enough to launch the vessel down the face of a wave, which may be exciting (it sure as hell is) but I'm all for an easy life. The last thing we want is our old tub taking the bit in her teeth and start *galloping* (surfing) off to the west'ard.

There's nothing magical about this rig; it's no more than bog-standard stuff, but when you get it *right,* it's a real pleasure to see the way she lifts to the swell.

Remains poised - for the crucial moment, as a lump of a sea passes under the boat.

Nobody busts his ass.

The vane stays in charge, and she slips into the trough, still on course, and as sweet and dry as you like.

The other good thing about this beaut of a sleigh ride is - it *is* all down hill.

We're running dry-decked before a boisterous trade. All we've got to do is, relax - and enjoy the extent of the Old Man's magnificent kingdom.

The view is superb.

The breeze is creaming the top off the swell.

The crests are white, the sea is blue.

The scudding clouds are puffball light.

The sun's as hot as Hades.

However, before we get carried away with the beauty (the *sheer* beauty of it all) it's worth keeping in mind we've still to clear the last of the Canaries.

We left Tenerife at 8 o'clock last night.

The distance to run, from the end of the jetty to the southernmost point of Hierro is roughly 72 miles, which gives an ETA off *Punta de la Restinga* of somewhere around 2 o'clock this afternoon.

Just what's needed; because we'll have time to sort a few things out before we take our final departure.

As things stand, after a night spent mostly sitting in the cockpit, I'm feeling a bit crinkled round the edges, with this coming about because I'm never too happy about getting my head down when there's a risk of shipping about. Fortunately, that threat is receding, even though we haven't cleared the islands, there's not much traffic (just another way of saying we haven't had sight of a vessel since 3 o'clock this morning) which doesn't mean it's permissible to take to your bunk and snore the forenoon away (that *would* be tempting providence).

So this does seem a good time to consider the seagoing system that I, and I think most other single-handed voyagers adopt, when faced with an ocean passage.

What we do is 'catnap'.

This means getting horizontal, in a nice warm bunk if possible, but wherever you kip, you adjust your body-clock to give you a nudge every 30 minutes (this figure being generally agreed as being ten minutes longer than the time you've got available between a first sighting, and being run down by a steamer). But if you've tried limiting your nap to a mere *twenty* minutes, you soon appreciate the value of that luxurious, even if life-threatening extra time in your bunk.

This caulk and wake, caulk and wake, caulk and wake technique does take a bit of getting used to. But when you come to terms with it, and you're sleeping in a small-boat berth that's conveniently arranged - you can stick your head out of the hatch, have a quick look around the horizon, and get your head down again (almost) without waking up.

Now, there is a bit of the old bugle being blown here, because you have to be sufficiently awake to be able to see if there's anything in sight. And no doubt we would all have to admit (when you've been popping up and down for a week or so) and haven't met any shipping, the tendency is, for the pop-up intervals to get stretched a little more.

However, this is a self-correcting indulgence.

There comes the time, when you stick you head out of the hatch - and you damn near die of heart failure, because *there*, on a guaranteed collision course with your pride and joy of a shell, is the forty thousand tons of cruise ship which is going to carry the barely visible scratch on her bow.

All that remains.

The *only* clue, which explains yet another 'mysterious' disappearance.

A tough enough outcome.

But these aren't the sort of gloomy thoughts you're concerned with when admiring the southern aspect of Hierro.

The island towers nicely out of the sea, even if it isn't as attractive as Tenerife.

The central feature, the plateau of Mapaso, is 1499 metres above sea level.

Our principle concern, is the aforementioned *Punta de la Restinga* (there appears to be some sort of a settlement, with a jetty, but we're too far off to make out the details). No matter, a vertical sextant angle from the top of the plateau down to sea level gives a reading of 7 degrees and 35 minutes of arc, and after not much of a battle with the simple arithmetic, we arrive at the distance-off, [15] perhaps not all that accurately, which works out at 6 miles; and this, in conjunction with a compass bearing, gives us a position we can use as a reasonable point of departure.

(don't worry about the introduction of sextant angles and compass bearings) the whole thing is as easy as - almost as easy as.

Hell - as easy as.

As easy as falling off a log?

You could say that - and there is an element of truth in it.

Nevertheless, there are degrees of sophistication concerned with what we know as celestial navigation. At it's most literal, the old saying is - *it's as much of an art as a science* - yet this is a bit misleading, because before you can practice the art, you have to understand at least some of the science, and it involves all sorts of sophisticated tricks.

Spherical trigonometry.

Sidereal time.

The sun's declination.

The watery look of the moon - all *kinds* of magical numbers.

My own preference, in a small boat, is keep it as simple as possible, and this fits in neatly with the straightforward philosophy underpinning our old tub.

Devoid of an engine.

Reliant on an oil lamp, and at least two boxes of matches.

Who wants a Global Positioning System (a sat-nav) when we've got an old vernier sextant [16] which is going to provide a day-by-day position, *and* an enormous amount of pleasure - just in the measurement of angles.

Now we've got our position (27 degrees and 34 minutes north; 17 degrees and 57 minutes west), we can stream the log, set the counter on zero, sit back and admire the view; which does stretch, in my mind's rollicking eye, at least two thousand marvellous miles to the west'ard.

The island's slipping astern.

The boat's dealing well with the age-old partnership (sometimes devious Davy and the bearded Old Man with the trident).

We're making what might be four knots, judging by the time it took to bring the southern point of Hierro abeam, but we could do with a sizeable onion.

No matter, the best thing now is get a day's run under our belt, and *then* see what sail changes are needed to get us to Barbados by Christmas.

As far as our immediate situation is concerned, it's the inner man who demands attention, and as some of the tropical heat is going to follow the orb over the western horizon, this is the best time of day to drum up some grub.

Nothing elaborate; when your galley consists of a single-burner primus and a bucket, *haute cuisine* sometimes proves to be just one saucepan too far, but a bowl of soup and a biscuit is not beyond the wit of man, and 'dinner in the cockpit' not a bad way of ending the day.

When the sun sets in these latitudes, it's not long before darkness sweeps up and envelops the boat.

Stars appear.

The breeze may moderate, veer a point, and it's necessary to juggle about with guys and braces to keep what was the white stuff (shades of silver now) square with the trade, while at the same time adjusting the self-steering gear to keep her pointing in the right direction.

In 30 minutes or so, it'll be time to go below and twiddle about with the radio.

This is another facet of the regime I've adopted over the years, when making long ocean passages. The alternative (reading at night, while stretched out in your bunk) would indeed help to pass the long night watches, but there are several practical difficulties involved with this indulgence.

Point A: there's only one cabin lamp aboard the boat, and it's located on the main bulkhead in order to illuminate the galley and chart table area (a grand way of describing the plywood box where the charts are stored).

Point B: I sleep with my head aft, six feet and several inches from the lamp, immediately adjacent to the companionway hatch; so although I can't read, I can hear, not only the below-deck creaks and groans, but also what's going on above deck.

Point C: if you *do* read at night, and then stick your head out of the hatch, to see if there's any shipping about, you are just about as blind as a bat, and it takes longer than you think to come into your night vision. Whereas, if you have been listening to the radio, [17] the cabin of your small boat stays as dark as the inside of a cow, and when you put your head out of the hatch, there's no problem with picking up even the glimmer of a masthead light, which may be lipping and dipping just above and below the horizon.

But it's a light you can *see*; because, surprise, surprise, you have the benefit of your *just out from the insides of a cow, searchlight-like eyes.*

By adopting this sensible approach, the night watches roll on, and a respectable lookout is maintained.

Yet it would be foolish to deny the first streak of dawn doesn't offer the prospect of a longer than usual caulk, which you probably think you've earned, if you've been conscientious about the Jack-out-of-the-cabin regime.

Just before dawn (have you noticed it rhymes rather nicely with *yawn?*) arrives, there are traces of grey feathering the eastern rim, as the fringe of the celestial curtain is ruffled, then raised.

And I'm always impressed, by the advent of yet another bright tropical day.

The striking assurance.

That the world *is* actually spinning.

As the sun climbs, majestically, above the eastern horizon, this is the time to start on the navigational chores (wrongly described). But however you view it, the fact that the Nautical Almanac provides the bearing of the sun at sunrise and sunset does help.

Because all we've got to do now is - ship the shadow-pin on the compass.

Note where the shadow falls.

Compute this bearing with the information in the Almanac.

And *hey presto:* the difference in the numbers is the error of the compass.

Didn't I *tell* you navigation is as easy as falling off a log?

And by George, it's coming on time for breakfast.

Always a nice time of day.

The sun's up.

The kettle's singing.

The chunk of bread, the lump of cheese, the crisply slicing apple.

After coffee, it's just a question of giving the old orb time to gain enough altitude, and we can get a sight which is reasonably free of distortion.

I'm delighted to take this first celestial observation.

In this running free, dry-decked instance, the 'art' that's involved is simple enough - consists of little more than making sure you have your bum wedged securely against the companionway scuttle, so that you can let your upper-body sway and accommodate the roll and lurch of the boat.

It's easy enough to check the sextant index error. [18]

This may be an old box of tricks, but it still delivers the goods, so as we know the instrument is just about error-free, it's only a question of bringing the lower limb of the sun *below* the horizon.

Swinging her back and fore until the orb has climbed a bit more, and the limb is just *touching* the horizon.

Shout *stop* (the old bosun reads the chronometer), then go below counting one, *and* two, *and* three, *and* four, *and* five, *and* six - until you can see the ship's clock, and after you've taken note of the time (and deducted six seconds) enter the numbers in the sight book.

Read the sextant.

Record the altitude.

Put the instrument carefully back in its box.

Go back on deck.

Read the log, then retire below to fire up the primus (did anyone say something about falling off a log?).

Because we're running dry-decked to the west'ard, before a moderate breeze, and taking an AM sight, [19] there's nothing too difficult about an observation which is going to provide a reasonably accurate position line. In contrast to the problems associated with the same man attempting to obtain a sight from the deck of a boat that's being thrashed to windward with two reefs tied in the main.

Deluged with spray.

Poised on the top of a twenty foot wave (where you have all of two seconds to bring the sun down, before you're plunged back in the trough), with the cloud cover so thick, you have to wait an age while trying to keep the sextant dry - until the boat's perched on the top of another wave that's high enough to give a clear view of the horizon *while the sun is actually out*. Then you find it's the *upper* limb that appears (when you've been anticipating the lower) and before you have time to make the adjustment, the pale shadow of a sun has disappeared *and the boat's back once more in the watery depths of the trough*.

By contrast, right here, it's hey-ho for the tropics, where the important things are in the navigator's favour.

There *are* clouds - but the trade is moving them nicely over the boat.

If the sun does disappear - it's seldom for more than a moment or two, so it's only a question of selecting the right shades.

Closing one eye.

Humming (*never* whistling) a few bars from The Flying Dutchman, [20] and you've made a decent observation.

Working up the sight isn't all that difficult either.

If you are using Sight Reduction Tables, the mathematics amount to a few additions, a few subtractions, and you arrive at a figure which only provides *one* position line - and you could be anywhere on it. But we have made a fair start at solving the problem of where will we be in a few hours time, when the sun's approaching the meridian and we're all looking forward to Noon.

The *fore*noon doesn't present a problem.

If you need to catch up on sleep, you can spend a couple of hours in your bunk, trusting to the fact that, now it's daylight, the chances of being run down should have diminished.

So it's nice to lounge in the cockpit, admiring the way the boat uses the trade.

Deals with the swell.

Slides in the trough.

Lifts to a sea, and dodges the crest as she slips along under a pair of headsails which seem almost too small for the job - but you don't need a billow of canvas to sustain this lope of a pace.

Aboard this hooker, it has long since been established that lunch is served *after* the noon observation's been made.

So, about ten minutes before the witching hour, I've got my backside jammed against the scuttle, watching through the well-shaded sextant telescope the golden old orb steadily increase its altitude.

The sun climbs towards its zenith, then slows to the point of suspension, before starting its slide towards the welcoming western horizon, and I'm always delighted to go through what has become the very important *big ship midday ritual.*

The whole procedure is so deceptively simple, and so amazingly satisfying. All that's needed, after the altitude's been obtained, is the sun's declination (lifted straight out of the current page of the Nautical Almanac).

If the sun is south of the equator (while the boat is north of the imaginary line) you subtract the declination from the zenith distance (the figure arrived at by subtracting the sun's altitude from ninety degrees).

And would you (could you believe it?) *that's* your Latitude.

While, naturally enough, if you and your boat are on the edge of the Arctic icepack, while the sun is also north of the line, you *add* the declination to the ZD to reach the same conclusion.

The other half of the Noon Position is almost as easily established.

Maybe a little more sucking on the stub of a pencil, but not really enough to discolour your teeth, because it's only a matter of running the AM position line up to noon, by the number of miles (about 10) recorded on the log since you took the morning sight. And again, *hey* precedes *presto,* because you know *exactly* where you are on this old planet, which is merely ninety three million miles from the sun, hurtling through space at fifty seven thousand, eight hundred and fifty-one nautical miles an hour, on its trip round the orb while rotating at a peripheral speed of one thousand five hundred feet per second (*great jumpin' Jehoshaphat* [21] *ain't it all enough to make your sagely nodding head whirl?*).

When all you are doing (*all* you are doing) is making a trade wind passage across the pond, and you've got your ducks in line to the point where you know where they started from - where you want them to go, and how you are going to shepherd them there, the whole thing may appear to be less than mildly spectacular.

As the sun rises, you check the compass.

Prepare breakfast, tidy the cabin.

Take the AM sight.

Enjoy a forenoon nap.

Observe the midday ritual.

Record the vessel's position.

Fill in the logbook, mentally deducting the day's run from the previously arrived-at great circle distance [22] (so you have a rough idea of *how far there is to go*).

Then, with a smile which would crease the face of a cast iron cat, retire below, secure in the knowledge you are well in control of events (perhaps you *are* aware that things may not be *quite* what they seem) that crook old Davy must be *somewhere* around.

But it's easy to be beguiled by the regularity.

The symmetry.

The astonishing *beauty* of it all.

As we've left the islands astern, I've been expecting the trade to freshen a bit; but there's been a slight falling off in the breeze, so to make sure we're going to keep to our planned arrival at Barbados, it's become necessary to set a bit more sail, as an extra bit of canvas, which entails tying two reefs in the mainsail, before the sail is hoisted, and rigging the pennant to lace down the last deep reef.

So what we've got now, in addition to the two running sails, is the peak of the mainsail, with the boom well squared off and the main preventer rigged.

This is quite convenient, because I can now steady my bum against the boom when standing on the coachroof, having moved from the companionway in order to gain personal altitude when taking a sight.

With the bit more sail, we've picked up the better part of an onion, but not enough to tempt the tub to even *think* about surfing down the face of an about-to-break wave.

So, as far as the skipper's concerned, the ducks *are* nicely in line, and it's time to indulge the common man.

If you have decided, for one reason or another, not to read at night, then the tropical afternoons are just the time to lounge in the cockpit (large straw hat and sun glasses) while deciding what to take out from the tub's well-stocked lending library (remember the day, in Tenerife, when we were lucky enough to pick up those Dick Francis novels?). So there's plenty of print available, particularly as the paperbacks have been added to the boat's usual stock of books. [23]

This 'afternoon read' is part of the ritual; perhaps not on the scale of the midday observation, but the sort of pleasurable habit you adopt when there's plenty of distance to go, no hurry about getting there, and a confident feel about the boat.

In this context, the vessel is running dry-decked before the reliable trade, being looked after by the self-steering gear.

The log is ticking up the miles.

The navigating officer has a smile on his face, because the distance sailed over the last 24 hours has been augmented by twelve miles of favourable current.

As far as the 'boat noises' are concerned, the occasional squeak of a sheave and the regular slap of a crest are punctuated by the pleasurable turning of Dick Francis' *Dead Cert* pages, and - a storm petrel has been following the boat for an hour or more.

This is about as good as it gets for a single-handed ocean wanderer.

Yet an even better thing is - tomorrow, the vessel will be running before the same reliable trade.

The log will be ticking up the miles.

The navigator will still have a smile on his face.

There will be the regular slap of a crest, but no protesting squeak (the sheave's been oiled) and what few shipboard noises remain will be punctuated by the pleasurable turning of the last few pages of *Dead Cert*, while the next Dick Francis saga has already been selected.

Also, what looks like the same storm petrel has been dodging about the boat for most of ....

Another wonderful seafaring day.

The other half (the pop-up half) of the watches are also falling into an acceptable pattern.

After the sun has set, and the evening meal has been prepared and eaten, by the time the dishes are washed and stacked away, it's dark enough to start fiddling about with the radio.

This neat bit of equipment is the product of Sanyo ingenuity, a battery-operated set that has band-spread on a satisfying number of short-wave frequencies. Many of the stations are broadcasting news of (let's hope) one unbiased sort or another; however, there's another string to this particular bow.

The very special string, that's concerned with the reason the radio has been allotted valuable shelf space in the first place; music is the key.

Sometimes not all that easy to come by in the crackling hash of endless political commentary. But if you persist, and make allowance for less than perfect reception, it's possible to listen to a performance which seems purpose-made for the place.

The trick is, you should position yourself in a small boat that's departed whatever shore you thought it appropriate to leave.

Pick a night which provides the first thin sliver of a silver tropic moon, lipping the horizon as a russeted blur, then climbing to shine amongst the star-studded spaces that sail above the trade.

Arrange for the Chicago Symphony Orchestra to be conducted by Georg Solti [24] in a performance of Beethoven's Ninth.

And after you've done that.

It's probably a good idea to move from the confines of the cabin, to sit in the cockpit, under the stars, nursing the radio with the headphones clamped to your ears.

Because she's allowed to stroll before the trade, the boat's moving quietly through the night, before the substantial lump of a swell.

The ripple of the bow wave, and the gurgle of the wake, are the product of a breeze which could be described as whistlin' in the riggin'. But it's a low key cliché, and when you stand in the companionway (recovering from *The Choral*) it's possible to hear splashes, grunts, squeaks - an expiration of air alongside the boat; leaving you in no doubt you're surrounded by who knows what, some of whom are apparently sussing you out, before going about their legitimate affairs.

Come morning.

The wheel's revolved once more, and the routine marks the start of yet another absorbing seafaring day.

I usually split ocean crossings into handy-sized chunks, which are allocated way-stations, intended to flag up the miles made good.

In this regard, as we're engaged on a 2,400 mile jaunt, it seems sensible to arrange some sort of a jamboree after six hundred miles (a quarter of the passage). There's nothing extravagant in these celebrations, partly because although they are 'counting down', there's an element of regret (the passage is slipping away).

So the 'quarter distance' recognition is nothing more than a looked forward to bath in the cockpit.

Then a meal, followed by a search about the ether for a concert.

On this occasion (the 600 mile milestone) it's Jimi Hendrix, [25] teamed with Mitch Mitchell, and I'm staggered by the sound they produce (a long way from Beethoven) and no doubt a slide on the riotous slope of the wild side, but a display of outrageous talent by the - bee/bee, bee/bee, bee/bee, bee/bee bloodyfull bucketful.

In this entertaining way, the passage proceeds.

I'm not bustin' a gut to get there, because the days are not proving in any way tedious.

The reverse is the case.

The sun is shinin'.

The breeze is blowin'.

The boat is sailin'.

The noon positions are marching across the chart in a satisfactory manner. And before you know it, the next milestone is around the corner, and we're coming up to the half-way point in the passage. (26)

This celebration *is* going to be more than just another sluice-down in the cockpit, because the consensus is - we've made significant progress.

Although there's a rule aboard the hooker which prohibits booze, anyone who is familiar with the way the 'tween wars prohibition distorted the social fabric in the U S of A, would surely agree that a tot wouldn't come amiss on this rather special occasion. So I'm going to fix the crew a meal that'll leave them just about satiated.

This requires, apart from a gin and tonic start, about a third of a tin of Campbell's cream of tomato soup.

The main course is going to be pasta spiked with a jar of Dolmio bolognese sauce (a Tenerife supermarket extravagance), and we'll complete the meal with mixed fruit, suitably enhanced with evaporated milk.

And then, another, not so small, half-way house gin.

The cooking is easy enough.

I've lit the primus so many times, I know to a 'T' how long it takes to pre-heat the burner.

And now I've actually got down to the task, and the primus is going, I've decided I might as well heat all the soup, then decant some of it into Sue Hutchinson's vacuum flask, because it means, come midnight, with the crew keeping what we all hope is a conscientious lookout, the steward will be able to serve the skipper a celebratory half-way across the ocean, cup of broth in the cockpit. This may seem a simple sort of a scenario (but when you're alone in the middle of the 'oggin) these sleight-of-hand indulgences all become part of the deal.

Including, an extravagant bath in the cockpit (the following morning) with the reasoning here being - because there's plenty of water in hand, the slightly hung-over feeling, occasioned by perhaps a drop too much gin, might as well be dealt with as soon as the sun's decided it's time to lift the lid on yet another, just about perfect, running our westing down day.

The muzzy feeling has been occasioned by only a couple of drinks, which if they'd been consumed ashore would have hardly been worth mentioning. But here, it's noticeable that even a modest snifter has an enhanced effect, and this heightened awareness (susceptibility?) isn't confined to the booze.

It really *is* extraordinary, how pleasant it can be - lounged in the cockpit of a boat you built yourself, with the tub rolling quietly towards Barbados.

The sea glinting under a tropical sun.

The trade, a companionable Beaufort 4 to 5; fresh enough to knock the tops of the swell, with the spray leaving the crests in a careless scatter of drops that are decking out the ocean with a host of sparkling rainbows.

In these conditions (the standard trade wind day) the crew would be a dull old dog indeed if he didn't appreciate how lucky he is, being in this particular place, at this particular time. And there are some times of the day that are even better than that.

Since the midway point (two days and a bit now) I've fallen into the habit of making a cup of tea, just before dawn, and then, suitably quaffed, standing in the companionway, watching the world spinning, with the sky above eastern horizon showing the first faint greying of the day as another tropical dawn winds up to make its spectacular entry (so I'm below right now) waiting for the billy to boil, and hardly conscious of the lift and roll of the boat as she's running before a handy lump of a sea.

Then in the matter of a moment.

What was the lee side - has become the weather side.

What was previously up - is now decidedly down.

The nautical almanac has been pitched from the chart table, across the cabin, and has knocked the kettle off the stove. I've followed the almanac and in the confusion have foolishly put my hand on the business-end of the primus, and as if that wasn't enough - the boat is lurching back.

Apparently corkscrewing her way into the trough of a wave, with another hell of a crash from aloft.

What was temporarily *up* - has now become alarmingly *down*.

The kettle, minus its contents, has slid across the galley and has lodged under the gimbals of the primus.

There's been another helluva crash.

The boat's corkscrewing again, with another whiplash of madly gybing canvas as she's thrown on her beam ends once more.

This is a crazy situation, and the immediate thought is - *get on deck as soon as possible.*

But the primus is flaring up, and a few precious seconds must be spent, either getting the gimbal working again, or easing the pressure in the stove. But by the time I've opened the valve, the boat's gybed again and I'm struggling to climb a companionway ladder that's inclined at an angle of about 45 degrees from where it damned well aught to be.

The scene on deck is surprisingly normal.

The boom's in the right place (held there by the preventer).

The peak of the mainsail is still there.

Both the headsails are up.

The running poles are intact, but while I'm looking at the rig, the boat is twisting off the top of another wave, and as she does so, the headsails are taken-aback and the vessel is slam-gybed again from one mad tack to another, completely out of control.

The next thing to look at is the self-steering gear.

It seems O.K., but when I put my hand on the tiller, it feels odd, as if there's no connection between the tiller and the wind vane (yet I can *see,* there *is* a connection between the tiller and the wind vane) so the problem must be deeper-seated than that.

She's been slam-gybed again.

So it's a question of making my way for'ard as quickly as possible, to get sail off the vessel. A situation where it's one hand for the tub, and the other for the skipper, if you don't want to part company with what *was* your pride and joy of a shell.

Now we're under a bare pole, the wild gyrations have stopped.

She's lying across the swell, rising to the height of the sea, before slipping once more to the trough. However, I don't trust the old cow, and I'm holding on to the mast, wondering what caused this mad state of affairs.

The trip aft isn't difficult, but I'm glad to be back in the cockpit, reaching for the tiller, hoping for the best - but expecting the worst.

The lines connecting the pendulum-servo to the tiller are intact, but there's no 'feel' to the tiller (when I've de-clutched the wind vane and let go the lines, the system's been disengaged from the rudder) and I should feel what should be the 'weight' of the helm, so the painful truth is beginning to emerge.

The self-steering's O.K.

The tiller's O.K.

But if I was a betting man, I'd be wagering a pony, [27] on the probability we're now in the middle of the Western Ocean

in a vessel which no longer possesses a rudder

CHAPTER SIX: PAGE NOTES

---

(1) Page 236. Line 8 .... *'bosun's chair'*.

A device carried aboard all vessels, consisting of a short plank (approx 24" long) modified in order that it can be supported by a rope cradle, which is attached to a halyard that is used to conveniently haul a seaman aloft (sitting in the 'chair') so that he may carry out work associated with the mast and rigging.

(2) Page 237. Line 10 .... *'Collette's twice-yearly overseas trips'*.

The trips Collette makes are connected with her work. She's researching a book, has it about halfway written, which deals with the problems facing the third world. The burden of this treatise is, you can't **give** anyone prosperity, all you can reasonably hope (from Collette's clinical viewpoint) is help them into a position where they should be able to earn it. Although she's not quite so forthcoming, when asked how she reconciles the act of *giving*, with the more charitable concept of *sharing*.

(3) Page 237. Line 12 .... *'entrée to the glittering casinos'*.

Pierre is, amongst his other accomplishments, a high-rolling gambler who spends time in Monte Carlo every year, and perhaps some of us may think the money wagered and usually lost would be better spent on famine relief in sub-Saharan Africa. But who are we to make judgements? Pierre isn't mean, and he may (probably does) contribute to charitable organisations which specialize in the distant end of his free spending lifestyle.

Perhaps of more concern, to those people who take a jaundiced view of outrageous ostentation, would be the example set by the yacht *Corporate Raider (nee Palatia)*. There are currently at least 40 super yachts of her type on order (to add to the many hundreds already built) and they are not getting any smaller, with an overall length of 50 metres being just about par for the course. These trinkets run out at 30 to 40 million US dollars a pop, with the top end of the market having $30 million spent on the *interiors* alone (bathrooms lined with rare marbles: solid gold fittings scattered liberally about). As good an example as any, of the profligate use of resources which could be better used?

(4) Page 237. Line 30 .... *'hurricane season has run its course'*.

In the North Atlantic, the season of tropical revolving storms extends from May to December, so it's technically inaccurate to say the 'season has run its course' when discussing a departure on a trade wind passage during the month of November. However, by far the greater incidence of these destructive winds occur in the summer months, May to October, and during this period a small-boat skipper would be making a serious and probably fatal error, if he contemplated being in the wrong place at the wrong time, when he can reduce the chance of catastrophe by being not only cautious, but patient.

(5) Page 239. Line 4 .... *'pot-bellied grunt'.*

Slang for a bacon pig; now offered in modern supermarkets, smoked and sliced in vacuum packs, so that, at a pinch, those vessels which don't have a refrigerated locker can enjoy bacon for breakfast, at least for the first week or so of a voyage (although, in a small boat it's advisable to be a dab-hand with a frying pan, to avoid the possibility of the scalding fat being slopped over the stove as well as over the cook).

(6) Page 240. Line 25 .... *'display of flowers'.*

There are approximately 1,800 plant species growing throughout the Canary archipelago, and many have been introduced during the long human occupation of the islands. Almost 500 are endemic to the Canaries, while nearly 60 are found only in this locality and throughout the rest of the group, made up of the Azores, Madeira, Cape Verde, and the Salvage Islands; so a significant part of the flora on offer to the observant yachtie who is visiting Tenerife can be seen nowhere else in the world.

Useful books, quoted above are; *Natural History Excursions in Tenerife* by **Philip ASHMOLE**, published in 1989 by Kidstome Mill Press, Peebles, Scotland; and *What's Blooming Where on Tenerife*, by **Herbert MOELLER** translated from the German by **Raul HOCKSTETTER** and published in 1968 by *Bambi*, Puerto de la Cruz, Tenerife.

(7) Page 241. Line 14 .... *'the mountain is magnificent'.*

It's not easy to appreciate the scale of Teide. The mountain dominates the island of Tenerife, which is roughly triangular in shape. The volcano rises from the northern edge of a vast cauldron, *Las Cañadas*, which is ten miles across, 47 miles in circumference, and at an altitude of 6,500 feet above sea-level. Running north-east from Las Cañadas are mountains, split by ravines that lead down to the sea. There are four recognisable ecological areas, ranging from the upper slopes, almost devoid of vegetation, through what used to be an evergreen forest (Laurels) now mostly pine, down to other areas that support an enormous variety of flora.

The publication already mentioned. *Natural History Excursions in Tenerife* (directly, even if briefly quoted here) is essential reading for anyone wishing to understand the complexities of this fascinating island, particularly the way Teide's trademark cloud bank is formed and maintained.

(8) Page 241. Line 39 .... *'Shank's Pony'*.

Slang for making a journey on foot; otherwise known as 'catching the marrowbone stage' or boarding 'Walker's bus'.

(9) Page 244. Line 3 ....*'Pierre's had his picture taken*
not as popinjay
(but Patriarch)
Moses, leaning on his staff, bare-headed, looking westward
a jewelled hand shading eyes that are searching now for Canaan'

The earliest reference to Canaan occurs in the Mari documents of the 18th century BC. This land, later known as Palestine, was conquered and occupied by the Israelites in the later part of the 2nd millennium BC. (perhaps a clue to the origins of the present disastrous conflict centered about present-day Jerusalem?).

MOSES: the Hebrew patriarch who was born in Egypt and led the Jews from bondage. During this epic journey he was able, by Divine Intervention (so we are told), when near the summit of Mount Sinai, to incise the Ten Commandments on tablets of stone, as recorded in the second book of the Old Testament (Exodus. 20).
   He died in Moab, within sight of the Promised Land.

(10) Page 244. Line 22 .... *'Hillary would have employed on Everest'*.

Edmund (Percival) **HILLARY** (1919-2008) born in Auckland, New Zealand; a member of John Hunt's Mount Everest expedition in 1953; being the first man to gain the summit, together with his Sherpa companion Tenzing Norgay. Hillary was knighted for this achievement and later gained renown for his establishment of the Himalayan Trust, a medical and educational charity that has built many schools and two hospitals in Nepal. His autobiography, *Nothing Venture, Nothing Win* was published in 1975.

Tenzing NORGAY (1914-1986); also known as *Sherpa Tenzing*. Born in Tsa-chu, Nepal. A prodigious mountaineer, being involved with British expeditions from 1935 onwards, climbing many Himalayan peaks. He was awarded the George Medal for his climb with Hillary and later became head of the Institute of Mountaineering at Darjeeling.

(11) Page 247. Line 20 .... *'scrimshaw work'*.

The term decribes the artifacts produced (as a means of 'passing the time') by the crews of whaling vessels when on long voyages in pursuit of their quarry.
   Following the hunting, harpooning, hauling-aboard, flenzing, and then rendering-down of the blubber to produce the whale oil demanded of the market they were serving, the crew extracted the teeth from the jaws of the animal and,

271

when they had the time, cleaned up the molars (filing smooth, and then burnishing) in order to establish the smooth surface required by their craft. This involved first the etching and then the application of indelible ink, which was necessary to highlight the scenes that had been scratched on the surface of the ivory. The end-result was an undoubted work of art, which commands high prices when displayed in those galleries which specialize in trading these relics of a bygone age.

(12) Page 250. Line 29 ………. *'adiós amigo, see you next time round'*.

As we left the marina, towed by Pedro, I couldn't resist a last minute smile at his involvement with *Bouton de Rose* and how Pierre has misunderstood the man he hired as a working addition to his crew, with the truth of the matter being not quite as simple as it looks.

Pedro might be an old man, and as such is representative of a previous generation; but his wife is even more upright than he is, and the result of *her* straight-laced background is, while our practical fisherman has adapted to changed circumstances, his *esposa* believes some of the people jumbo'd in by the tourist industry have reduced what was once an attractive fishing village to (what *she* sees as) little more than a brothel.

(13) Page 251. Line 2 ………. *'Blondie can take charge of the vessel'*.

The distinguished soldier who was known throughout the international yachting community by his nickname was born in Dublin on February 27th 1914, during the time his father, Lt (QM) A.T.Hasler, MC., RAMC, was temporarily stationed in Ireland. His mother's family also had a military background, so it was natural for her son to choose the profession. After attending *Wellington* (English 'public' school) Hasler commenced his probationary period in the Royal Marines in September 1932, and obtained his regular commission 3 years later, having served afloat for a short training period in the ex-battleship *HMS Iron Duke* and then an operational posting aboard *HMS Queen Elizabeth*, at that time the flagship of the Mediterranean fleet. During these formative years he made significant progress, gravitating naturally to the small-boat end of the service, being appointed Fleet Landing Officer to the then re-forming Mobile Naval Base Defence Organisation in 1937. He was promoted Captain on May 23rd 1939, and so was well trained and positioned to take part in the war with Germany which was declared in the September of the same year.

Anyone interested in Colonel Hasler's career could do no better that read **Ewen SOUTHBY-TAILYOUR'S** biography, entitled *BLONDIE,* published in 1998 by Leo Cooper (Pen & Sword imprint) designated ISBN 0 85052 516 0. This well researched book records the pre-war years. Describes an engagement that took place during the first few months of the war, in the Norwegian theatre, where Blondie served alongside a detachment of the French Foreign Legion. After recording this relatively minor skirmish, the author deploys the main thrust of the book, describing Hasler's involvement in the conception, planning, training, and courageous leadership of an amphibious assault team which, because of its clandestine nature and breath-taking audacity, not only earned an honoured place in British military history, but became the forerunner of the special undercover (boat) service, SBS.

After the war, in which he served with such distinction, Blondie decided to take up the challenge presented by the events organised by the Royal Ocean Racing Club, but in a vessel, *Tre Sang,* which most people at the time thought unsuitable for the task. Even now, an argument could be made that a 30 square metre, developed in Sweden in 1908 for Baltic (relatively sheltered) water conditions was perhaps not an ideal craft to undertake passage racing, some of which takes place on and about the eastern seaboard of the North Atlantic Ocean. However, although her crew would occasionally describe the vessel's performance as something akin to driving to windward aboard a half-tide rock; under Blondie's expert guidance *Tre Sang* was entered for six of the seven races in the RORC's small-boat section (winning three of them) and in 1946 won the Class 3 Championship and the *Ortac Cup.*

Having successfully explored this avenue, Blondie conceived and organised competitive single-handed ocean racing which was, at the time, perhaps a step too far for some of his contemporaries. With the hardship imposed by *Tre Sang* no doubt in the forefront of his mind, he decided on a different approach (vis-à-vis single-handed sailing) relinquishing the concept of the half-tide rock and altering a Scandinavian Folkboat (25 feet overall) so she could be sailed by one man, who stayed *dry.* The result was *Jester,* perhaps the most famous small ocean-going vessel since Noah embarked in the ark.

From the year of the first organised single-handed trans-Atlantic race (1960) *Jester,* or her replica, has made eight Atlantic crossings, mostly sailed by Michael Richie (for 40 years the Director of the Royal Institute of Navigation). When honourably retired, the vessel (as a replica; the original boat being lost at sea) will be placed on display at a (yet-to-be-chosen) Maritime Museum.

Amongst Blondie's other gifts to yachting, the pendulum-servo steering gear remains high on the list, and anyone interested in this device should consult *Self-Steering for Sailing Craft* by **John S. LETCHER, Jr.,** published by International Marine Publishing, Camden, Maine, in 1974. The *Jester* saga and Mike Richie's central position in it is set out in **Classic Boat**, July and October editions 1992. The **Jester Challenge** (lately of the Jester Trust) can be contacted at:
www.jesterinfo.org

Blondie married late, eventually meeting the right person (Bridget Fisher, the daughter of a distinguished Admiral) with the wedding taking place at Aberfoyle on October 3oth 1965. There were two children, Dinah and Tom, who were brought up on the Scottish farm Blondie retired to, towards the end of his, by any standards, quite extraordinary life.

He died on Tuesday, May 5th 1987, admired by all who had known him. Mourned and undoubtedly missed by the select and without doubt proud group of people who had served their country with him.

(14) Page 253. Line 2 .... *'second of the running poles'.*

Just to keep the record straight, aboard this vessel the description *'running pole'* is interchangeable with the term 'spinnaker pole'. They are the self-same article, used on different sails.

(15) Page 255. Line 23 .... *'arrive at the distance off'.*

This figure was calculated by multiplying the height of the plateau in metres by 1.854 and then dividing the result by the sextant angle in minutes. But if you feel the need, you can divide the height of the plateau in feet, with the sextant altitude in minutes, and then multiply the result by 4, then divide the lot by 7.

(16) Page 256. Line 7 .... *'vernier sextant'.*

Perhaps looked on now as an old-fashioned instrument (the modern sextant has a micrometer read-out) but there's nothing like peering through an eyepiece in order to interpret the vernier. An ingenious device invented and named after the French scientist **Pierre VERNIER,** who was born at Ornans near Besançon in 1580.

(17) Page 257. Line 15 .... *'listening to the radio'*

The inclusion of a short-wave radio in the vessel's inventory has been the subject of a certain amount of soul searching. Simply put, how down to the bare essentials are you, when you can tune into the BBC and keep tabs on how the Dow is doing today?

(18) Page 258. Line 22 .... *'sextant index error'.*

The quick way of checking the index error of a sextant involves observing the horizon with the instrument set at 'zero,' (more than likely the horizon will appear to be 'split').
   Adjust the instrument until the horizon appears as one straight line.
   Read the sextant.
   If the reading is 'on' the arc, then the amount must be subtracted from an observation. Conversely; if the amount is 'off' the arc, a positive correction must be applied. This method does require a decent (i.e. a 'hard' horizon) but that said, the procedure is quick, and the result accurate enough.

(19) Page 259 Line 1 .... *'taking an AM sight'.*

The description AM (*f. ante meridiem:* belonging to the forenoon) is given to an observation intended to ascertain the longitude of the vessel. In its simplest terms this involves measuring the height of the body above the horizon, taking the time of the observation, then calculating the intercept (the distance between the actual as against the assumed, dead-reckoned position). The resultant position line is run up to noon and, combined with a meridian altitude, fixes the vessels position. The important phrase here is, *in its simplest terms*, because the art and science of navigation, both coastal and celestial, is an intricate even if absorbing subject.

Perhaps the definitive volume on the history of navigation is **E.G.R.TALYOR'S,** *The Haven-Finding Art;* a masterly work, published in 1956 by Hollis and Carter. Ms Taylor was professor of geography at London University, and an Honorary Member of the Institute of Navigation. Her book is all-embracing, from the time of Odysseus to Captain James Cook, and anyone interested in her subject would be hard put to find a better teacher. The bibliography runs to some seventy items and (for the time covered) is comprehensive.

For those who seek an introduction to celestial navigation, **Mary BLEWITT'S** *Celestial Navigation for Yachtsmen*, first published by Yaching World in 1950 and subsequently by Stanford Maritime Ltd., satisfied a need. But the more up-to-date work is **Tom CUNLIFFE'S** *Celestial Navigation* (subtitled *'what the Ocean Yachtmaster needs to know)* published by Fernhurst Books in 1989, which quotes **J.W.NORRIE** from his mid-nineteenth century *Norrie's Practical Navigation*:

> *navigation is that art which instructs the mariner*
> *to conduct a ship through the wide and trackless ocean*
> *from one part to another*
> *with the greatest safety*
> *and in the shortest possible time*

To bring it up to date, **J.E.D.WILLIAMS'** *From Sails to Satellites* (*The Origin and Development of Navigational Science*) published by Oxford University Press in 1994, is well worth its cover price (£13) and although the author claims 'the book is not a product of scholarly research' that statement should be discounted, because it's very well produced and deploys a range of information which makes it obligatory reading for anyone interested in the subject..

(20) Page 259. Line 22 ....'*humming, **never** whistling, a few bars from the Flying Dutchman'*.

The relevant information in this item is that, at sea, the old-fashioned seamen were rather careful **when** they whistled. This prompted by the superstition that when a ship was becalmed, a wind could be raised **by** whistling, so when there **was** a bit of wind about (and some idiot whistled) the chances were, that the vessel and those aboard her would be beset with far more wind than they wanted.

Mention of *The Flying Dutchman* merely indicates a choice of music; in this case Wagner's romantic opera, given a first performance in Dresden in 1843 with the composer's libretto based on the legend of a spectral ship, alleged to appear off the Cape of Good Hope. This vessel was under the command of a captain condemned to wander the oceans until the Day of Judgement (because he refused to heed the warning of God *not* to round the Cape).

The note referring to *Paddy's Hurricane* (Item 10, Page 180, line 23) suggests other methods that may be used to conjure up a breeze. In the Royal Navy there was an edict that *prohibited* whistling aboard His/Her Majesty's vessels, on the ground that careless whistling may interfere with the skirl of the boatswain's pipes which were used to convey orders to the ship's company.

(21) Page 260. Line 32 .... *'great jumpin' Jehoshaphat'*.

It seems the reason for the supposedly characteristc 'jumping' has been lost in the mists of time.
   The man himself was a King of Juda. His alliance with Ahab (King of Israel, and Melville's choice for the command of the whaler *Pequod*) proved disastrous, and he barely escaped with his life (aboard the *Pequod*, he didn't). A trading venture to Ophir resulted in the fleet's destruction in the Gulf of Akaba, but his campaigns against Moab and Ammon were more successful and he is credited with some useful internal reforms.

(22) Page 261. Line 7 .... *'great circle distance'*.

The 'great circle' distance from our point of departure (27 degrees and 34 minutes North; 17 degrees and 57 minutes West) to a position 5 miles South of the southern-most point of Barbados (12 degrees 58 minutes North; 59 degrees 32 minutes West) turns out to be round about two thousand four hundred and eighty four nautical miles, on an initial course of 258 degrees, true. But on this particular passage, we will be getting to the south'ard of the great circle track (steering roughly sou'west from our departure point, before heading off to the west'ard) in order to get into the best of the trade wind as soon as possible. But it will of course entail sailing a little further than the great circle distance.

This 'getting down into the trade' has been a regular practice amongst seamen since the days of Columbus (1451-1506) who made the first recorded passage to the New World (departed Palos August 3rd 1492) sighted what we now know as the Bahamas on October 12th of that same year.

(23) Page 262. Line 1 .... *'the boat's usual stock of books'*.

The vessel's bookshelf contains, as well as a selection of novels; *The Book of Common Prayer*. The *Seafarer's Guide to Marine Life* by **Paul HORSMAN**. *A Guide to Seabirds on the Ocean Routes* by **Gerald TUCK** (Captain G.S.Tuck DSO Royal Navy). *The Sea Around Us* by **Rachel CARSON.** *The Proper Yacht* by **Arthur BEISER,** published by

Adlard Coles in 1966. And finally, a quaint old publication, but a permanent fixture aboard the tub, *The New Standard Encyclopaedia*, published by Odhams Press Limited in 1932, with an introduction by **The Reverend C.A.ALINGTON**, the headmaster of Eton, who was no doubt pleased by the inclusion of Jehoshaphat.

He (Jehoshaphat) reportedly died in 851 B.C., but recent work by the Israeli archaeologist Professor Ze'ev Herzog challenges the traditional biblical account.

(24) Page 263. Line 11 ………. *'Georg Solti'.*

It is 'Georg' without an 'e', (and his surname is pronounced **Sholtee**) was born in Budapest in 1912 and, as an exceptionally talented individual, embarked on a musical career; becoming principal conductor of the Budapest Opera by the outbreak of WW2. Threatened by the holocaust, he escaped to Switzerland, but after the war became director of the Munich Staatsoper, later moving to Frankfurt (1952-1961), and Covent Garden, London (1961-1971). Solti famously conducted the Chicago Symphony Orchestra (1969-1991), and the London Philharmonic (1979-1983), then was artistic director of the Salzburg Easter Festival (1992-1993). Previously he had been granted an honorary knighthood in 1971. However, by taking British nationality in 1972, was able to modestly display the accolade he certainly richly deserved. He died in 1997.

Ludwig Van BEETHOVEN (1770-1827) was born in Bonn, but later moved to Vienna where he took lessons, briefly from Mozart, then with Hayden and Alrechtsberger. Without doubt he strides the world as a figure of immense stature. Nine symphonies; 32 solo pianoforte sonatas; 5 concertos for pianoforte and orchestra, as well as a prodigious body of other significant work. His achievement can be divided into three periods, with his greatest pieces composed between 1802 and 1814. And all this, while, from about 1802 onwards, suffering from incurable deafness.

Esteban Buch's recently translated, ***Beethoven's Ninth: A Political History*** (University of Chicago Press: paperback edition 2004, ISBN: 0-226-07824-8) provides a fascinating insight into what must be regarded as a monumental work.

(25) Page 263. Line 39 ……*'Jimi Hendrix, with Mitch Mitchell drumming up a rage'.*

The stage name of **James Marshall HENDRIX** (1942-1970) singer and songwriter who was born in Seattle. USA. He was self-taught, but ultimately recognised as an immensely talented musician who, after straying around, came to London and formed his own group, the *Jimi Hendrix Experience,* with the band's first single *'Hey Joe'* being an immediate success.

His work can be described as being psychedelic (for want of a better word). An immense outpouring of complex rhythms and harmonies that involved intuitive trips to (sometimes, it seemed) only Jimmy knew where. Tragically, he fell prey to alcohol and barbiturate addiction, which brought his astonishing career to an untimely close.

Mitch MITCHELL: the drummer/percussionist on many of Jimi's famous tracks, from *Purple Haze* (1967); to *Night Bird Flying* (1970) which turned out to be one of the last songs laid down at Electric Lady Studios, the Hendrix state-of-the-art facility located in Greenwich Village. NY.

(26) Page 264. Line 14 ………. *'halfway point in the passage'.*

The halfway point turns out to be 19 degrees 10 minutes North, 36 degrees 04 minutes West. From this position, the distance to Barbados works out at approximately 1,200 miles. As the elapsed time from the departure date of November 17th amounts to 12 days, our average speed works out at a stroll-along 100 miles a day, which is just what the doctor ordered for a relaxing single-handed trade wind passage. Particularly when note is taken of the fact that we have the benefit of the North Atlantic drift (10 or more miles per day in a westerly direction).

(27) Page 267. Line 6 ………. *'wagering a 'pony'.*

Old-fashioned betting slang for £25 Sterling, with the amount no longer relevant to the price of a 21st century nag. In cards, the person on the right of the dealer is called the *pony*, from the Latin *pone*, meaning 'behind' (behind the dealer).

IT SEEMS THE VESSEL
HAS LOST ITS RUDDER ?

A correction is needed here, because to say 'it seems' the vessel has lost its rudder is a fatuous statement. The vessel *has* lost its rudder, with the inclusion of the phrase 'it seems' being an indication of how tempting it is to adopt a subterfuge, when the person concerned has yet to come to terms with an unpalatable fact.

THIS well enough illustrated when you stick your head out of the companionway hatch, and find what had previously been thought of as 'the pond', has somehow got a little bigger - taken on the aspect of an ocean, with a breeze blowing over it that has raised more than a modest sea and a hefty lump of a swell, because what's blowing now is fresh enough to form a succession of crests breaking endlessly to windward, offering a vista that's inspiring, but carrying with it the rude reminder that it's over a thousand miles to land in any sensible direction.

In these circumstances, it takes an effort of will to come to grips with the gut-emptied void which is occupying the position where your stomach used to be, so it's absolutely vital to get down to practicalities.

Take the necessary steps.

Move away from speculation.

Start *thinking* about the mundane problem, which is nothing more nor anything less than regaining control of the boat.

There are tools aboard the vessel, because only a total idiot is going to sea without a basic kit that will enable repairs to be made.

Aboard this boat it consists of a handsaw.

A mallet as well as a hammer.

Several wood chisels.

Two screwdrivers.

A brace, with a selection of wood bits.

A small hand drill, together with a box of high speed bits.

A Stanley wood plane.

An 'Eclipse' hacksaw frame together with 2 metal cutting blades.

There are some other items, which were well worth carrying along.

There's an oilstone, used to keep the ship's assortment of knives in razor-sharp condition.

Three double-ended spanners, as well as an adjustable spanner big enough to fit any nut found aboard the boat.

And to complete the kit, there's a selection of 'G' clamps which are always useful to have.

As well as the tools, there are odds and ends of both brass and bronze screws.

A few small bolts and set-screws of various sizes.

A supply of nails, both galvanized and copper.

And lastly, a tin of powdered marine glue, complete with a bottle of catalyst.

This may sound adequate - or not even the barest of bare essentials (depending on what sort of workshop you've been used to in the past), but when it's all you've got, you really have to be satisfied with it, because once you succumb to the *'if only we had'* type of bellyache, you are undermining the confidence otherwise known as morale.

While this necessary stock taking has been going on, the boat's been lying quietly under a bare pole, and it's tempting to think - that if a rag of sail was set well for'ard, and a jury rudder constructed, it may be possible to get the vessel underway with some sort of rudimentary control.

However, before getting down to the task of constructing a jury rudder, the thought occurs (dredged up from some long-forgotten seamanship lesson) it may be possible to 'steer' the boat by towing, say, a bucket, and by moving the towline from one side of the counter to the other, influence the course the vessel's encouraged to make.

This is certainly worth trying.

The problem is, in a vessel that combines a canoe body with a deep fin keel, and only offers the narrowest of counter, even if you *do* tow a bucket (the same old plastic bucket) it doesn't provide any meaningful control of the boat.

Not in this sort of weather.

The breeze is fresh; Force 5, bordering Beaufort 6, and the sea is what you would expect to have been raised, by a trade which has the benefit of a thousand miles of fetch, and an unimaginable age to blow unhindered over it. So, juggle though you might, with only a rag of canvas offered, as soon as she gathers way, the tub develops a mind of her own, regardless of how you play about with the bucket, which might as well be hauled aboard and revert to its original duty.

This is not really a setback, or demotion for the bucket.

Merely confirmation that whoever offered the old-fashioned advice in the first place, was no doubt talking about a long-keeled, heavy displacement vessel, that had been blessed with directional stability; not the sort of competitive cork which, while it may be 38 feet overall, sports a keel that's only as long as it's six feet deep, the sort of design meant to provide minimum wetted area, combined with maximum righting moment as well as developing lift.

Plan B: constructing a jury rudder, seems a better proposition, because although the boat's main rudder has been lost, the self-steering mechanism is intact and does offer encouraging possibilities.

The pendulum blade, although narrow, is hung in bearings which provide two arcs of travel, so if the pendulum action is restrained, there remains the rotational movement normally controlled by the vane.

By de-clutching the vane, and preventing the pendulum swinging, a small rudder-type device becomes available, whose only real drawback is the narrowness of the blade.

It doesn't take long to arrive at this conclusion.

And not much longer to re-position the tiller lines, and use them to lash the pendulum in the vertical position. The rest of the self-steering mechanism (the vane, and a bit more) is little more than a hindrance, which is best dismantled and stowed safely away below.

Now the gear's been stripped to its bare essentials, it confirms the supposition that if the main tiller can somehow be connected to the top of what used to be the pendulum, then, when the tiller is moved, the blade is going to rotate in the appropriate direction. This is not an insuperable problem, because the pendulum has got a short stub-tiller of its own, an integral part of the ingenious design, which has been converting vane-powered rotational movement, by reason of the servo-mechanism, into more than enough power to retain control of the boat.

This stub-tiller is a hefty item.

A stainless steel bar, barely a foot long, but getting on towards three quarters of an inch in substantial diameter.

All that has to be done, is connect the tiller lines to the small tiller; and to anyone firmly ensconced in an armchair, it would seem the easy-going solution to this little problem would be a neat clove hitch, formed in the bight of a rope, and then cast over the bar.

If only it were so; because the truth is, no matter how well you tie the hitch, the knot works out of position, which *has* to remain at the end of the slippery bar, by reason of the limited fulcrum provided by the stubby little tiller.

The skipper of this hooker is aware there may be an alarming number of readers who, if not already squirming in their chairs, are beginning to wonder how long this talk of vanes, blades, pendulums, tillers, stub-tillers, hammers and spanners and the like will have to be endured.

The trouble is, when you are stuck in the middle of the Western Ocean, without any means of controlling the boat, you *have* to address these items. The problem has *got* to be solved (however, if it's giving you a headache, perhaps it would be better to skip a few pages until the nuts and bolts of the situation have been dealt with).

Meanwhile, the crew (who can't opt out) are faced with the problem of boring a hole in a stainless steel bar, using a hand drill which has been fitted with a high speed 5/16 diameter bit.

The size of the bit has been dictated by the fact that the hole in the stub-tiller must be big enough to accommodate the pin of the shackle which has been dug out of the bosun's locker. As a matter of fact, *two* shackles have been selected, one larger than the other, both having pins which, if this plan can be brought to fruition, should provide a neat solution to an awkward problem.

But it all depends on boring a hole in the bar.

The sort of job which would take, say, little more than a minute or two if you were operating a powered drill press.

However, if you happen to be using a hand drill, it may take longer than that (would anyone believe *three and a half hours?*), and this is real time, which doesn't include stops for tea, calls of nature, and the runs out of steam that are bound to occur when you're engaged on a task that goes on, and on, and on, for hour, after hour, after hour.

This may seem excessive; yet the truth of the matter is, to even *start* the job raises its own particular problem - because there's no centre-punch in the tool kit.

A drawback not all that difficult to circumvent.

It just means sacrificing the well ground corner of a nice bevel-edged chisel, which has to be tapped by a more or less reluctant hammer.

Nevertheless, doesn't this troublesome start illustrate how small things are apt to influence the outcome?

The other small thing is the difficulty in keeping an edge on what used to be called a *high speed* twist drill.

This particular bit was not very sharp in the first place, and you can kick yourself for that, because not having a grindstone on board means the bit must be edged-up on the oilstone, with this task not as easy as it sounds.

It comes close to being a nightmare, particularly when you know one delicate touch on an emery wheel would provide the correct bevel, and a leading edge that would cut cleanly into whatever grade of stainless steel it encountered.

However, trying to get the correctly fashioned point when you only have a hand-rubbed oilstone ....

This is hardly worth loitering over, because the hole *is* drilled in the bar. And the shackles do provide a neat solution to the problem of attaching the tiller lines to the slippery stub of a tiller. But only after several more hours have been spent reaming out the threaded hole in the *smaller* of the two shackles, in order that the pin of the *larger* shackle can pass through and enter the threaded portion of *its* receiver.

By this time, Plan B has just about run out of steam, principally because day one has run its course and night is about to fall.

Day Two starts as soon as there's enough light to enable the job to recommence, with the first task being a trial run for the modified pendulum blade.

It works well enough, although it becomes obvious it's too narrow, it doesn't have the necessary surface area to provide the turning moment required to steer the boat.

With only a rag of canvas set on the forestay, which gives the vessel minimal steerage way, in these wind and sea conditions, as soon as the boat is being overtaken by a following crest - she gathers speed, slipping down the front of the advancing wave, and even when you apply all the helm you have at your disposal (hard over, with the modified pendulum-servo) it's insufficient - she careers away from the course you're steering, ending up broached, amid a flap of canvas and the sound of a rude seaman's curse, which leaps unhindered from the mouth of the frustrated man at the helm.

The solution to this problem is easy enough to arrive at.

Yet not all that easy to accept, because the only material available to modify the blade area is the cabin sole, which has to be - not ripped up, but dismantled, and cannibalised in order that the recovered material can be used to increase the size of the blade.

So what we have now, after the blistering forenoon of day 2 has been spent on the work, is a vessel which has lost its rudder - has had the action of the servo blade altered and its surface area enlarged [1] (see sketch at end of chapter) with the skipper feeling quite pleased with himself, because the contrivance does work, even if it's difficult to manage.

The steeper swells still present a problem.

The vessel is just as inclined to run ahead of the advancing face of a tumbling crest, and gathering speed while she's doing it, which means the helmsman must be continually, as it were, 'on guard' against yet another embarrassing broach.

In these conditions, you have to try, indeed it's essential you anticipate what's likely to happen.

Keeping a weather-eye lifted to windward.

And when you see a larger than normal swell approaching (and they always turn up, sooner rather than later) you *must* keep her stern up a bit, temporarily abandoning the course you're steering, in order that she's encouraged to lift cleanly, and not allowed to slew across yet another tumbled down curse of a wave.

Two hours engaged on this task may be a just about acceptable trick, but it's hard work, and after a late lunch, with the vessel left to her own devices under a bare pole, to have to return to the tiller, for what's left of an endless afternoon devoted to steering, means the crew is beginning to realize how convenient it is to have the use of an absolutely reliable, tireless, and uncomplaining *self*-steering gear - because, by nightfall, on day 2, the crew is as close to being exhausted as makes no significant difference.

Glad to get below, and go through the motions of preparing and wearily tasting, yet hardly touching an evening meal, before retiring to the welcoming arms of his cart (but the degree of tiredness experienced is only partly the result of the physical effort involved).

There are two other significant factors; one being the enervating effect of occupying the cockpit for the whole of the blistering day (a twelve hour fry under the relentless tropical sun) while the other skin-tightener is - shall we just call it a touch of *anxiety* ? And the man who denies that, is certainly not telling the truth.

Day Three dawns as bright and challenging as ever, and, after a restless night, it's a relief to settle to the task of once again steering the boat - able to put yesterday's experience to good use.

Which is another way of saying - that no matter how hard the task, if you stick to it, you will eventually get somewhere near the hang of it.

This means an attempt has been made to rig an awning, in order to obtain at least a modicum of shade. However, the seemingly sensible idea has provided a complication of its own, because the 'awning' is the smallest staysail, rigged horizontally between the standing backstays and the runners - amounting to no more than a lash-up.

Nevertheless, it has provided some shade, which was the purpose of the exercise. Unfortunately, it has also provided additional sail area, and in just the wrong place (in the after part of the vessel) which in its own irritatingly disproportional way, is now making the boat harder to control.

The extra speed is no more than a fractional part of an onion, but it means that full-blooded heaves on the tiller are required, at the crucial moment, when she's perched on the top of a crest, otherwise the inevitable happens, and she slides across the face of the wave, to end once more broached in the trough.

This is a wearying business, and by lunchtime the decision has been taken, to not only do away with the awning, but radically alter the work schedule, because it now seems daft to spend the whole of the day labouring (and that *is* the correct word) *labouring* throughout another blistering afternoon, when the time spent at the tiller could be postponed until the sun has set (in other words, try to sleep during the day and steer throughout the cooler watches of the night).

This is a radical proposal, yet there is a positive element that helps clinch the sensible decision, because there's sometimes a reduction in wind speed in the evening, which if it does little else, may ease the enormous strain the jury rudder is being subjected to.

That's the theory; but it's not easy to put into practice, because, until you have actually climbed on deck, just after the sun has set, and settled yourself in the cockpit, to face another twelve-hour trick at the helm, knowing there are more endless days, running into weeks, of this sort of effort before it's going to be possible to arrive at any sort of a landfall ....

But regardless of this dismal thought, you *have* to set the sail, and start on the task. Then you bump into another complication, because when it *is* black dark, and you're steering, while hoping against reasonable hope to catch star-lit sight of the next extra-large wave, you are continually getting caught out - having to apply extravagant amounts of helm, just to keep her pointing in the right direction, so what happens next should have been easy to anticipate.

By midnight, the tiller is starting to feel a bit 'soft', and the first thought is, the rapid rudder movements associated with excessive use of the helm have stretched the tiller lines; yet the hope remains, that this will turn out to be a minor problem, which can be solved by merely tightening the over-strained lines themselves.

But when this job has been done, the tiller feels as slack as ever, so there must be something else to look for. This means taking in the small jib, and letting the boat lie under a bare pole, while the crew gets on with the job of examining the jury rudder by the light of the ship's torch.

The trouble turns out to be nothing to do with the tiller lines; it's the guts of the gadget itself. The stainless steel frame, on which the pendulum swings, is coming apart at the seams, leading to the inescapable conclusion it's not worth carrying on, as it's obvious the whole thing is about to disintegrate.

To say **Day Four** opens on a down-beat note is hardly an exaggeration, because on further daylight examination, it's obvious the jury rudder is well and truly stuffed, so the first job will have to be the unshipping of the twisted remains of it, and stowing the wreck of a hope on the foredeck.

Plan C seems to have risen to the top of the heap. This entails removing the cast aluminum heel fitting from one end of the shorter of the two running poles, and after a slot has been cut in the alloy tube, fitting a wooden blade which effectively transforms the pole into a sweep. The timber used to produce the blade for this device has again been stripped from the cabin sole, and there's now very little of that useful item left to grace the length of the saloon. All that remains of what was recently a nicely fitted deck, is a small board located under the companionway ladder, so when the crew goes below, he has somewhere to put his feet.

The rest of the saloon is now open to the bilge, and while it's not very deep, it's hardly a thing of beauty and is amazingly slippery to stand on.

It's worth noting, that the failure of the self-steering assembly has not been brought about by any inherent weakness in its manufacture, but because it has not been designed to accept the strains it's being subjected to. The labour-saving skip and spot welding techniques have not contributed to its failure, regardless that to a casual observer it looks like a question of - *when opening this parcel, please rip along the dotted lines'.*

The next thing of note is that the spinnaker pole, converted into a sweep (hopefully another word for a steering oar) although offering the possibility of regaining control of the boat, does have two serious drawbacks. The first thing being - the alloy tube is too large in diameter to enable it to be manhandled. It can't be grasped, in the way which allows your fingers to close on the object (and when you think about that, the difficulty, although hard to describe, soon becomes apparent).

The other significant problem is the awkward length of the pole, because when the blade of the 'oar' has been manoeuvered through what remains of the self-steering cradle (in order that it can be lashed in position, prior to being brought into use) it's difficult to control.

Even an enthusiastic seaman, let alone a sensible one, would think it prudent to don a safety harness, before attempting the balancing act demanded of anyone bold enough to stand on the afterdeck of a 38 foot ocean racing cutter, bobbing about before a sea raised by a breeze which has some of the charm (and also some of the threat) of an all too boisterous trade.

This engaging drama has now reached the stage where the crew should go for'ard, and set the small jib; but before doing that, we all decide, by common consent, that he may as well have something to eat.

Day Four has dribbled away well beyond the reach of the forenoon, and as it seems what's being attempted could turn out to be a protracted exercise, it might be sensible to at least start the job on a full belly (shorthand for a cup of tea and a biscuit). However, this seemingly sensible decision does have, tucked away within it, a less than barnstorming motive, because part of the reason the crew opted to spend time in the galley is - it's a way of postponing the task facing him on the afterdeck, which has now assumed the proportions of a high-wire act that could well hold its own in a circus.

There is a degree of exaggeration here. But not much, because until you have taken up station on the afterdeck of a small boat which is running, albeit as slowly as possible, before a substantial sea and a swell, and then tried to influence how the vessel behaves by mucking about with what used to be a spinnaker pole - you find the problems you face are ....

(1) associated with the length of the boat.

(2) the height and particular form of the swell.

(3) the distance between the recurring tops of the waves.

What this means, in practical terms, is when the boat is *in* a trough, you can keep the blade of the steering oar in the water. But when the vessel rises, as she must, before the next advancing swell, there comes a time when she's balanced on the top of a higher and steeper than usual crest.

And when she is, the business-end of the sweep is apt to come *out* of the water (which is not the end of the world, you may think).

But as the wave moves on, and the boat is once more lowered into the trough, the oar is then slammed *by* the water, and if, as is sometimes the case, the blade is not absolutely vertical, you have what could be fairly described as a small problem on, and more importantly in, both your blistering hands.

In this situation, it's easy to lose your balance, or just play the Bold Buckaroo for a fraction of a second too long, because there's no prospect whatever of controlling the brute. The beast you're dealing with is so much bigger than you are, and kicks like a mule, so even if you carry on foolishly fighting the pole, you soon learn the next time she slams in the trough, and you hang stupidly on to the sweep, you stand a good chance of being catapulted *off* the afterdeck - to end, not *swimming for home* - but being towed by whatever length of lanyard you previously thought appropriate to rig on your safety harness.

This is not the sort of Russian roulette you want to indulge in, even if there doesn't seem an alternative to it.

So it's only the matter of one more narrow escape, before the decision is taken to pull the jib down, unlash the sweep, and manhandle the awkward bag of tricks to the starboard side of the foredeck. Slotting the discarded idea into the pair of sculpted wooden blocks which have been designed to keep the running poles in place, secure on deck, yet easily available. All that has to be done now, is spend a minute or two on deck, amidships, leaning over the boom, admiring (*trying* to admire) the seascape; and when you've had your fill, and a quiet think about it.

Retire below, having decided this is probably as good a day as any to indulge in a seagoing snort. A stiff aperitif, while wondering what to russle up, for what will probably turn out to be a not very exciting evening nosh-up.

but isn't a meal that's going to eaten
in somewhat unusual circumstances ?

CHAPTER SEVEN: PAGE NOTES

(1) Page 284. Line 7.......'*action of the servo blade altered and its surface area enlarged'.*

Wind sensitive self-steering devices for small vessels fall broadly into three categories. The first and perhaps the simplest being sheet-to-tiller arrangements that were originally developed to control model yachts. This type of device utilises a rope link between the mainsail sheet and the vessel's tiller, so that when the craft strayed off track, due to (amongst other reasons) an alteration in wind speed, the varied pressure on the sail and thus on the sheet was transferred to the tiller, with the rudder response resulting in an appropriate alteration in course.

A subsequent development in self-steering for sailing craft employed a trim tab on the trailing edge of the vessel's rudder, with the tab controlled by a vertically pivoted vane, free to rotate in response to the varying direction of the breeze. Although apparently simple, this proved a sophisticated device, because when correctly designed, and fitted, it was possible to provide either negative or positive feedback, and in that way counteract the tendency to over-steer, which is inherent in most self-steering systems. There are limitations associated with a trim tab (it can only be used if the craft concerned has an externally hung rudder) with those vessels without this facility offering under-water linkage problems that are difficult to solve. However, Blondie Hasler (ref: Page 257, Item 14) came up with the pendulum gear, an ingenious development that could be fitted to virtually any hull shape, and by harnessing the passage of water past the hull, and utilizing the mechanical advantage offered by a cradle-hung blade, provide enough energy (the *servo* part of the pendulum servo) to control sailing craft up to 50 feet in length. As a final comment on self-steering gears, it's necessary to point out that these gadgets react to the apparent wind - they don't steer a compass course, and if the breeze veers - so does the vessel.

The sketch now offered has been developed from an illustration appearing in **Gerard DIJKSTRA'S** *Self Steering for Sailboats,* which was published in the United States by Sail Books Inc in 1979, with the material being drawn from a series of articles entitled *Windvaanstuurinrichtingen* which appeared in Maanblad Watersport in 1973/4.

The hatched area shown at the bottom of the pendulum illustrates the extent of the material added to the blade, and by implication, the extra strain this modification imposed on the cradle in which the mechanism was hung. The sketch also makes clear how, if the wind vane is removed, the pendulum lashed in the vertical position, and the tiller lines re-routed to connect directly with the stub-tiller, the pendulum blade is converted into a rudder which, although narrow, does at least go some way towards offering control of the vessel.

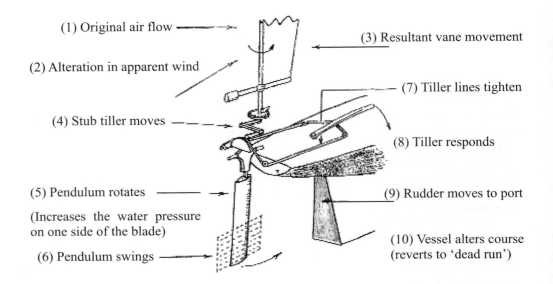

(1) Original air flow

(2) Alteration in apparent wind

(3) Resultant vane movement

(4) Stub tiller moves

(7) Tiller lines tighten

(8) Tiller responds

(5) Pendulum rotates

(Increases the water pressure on one side of the blade)

(9) Rudder moves to port

(6) Pendulum swings

(10) Vessel alters course (reverts to 'dead run')

A TOUCH OF THE BLUES

WHILE the crew of our old tub has been attempting to cobble together some means of regaining control of the boat, he's been totally absorbed in the task, and this is hardly surprising, because making a jury rudder, or transforming a spinnaker pole into a sweep requires an effort that blots out everything else. But when you've given 'the situation' your best shot, and failed to solve the problem, you have to sit down and scratch your head.

Perhaps what you should have done in the first place, because even if the jury rudder, or the sweep had proved to be effective, the position of the boat relative to a landfall means the distances involved are bound to influence the outcome. To blithely assume you may be able to *sweep* the boat into harbour, means you haven't come to terms with your geographical location, so it's time to go below and take another look at the chart.

It's not a reassuring picture.

Four days ago, we were twelve hundred miles from land, and what's been made good since has only reduced the figure by a marginal amount.

There's still the little matter of a thousand miles, and more, of boldly rolling ocean to negotiate before we'll be able to approach any sort of a beach, and this assessment of the position conveniently ignores the difficulty of *where* we're going to make the landfall. A conundrum which takes time to come to terms with, so it's worth pouring a tot, [1] which may as well be lingered over, in what is perhaps the best place in the world to confront an enigma of this sort.

In this context (could also be contest) the companionway ladder of a small vessel is a handy little item.

As you ascend the steps, your head emerges from the confines of the boat.

When you move up another rung, you are head and shoulders into whatever breeze there's blowing.

One more step and you can lean over the coaming.

Resting your elbows.

Lounging the deck.

Surveying an ocean that heightens, then rolls, with laughing old crests which tumble and play in the sun.

Down under the lee, the topple-backed waves move easily off, having dealt with the boat as a plaything, while away to the west'ard the endless red road taunts the reticent stance of the seaman.

But whatever shapes the outlook.

The trade has raised a substantial swell that approaches, then lifts, as it shoulders the boat on the curl of a wave which offers no threat of breaking aboard.

Though some of them burst with a slap on the hull, and a shower of spray that trickles once more to the ocean.

As scattered white clouds scud high in the trade.

To drift over the boat.

And dapple the scene.

As they sail between seascape and sun.

This is the vista facing you, as you stand on the companionway steps of your small vessel, in order to elbow-lounge the ocean.

And ordinarily, it's a view that satisfies the most fastidious seaman.

While the sun sets, the orb softens and swells the dominant flame.

To no more than a ball which hangs.

Poised for a moment.

Then dips to the beck and turn of your wet-centred world.

As the glare diminishes, with the sun half-way set, the man waits.

Squinting, while hoping for that tease of a moment, when the flame slips from view.

Flaring what may or may not mark the end of his day, [2] as shadows lengthen.

Smoothing the outlook.

Yet raising it seems, for one weighted moment, what he previously thought was the height of the swell.

While far overhead.

The puff-balled white clouds have grey'd themselves out.

All the way to the eastern horizon.

Drifting from view, as twilight sweeps on from the rim of the world.

Time to retire.

Must go below, before more stars appear.

And this *insignificant* feeling gets any worse.

Whatever may be said about the platform offered by a small boat engaged on an ocean passage, to feel obliged to retreat from it, to what you hope is a more amenable location (the homelier feel of the cabin) is a notable step in the deterioration which has taken place in the relationship between the seaman and his always wet and often windy world, because when you descend the companionway steps and thankfully shut the hatch, an attempt has been made to move from a larger than life environment - to one of assuaging domesticity, where what's brought into focus is not the height of the swell, the strength of the breeze, or even the scud of a cloud, but something easier to live with. The situation being reduced to manageable proportions (the skipper trying to decide which tin of beans to lever open for this day's evening meal).

No doubt, what we're contemplating seems a long way from red setting suns, tumble-backed waves and laughing old crests - to recall just a few of the seascapes.

Even then, it's not far enough, because though the glow of the cabin lamp does offer some comfort, and the can opener *is* in its usual place, the fact remains there's been a dramatic change of outlook - the crew not quite the braw lad he used to be, as he tries to face up to the fact that what was previously a 38 foot, ocean-racing cutter, has now become (in his mind, anyway) little more than a log-sogged, wallowing raft.

This down-turn in morale has been on the cards ever since the rudder fell off the boat, but has been postponed by the physical effort involved in trying to solve the difficulties concerned with trauma of this sort.

However, now several avenues of escape have been painstakingly explored, and reluctantly abandoned, those hard-worked days no longer provide protection from the gloom which pervades the cabin, even though this domestic haven is partially illuminated by the light from the paraffin lamp.

In this situation, while it's possible to see things which were previously deemed of some importance (the ship's clock, screwed to the saloon bulkhead, and the primus, suspended in its gimbals, waiting the call of the cook) the sight of these familiar items doesn't offer reassurance, as perhaps they might be expected to.

To the contrary, they cast even more shadows, which have as their morbid background the sullen wash of oily water in the indecently open bilge; an awkward reminder that the despoliation of the cabin's been to no avail, with the situation appearing to be worse now, than it was before.

Probably, the onset of depression can be as difficult to avoid, as it is to describe, and this is partly the case because there's no recognisable point which is shuffled past - and when looked back on, can be flagged-up as the moment when the person concerned became convinced the game had turned against him.

If this were the case - if there *were* recognisable signposts to, and then leading thankfully from, the debilitating spiral - the age-old, but ill-considered advice to people who suffer a clinical reverse (that they should pull themselves together and *snap out of it*) may be just about acceptable.

However, when you have *entered* the depressing world, this impatient comment does little more than beg the dubious question, because if you *could* snap out of it, *you wouldn't be damned well in it,* so all that can be said, with any degree of certainty is - when you find yourself in line for a serious fit of the glums, you should try to avoid ending up on the bones of your bare as a badger's emotional arse, when you're alone, at night, in the middle of the dismal North Atlantic. Apart from anything else, there must be better places to hit rock bottom, and this is regardless of the two thousand fathoms of ocean swirling under (although you're doing your best to forget it) the keel of your rudderless boat.

In these circumstances, what have you recourse to?

The bottle, of course, is as handy as ever, and there's a supply of the usual goodies if you're seriously considering a pig-out.

But whether these temptations offer a solution to the problem remains a matter of doubt, because even when a gluttonous proportion of the ship's stores have been eaten, and yet another mind-bending slug poured out, the outlook remains as bleak as ever.

You can, of course, persist with the treatment - open another tin of sliced and slippery peaches, and down another debilitating tot.

Yet if (when) you do, sooner or later, you will have to admit that while alcohol may be handy as a social lubricant, its use as a morale booster seems to have been exaggerated - though the stuff *is* having a strange effect on the ship's clock, now ticking assuredly away, but apparently gone slightly awry.

Can it be midnight?

The very time when, aboard this lugger, the crew would normally be handily asleep in his cart; while here he is, making something of a fool of himself by experiencing a dismal attack of the hab-dabs, taking the form, in this depressing instance, of the skipper being unable to get mentally out from under the problem of how to move the boat on from where it now happens to be.

And this is not merely a mental difficulty.

It has a physical, a clammy, not to say sweaty dimension, because this move down hill has brought the crew to the point where he finds the cabin, previously handy as a bolt-hole, has turned into a cubicle that's much too small to live in.

But when he climbs the companionway steps, in order to escape from confinement - he now finds the view from the cockpit presents a world that's *much too large to look at.*

And there doesn't seem an easy solution to this step-by-step denouement, because if he goes below for a sweater, more booze, and a cushion, when he gets back on deck and resettles himself in the cockpit, he finds he's just as unsettled as ever.

What's worrying him now is ....

It's such a dark night.

The breeze is also sighing in the rigging, and when he looks aloft, there are far - *far* too many stars in the sky.

Prompting the thought, that one possible way out of this frightening glimpse of the firmament, may be to hang the old lamp in the rigging, even if it does entail another sweat-raising dive down below.

But when the lamp *is* hanging in the rigging, responding to the lurch and sway of the boat, it illuminates the encircling ocean, emphasising, as well as confirming the skipper's maudlin outlook - that hasn't been helped by the trip down below, because when he was fuelling the lamp and scratching about for the matches, he just happens to put his hand on the bottle, and then, when he's climbed back on deck, made himself comfortable and dozed inexplicably but probably alcoholically off for a moment, he's prey to an amazing delusion.

That he's not aboard *this* boat - has somehow been transported, to a specialist Round the World ocean-racing yacht. A state of the art machine that's not only fully-crewed, but has a skipper with sufficient guts to run before a gale of Southern Ocean nightmare, surfing the vessel down wind under a heavy weather spinnaker, with the speedo off the clock and only a matter of time before she slews uncontrollably across the face of a towering, ice-fingered wave, which breaks - washes the helmsman overboard - leaving him dependent on how long she takes to right herself and the length and strength of his safety harness.

This being a development of the sport of sailing which takes the whole thing well beyond a leisure pursuit (raised it to Formula One) particularly so, when, as the crew find they've still got a rig aloft, they get themselves together and do it all over again. But this monumental flight from reality has done nothing to bolster morale, because when he opens his eyes, (our skipper) finds the courage displayed has been carelessly left in the other boat's wake.

That *he's* still on the bones of his emotional arse, still trying to escape from the shadows.

So could it be?

Could it possibly be, the time has come, when contact with the *outside* world may provide some way out of his difficulty?

There are two possibilities.

First, there's the boat's radio, with its flick of the on and off switch hooked-up to convenient headphones.

This requires another trip to the cabin.

But it might be worth it, because music has provided welcoming balm in the past. Yet just when it's needed, all that's available is a post-modern *atonal* concert, preceded by the avant garde announcement that what's about to be performed *could be* (in a pig's ear it could be) one the Brandenburg Concertos of *our* time, [3] (a hideously-shaped joke of the age?) demonstrating, as it does.

If polytonality be perpendicularly, instead of horizontally considered (that is, harmonically, instead of contrapuntally constructed) we already have atonality (the absence of a key) because, looked at in this way, the keys brought into combination are mutually destructive. The chords produced by their impingement being referable to no acknowledged key whatever.

So it's but one small step, to abandon all pretence of a key, in any strand whatever, with this staggering lack of accessibility [4] followed by a succession of squeaks.

Clashes on a cymbal.

The double-based grunt of what sounds like a sousaphone, followed by the faintest of tinkles on a tiny (could also be *tinny*) little triangle, and another apparently unrelated tap on a determinedly out-of-step drum. The whole of the kitched-up cacophony blasting through the head phones, leaving the seaman searching frantically for a sensible, or indeed *any* possible line of retreat.

Then, when he twirls along the wavelength, comes across the BBC booming through the ether, reliably informing the oceanic listener that the world's sad wars rage as cruelly as ever.

That armed-to-the-teeth tribesmen, sophisticates and others, now control over two-thirds of their mutinous and mountainous, land-locked, sea-girt, verdant, or dry as a dust-bowl countries, and it's only a matter of time before the other third will be ravaged - forced to return to medieval barbarism and submit, *submit*, **submit** to the God-dictated (?) rule of their 'Law'.

Another twirl to the dial, and the news is - baseball still holds centre-stage, with a million fans out shouting *they can do it one more time*.

That we're all agog at the clash-of-titan's drama that's involved with this year's cherished Rose Bowl, *and we-all can't wait*, until the Yankees are winding-up to take on, *what they think of as*, the rest of the 2nd class World.

Meanwhile, back @ the Beeb, in yet another Eden, another 18 innocents (2 babies, 4 adolescents, 8 women, and assorted octogenarians) have just been brutally murdered, bringing the five-year abominable aggregate to an unbelievable thirty-five thousand citizens with their lifeblood ebbed in the sand. And this works out, just in passing, to 1,1,1,1,1,1, 1,1,1,1,1,1,1,1,1,1,1,1, hideously throat-cut victims every, *every*, **every** day of those five revolting years.

So it's on with reluctant fingers to another twirl of the wavelength, where Vatican Radio is broadcasting *The Truth*, as *Revelation* sees it, trailing next month's sermons with details of oratorios, initially from Cavalieri's *Soul and Body*.

Then on to Handel's *Saul*.

Beethoven's *Christ on the Mount of Olives*.

Mendelssohn's *Elijah*.

Sullivan's *The Light of the World*.

Gounod's *Redemption*.

Dvorak's *St. Ludmila*.

Stanford's *Eden*.

Elgar's *The Dream of Gerontius*.

And there are over a hundred others to choose from, with this night's offering being an extract from Handel's *Messiah*, about to be performed by the London Philharmonic Orchestra, from the Albert Hall, with a suitably full-throated chorus.

Handel's masterpiece (overplayed?) but still this seaman's favourite, echoing around the world, after bouncing off the Heaviside Layer [5] then hovering above the boat, before being netted by the vessel's short-wave radio aerial (her antenna) not in any way related to Prospero [6] and transposed into a series of vibes in the headphones, which are now clamped tighter than ever about this drunken seaman's head.

Followed by another 87 bars.

The last three loud enough to wake any sleeping Host, with the chorus enhanced by the glorious appeal of the organ, and voices raised in tribute to *Christ the Only Begotten Son - the Anointed One - sent by God to Save the World*, an expression of Faith made accessible to the sometimes wayward rest of us by the inspired insight of one man's glorious score.

Then the sermon, containing, amongst other things, the news that the Holy Father (with perhaps a glance over his shoulder at the burgeoning feminist movement?) has decreed that we should no longer think of God as, an old man with a beard, who lives - *up there.*

This raising a smile on the same three-sheets in the winded old seaman, who has long since believed the three tier (could also be tear, with a salt-glistened drop, which glints with the depth of your anguish), that the three-tier universe of *God the Father; God the Son;* and *God the Holy Ghost* ....

This image has long since gone the way of all flesh.

Perhaps since the Age of Enlightenment, and most of us (well, many of us) now subscribe to the view that, what *we* are concerned with, are the amazingly varied hypotheses that attempt to explain

Man's intricate relationship
with his oh so clouded destiny
(7)

CHAPTER EIGHT: PAGE NOTES

(1) Page 291. Line 22 ………. *'worth pouring a tot'*.

In this context, it might be as well to remember that Gin is supposedly a *downer*, while Vodka acts as an *upper*, and Scotch has the enviable reputation of being a middle of the road, reflective balm of a drink. But perhaps distinctions of this sort are inconsequential in these particular circumstances?

(2) Page 292. Line 27 ………. *'flaring what may, or may not, mark the end of his day'*.

A reference to the green flash, thought to occur as the upper limb of the setting sun dips below the horizon, although countless observers seldom see this perhaps apocryphal phenomenon. Nevertheless, the tradition persists, and provides entrée to the sun-downer's tête-à-tête - *'did **you** see the green flash?'* as glasses are raised to the glory unseen.

(3) Page 296. Line 20 ………. *'one of the Brandenburg Concertos of our time'*.

The Brandenburg concertos mentioned by the radio announcer refer to the work of **Johann Sebastian BACH** (1685-1750), recognised in his lifetime as 'the greatest organ and clavier player who ever lived'. His Brandenburg Concertos, six in number, were commissioned by Christian Ludwig, Margrave of Brandenburg, and have become a valued, not to say priceless part of Man's musical heritage.

(4) Page 296. Line 29 ………. *'lack of accessibility'*.

This is a reference to the previously mentioned *atonal concert from the 'States* (supposedly the Brandenburg Concertos of our time) when what is on offer seems to have more in common with 'sound effects' than what most of us recognise as music, which the **Shorter Oxford** defines as *'one of the fine arts, concerned with a view to beauty of form, sounds in melodic or harmonic combination*. An explanation which puts atonal music on the other side of a very wide street for this old seaman, who wonders if - should you manage to gain access to the atonal composer's intention, you would find anything there worthwhile?

The comment on atonal music is drawn from **The Oxford Companion to Music**, published by OUP as a 10th edition in 1970 and given a 22nd impression in 1996.

(5) Page 297. Line 37 ………. *'bouncing off the Heaviside Layer'*.

One of the ionised regions (found at a height of approximately 115 kilometres above the surface of the earth) that reflect waves from a transmitter. An essential part of short-wave radio communication which would otherwise be lost in space. Also known as the E-layer, or the Kennelly-Heaviside layer, after those scientists who first commented on this phenomenon.

(6) Page 297. Line 39 .... *'the vessel's radio aerial (her antenna: not in any way related to Prospero)'*.

Those familiar with *the Bard of Avon* (1564-1616) will recognise this side-ways, but still appreciative glance at two of his ethereal characters.

(7) Page 298. Line 23 .... *'Man's relationship with his destiny'*.

This far-reaching remark was drawn from Professor Julian Huxley's **Religion without Revelation'**, published in 1927, with a 2nd edition in 1957, putting forward a view of the world which stands in dramatic contrast to that constructed about the following incident.

On May 13th 1981, **Pope John PAUL** the Second, was shot, while he was in St Peter's Square, Rome, in the act of blessing over 20,000 people. The gunman, *Mehmet Ali **Agea*** (23) used a 9mm Browning automatic. The Pope was hit by four bullets, several of which lodged in his lower intestine. Two women standing near him were also hit, and one was seriously injured.

When he had recovered (after extensive surgery) the Pope declared it was *Divine Intervention*. A magical sort of a sortie, expressed as a supernatural act by the Virgin Herself, which had deflected the bullet ....

'after' it had entered his body.

(but how many people believe it ?)

WITH A RATHER UNUSUAL PADDLE

I don't suppose for one moment everyone will be prepared to accept, or even be interested in a public expression of doubt (questioning the usual form of Belief).

Why should it concern anyone else?

Isn't it a private matter, that should be decently held over for a more suitable occasion?

Yet there are plenty of instances where, in the midst of adversity, a great deal is made of the power of prayer, and some of these experiences are written-up and find their way into those annals that record how the person concerned thanked God for his or her deliverance. And this is fine; it is certainly thought to be fine by the Establishment, who then make use of these role-models as and when they think it appropriate to do so.

To quote two, out of many examples.

There's the well known 'professional' adventurer who, having come seriously unstuck in the middle of the Southern Ocean, recorded and published the news that he wasn't worried, because he was absolutely sure the Almighty would look after him, *that HE, knew he was there*, it being only a matter of establishing contact, through prayer, and the ugly situation would be dramatically resolved.

Then there's the famous polar [1] explorer (who happens, by contrast, to be every seaman's favourite) who survived appalling hardships as he led a band of men through ice-bound seas and, having survived the ordeal, struggled with a hand picked group over a glaciered, snow-covered mountain, in order to summon help for those comrades who had been necessarily left in their wake. Having accomplished this astonishing journey, the acknowledged national hero quietly informed his friends that throughout the endeavour he knew someone else was present, who had joined him and his party, and while there, had not so much relieved him of the burden of leadership, but guided him in the difficult, indeed almost impossible task.

This is great stuff - the sort of fare most of us are raised on - but as we grow up, although prepared to accept these accounts as a truthful record of how the people concerned interpreted their private circumstances, in that particular place, and at that particular time; we may later question the proposition that there's a supernatural world *out there*, with an army of visiting angels who, if the Almighty happens to be otherwise engaged, will pay the necessary visit and solve the troublesome problem.

There is a snide little edge to the last remark, yet this apart (and the apology given) there *is* a real dilemma involved, and it's easily set out.

If you question the existence of the supernatural world (which some theologians, for example Tillich, in his *Systematic Theology*, seem to be trying to finesse when he changes it to *supra*-natural) then, when you're caught with your schoolboyish pants down (stuck in the middle of the Western Ocean without apparently being able to do much about it) there may be an urge to get down on your knees, and ask for the help you have been brought up to believe is there - if only we have the necessary Faith to accede to it.

This is serious stuff - it may even be found to be boring - yet it does provide an amusing aside, because it's now become apparent there are two sorts of *Creek* which we normally do our best to avoid.

We are all familiar with the first of these locations (up shit creek) which is usually referred to as the one that's devoid of a paddle; however, it now appears there's another, even more embarrassing inlet.

This is the creek you are well and truly *up* (no doubt about that) but it seems now - you have thrown the damned paddle away, and *that's* the embarrassing part of it.

In these unfortunate circumstances (having suspended Belief) you have been tempted to pray.

And *this* is the challenge, because (who to? And for what?) when you've been persuaded, by people who claim they know a great deal more than you do, that prayer is sometimes little more than a knees bent, head bowed, begging letter. And these doubtful messages could be - either being posted to ourselves - or are of the type we resort to when we have lost, or perhaps have never actually gained, the ability to stand on our own two undoubtedly clay-laden feet.

This is navel gazing with a vengeance (that will be *mine*, says the Lord) which sounds like a threat straight out of the Old Testament, by Yahweh. But there's no need to lose much sleep over it, as more than likely this has all come about because, last night, I not only had an attack of The Dog, black, brown, or brindle - but probably had one gin or more too many (however, quite honestly, and with just the trace of a smile) I don't *think* it was the gin. It's just not as easy as that.

Last night, there was a real downturn in morale.

The sort of night where there seems no light at the end of the tunnel, which has already been alluded to as being very hard to describe.

As indeed is recovery, which arrives unannounced, seeming to take little more than the advent of a brand new day, and the effort involved in the brewing of a steaming pot of coffee for the sufferer to emerge from the gloom.

Able to look around the boat, which, somewhat to the seaman's surprise, seems to have escaped the ordeal.

Apart from the untidy state of a cockpit that's littered with blankets, cushions, and a nearly empty bottle, which I can see out of the corner of my other bloodshot eye.

Having negotiated this escarpment, and tried another scalding sip of coffee, it's tempting to pick the bottle up, and hurl the lot over the side, even though there's still some of the fatal liquid in it.

A gesture intended to demonstrate (but to whom?) the days of introverted stumbling are over.

That the crew of this old hooker may have suffered a fit of depression, but he's over it now and is keen to get on with the job.

At the same time, there are imps at work, whispering the tantalising message that - to *demonstrate* you are on top of the problem (but which one?) it would be better to keep the drop of gin as something of a talisman, and then, when circumstances allow, pour the snifter into a celebratory glass which can be raised on the leeward side of the ocean. But what's not been mentioned, because it may give offence - came the dawn, the crew is buoyed by the knowledge that he *hasn't* succumbed to temptation.

Didn't, get down on his knees and wailed about for assistance.

But all this backing and filling is getting in the way of the job in hand, which is difficult enough, because the sun's well up, and the time has certainly arrived to stop feeling sorry for yourself (myself) and make a determined effort to get into shipboard routine, regardless of the fact that both the skipper and the tub are wallowing about.

Nevertheless, this doubtful motion has a bright side to it, because as the boat is lying under a bare pole, it's easier to stand on deck, lean against the boom, and take a hard enough look at the ocean.

And if, previously, everything was in the dismal arse of the introverted world. At the other end of this now extravagantly zooming but thankfully extroverted spectrum ....

Everything's as marvellous as it all could possibly be.

Because it's as plain as a pikestaff, the good old trade's still blowing away.

As fresh and clean as ever.

That the new day's sun sparkles an ocean, which is blue.

As blue, as the bluest of seas could possibly be.

While young Neptune's kites (the puff-balled clouds) are flying high.

As high as kites can be coaxed to fly.

When they're headed for the rarefied height of the firmament.

In commonsense terms, they're just scudding away to the west'ard, occasionally obscuring the sun.

But only momentarily, as the glare of the orb encircles the scene, making sure there's not the shade of a shadow in sight.

The sort of extravagant picture, a forenoon may be spent mooning over, if you can put up with the mood-swing which produced this astonishing touch of euphoria.

By watching the way the swell lifts, and then plays with the boat.

The way a crest curls, and then doesn't just break, but tumbles instead as old Neptune trips over his foot and his feat (probably admiring his kids with their kites) in this light-headed part of the ocean.

If it wasn't so blisteringly hot, I'd spend more time on deck, lounging about, but this isn't a practical option, because there's shipboard work which needs attention.

First up - I would have to engagingly admit, I don't know where the vessel is, precisely.

It's four days and five nights since the rudder fell off the boat, and during this time, although much effort has been expended trying to regain control of the tub, there hasn't been the slightest concern regarding her day by day position.

Then there's the matter of stores.

The boat was vittl'd for the trade wind passage from Tenerife to Barbados, with the assumption made, that the two thousand four hundred mile trip would take no more than twenty-four days; give or take an unlikely change in the weather.

As half the passage has been completed, getting on half the stores have been consumed, leaving a question mark over the sensible rationing of the grub that remains in the locker, which leads to the serious matter of water;

the drinkable sort, not the oceans of stuff surrounding our disabled old hooker.

We started this trip with a seamanlike amount.

A figure obtained by estimating the duration of the passage, and then adding to the 'gallon a day' rule of thumb, the usual sensible margin (+50%) to arrive at a figure of 36 cautious gallons, which were then stored, carefully distributed, in nine 18 litre jugs.

About nineteen gallons remain, which sounds a lot; but it brings into question the advisability or otherwise of those baths in the cockpit, taken to commemorate what had seemed, at the time, to be small, yet nevertheless significant waypoints.

But it's no good bellyaching about what we've got, or haven't got.

The first job is - to find out exactly where we are.

This means an AM sight, and spending the next two and a half hours profitably enough, praising the beans, counting the carrots, sorting the spuds, generally stock-taking and tidying the cabin until it's Noon, and we can arrive at a reasonable position, which turns out to be ....

Eighteen degrees, thirty-four minutes, north; forty-two degrees and eighteen minutes, west.

Indicating Barbados lies approximately 1050 miles in a west sou'westerly direction, while the mainland (Guyana, Suriname, Guyane-Française) is about the same distance, but further south again.

These are substantial, even if rounded-out figures; nevertheless, there are one or two things running in our favour.

There's the North Equatorial Current [2] which is moving in the right direction. And there's the surface drift provided by the trade, because it seems we've been blown about 100 miles to the west'ard since we encountered our little local difficulty.

This figure is complicated by the fact that, during the last four days, time's been spent mucking about with the jury rudder and the spinnaker pole. They may not have been an unqualified success (and let's hope this wildly unreal description *is* the last faint twitch of euphoria) but some progress *was* made, and it's difficult now to differentiate between current, drift, and actual miles made good when struggling to steer the boat. But the real centre of interest lies in the number of days that may elapse before a landfall is made.

Let's suppose, taking a worse-case scenario, we have the benefit of about half-a-knot of current to the west'ard.

Add another half-a-dozen miles of favourable drift - this means 18 miles made good every day.

Divide this figure, into the getting towards eleven hundred miles which lie between us and Barbados, and you don't have to be a mathematician to conclude the passage may take another - sixty-six days? It may take more, if we can't make a satisfactory landfall and get blown past the islands, into the Caribbean, to end up at Caracas; or further along the coast, past the Gulf of Venezuela.

These are the sort of idle and not so idle thoughts which occupy your mind when writing up the log book, and inserting the symbol on the passage chart which records this day's noon position. From here, it's just one more step to arrive at the disturbing conclusion that the estimated duration of the voyage (sixty-six days) when divided by the number of gallons remaining (19) provides the sparse figure of roughly two and a half pints of fresh water per day - thankfully an adequate, if not generous amount.

But if this drift of a passage extends *beyond* the estimated sixty-six days, the figure will have to be reduced, which wouldn't present much of a problem if we were up north.

However, we're in the tropics, where water intake is important, with the consequent risk of dehydration something much too serious to be foolishly ignored. So taking one tight-lipped thing with another, we will have to be careful with the stores, most particularly the water, until we see how this dry old cookie crumbles.

In the meantime, back on deck, the view from the cockpit is very much what you would expect in this favoured part of the ocean.

The nor'easterly trade is Beaufort 4 to 5.

The sea-state matches the breeze.

The swell's as substantial as ever.

The old tub's as dry as a cork, and likely to remain so.

So what's the on-going problem?

The problem is - it's too much of an iffy equation.

It's all very well assuming we'll be home, and hopefully not too dry, at the end of - who knows how long the passage will take? Yet this assumes we will not only manage the distance, but *find* a convenient beach, before being dried out (the skipper reduced to a kipper) and that's by no means a forgone conclusion.

The prospect of drifting towards, and through the Windward Islands, to end up sculling about the Caribbean, looking for a convenient spot to land on (swim to?) is not something to be idly dismissed.

This is an outcome that's apt to concentrate the mind, particularly when you're lounged in the cockpit, late in the afternoon, toying with the idea of making a cup of tea (the indulgence enjoyed, as you admired the way the old boat was running her westin' down at the rate of a hundred comfortable miles a day). While now, there's a nagging doubt, prompting the thought that, though you would *like* a cup of tea ....

This is a situation which has only one outcome (you don't have the tea) because the consensus is, it would be better to wait until the sun's about to set, and at least some of the heat's gone out of this scorching tropical day. Then, when the sun *has* set, and you're enjoying the tea - and it's not *such* a sweaty occasion - you can consider what to rustle up for the evening meal.

Not a difficult decision, when you know exactly how many tins of beans, sardines, soup, tomatoes, peaches, pears, tuna in oil, tuna in brine, corned beef, stewed beef, and other odds and ends of shipboard grub, which includes sprouting potatoes, limp carrots, still-juicy onions; previously fresh (but about to get rubbery, beetroot), together with uncounted packets of Danish crispbread that goes so well with cheese.

English Cheddar, or a chunk of doubtful Double Gloucester; possibly a piece of almost tasteless, last-for-ever Edam, *all* of which are available on this not exactly famished old tub.

And that's saying nothing of three screw-topped jars of sweetly pickled onions, which go so well with cheese of any sort.

And further on even than that. If you, or I, as skipper, feel like breaking the strict rule governing the crew of this old hooker, there's always the possibility of a civilized tincture of pink to use up what's left of the gin.

A staggeringly different outlook to the previous night's gloom and unrelieved doom, when the cabin turned out to be an inhospitable place; a half-tide rock, awash with stuff deep enough to wallow in.

There's even been the gleam, so far unannounced, of what might turn out to be a sensible idea (but that'll have to wait 'til the morning).

What we're faced with now, is another night aboard the crippled old boat, yet buoyed with a completely different focus; and, as so often happens on these newly-recovered occasions, the visitors (invited aboard via the radio) are more than prepared to play-up to a crook-looking smile from the crew.

No more atonal concerts, very little mayhem, only a couple of murders.

A 'quake in Guatemala.

Another flood in Bangladesh (15,000 dead) 100,000 homeless.

A rape or two in Runcorn: but apart from that ....

The only excuse for this callous attitude is - if you've come to terms with being adrift in the middle of an ocean - you could be prey to the sneaky little feeling that you are well removed from a conscience-driven scene; because (and here's something that maybe worth a second glance) it seems a *sense of isolation* doesn't necessarily come by itself.

However (whatever?) now the woe has been shuffled past, shelved, or simply marked down as someone else's problem, it is easier to get a good sleep on the basis of - why not let tomorrow simply take care of itself?

Another day is another day, which breaks as all days do, when viewed from the cockpit of a small boat.

As the world turns, the sky lightens.

The trade freshens, and before you know where you are, the sun climbs over the horizon, just as bold and as brassy as ever.

The breeze is still blowing from a nor'easterly direction, still raising the same old lump of a swell, and the same old curl of a wave; endlessly displaying the face and pace of an ocean that's rolling towards the boat, with a succession of lowers and lifts, as the Old Man flexes his muscles (just keeping his triceps in trim).

A well-equipped sailor would be taking advantage of a smoke-free ride to any old port of his choice.

But if you're aboard a disabled vessel - and you can't set any canvas, it seems that last night's gleam of an idea might be worth - at least another not-so-doubtful look.

This hopeful thought, concerns the way a boat can be made (*persuaded*, is a far better word) to behave in adverse conditions, which may or may not seem relevant to our present awkward circumstances. But when you're sitting in the cockpit of a boat that's bobbing up and down, but going absolutely nowhere, while there's plenty of wind about, you're tempted to think there must be *some* way out of this vexing situation.

What I have in mind, is trying to get the boat to heave-to; because if this can be accomplished, we might be able to make use of at least some of the breeze that's whistlin' over the deck.

There's only 15 knots or so, but if we can set some canvas, even a modest amount will be enough to get the old tub driftin' downwind, leaving the sort of slick which is vital when weathering storm conditions.

This is not a bad idea, worth looking at in some detail.

When a small boat is faced with a life-threatening gale (Beaufort 8, and more) in order to survive, even the lower numbers, it's necessary to reduce canvas, and keep on reefing until the vessel's no longer making headway, but lies 4 to 5 points off the wind, establishing a square, life-sustaining drift. This being one of several old-fashioned, nevertheless classic examples of heavy-weather seamanship, which ensures the boat's not driven *under* a potentially damaging crest, but allows the hull to move *with* the onrushing breakers, bodily to leeward, so the amount of heavy water coming aboard is limited to survivable amounts.

Of course, there are variable factors that have to be taken into consideration before a skipper decides to adopt this particular tactic, which could be likened, in pugilistic terms, to *rolling with the punch.*

In this regard, there's the severity of the gale.

How much searoom you've got under you're lee.

And the sort of yacht, which may or may not be adequately equipped to survive the storm and complete the ocean passage.

However, there is one factor common to all small boats in circumstances of this sort. And that's the advisability of exercising more than just a modest degree of caution.

Making *sure* you are hove-to, *before* the ill-tempered Old Man is allowed to get what he always wants to get, which is never anything less than the destructive upper hand.

Having called your own time-out, in your own particular gale (and now riding duck-like, bobbing up and down with *your* neck safely tucked under *her* wing) the observant seaman notes, that the boat is being driven bodily to leeward, by the weight of the wind in the rigging and the action of the sea on the hull. And as she makes her strategic square-on retreat, she leaves a slick (a 'smooth' on the surface of the water) which may seem of little consequence. But when you take a closer look, even a duffer can see that *in* the slick, which may extend from one wave crest to another, the incidence of breaking waves has been reduced. And this despite the fact that the howl of the wind in the rigging is as dauntingly high as ever, and the role (together with the *roll* of the sea) remains substantially the same.

When you understand this strategy, it's only a matter of time before you want to put it to the test.

The trouble is, the old tub doesn't want to cooperate.

As soon as even the hint of a mainsail is set, she gets restless, and when the small staysail is coaxed up the inner forestay, in order to balance the main, she's charging about, rushing off here, darting off there, in a mad scramble; leaving the crew wondering if it will be possible to get her under even a semblance of control.

This wild behaviour can also be dangerous (don't get hit on the head by the boom). So it doesn't take many involuntary gybes to convince the skipper it would be a good idea to set up the main boom preventer. However, when this useful bit of equipment has been rigged (to restrain the boom) the next time the mainsail's set, she still takes charge - executing another crazy gybe - but this time it's a Chinaman, [3] which is more embarrassing than usual, because not much can be done about it, apart from hand-the-main, and get the small staysail on deck as soon as you possibly can.

Meanwhile, the forenoon's well advanced, and it's time for the obligatory AM sight. But when the necessary few bits and pieces of the mathematics have been sorted out, the rest of the morning can be spent trying to make sense of the really important conundrum.

Part of the trouble is - when the mainsail is hoisted, and flutters about in the breeze, the sail is well above deck-level - then, when the staysail is hoisted, in order to balance the canvas, this area is close to the deck and the lack of 'match' doesn't suit the rudderless hull, because she's rushing off in what could be any one of the 32 points of the compass.

In these circumstances, you can spend time experimenting with all sorts of combinations of sails.

Two reefs in the main, and a small staysail.

A trysail instead of the main, and a storm jib in place of the staysail.

A full mainsail, and a large jib set on the outer forestay.

Two reefs in the main, and a *staysail* set on the outer forestay.

Three reefs in the main, and the staysail set on the *inner* forestay.

One reef in the main, and a small yankee,[4] set on the outer forestay.

Hell's Bells and buckets of blood, when you come to fiddle about with the variables, it seems there are *endless* combinations of sails, both large and small, which can be set here, there, and every damned where else. But whatever permutation is chosen, the crazy old coot has no intention of behaving herself.

She still takes charge, not only to the embarrassment of the skipper, but coming close to *infuriating* the same man, who, when he looks at the ship's clock, can hardly believe the forenoon's melted away and it's time, indeed more than time to get an altitude (because of the slippage, it has to be an ex-meridian) [5] before this day's noon position can be worked out, and entered on the chart.

After these details have been taken care of, it's time for a cup of bloody coffee (feel free to pick the adjective that suits you) while *my* ill-mannered solace is *not* tempered by the knowledge that the calculations have revealed, that we can't count on much more than 18 miles made good each day; which brings into question the number of cups of coffee, or any damned thing else for that matter which might be frugally available before this aggravating arse of a passage is well and truly over.

Time to calm down?

Yes: because there's little to be gained by losing your temper when you're dealing with an inanimate object (the old bosun was, and still *is* right about that) so after lunch (an apple, crisp bread, and a slice of all-too-rubbery Edam) together with half-a-cup of water, with just a little limejuice in it, perhaps it'll be a good idea to sit down and *think* about it.

To see if a little *rational* thought can be brought to bear, on what seems an intractable problem.

(an hour later) enough time has been spent on the task, to enable at least one sensible conclusion to be drawn.

When I think back on it (referring to the canvas) things started going wrong as the mainsail was *being* hoisted, with this unfortunate state of affairs brought about because the lee runner is preventing the boom from being squared-off.

And because the boom *can't* be squared right off, the sail hasn't got 100% freedom of flutter (for want of a better description) but fills, just a little, and as soon as there's any weight of wind in it, off the old cow goes, in whatever direction she chooses, regardless of what combinations of canvas the crew's been tempted to try.

This may seem a tangled argument, yet there's sense in it, certainly enough to start on the task of unrigging the runners, and when they've been attended-to, slackening the inner forestay bottlescrew, and when *that's* done, unhitching the stay and bringing it back to the mast.

The net result being, the boat's now rigged as a sloop; the mast being more than strong enough to stand with what's left of the rigging, amounting to twin standing-backstays, the shrouds, and the outer forestay.

While the battle's been raging, it's become apparent that another difficulty is the near impossibility of correctly sheeting the high cut headsails (hauling the clew out to windward, in the classical hove-to position).

So what I'm going to do now is, rig the second spinnaker pole, with the

311

heel well up the mast, and by making and fitting a rope grommet [6] which slides along the pole, arrive at a lash-up which allows the crew to sheet the chosen headsail in just about any position, as this moveable in-and-out block amounts, almost, to a useful skyhook.

The upshot of this blood, sweat, and not so occasional rough seaman's curse is - the boat's brought under control.

After another five hours of hit and miss experiment, the starboard runner's been restored.

The inner forestay's been taken for'ard to its original position, and the storm jib set on it.

The trysail has been set, and sheeted flat as a board.

The clew of the jib has been hauled outboard to effectively 'bisect' the breeze, utilizing a mad cat's-cradle of inhauls and outhauls that's achieved a balance between trysail and jib, with the old tub now leaning away from the trade, lulled to rest, but being blown downwind (the object of the exercise in the first place).

It may not look in any way pretty, because it's not too-attractive a rig; but it's the best we can do for the moment.

And who cares what we look like?

It'll be dark soon, yet our old wreck will be soldiering-on, rocking quietly across the breeze; nodding here, drowsing there, plodding on, while her skipper enjoys a well-won nod of his own. A good night's kip that's almost worry free, while the old tub looks after herself (as all good boats can be expected to do) *if you treat 'em the way that you should.*

And ain't it marvellous, to wake in the morning, knowing we're moving in the right direction?

That the crew, and the craft, have contributed - just a little.

That he and she (she & he?) have added their small but useful mite to progress, which was previously only on offer from the crafty Old Man himself (the north Equatorial Current), with the outcome being, we have probably more than doubled our rate of drift towards Barbados.

So having solved at least part of the problem, there's time to look about the boat.

Finding the trade remains as it has, for all those millions of yesteryears, and when you face it, is still wonderfully fresh in the morning; while a lump of a swell moves under the boat, lifting the hull as she leans from the breeze, with the vessel showing more of her topside than usual, as she wipes the smirk off a face, that, until a moment ago, was *absolutely sure* it was a roll-aboard dollop of wetly-toppling wave.

So it's - *Hey Ho, and up yours Davy !*

In these slap-happy conditions, when you look carefully at the surface of the ocean, you see the top of the 'oggin's been modified.

That close to the boat, it no longer popples about - it's been *smoothed*, and the ripple (the broad ripple just upwind of the boat) has little to do with the way the breeze influences the rest of the tumbling seascape.

We shouldn't make too much of this, because it's not an unexpected development. However, it is the sort of thing you notice when - either, you're attempting to weather a gale, and, *for your life*, you *have* to remain in the slick.

Or, you have plenty of time on your hands, lounged on deck, looking into the depths of an ocean that's become accessible, because the slick is easier to see through.

Easier to see through?

Indeed it is.

When the vessel is making way through the water, sailing under a blue and cloud-capped sky, it's difficult to see *below* the surface of the ocean, because the boat, and the wind-induced movement of the interface, is displaying the broken, bright-eyed reflections of those puff-balled clouds. And this distracting combination is reflected off the surface of the sea, disrupting an observer's *view*, even if it leaves his *vision* unimpaired.

However, now we're all-but-stationary, merely *drifting* down wind, it's possible to obtain a clearer view of what's about and under the boat. And even a cursory glance indicates there are interesting items down there.

The trouble is, I can't spend time mooning over the side, admiring shadows. The clock has marched towards noon, and the fascinating underworld will have to wait, until we've made an appraisal of where we are, and what's been made good, over the last 24 hours.

The sights, when worked up, show we've progressed nearly 30 miles to the west'ard (so fiddling about with the canvas has significantly increased our rate of drift). But we still don't know how to apportion the progress made between current, *and* drift.

Not that it matters, as the figure we're using for current (0.5 of a knot) is only an estimate, and what we're really concerned with is the aggregate figure, which will steadily, even if slowly, reduce the number of miles remaining to any sensible landfall.

It's now six days since the rudder fell off the boat.

A barely credible figure, which indicates how the days merge into each another when you're well and truly adrift on an ocean (or anywhere else, for that matter). And during the interval, although the face of the place has been observed, casually or otherwise, as time has rolled by, it's now apparent there's been a significant change in the relationship between man, boat, and the Old Man's place of abode.

Because I have learnt, during this odd Neptunian initiation, although I've spent years cruising-about *on* the 'oggin (and have come to feel very much at home on it), it now appears, since we fell into the soft stuff, but have partially recovered from that unfortunate condition, this old seaman now feels, not only at ease with the ocean - *but more at ease with himself.*

This could, at first glance, appear a fanciful suggestion.

But now the navigational chores have been dealt with, and another sparse lunch prepared and eaten; the afternoon stretches away towards evening, providing time to explore the possibilities that were vaguely recognised during the quick look-over-the-side of the vessel (the glance that took place just before noon).

And I have found, lying prone on the sun-blistered and blistering deck, bare belly protected by the spreading of a blanket, with my head cantilevered outside the lifelines, and using an old chart to shut out the reflection of the sky - I can peer into the depths of an ocean which stretches away from the drifting boat ....

As the green sward rolls unhindered from the favoured hills of Kerry.

An amazing, twice-removed scene, embellished by the notion that, *above* the wind-blown surface - everything's blue and white and bowls about in energetic motion.

While *below* Old Neptune's navel, looking at what was, until recently, his very private-parts, all's at rest.

The rolling swell.

The scudding clouds.

The whitely toppl'd seascape.

All that, and more, belongs to a mere seaman's view of the sea.

And is by far the lesser part of it.

Because, now I can see what's going on *under* the boat, it's obvious there's far more there - even than I thought, with the first thing being ...

The vessel is casting a shadow.

Our tired old tub, is making her very own imprint, not only on, but in, the boldly rolling ocean.

And I can see - have just become aware - there's a shaft, formed in the green sward on its silent way to that abyssal plain [7] which lies a full two thousand fathoms five, sunk below the keel.

How *far* our shadow makes its presence felt, is not the thing in question (as divers - don't we soon run out of candle?), but at and near the surface, we're making a significant difference.

There are fish, enjoying the parasol provided by the shadow of the boat, one quite large Dorado (also known as a Mahi-mahi); [8] and there are tiddlers, some no bigger than a matchbox, keeping close to the hull. Then, when Big Boy makes what could be interpreted as a predatory move, the small-fry nip around, either the leading or trailing edge of the keel, depending which is the favoured escape route of the moment.

In the sunlit portion of the ocean, the sea is blue.

(but hear this) the bright blue swathe has a *translucent* glow, and when it's eyeballed, you're aware of endless creatures in it.

Some are small (indeed, *so* small they're only visible as a barely recognisable dot), yet these are the millions (as many billions of millions you can wrap you're mind around, *then to the power ten*) of exponential dots that are altering the colour of the sward which supports our floating home.

These plankton are *dancing in the sunlight,* and the translucent nature of the deep is partly the outcome of their light-reflecting presence.

This gazing into the ocean may be fascinating, but it's giving me a helluva crick in the neck (because I'm cantilevered outboard of the lifelines) and what's more, the blazing afternoon sun is beginning to play merry-hell with my back.

I'm already as brown as a berry, but a sunburn is a sunburn, in anybody's language, so the sensible thing is - go below and dig out a shirt.

But when I'm back in the cockpit, sporting a tattered old T and a hat, there's still no escape from the lariat the crafty Old Man has cast about the boat.

Now I'm lounged, not flat on deck, but sitting in the cockpit, and once more taking note of what's happening round and about the boat, I can hear water trickling, gurgling, and occasionally surging round the hull, with the movement depending on the position of the vessel - whether she's dropped in the trough - or poised on the crest of a wave.

This stream of water seems innocuous; yet when you look at it again, you must take serious note of it, because when you do, you see it isn't just a stream of water.

It may be a stream of common-or-garden water.

It *is* a stream of common-or-garden water.

But it's also a stream that's shouldering a cargo - the sort of cargo I haven't had the opportunity of observing before.

This stream, gurgling round the hull, forms the slick the boat is leaving as she's drifting down the trade. And the significance of this stream is; the surface is relatively flat (it bears little relationship to the wind-blown popple which disturbs the surrounding seascape) and on this smoothed-out surface there are ....

Insects.

Insects?

Here?

In the middle of the ocean?

You're kidding!

There *can't* be insects, floating on the ocean.

(I'm tellin' you, friend) there are *insects*.

Scuttling about on the surface of the sea.

These bundles of wonder, having been swept round the hull, are moving towards the middle of the slick (the pond that we're creating) and once there, the bolder larrikins are taking stock of their position, by exploring the parameters of what must now be, to them, an easy-peasy world.

Some of them are venturing close to the boat (so I'm cantilevered out again, in order to get a bird's-eye view of this fascinating scene) and at first it's difficult to tell if the little devils are actually coming or going - the only sure indication is, when they race off in a particular direction - but now I can get a closer look at them, I can see they resemble the 'skaters' we all admired as kids, yet this is the first time I've seen them in this wow of a natural habitat.

Horsman says, there are more than 500 species of water striders, otherwise known as 'boatmen' (Heteroptera) and they're distributed world-wide, most commonly found on stagnant ponds, coastal swamps, lakes, and the back-waters of slow-moving rivers.

Five species of sea-skater have colonised the surface of the ocean, and these (Halobates) [9] are described as the only known ocean-going insects.

That's fine, as far as it goes.

But it doesn't go far enough.

How do they float? Where do they breed?

What's their lifespan? What do they feed on?

Who are their predators?

Can they make ocean passages?

How do these Halobates weather a gale?

Do they boat-oars ....

And lie to a drogue, as a clewed-up seamen would? [10]

This is a bewitching image.

All those gallant boatmen, holding on to their hats, as an out-of-season hurricane storms across the pond.

Yet here they are, rowing merrily away, seemingly without a care in the world.

Blading about, feathering beautifully, [11] on the slick our old tub is leaving, as she slides across the ocean by making use, in her own small way, of a rather unusual paddle.

In these circumstances, it's possible to spend considerable time admiring the wonders of the natural world. But this world spins, and before long I'm forced to abandon my grandstand view of the boatmen.

Partly because the sun's about to set, and there are shadows darkening the surface of the sea. But also because it's time for the major meal of the day, and it's better to do the modicum of cooking involved when there's a bit of daylight about (so the cabin lamp doesn't have to be lit) and once fired up, add its sweltering stum-down [12] to the already stuffy cabin.

Then, after the chores have been attended-to, it's back once more to the cockpit, carrying the grub, because this *is* the place to spend the closing minutes of the day, whether you're knife and forked or you're not.

The sun seems to gather momentum as it approaches the western horizon, prompting the lounged-about mariner to question - has it really taken such a fast-moving object a full twelve hours to zoom from rim to rim?

Then, having set the conundrum aside, the skipper enjoys a cup of steaming coffee as darkness smothers the boat.

Reassured - that the ocean *can* be a companionable place.

That the stars, now beginning to appear, don't necessarily intimidate a person, whose only real hope of a card game is ....

a dog-eared twist of greasy solitaire

CHAPTER NINE: PAGE NOTES

(1) Page 301. Line 21 ....*'famous polar explorer.'*

Ernest Henry SHACKLETON (1874-1922) born in Kilkee, Ireland and educated at Dulwich College, later entered the Merchant Service and qualified as a Master Mariner.

He accompanied Captain Scott RN on an Antarctic expedition 1901-1904; and in 1908 sailed from New Zealand in command of the *Nimrod,* heading an expedition that got within 100 miles of the South Pole. On returning to the U.K. he was knighted for this exploit, which was thought a model of its kind.

In 1914-16 he made an attempt to cross the Antarctic continent, and it was in order to summon help for his marooned crew that he undertook the epic journey mentioned in the text. In 1921, in command of the *Quest,* he led another polar exploration, but died of a heart attack during the endeavour.

Shackleton's powers of leadership were outstanding (he never lost a man) and his achievements, sometimes with limited resources, were generally recognised as being extraordinary. His books include *The Heart of the Antarctic,* and *South;* with this volume first published by William Heinemann Ltd in 1919, but recently reissued (1999) in a Pimlico edition by Random House, London, edited by **Peter KING**, with over a hundred of **Frank HURLEY'S** original photographs beautifully reproduced.

(2) Page 305. Line 25 .... *'North Equatorial Current.'*

The **North Equatorial Current** runs west'ard in these latitudes, at a rate that varies from 0.5 to 1.5 knots (Admiralty figures).

(3) Page 310. Line 7 .... *'it's a Chinaman.'*

A slang reference to an involuntary gybe (a 'Chinese' gybe) when the boom remains on one side of the boat, while the mainsail's been slammed on the other - sometimes amusingly known as a badly twisted nautical knicker.

(4) Page 310. Line 27 .... *'small yankee.'*

A **yankee** in this context is nautical usage for a headsail which may vary in size, but is always high-cut, thus requiring aft sheeting arrangements (see back cover illustration).

(5) Page 310. Line 37 .... *'has to be an ex-meridian.'*

An **ex-meridian** is an observation that becomes necessary when the navigator is seeking to establish his latitude, but is unable to obtain a meridian altitude (taken at noon precisely). The ex-meridian facility is particularly handy in weather that offers heavy cloud, with only occasional breaks, which means that the sun may be visible for only a brief moment (but not on the meridian) before being lost behind the cloud bank. The standard *ex-meridian tables,* convert an observation that was not taken at Noon, to an altitude that provides an acceptable latitude.

(6) Page 312. Line 1 .... *'rope grommet.'*

A **grommet** (also known as a *grummet*) is a ring of rope, made up by paring back (unlaying) a piece of three-stranded stuff, and then relaying the material in a circle, ending up with what looks like a deck quoit.

(7) Page 314. Line 39 .... *'Abyssal Plains.'*

The extensive areas that form the ocean floor at depths of 2,000 to 5,500 metres, lying between a continental shelf and a mid-ocean ridge. The plains are flat or gently sloping, classified as gradients that don't exeed 1:1000. They are formed of fine-grained sediments of clay and silt, amounting to several hundred metres of deposit which have taken (literally) an age to accomplish this blanketing effect; but as a result of the accumulative process, offer a smoothness unparalleled on the surface of the planet.

For mere Man, this is *the* hostile environment. The fleshed remains of shipwrecked seafarers (*should* they reach the bottom) are quickly eaten by those rare species of fish that can survive the immense pressure found at abyssal depths. The bones, stripped clean, are attacked by bacteria; but as our young Adam's Ribs are composed of soluble material (mostly calcium phosphate) they anyway disappear completely, leaving the basement floor of the Old Man's watery kingdom devoid of any trace of human form whatever.

(8) Page 315. Line 6 .... *'one quite large Dorado.'*

Every seaman knows a **Dorado** (*Coryphaena hippuris*) when he sees one, and is aware this animal is also known as a dolphin (fish) which may be descriptively confused with the other sorts of dolphins; part of the group of marine mammals knows as toothed whales (*Odontoceti).* In Hawaiian waters, the dorado is known as Mahi-mahi..

(9) Page 316. Line 36 .... *'Halobates.'*

Although **Paul HORSMAN'S** book *The Seafarer's Guide to Marine Life* offers an introduction to these fascinating creatures, the acknowledged world authority is Dr **Lanna CHENG** who, after graduating from the University of Singapore, went to England on a Commonwealth Scholarship and obtained a D.Phil from Oxford University in 1969. She now works as a research biologist at the Scripps Institution of Oceanography, University of California, San Diego; and since the early 1970s has studied marine insects, and particularly Halobates, the world's only oceanic insect.

Although noted and described by the Estonian naturalist Johann Eschscholtz as long ago as 1822, until the late 1960s, few entomologists were familiar with these creatures, and even fewer oceanographers were aware of their existence, while today, even after the publication of *Marine Insects* (1976), edited by Lanna Cheng, few seamen realize the oceans they traverse support an insect population.

Although sometimes described as 'distributed world-wide', Halobates are confined (if that's the right word) to tropical or near-tropical locations. There are 44 known species, mostly found on coastal waters, one of them being *Halobates lannae* and named after Dr Cheng. But there are five ocean-going skaters, and amongst a host of intriguing characteristics, their diminutive size compels attention. These critters (Dr Cheng's affectionate familiarisation) are tiny - a body length of about 6mm, and they depend on surface-tension to stay afloat, utilizing water-repellent hairs on their legs to spread the 'load', which amounts to all of 8mg. But although small, these creatures are relatively fast (a metre per second) with this mobility displayed in bursts of frenetic activity as they skate from place to place.

Confined to the air-sea interface, Halobates are, during the day, continually exposed to the sun, but are apparently immune to damage from ultraviolet light, although devoid of the substance *melanin* which was previously assumed to be the normal source of protection. Thus raising the intriguing possibility, that these skaters will provide a scientific lead to a novel substance, which may ultimately benefit those of us who are not immune to the debilitating effect of sunlight.

Halobates are true bugs (they feed by sucking fluid from their prey) and the staple diet appears to be zooplankton, caught at the sea surface; but they also feed on fish eggs and larvae. A mature female carries up to 30 eggs, which she lays on just about anything that floats; while the nymphs, when hatched, initially may rely on the organic film that coats the interface. When faced with storm conditions, these creatures survive immersion for short periods on the bubble of air they trap about their body, utilizing a 'mechanical gill' (Dr Cheng's description) which enables the animal to diffuse oxygen from the seawater and thus prolong survival; while this life-saving bubble, in normal conditions (held against their bodies by hairs no more than 1.5 microns in length) provides the buoyancy needed to survive on the surface of the ocean.

Taking one amazing thing with another - shouldn't the most hardened dog doff his hat to Halobates?

(10) Page 317. Line 6 .... '*lie to a drogue, as a clewed-up seaman would.*'

The expression *clewed-up* stems from the usage of drawing the lower ends (the clews) of square-sails to the upper yards, as the sail is being furled. But in the context of the text, 'clewed-up' means *on top of the job*; leaving nothing to chance.

A *drogue* (another word for a sea-anchor) is a hooped canvas bag, towed from the stern of a small vessel, in an attempt to prevent her broaching-to in heavy seas.

(11) Page 317. Line 12 .... *'blading about, feathering beautifully.'*

A reference to the technique used by oarsmen (and of course, oarswomen) who indulge in the upper-echelon sport of sliding-seat rowing. In this environment, plain old-fashioned oars are promoted to 'blades', so that a racing shell can be fairly described as being 'bladed-about'.

The expression 'feathering beautifully' is an accolade presented to those people who really do know how to row. The cognoscenti who understand the importance of 'catch'; 'length of stroke'; 'leverage applied'; and then the feathered, well-swung 'recovery', when the blade (of the oar) is rotated through 90 degrees in order to reduce wind resistance during that part of the manoeuvre. A marvellous sport, which not only exercises just about every muscle in the human frame, but requires a degree of mental discipline that makes no bones about sorting the dull old sheep, from the mountain-climbing goats.

(12) Page 317. Line 22 ....*'sweltering stum-down.'*

A **stum-down** is slang for a situation exemplified by lack of air. A right royal example would be a crowded room, where far too many of the people present are puffing Meerschaums, stuffed with Capstan full strength tobacco, regardless that the location lacks any form of ventilation and the temperature is nudging a high-humidity ninety.

A FASCINATING SLOPE

(could be a learning curve of a sort)

WHEN faced with a long haul, in difficult circumstances, it's important to adopt a stance which maintains a level of morale that avoids mood swings of one embarrassing sort or another. And this may sound easy, a truism, something within the compass of any competent seaman.

But this facile judgement ignores the effect of happenings that have, tucked away within them, private dramas which all too easily turn into the small, yet not so minor traumas that seldom see the light of an ordinary day (when what you have to deal with is the character of the person you *are*), which may be more than one step removed from the person you would *like* to be, and another step again from the person you thought you were.

There's nothing complicated about this argument.

We are all capable of deceptions that go personally unnoticed (usually because we are not always in a position where our frailties are exposed, when we have the alarming mirror in our hands). And then, when we find ourselves *with* those frailties cruelly exposed, the tendency is to keep our mouths shut (put the mirror carefully aside, and shuffle-on) in the hope that the cavalcade of events will divert attention from a situation which may deteriorate, into what's sometimes known as a sorry state of affairs.

And I reckon that's more than enough navel gazing for the moment, because I have every intention of keeping everything low-key, and intend to soldier on (even if this is a poor choice of phrase for someone adrift on the briny).

Last night was a case in point.

All was going well.

The old boat lying across the trade - sliding to the west'ard easily enough, while I spent time in my bunk, fiddling about with the radio.

I *was* popping up as the Old Man's rules of engagement require, conducting the head out of the companionway look round the horizon every thirty minutes or so. But as we haven't had sight of another vessel since we left Hierro astern, I must concede my '*look-outs*' had dragged out a bit, with the actual watch keeping intervals no doubt longer than that.

323

So I felt guilty when, during yet another pop out of the hatch, squint round the horizon, at three o'clock in the morning - there's a ship, hull down, and by the alignment of her masthead lights, raising the doubt that she may not pass clear of our drift-about cutter.

Normally, I watch how things develop, and if an approaching vessel *is* on a collision course, I take appropriate action.

Make a decisive alteration.

Moving well out of the way, to offer a change of relative bearing that should show up on a radar plot (assuming we appear on this handy bit of equipment) and the steamship's watch keeping officer has noticed the blip we've hopefully made on his screen.

However, if you happen to be aboard a small boat which can't be manoeuvred, the probability is you're in for an interesting ten minutes or so.

The feeling of vulnerability grows with every passing minute.

As the ship approaches, comes steaming over the rim, her sidelights appear, confirming your cockleshell is smack in line for a confrontation with something a great deal larger than you are.

There's no need to extend this little drama, because the vessel I noted has just made her own significant alteration, and is certain to pass half a mile to the nor'ard, which may sound ample enough.

In seafaring terms it's biscuit-tossing range.

Close enough to smell and *feel* her upwind presence.

A supertanker, lit up like a Christmas tree, and as she's running 'light', [1] hear the blades of her massive propeller break surface with a regularity that has all the appeal of a count down to what could have been a calamity.

However, there's nothing to worry about now.

She's steaming on to the west'ard, and in another ten minutes will be hull-down again, passing out of sight.

Just a ship - popping over the horizon.

A bit of a surprise. But hardly something to keep twisting your knickers about, because she *has* passed clear.

Yet the fact is, I've just made a foolish mistake. [2]

This is the first vessel we've seen close-to since making our departure, and I might as well admit, that if this sighting had occurred soon after the boat had become disabled, the probability is, given the state of my morale at the time, I would have been diving for the tub's torch in order to make 'Morse' [3] contact, with the object of organising a pick up, after I had pulled the plug and taken to the life raft.

That didn't happen.

And I'm very glad it didn't, because the gloom and doom has been left astern.

The penny not only dropping, but landing right side up, with the outcome being, that I now feel confident this odd sort of a passage can be successfully accomplished, while at the same time providing interesting sailing (if you can describe this drift across an ocean as 'sailing' in the accepted sense of the term).

Comes the dawn, and it's another beautiful day.

The trade's picking up, with the breeze fresh enough to knock the tops off the swell, in a scattering of spray which the sun decks out with rainbows, before the crest moves on, the droplets fall, and the boat slips back into the trough - while the crew stays lounged in the cockpit.

Frying in the tropical sun, yet admiring the way the old girl leans from the breeze, as she *slides* her way to the west'ard.

In these conditions (hove-to, dry-decked, and nicely sun-drenched) as the forenoon advances, the cabin gets too hot to offer much in the way of comfort.

Yet there's a question mark about rigging an awning, because the rig we're 'sailing' under is so delicately balanced.

A trysail and a storm jib, with the clew hauled out to wind'ard (the classic hove-to position) may sound a simple contrivance - but without a rudder it's a tricky sort of a do.

However, here we are, not all that far north of the equator, and it *is* damned hot, so it's worth taking a chance.

Hoping the extra bit of canvas, offered by an awning, isn't going to disturb the status quo.

This 'awning' is really a small staysail, but when it's rigged and stretched horizontally, utilizing all sorts of lanyards and out-hauls it does offer a modicum of shade, and fortunately, the extra area hasn't disturbed the balance of the boat, although there were one or two anxious moments when the sail was flapping about.

Now we've got a bit of shade available, the next thing on the list involves stripping the starboard pilot berth (I'm sleeping, as always, in the lee cart), lugging the mattress on deck, and lashing it on the coachroof; so we now have an out-of-the-sun chaise longue of sorts.

A delectable spot which any old hound would appreciate, because when you're spread there, admiring the 'oggin, it's difficult to deny the sea *is* beautiful, in a blasé sort of way, even if all it amounts to is the same old crests, driven by the same old trade, drawing the sun-shaded eye to the same old rainbows, that are *still* being blown from the tumble down backs of those same old play-about waves.

Nevertheless, while it looks very attractive, there is rather a lot of it (particularly between here and Barbados) so I reckon this as good a time as any to draw up a working agenda.

It will soon be time to arrive at the noon position (run up the position line provided by the AM sight, to cross with a meridian altitude) and during a normal passage this develops into a ritual.

The daily runs made good are entered in the log, with the reducing 'distance to go' being an enjoyable part of the game.

But as we're *drifting* across the ocean, to keep on measuring our not much more than snail-like progress could turn out to be a pain in the proverbial butt (because it draws attention to how little mileage has been made good on that particular day), so I reckon, a good decision would be, to leave the sextant in it's case for a while, at least until a sizeable amount of progress has been made.

This sounds sensible, and with roughly twelve hundred miles to cover, to break it down into three hundred mile chunks also seems reasonable. In man-management terms - wouldn't this be recognised as aligned to 'attainable objectives'?

Whatever, I feel happy with it, because it provides not so much a time-scale, as a 'distance made good' compilation, which suits the job in hand, with the result that I won't be worrying my guts out every day concerned with the lack of progress.

The newly-rigged chaise longue is also working well (the crew can lounge on deck, mostly out of the sun).

I've also rigged a headrest, utilizing one of the saloon settee cushions, wrapped round the mast to provide another touch of luxury.

So taking one thing with another, I now feel better organised, and not only in a physical sense, with a well-rounded view of the world.

The main attraction, on offer for this day's cinéma vérité matinée performance turns out to be the well-heralded arrival of a troupe of itinerant flying fish. [4]

Scores of these nautical illusionists are streaming off the surface of the ocean, launching themselves from the top of the swell by self-propelling tail-lashing wriggles, to arc down wind, splash into the 'oggin, then drive on and upwards again, very much like the pond-hopping stones we skittered about as kids.

Strictly speaking, these fish don't 'fly'.

They glide through the air, supported by elongated pectoral fins.

And another thing not immediately apparent is - these fish are 'flying' because they are *fleeing for their lives,* pursued by predators, probably dolphins, who are fast enough to follow the school in flight, then snatch lunch in a brief boil-up which barely disturbs the surface of the ocean (it's over and done with in two seconds flat). Leading the casual observer, to the cynical conclusion that, although - Davy Jones & Company, - *Entertainers Unlimited* - provide a marvellous display, very well cast; it's an expensive production, particularly if you happen to be a flying fish.

This bit of unabashed butchery has reminded me we have (or anyway, had) a pet dolphin, enjoying the parasol our old tub's providing. I can't see him now, and I suppose it's possible that he (or it could be she) has joined the fun provided by the hunting party that just galloped past, halloo'ing on their way.

The afternoon performance, for those of us seated in the stalls, is the arrival of a loggerhead turtle. [5] This stately gentleman swims alongside, takes a look at the tub, then meanders off in a westerly direction (bound for the Windies?) but wherever he's heading, he will certainly be making his landfall long before we're likely to.

The day drifts on, blisteringly hot, even under the awning, and it's tempting to raid the water jug. However, this wouldn't be a smart move, should certainly be resisted, as the master plan requires an intake of no more than two pints of fresh water a day. This isn't an absolute figure, because it doesn't take account of the liquid contained in a tin of beans and, more obviously, a tin of soup; but two pints of water isn't a lot, and boils down to taking a sip when you would normally indulge in a cup, of tea or coffee.

So there's a feeling of relief as evening approaches, and the sun's about to set.

After the meal's been prepared and eaten, it's nice to sit in the cockpit, waiting for the cabin to cool.

Looking forward to Davy's evening performance, because, not long after the sky has darkened, and stars appear, there's an amazing change in the ocean. [6]

During daylight hours, the majority of pelagic species [7] vacate the upper layers of the 'oggin, to spend their time below. But after sunset, there's a realignment, and some of the denizens make their way to the surface. The champions being a species of lantern fish, which swim from depths of 1,500 metres (taking three hours to make the trip). Then just before dawn, these *Ceratoscopelus* prefer to keep themselves to themselves, and return from whence they came. Nevertheless, there are some gregarious lanterns who, when they're lit up and out & about, can't resist the lure of the footlights (the ship's torch, shone over the side of the boat).

These inquisitive devils come to the side of the vessel.

They're not very big (5-10cm) having brightly silvered sides.

Hove-to, they position themselves in a semicircle, looking directly up at the tub. A row of bright red eyes, peering at the skipper, who stares back, fascinated by yet another example of the tricks old Davy's got stowed in his locker.

The night and the boat drift on, with the crew spending as much time out of his bunk as in it, because the light over the side temptation (for viewer and for visitor) has attracted a bunch of squid. [8] These lads are bigger than lantern fish, perhaps averaging 30 centimetres, with some of the big boys approaching a metre in length.

They keep out of the spotlight.

Lurk in the shadows, but when they see an opportunity, make darting runs across the brightly lit arena to nail whatever's available. Then, come morning, with the sun up, having rung the curtain down on last night's cavalcade, we're back to the rolling ocean.

Blue skies.

Scudding clouds.

A freshening trade.

Rainbow-driven spray (all the run of the mill, common or garden old stuff).

By the middle of the forenoon there are Portuguese Men of War [9] to leeward, and it's not long before we're drifting through the fleet.

These newcomers resemble blue light bulbs, bobbing on the surface of the ocean.

As we take close order and drift amongst them, it's possible to see trailing tentacles extending metres from the float. And there could be more to 'em than that, because these jokers are sometimes described as a group of animals that have developed inter-dependent roles.

The bulb provides buoyancy.

The lucky ones are involved with reproduction, while the third group (the tentacles, not the testicles) are responsible for the collection of food, having stinging cells (nematocysts) they use to paralyse their prey, that's then generously shared with their mates.

Amazing, isn'it?

But as Jolson said - *you ain't seen nothin yet'*, [10] because in amongst the poisonous tentacles, swim a species of fish called *Nomeus,* who either enjoy an immunity from the toxins, or are smart enough to keep beyond waving-tentacle reach; nevertheless, they must benefit in some way from their proximity with the Men of War.

Else why would they be there?

Mixed up with the PMOWs are other jellyfish (Vellala) known by old dogs as 'Sailor by the Wind'. They are only an inch or so long, but make up for lack of length, by the number of their bretheren scattered on the ocean, which they share with another small jelly (Porpita); also blue, which supports itself by making use of a calcareous gas-filled disk, about an inch in diameter, from which hang an array of fine blue tentacles.

Both these species are preyed on by a sea snail (Ianthina), boasting a toothed mouth called a radula, which they use to rasp away at the jellyfish.

All the jellies are preyed on by another shell-less snail *(Glaucus),* which resembles a sea slug, having bunches of finger-like projections *(cerata),* radiating from the sides of its body.

This slimy wobbler is able to eat the stinging cells of the Man of War without discharging them; passes them through its gut; and then rearranges them on its cerata, so is able to defend itself from predation by the use of second-hand cells, while this cost-conscious meanie keeps itself afloat by swallowing air and distending parts of its body.

We have only been at this game for something around a week, yet it's already taking on a shape of its own.

At night, there's so much going on, we're faced with an embarrassment of riches; and when the sun's up, there are other, equally outrageous scene-stealers about.

A school of smiling dolphins. [11]

The bottle-nosed variety, who are probably wondering why our tub is hove-to, in a breeze which provides perfect sailing conditions.

They usually sport about in the bow wave, but as we haven't got anything resembling a bow wave, they've come alongside.

Hanging in the water; sussing the place out.

Taking a good look.

Circling the boat a couple of times; then, *'morning all'* and off they go, looking for someone to play with.

The sharks - small blues (*Prionace glauca*) about eight feet long, have a more cautious approach.

Sure enough, they circle about the boat, but as solitary individuals, conducting a careful reconnaissance before making a pass; then, when they swim alongside, reveal themselves as graceful creatures, perfectly proportioned, athletic to the point where the lazy movement of a tail provides the effortless mobility the top-dog predator has in such run'em down abundance.

With all this, the bare truth is, I don't know exactly how many days have elapsed since we fixed the boat's position.

It's got to be eight (could even be nine) so it's worth taking the plunge.

Arrive at a noon position, which turns out to be 16 degrees 52 minutes north, and 47 degrees 42 minutes west.

Not a bad result, as it means our rate of progress amounts to a bit more than thirty miles in 24 hours.

Better than the original estimate, and probably due more to the current, running at the best part of a knot, as against our slide down wind, which can't be providing much more than a dozen miles made good.

So who's worried?

Not me: even if there is a long way to go. Although we do have a dilemma gathering on the horizon, that involves - not our rate of progress (couldn't expect much better) but it seems we're being pushed to the nor'ard of our Barbados-bound track, [12] yet what we can do about it remains something of a mystery.

The days drift by.

Not without the occasional surprise.

A storm petrel has been dodging about for several days.

These miniatures are known to the brethren as *Mother Carey's Chickens* and have the reputation of being shy, to the point of reticence, as they flutter about, but keep their distance.

Appearing to flirt with danger - they fly *under* the toppling crests, dancing on the surface of the ocean, and so at home in a gale of wind they're surfing around, *tubing* with the best of them, [13] so I was surprised, come dawn this morning, to find a storm petrel, perched on a sail bag, [14] in the for'ard part of the vessel.

A petrel? Come aboard the boat?

Yes, a petrel.

Come aboard the boat.

Must have been during the night.

Flown through the for'ard hatch (kept open, to ventilate the hull) and when I crawled out of my cart, with visions of brewing a cup of morning coffee ....

There she is.

A *petrel*, perched on a snow white sail bag.

There are three things here.

The first is - *nobody* is going to believe a petrel flew aboard the boat.

The second thing is, I'm not going to have a cup of coffee, because it would involve moving to the galley, firing-up the primus, and probably disturbing the visitor. The third thing is; my family bible measures 17 inches long, 10 inches wide, 4 inches deep (rounded-out figures). It weighs 16 pounds (7.26 kg) and is stored in a purpose-made oak chest (I took great pleasure making this piece myself).

This good book belonged to my maternal grandfather, who hailed from Berkley, Gloucestershire, and he passed down, what is certainly my most prized possession (first entry dated 1820).

That said, I would be quite prepared to put my hand on this heirloom and declare - a petrel flew aboard the boat - and spent time, not only on, but *in,* this most fortunate vessel. (15)

It's coming on towards Christmas, and I'm beginning to wonder what to rustle-up for the celebratory meal.

There's no hurry, the crew have plenty to occupy their days.

Lounging on the chaise longue.

Trying to keep out of the sun.

Enjoying the current Dick Francis thriller (he always turns up trumps, usually gets the girl, and *invariably* beats the criminals) while I'm admiring the ocean, not bothering to keep much of an eye open for steamers; noting the trade's eased a bit and now has more of an easterly component than hitherto, while I'm looking about, and over the side of the boat - an endlessly fascinating pastime, because there's such an amazing variety of stuff there.

What caught the eye today, after Paula the Petrel took wing, were some of the creatures which occupy the upper reaches of the 'oggin.

These are mostly blue, having adopted (been allocated?) (Darwinianly arrived at?) [16] this colour, because it offers protection from both aerial predation and ultraviolet light.

These neustons (the wee beasts associated with the interface) are also transparent, and not all that easy to see.

If you take a close look, there are millions (millions?) hundreds of billions of trillions of bright blue *Copepods* - the ocean's most abundant planktonic animal.

Then there are the *Pontellids*.

These punters (I reckon they are aspiring Tattersall members) [17] have taken a look at the odds, and decided an each-way bet is the only way to go (or perhaps more correctly - the best way *not* to go) because they have developed optics divided into two halves.

An eye focused upward.

To guard 'gainst danger from above.

The other focused downward, to search out dangers from below. [18]

They move around a lot - jump out of the ocean as quick as any Jack in the Box, playing hard to get, displaying the sort of neurotic behaviour which goes hand-in-hand with the nervous thought that, in their part of the world, if you adopt the notion - *ignorance is bliss,* there are serious problems ahead.

All this while, and it amounts to several more days, my own little problem has revolved around - what are we going to have for Christmas Dinner?

(I have to mention this, because I have a serious admission to make).

The dolphin *Coryphaena hippuris* I noticed when we were first hove-to is still hanging around the keel.

It may not be the same dolphin, but it *looks* like the same fish, and one of the notable things about this species is - they're very good to eat.

Another thing is; as they die, they display an astonishing array of colour, displacing natural blues with scintillating greens as their lifeblood ebbs away.

Yet another thing is, in the port settee-locker (the longest locker aboard the boat) there's a spear gun.

I've owned this gadget for years, have dealt out more death and destruction to parrot fish *et al*, than I care to remember, and although the rubber wham-bands are not as good as they were, I'm sure there's life in the old gun yet.

Or is this the case of a callously (even if it is a deliberately) inverted phrase?

An old dog's attempt at black humour? *(life in the old gun yet)*

Whatever: the thing is, I'm seriously considering overhauling the weapon, selecting the best point, and finding if my hand-and-eye co-ordination (allowing for refraction) is as good as ever it was.

I can't say I'm entirely happy with the idea; and to go some way towards counter-balancing the temptation, I've hit on the notion of christening the dolphin *Percy*, on the wobbly-logical ground that it won't be so easy to despatch poor old *Perce*, as it would be to spear just any old fish.

There may be more to this conundrum than meets the immediate eye, as this 'Christmas thing' has more to it than - *what are we having for dinner*; because as *der tag* [19] approaches, I find my thoughts diverted from our immediate surroundings, to what's going on in Barbados and further afield than that.

Where, previously, the ocean, the boat, the fish, the birds, the sea, the sky, the stars - the whole gamut of my physical world - have been more than enough to occupy my mind, I now find my thoughts strayed towards *'people'* (and having a fish below the boat, who has been recently endowed with a rudimentary personality, seems to have prompted my unconscious mind to start flirting with all sorts of crazy ideas).

This is just another way of saying that during the long night watches, when I should be keeping a more or less efficient lookout, I've been doing a bit of snogged-off [20] dreaming; some of it innocuous enough, involving strolls through fields of new-mown hay - then wandering back to the homestead.

Which is a bit odd, because here we are, in the middle of the Western Ocean. But when I'm turned in, fallen asleep while listening to music on the radio, I'm transported all over the place. Able to indulge in pastimes totally unconnected with sailing - and all of it out of the blue.

Not the blue of the ocean.

These are memories that may not be easy to bring into focus, because they're so wildly remote from the boat.

After a stroll around the farm - wandering across to the stables, where McGinty knows very well this is a hunting day, and it won't be long before he'll be saddled-up, and we'll be clip-clopping along the country lanes, hacking our way to the meet.

This old 'oss is a character (sometimes, I think he knows more about me, than I know about him).

We bought him from the Jeff Lloyd-Davies's who were farming then near Fishguard (Trebover) and hunting with the North. [21] Jeff's wife Pat had a reputation for producing just the right sort of heavyweight, and being new to the game, I was glad of her advice - even had the sense at times to take it.

McGinty's a well-mannered gent.

Big enough; 16 hands and an inch or two - not all that beautiful (has an unfortunate Roman nose) but turns out a marvellous ride.

He is a bit tentative over the first few fences (offers the endearing characteristic of a high-couraged animal with a nervous disposition) but after he's got his dander up, he'll jump anything.

Push through a blackthorn thicket.

Plough his way through a girth-deep Pembrokeshire bog.

With a horse as good as Mc-G., we can hunt all over the county, often having a day out with neighbouring packs.

Memories of the Towy & Cothi (the Jones Boys up on the hill).

The Tivyside.

The Carmarthen.

The unconventional character, John Dix, with his private pack, also up on the hill.

The Gogerddan (with m'Lady Pryce-Pryce) north of Aberystwyth.

The Banwen Miners; with Twm, the Master, presenting a good-natured caricature of landed gentry, with this old sailor and his nag having a marvellous time (even if the jock was sometimes reduced to clinging to the hell-for-leather galloping of good old 'Ginty's mane). [22]

See what I mean by *dreaming*?

So the question is - how far can this indulgence take you?

Because, there are all sorts of dreams.

Some, not so easy to pin down.

and there are others
much more slippery than that

CHAPTER TEN: PAGE NOTES
---

(1) Page 324. Line 26 .... *'running 'light'* .

The expression describes a commercial vessel making a passage, but not carrying cargo. A tanker, having taken crude (oil) from, say, Venezuela to a European port, would return in ballast, because her owners would be unlikely to find an operator wishing to ship crude *out* of Europe. When running 'light', a vessel, particularly if she is a single-screwed ship, creates a characteristic noise, with this condition brought about because her ballasted draft is insufficient to fully immerse the propeller and the tips of the blades, as they break surface, create the, *'prop-noise'* which carries several miles down-wind.

(2) Page 324. Line 34 .... *'just made a foolish mistake'*.

The observant reader has probably noticed there's a hole in the bucket (that it's all very well admitting to a 'mistake'; but not all that clever to then conveniently fail to mention what the mistake is). Even now, I'm not too keen on discussing it, because the error, and it's a revealing one, is that the opportunity of getting a message home was squandered. The people (and there are lots of them) who expect me to turn up at Barbados for Christmas have been left swinging in the wind, while I'm mucking about in the middle of the ocean.

(3) Page 324. Line 39 .... *'in order to make 'Morse' contact'*.

A means of communication devised by Samuel Morse, in collaboration with Alfred Vail, in 1837. The letters of the alphabet are represented by a combination of dots and dashes, with numerals and punctuations marks similarly transcribed. The system can be employed during daylight hours by means of flags, and at night by the use of a lamp that is designed to produce the necessary flashes at the required rythmic intervals.

Perhaps the most easily recognised group being that of (what used to be) the emergency signal S.O.S. (three dots, followed by three dashes, followed by three more dots) which is generally supposed to indicate the phrase, *Save Our Souls*. Although, in dire circumstances, perhaps those at risk would prefer to have their physical wellbeing attended to, as a *first* priority, secure (?) in the knowledge that their souls could be saved (?) at a somewhat later date.

(4) Page 326. Line 37 .... *'troupe of itinerant flying fish'*.

There are approximately 50 species of flying fish, classified as *Exocoetidae* in the order *Atheriniformes*. These trade wind Atlantic fish are probably *Exocoetidae volitans*, as they are dark brown, with a white splash on the back behind their pectoral fins. They rarely exceed 10 inches in length, although the '**great** flying fish' found along the coast of California (where else?) can attain a length of 18 inches or more. There are all sorts of yarns about hanging a light in the rigging, at night, and then enjoying the lured-on-deck catch for breakfast (must try it one day).

(5) Page 327. Line 20 .... *'Loggerhead turtle'*.

One of a group of ancient animals with, in this instance, the common name for *Thalassochelys caretta* being influenced by the usage of 'loggerhead', as something appropriate (to other animals as well) that have heads out of proportion to their bodies.

(6) Page 327. Line 39 .... *'an amazing change in the ocean'*.

Amongst the no doubt many hundreds, running into thousands, of available studies, an illustrated guide entitled *Oceanography*, edited by **C. P. SUMMERHAYES** and **S. A. THORPE** and published by Manson contains much fascinating material; together with *Deep Oceans*, edited by **M. R. CLARKE** and **P. J. HERRING**, published by Arthur Barker in 1971.

(7) Page 328. Line 1 .... *'the majority of* pelagic *species'*.

Found on the high seas, as distinct from those encountered in shallower waters, nearer the coast. Also applied to those species living near the surface of the ocean.

(8) Page 328. Line 18 .... *'a bunch of squid'*.

A varying species of cephalopods, belonging to the family *Loliginidae, Teuthididae*, or *Sepiidae*, commonly known as cuttle-fish (calamari) or pen-fish.

(9) Page 328. Line 31 .... *' Portuguese Man-of-War'*.

The view that the Portuguese Man-of-War (*Physalia physalis*) consists of a group of animals is put forward by Dr **S. K. SUTHERLAND,** of the Commonwealth Serum Laboratories, in his book *Venomous Creatures of Australia* (*a field guide, with notes on First Aid*) published by Oxford University Press in 1981. The PMOW is distributed world wide, and is known as a 'Blue Bottle' in Australian waters; not to be confused with a Sea Wasp (the Box Jellyfish, *Chironex fleckeri*) which also has poisonous tentacles with 70 recorded fatalities, as against (according to Sutherland) none for the Man of War. Further reading could include *Marine Animal Injuries to Man* by **C. EDMUNDS**, produced by Wedneil Publications, Newport, Victoria, Australia.

(10) Page 329. Line 6 .... *'but, as Jolson said: you ain't seen nothin' yet'*.

A reference to the Russian-born singer (Asa Yoelson, 1886-1950) who, using the stage-name Al Jolson, strode the boards of 'Music Hall' ('Vaudeville' in the 'States) to such magnificent effect. He made the Gershwin song *'Swanee'* his widely recognised trademark, and amongst other things appeared in the first full-length 'talking' film, *'The Jazz Singer'*, screened in 1927.

(11) Page 329. Line 35 .... *'a school of smiling dolphins'*.

Although bottle-nosed dolphins are mainly found in coastal areas, there are offshore varieties, and these deep-sea populations form larger groups than their inshore cousins. Although they have been hunted commercially, it seems pollution and decimation of their food species have caused almost as much damage as direct killing. These beautiful creatures belong to the family *Delphinidae,* in the sub-order *Odontoceti* (order *Cetacea*), classified as *Tursiops truncates* (so no wonder they sport an amused, deprecating air). But they have long been favourites with seamen, who appreciate such fascinating, and fascinated, fellow citizens (it most certainly is, a two-way street).

(12) Page 330. Line 27.......... *'pushed to the nor'ard of our track'*.

This refers to the fact that the vessel is being swept to the nor'ard of Barbados, and although an effort has been made to counteract this tendency (by altering her hove-to position, so that she has the breeze on her port beam) the small amount of fore-reaching available isn't enough to significantly alter her direction of drift.

(13) Page 330. Line 37.......... *'tubing with the best of them'*.

A reference to the art of wind-surfing, where those who are sufficiently skilled indulge in 'tubing'. That is, surfing *under* a breaking crest, with all this entails in the mastery of a fascinating sport.

(14) Page 330. Line 38 .... *'a . . . **petrel**, perched on a sail bag'*.

There are over 20 species of petrel, but I think the visitor is **Wilson's Storm Petrel** (*Oceanites ocean*), probably the world's most numerous seabird; certainly the smallest, as fully-grown they weigh about 32 grams. They range from Antarctica to as far North as Labrador, so they are truly oceanic. But in a lifetime of mucking about in boats, I have never heard tell of a petrel dropping in for breakfast. There are Norse legends that describe petrels as 'water sprites', and Irish folktales which suggest they represent the souls of sailors lost at sea. The English, *'Mother Carey's Chicken'*, seems to derive from the Spanish term *'Madre Cara'* (referring to the biblical Mary, Mother of Christ) as being the real mother involved.

(15) Page 331. Line 23 .... *'in this fortunate vessel'*.

It's worth emphasising the inherent shyness of petrels. They only come ashore to breed, and when they do, it's usually under cover of darkness, to enter underground burrows; so it would seem that very few people have had the privilege of being able to offer an ocean-going lift to one of these attractive birds.

(16) Page 332. Line 1 .... *'Darwinianly arrived at'.*

A reference to the work of **Charles Darwin,** the English naturalist (1809-1882) whose revolutianary book, *On the Origin of Species* was first published in 1859. This stemmed from the five years he had spent aboard HMS Beagle, which led him, ultimately, to the realization that natural selection is the basis for evolutionary progress. His other, ground-breaking publications are *The Descent of Man, and Selection in Relation to Sex*, followed by *The Expression of the Emotions in Man and Animals*. There was other important research on plants, and also a far-reaching examination of earthworms and their effect on their habitat (the soil).

His place in the march of scientific progress is unrivalled, and he has been acknowledged as one of the monumental figures in human history.

The religious establishment of his day disputed all he stood for; but the march of time has unequivically supported his quality of character and the supreme standard of his scientific work, with emerging fossil evidence, over the years, adding further support to his original hypothesis.

The work of Alfred Russel Wallace should be studied alongside that of Darwin, as the two men, perhaps by different routes, reached almost identical conclusions.

(17) Page 332. Line 9 .... *'aspiring Tattersalll members'.*

For people unfamiliar with the horse world . . . *'Tattersall's'* dates back to 1766, when auction rooms were established in London by Mr Richard Tattersall, near Hyde Park Corner; since moved (1865) to Knightsbridge. The establishment became famous, not only as a location where race horses were bought and sold, but as a meeting-place for betting men to settle their accounts.

(18) Page 332. Line 15 ...... *'the other focused downward, to see what's going on below'*

A good example of how the *Pontellids* (those aspiring Tattersall members) have successfully played the evolutionary percentages.

(19) Page 333 Line 12 .... *'der tag'.*

A reference to **'The Day'**, when the German Grand Fleet, under the overall command of Vice-Admiral Reinhard Scheer, and Vice-Admiral Franz Hipper (commanding the scouting forces) took to the high seas with the object of engaging the British fleet under the command of Admirals Beatty and Jellicoe. The resultant engagement on May 31 and June 1, 1916 (the Battle of Jutland) proved indecisive; certainly not satisfactory from the RN point of view, because although they had the superior force (149 ships against 110) the British losses were significantly larger than their opponents. Nevertheless, the German fleet never embarked on a second engagement.

(20) Page 333. Line 23 ………. '*snogged-off*'.

Slang for 'sleep'; not to be confused with *snogging* (not listed in the Shorter Oxford Dictionary, Book Club Associates Edition 1983, reprint 1992). But *canoodling* is mentioned and other editions of the Shorter Oxford *do* mention 'snog'; both terms (snogging and canoodling) concerned with a type of (usually, but not exclusively) adolescent sexual foreplay, which sometimes leads to the sort of situations nice young girls have been warned about (but with little effect?) since time immemorial.

(21) Page 334. Line 1 ………. '*hunting with the North (Pembrokeshire Hounds)*'.

The Pembrokeshire hunting country is divided into halves, the 'North' having kennels just outside Haverfordwest, while the 'South' are based at Cresselly, where the Allens (later becoming Harrison-Allens) have lived and 'Mastered' the pack for generations.

(22) Page 334. Line 24 …… '*the hell-for-leather galloping of good old McGinty's mane*'.

There are lots of people who can't stand the thought of 'blood sports', with fox hunting presenting (to them) the image of loudly-spoken 'County' types, seemingly intent on murdering a creature, merely to enliven what might otherwise be a boring afternoon. But this is as far from the mark as the other side of the argument, which declares that hunting is a 'way of life'. The truth is (not always acknowledged) if there are 50 people out 'hunting', only three or four of them are doing so. The rest are 'followers' engaged on a country pursuit, which in their case involves attempting to match the equestrian skills displayed by a professional huntsman, and his experienced whippers-in, who are usually better mounted than they are. These followers are kept in their place by a Field Master, who makes sure that they (the ***spectators***) ***do*** keep out of the way of the huntsman.

However it's turned out, there's no gainsaying the fact there's an element of cruelty, as well as more than a smidgin of snobbery involved, even in so-called farmers packs; with the likes of the Beaufort, the Quorn; and, in his heyday, Captain Ronald Wallace with the Heythrop, representing the well-polished display of the self-assured elite.

Ronnie WALLACE (1919-2002) was the outstanding huntsman of his generation, having taken the field with foxhounds, beagles, harriers and otter hounds during what could possibly be described as the golden age of that type of sporting activity.

He was educated at Eton and Christ Church, Oxford, where he read history. While at school he became, at 18 years of age, the master of the Eton Beagles, gaining as a secondary honour the *Silver Horn,* much to the displeasure of some of the older students, who were undoubtedly jealous of his empathy with hounds.

During his first season (1936-1937) in charge of the Oxford pack, they accounted for 60 brace of hares (and a solitary fox), and then a further 75 brace of hares and three more foxes during the following season.

During the second World War, after general service, he was posted to an organisation called *Phantom,* (they were charged with the demanding task of gathering information in forward areas, in France, after D-Day). On demobilization, Wallace became master of the Ludlow in Shropshire, and then went to the Cotswold Hunt in Gloucestershire; eventually becoming master of the Heythrop, where some of the 'days' became legends of their time. He gave up the Heythrop in 1977; but then, instead of retiring, moved to Exmoor, and became Master of that hunt for more than 20 years.

His vast experience and success in his chosen profession cannot be challenged, although he was judged by some (almost certainly his inferiors) as being somewhat autocratic and opinionated. Yet he commanded the respect of the hunting fraternity far longer than anybody previously concerned with hounds.

DOESN'T EVERYONE DREAM ?

OUR grey-bearded bosun does, because, amongst other things, it allows him to look back, as well as glance astern, and the perceptive dog is immediately struck by an ambitious thought.

That in a perfectly ordered world he would provide himself with two boats, one to sail, and forcefully enjoy, while keeping the favoured vessel comfortably upwind, within admired sight of the other mirrored image of his dreams.

You don't believe me?

I can tell you (stretched out in *my* bunk) the bay *the bosun* views is peaceful. As easily as that, he can see a vessel lying quietly at anchor, off the same old sandy beach, as a glowing blob of light set against the inked-in blue/black image of this blurred-edged dream of an ocean.

An ocean - the reef has moulded to a sea.

Let trickle - through a thousand silting channels, to what's become a lake recalls the ocean's surge, as a wavelet, bolder than the rest, runs higher up the beach and wets his feet.

Warm, caressing, carrying none of the power of the sea; but something more persuasive; a shy, yet sly reminder, not of the wonder of another world, just the self-indulgent world this dreaming seaman lives in.

He can take off his clothes.

Throw them on the sand.

Walk to the waters edge.

Stride the few short seaward yards.

Plunge.

Enjoy the swim (which frees him from the shrift of a booze and sun-soaked day).

Regain the beach.

Dry as best he can - then on with shirt and shorts as some protection against the chill night air, which now seems cooler than before.

The dinghy's hauled out, above high water mark, but easy enough to carry down the sloping beach, launch into the sea, and pull back to his boat.

Back to his own boat.

Five unexceptional words, yet nothing less than a fascinating hinge, supporting a door that creaks and swings for an ocean wanderer who has spent an entertaining evening ashore, and is now returning, snail-like, to his shell.

There are other vessels in the bay, and our old seaman makes a point of rowing to and through them.

Admiring the odd one here.

The even odder there.

Murmuring a greeting to a figure who appears, as a spectre, unexpectedly on deck.

But it's back to his own boat now, because there's nothing in the world to compare with the pleasure this manoeuvre gives him.

And as he rows, he reverses the motion of the punt.

No longer pulling on the oars, but leaning on them, in the old-fashioned way of professional watermen the world over.

To enjoy the dark water, dripping silver from the paler paddle ends.

The mirrored starlight, as it wobbles the reflective surface of the sea.

With each movement and the sluicing rhythm of the leaned-on blade, propelling the chuckling dinghy nearer home.

As an effortless progression.

Pushing the punt further into the bay.

Away from the safety of the beach.

To meet the full strength of the tide.

Towards the boat he knows is anchored in this haven.

Yet he'll not board her now.

Our old bosun will - dawdle.

Admiring the vessel's lines (her mast, towering above the hull, is strong and admirably suited to the type of craft she is).

The long sleek hull, with a reverse sheer, and a low flush deck - not because the combination is aesthetically satisfying, but because it makes for safety on and about her lighter-carried ends.

And the same dictat has influenced the size of the cockpit.

A stranger may say, the cockpit's too small; and the bosun would have to admit that it *is* cramped.

He also knows, it's too small, even when flooded, to retain sufficient water to depress the stern and render the vessel vulnerable to a succession of steeply breaking seas.

These indulgent thoughts trickle through his mind, as he admires the vessel that he built himself, then sailed this satisfying distance.

Anchored off this dream of a beach - with bosun, crew, *et all*, too much betwixt and between their shadowy worlds to attempt the measure of his rightful context.

Yet not too bemused to climb aboard, and secure the dinghy.

Making absolutely sure the turns are doubled-up, and there's not the slightest chance of a slippery hitch, which lets an idiot wind up later ....

Not only with an astonished look.

But to find his dinghy ....

Gone.

However, now, as a *careful* seaman, he's standing on the deck of the parent vessel, enjoying the pee that gets rid of the last pale shadow of the evening's ale, while making the reassuring glance at the inflatable lying safely astern.

Thinking, it's good, marvellously good, to feel the solid stucture of his own boat under the barefoot adventure of his evening's steadily unfolding dream.

Home at last.

And after the vicissitudes of the evening, going below to the cramped but comfortable cabin, reinforces the mistaken belief that everything's the same.

That there's not the slightest need to match-up the cabin lamp before turning in.

What need now of a light?

Our seafaring dog knows to an inch where everything is aboard this hooker.

From stem to stern.

Beam to beam.

Above and below.

Aloft and a'low.

He knows this vessel intimately.

There was a time, when he would have confidently added, that he knows this vessel as well as he knows himself. But even in his dream-like state, he can see the naïveté exposed by that remark.

Port bunk's favourite tonight.

Shorts and shirt soon stripped off, roughly folded, and placed on the starboard settee.

Then the unfolding of the cool clean sheet, which (blind though he may be) he *knows* is white, giving, as it always does, the moment of sensuous pleasure.

Climb into the berth.

Arrange the pillow, and the sheets.

Body horizontal and relaxing.

Framed in the square of the companionway hatch there are stars.

And through that hatch, to line the womb of his small vessel, where he now nestles, starlight, falling silently, as only starlight can, gossamers the eyes; and he's all acceptance, rejecting nothing, as he feels the daily wash of care slip from his mind, as heavy limbs lose weight and aching tendons melt to marrow on his India rubber bones.

Except for one small item.

Through the vacant spaces that were filling up with velvet, the strain of muffled echoes reverberate from wall to curtained wall.

Sometimes distant, sometimes closer.

But time, and time was, and not so long ago, Time was no longer important (the bosun's long since done with such inconsequential tinkering); yet now, to be dragged back by the aching eyelids, to the incoherent present.

This is the height of indecency.

To have to re-orientate his mind.

To have to wonder - what in hell is going on?

(there's knocking of a sort)

A repetitive tap followed by tap, and again tap upon tap upon tap, so a conscious effort has to be made to remember - where on earth (?) he is.

There it is again.

And now, no longer a mystery.

Because it's 2 o'clock in the morning.

And someone's knocking on the hull.

Time, now, has become no better than old-fashioned knicker-elastic, that's gripping - not a hot fat thigh, but leaving rumpled creases on his mind.

It's 2 o'clock in the morning.

It's 2 o'clock in the morning.

And someone's outside, tapping on the hull.

There *can't* be anybody outside, tapping on the hull.

However, what the bosun means is - he doesn't *want* anybody to be outside, tapping on the hull.

But someone's there, and he has to get up from his bunk, before the insistent tap/tap/tap drives his mind clear out of his skull.

Rolling out of his cart, isn't as easy as perhaps it should be.

Neither is sticking a head out of the hatch, while standing on his (the bosun's) locker, to gain two feet of height and have the deck at waist level.

There's a breeze.

And after the warmth and comfort of the bunk, the night air cuts across a shirtless back with the intemperance of a needle-cold shower, matching exactly the lack of warmth expressed in the irritable question.

'Who's there?'

'It's me.' (what a damn fool answer).

'Who in hell is me?' (as if he didn't know).

'Do you know what time it is?'

The only answer to *this* damn fool question is a barely restrained giggle, and the overwhelming feeling now is - the chill of the cool night air. And a slight shiver, running uncontrollably from shoulder to thigh, forcibly reminds the bosun of the fact.

It's tempting to go below and grab a sweater.

It's equally tempting to climb on deck and kick the boarding ladder over the side. A movement of the foot which allows the invitation to snake out over the toe-rail, rattle against the vessel's hull, and splash its last three inviting rungs into the sea.

Looking outboard, he can see she's pulling at, then submerging the floating ladder.

Placing the bottom step under her foot, in order that she can climb with practised ease.

Taking a proffered hand, while stepping over the lifelines, not because assistance is needed.

Because it's the natural thing to do.

'You must be out of your mind.'

'I just felt like a swim.'

'At this time in the night?'

'Why not?' (there are more than a dozen reasons: '*why not*', is merely an attempt at an all-too-private joke).

But who lays claim to reason now?

Our old dog is feeling chilled, and although he doesn't have a stitch of clothing on, this may be brought about by rather more than just the waft of cool night air.

'I have to get a sweater.'

'I could use a towel.' (there's nothing to be gained by staying on deck, so he's on his way below).

345

'Hold on a minute, while I light the lamp.'

Matches in their usual place.

One quick scratch, and the flame kindles in the hurricane lamp.

The wick illuminates the cabin, and into this yellow pool, two brown legs dangle, search experimentally for a foothold, soon finding the top of the locker - and having located this safe place, she steps down, to stand, unconcerned as maybe, on the cabin sole.

Her torso is patterned - displays bikini top and bottom outlines of discarded clothing.

Droplets of water hang proud on the oil of sunburned skin.

Silver disks fire golden arrows through the haze of dimly risen lamp light, as she pulls a golden swatch that's held in place by a yellow-ribbon'd hair clip.

'I could do with the towel.' (and she smiles, as she makes the remark) blue eyes twinkling - seeing he's a trifle disconcerted.

'What's the matter?' (while he's getting the towel, he's denying anything *is* the matter), yet somewhere along the line, there's been a slightly embarrassing twitch.

The sort of twitch that's got our bosun wondering.

If he's about to suffer a rare attack of conscience?

(that'll be the day)

But it's not an assault of conscience, neither is the problem of tomorrow's complications going to put a stopper on proceedings.

The twitch comes, partly because the initiative has been all hers.

Even in this free-wheeling yachtie community, where a nod is every bit as good as a wink, it's still old Adam who has most of the nodding to do.

But here, the boot's been on the other foot.

And she's capped it all - by swimming in the night.

'Sorry to be so long about the towel.' (and again, she bestows on him the sauce of a quizzical smile).

Towelling off, she bends forward.

Long hair flipping, then dangling from her head as she dries carefully between her toes, displaying brown shoulders and a well-muscled back with knuckled vertebrae running down to a delicious broadening of bum.

Having dried her feet, she works up calves, knees, thighs.

Running the towel between her legs.

Smiling, as she raises a foot and rests it on the edge of the settee.

Another twinkling smile, as she roughs-up pubic hair, and then delicately pats between her legs.

'Anything to drink?' (that thought too, had been bobbing in our rough old seaman's mind).

'Red wine?'

'Couldn't be better.'

'Anything to smoke?'

He rummages around - looking for the cigarettes kept for visitors, while she has the towel across her back, working energetically, one angular elbow up and then another.

Drying between her shoulder blades, and with a white-toothed grin, a quick wipe under the singular raising of each bobbed tit.

Then she sits herself down.

Knees slightly apart.

Hunching forward, as she towels off her hair.

Satisfied, she threads the yellow-ribbon'd clip on a finger, slips it over her ponytail - all in one svelte movement.

Our bold (and surely fortunate?) bosun has the wine poured - has even found some cigarettes (not the joint she asked for); in any case, she doesn't need the lift.

A supremely confident young woman.

At ease.

Comfortably seated.

Holding a glass of wine in one hand, and a cigarette in the other, waiting for it to be lit.

He lights it.

The flare of the match highlights her face.

Arched eyebrows.

Fair complexion.

A strong lean neck, and those impudent blue eyes.

'Are you warm enough?' (a level gaze, just the suspicion of a nod).

'Yes, I'm warm enough.'

So is he.

The wine has done much more than warm him up.

Coursing through his veins, it's converted an incipient shiver into a glow that's spread throughout his body; and our randy old roué, having settled on the tack he's taking, now has a flaccid erection dangling over the edge of the starboard settee.

They're seated opposite each other, in the narrow cabin, so it's possible to put a foot up on the facing upholstery (this is handy enough in a seaway, with the vessel hard on the wind), and now it enables our fortunate voyeur to position his feet on either side of her bum.

By gently flexing his ankles, he can massage the outside of her thighs, and while doing so, note that the devil-may-care smile has all but left her lips.

It's not that she's *not* smiling (she is).

But it's a smile that has deepened.

A smile spread through her, expressing what doesn't need to be said.

'The bunks aren't much good, I'm afraid.'

'I know.'

'Too narrow, and not enough headroom.'

'Yes.'

' Perhaps we should put one of the mattresses down on the cabin sole?'

'Let's do that.'

They do so - setting nearly empty glasses aside; dragging upholstery off the pilot berth, placing it carefully on the decking, fitting one end tight against the mast.

'Do you want a pillow?' (*she*, the night-time swimmer, is asking this old lecher if he wants a pillow).

'What about you?'

'No: I'd rather go on top.'

(what a good start).

Now, he certainly does want a pillow (rolled up and placed at the foot of the mast it makes a good headrest).

So here they are - he's lying on his back, she's standing above him, with a foot each side of his belly, while finishing her wine.

What he can see of her is delightfully foreshortened.

Long brown legs rise from slender ankles to a swelling of seductive thighs.

All set nicely off by an attractive thatch of crinkled pubic hair.

And that's it.

She's leaning backwards, tippling her wine, and from his worm's-eye view he's treated to an appreciative eyeful.

But she's well aware of that, and instead of draining her glass, she dumps what's left of the ruby liquid - rather more than just a drop, which narrowly misses what she aimed at.

Nothing flaccid now, about our old dog's quivering dick.

She's above him, lowering down, placing hands on his shoulders, while he fondles the gentle swelling of her breasts.

(isn't there a lot to be said for this position?)

He can run his fingers up and down her spine.

Span her waist.

Fondle her buttocks.

And as she adjusts - inching forward on her knees, to accommodate the length of her own long thighs - to get it all just right.

He can reach up, surprising her a little, by taking the lobe of her ear between his thumb and rude forefinger.

Making her look (not at the moment of contact, when even this uninhibited gal must shut her eyes), but just a little later, when the preliminary movements have completed their delicate task, and allowed the slide of lubrication to confidently flow.

So that, *now*, he can look her in the eye.

She's on top, and their principle point of shared endeavour ....

(that erection) has become a greasy pole.

Not his.

But common property.

Not to climb (at least, not yet) but certainly to slide on.

A reciprocating see-saw, that either he, or she, can set in motion.

She bears down, so gently, and rubs, so softly, while he tips and taps his fingers over her flanks to encourage her.

And as she's doing well, locate her coccyx - to rub her vestigial tail, while quietly smiling to himself (the sly-sided dog), that the tail she's tempting to its task, is so much better than the one long lost.

And then, as she's shut her eyes (and on that he would bet his bottom dollar) he can take each puckered nipple, between the same careful thumb and rude forefinger, to administer a playful tweak.

Not to hurt her - just to bring her, before she flies off with his proud as a peacock's pumped up moon-stick - back to earth.

Just a playful tweak on a gently swinging tit.

But unbeknown to Mothers Superior, there's a time and place for everything.

Even the tweaking of a maiden's nipple, because this gal's all steamed up, and pressure everywhere is rising.

So he's tweaking her nipples, laying hands on the rounded fall of her breasts (they have the feel of jelly-wobbled custard).

Tweaking again, and not too gently, on her gorgeous lick of a tit.

(she takes no notice, she's off on her trip to the stars)

Much too quickly, and if they're not careful, there's the risk of a broken moon-stick.

(then they'll both miss out on the trip).

But doesn't this position still have something to offer?

Control is possible.

By pushing upwards, with the cupped palm of his hands on her hips, he can ease the weight off the scalding tip of his cock - but in doing, so he disturbs her rhythm.

And now she opens her eyes (a quick glance, to see if there's a problem).

But another smile says all that's needed, because he knows (or hopes he does) that if he keeps her off the sensitive ridge - all will be well to the end.

She can have her slide to the moon.

Launching herself on a glide path, that'll take her beyond - on and on to the stars.

Watch, now, and you can see the tension in her face.

Her head held a little to one side.

Her neck arched, highlighting sinews that are corded from clavicle to ear.

Eyes shut.

Peeping white teeth, clenched over her lower lip.

Breathing hard, with a flare to her nostrils, as her belly ripples, knots and un-knots, hollowed from her ribcage, columned from her loins.

Nothing can stop her now.

The blood-red orgiastic bomb is primed, inexorably ticking.

And she's done it all herself.

Yet even now, poised as she is, with no road back - there's a moment's hesitation. A low moan, and then a slowing in her rhythm.

Another moan; and she's ground now to a halt.

A faltering, and our reminiscing bosun is wondering - if there's some voice, or some instinct, primitive or otherwise, applying some sort of a restraining hand?

Or is it because - she *thinks* she knows what it's going to be like. But the intensity of the feeling always comes as a shattering surprise?

Does it matter?

She's reached the excruciating point.

Coming?

Yes, but *not now* (oh, for just one moment longer).

Bursting?

Yes, and also - not wanting to be burst.

Yet a little movement (his hands on her flanks) exerting a light, but immodest pressure, *down*, as he brings her to the point.

Just the flexing of a muscle, the beginning of a ripple, is enough to threaten the whole of the delicately tethered balloon.

A quick intake of breath.

(his cause célèbre, by pricking in the bubble).

And the contracting spasms begin.

Squeezing her loins.

Putting pressure on her thighs.

Caving in her belly .

Until the prospective pips are squeaking.

'Oh.' (she says, not knowing, or having any control now, over what she breathlessly says or does).

'Oh, Jesus.' (says this well-bred girl, who's not given to profanity).

But if this girl were a Princess of the proudest Arab Kingdom, you could brand her with the Star of David and she wouldn't know the difference; deluged as she is, in a torrent that's giving her no time to draw even a reasonable breath.

'Oh God.' (she chokes; a whimper, that comes close to an entreaty, as she tries to close her legs).

An involuntary movement - that has nothing to do with what she wants, or doesn't want. For her, there's no before or after. The happening is everything, as she finds herself an incandescent blob that's frighteningly beautiful, and a light, that's lighting up the cavities that lie behind her eyes.

'Oh.' (for the torment) as the centrifuge rotates, to recreate the void into which she has to pour her being.

'Oh.' (while being drawn *into* the vortex) and the longer drawn out ....

'Aahs,' as the contractual grip of ecstasy grabs her by the throat.

Look, at this delineating moment, and you can see that she is melting.

Being poured, brimming moulds, having lipped the others full.

But in the filling, there's fulfilment.

An immense relief of the overwhelming pressure; an unwinding of the harp strings that have twanged throughout her body, first straining, then easing, those tension-laden sinews.

Draining the anguish from her face, relaxing her thighs, even allowing her to breathe (a quick intake of breath, that's all she can manage before another spasm shakes her).

That he can *feel*; along the embracing length of arms, the digging-in of nails, and the clinging tips of fingers.

Another intimate tremor shakes her. And he's beginning to wonder how he's managed to contain himself. Throughout her personal adventure, this old hoss has remained little more than an encouraging spectator; a privileged voyeur, who's only justification is the saddle he provided.

It's been her ride.

He didn't even tag along.

And wouldn't it be nice, to be able to claim it's nothing to do with the special circumstances of this particular gallop?

If only it were so.

Because even our hairy-arsed roué would have to admit, that with a normal up-and-tumble, he would have been brought to such a pitch of excitement, that he would have been drawn, irresistibly and panting, even slavering to the post. Both balls braking to avert the skid to slimy dissolution (the loss of control, that would prevent them both arriving at the delineating moment), so he's doing his best to avoid that embarrassing debacle, but being drawn along by the pace and depth of the tumultuous emotional storm.

However, now (can anyone believe it?) she's just this moment realized, there's everything to play for.

Having had her trip to the moon, she's just returned, through all those piles of fleecy clouds, to base; only to find, back on the launch pad, the rocket vehicle not only there, but brazenly steaming.

She seems surprised, and quietly giving.

What's this?

A rueful smile?

` She's relaxed now, lying above him, a gorgeous frog, and damp too, settled over his belly and his chest; her face inches away from his (but everything else is touching) and she's smiling this rueful smile (he has to push her away, just to make sure he's not mistaken), but it is so ....

Her little smile is, rueful.

Some oaf might say - this is the time to wipe the smile off her face.

But isn't it a puerile thought?

Not worth entertaining.

So can it be - she's disappointed?

No.

And because he's privy to this knowledge (he knows it, just as well as she does), our bold old bull is so cocksure of himself, that he's no longer bothered by the male-demeaning message. The big-balled boy has long since rid himself of that nagging little doubt (the momentary lack of confidence, that troubled its way to the surface when she stepped aboard the boat).

So it would seem - the rueful little smile is all of her own making.

But for the bosun's peace of mind, he should place it in its rightful context, because *she's* the person who's boasted she's devoid of inhibition, declaims it blatantly enough, when waving her own flag, making the position crystal clear - she's a swinger, and no mistake about it.

Yet she does have one remaining inhibition, tucked away in the innermost recesses of her very private being; for her eye alone (thus hard to view from any distance) even though he's as close to her now as anyone will ever get.

This is something she finds difficult to come to terms with, but the weakness (or is it a necessary defence?) has just been shamelessly exposed.

You (probably not the bosun) need to know the secret?

Simple, but true.

Her little smile is rueful, because she knows, she's just been - *watched*.

To be seen naked is trivial by comparison; indeed, this condition between merely friends as well as lovers has become so commonplace it no longer earns a second glance.

But at that private moment, when the defences really *are* down; the moment in coitus, which has inevitably led from coition, when she's not only *in* the crucible, but has *become* the crucible.

At *that* truly defenceless moment, her innermost conviction is ....

There should be no prying eye.

Everything else has been prized apart (but please; please: leave me one last modesty?). But it has been lost, and this is why she offers up her rueful little smile.

Our snorting bull, not only rampant, but Minotaured as well [1] is now convinced he's possessed of a sword, quiveringly tempered, which boldly swung would cleave a plank of roughly knotted oak. But what a fool he would be to bulldoze his way in, when there's no need; when what should be exercised, is not broad-shouldered manhood, but just a little patience, and the necessary care.

Not a brutal entry, or the tactic of obreption.

A fond consideration - making sure he has no startled fawn, but an acquiescent partner.

Who accepts the tip.

The delightful probe, that feigns the very last encounter, on its tempting way to foxglove; then retreats, not all the way, just leaves the key in the escutcheon, which tremors as the lock is turned - not forced.

So up the velvet pathway they can move ahead - not parting, but two becoming one.

She, softly muscled.

The bosun, hard, but caring.

The gorgeous fit between two lovers, that leads to life's most wanted music - a little sigh, which she has made, not all alone, but just for him.

Now: he can open his eyes, and she will follow suit.

Two deep blue pools, which he can look at, and watch them blur, by just a stirring of the loins that, should he care to, can bring to ruin this most perfect moment.

But not quite yet.

Just push up, firmly, while holding her by the palmed-down pressure on her back (there's no movement, merely confirmation that the tender trap is fully set). Yet one more thing; even though she's now spread-eagled, gorgeously pierced by life's bold pin, she's not quite naked.

Remember (the bosun does) her yellow-ribboned hair clip?

And having remembered it, run a smooth hand over her forehead, over her hair, the nape of her neck - seeking the talisman, which has now become a symbol.

Find it.

Remove it.

And then just watch her smile.

Because this is the measure of your shared indulgence, as you (to hell with the bosun) carefully arrange the still-damp tresses, that fall in long blonde coils about her shoulders - just *feel* the way she snuggles down and nuzzles.

Rubbing her face against your shoulder.

Allowing you to understand - by a voluptuous twitch (the most intimate signal, that *any* man, can *ever* get).

Oh, more than acquiescent woman.

Oh, woman gained, not taken.

What pleasure now that she can give, which you could slake, but two of you should share.

The slow withdrawal.

Just to make re-entry, and then retreat.

So tender tip breaks contact (a little tease).

Then once more, the swirl of love's sweet waltz, that slowly enters dreamtime, and then withdraws - but only to ensure the echo of the tune.

And while you play it, just knuckle-up each buttock, with a little push that accentuates the rhythm with increasing penetration.

Love's piercing lance, which has her panting.

Clinging, to the slow withdrawal.

Gasping at the speed of entry.

But before you get carried away, it may be as well to remember the baton being wielded is a perishable item.

You may be conducting the delightful old tune, 'Everyman His Own Artist,' yet it wouldn't do to run out of steam.

So?

Stop.

When fully entered?

Yes.

Stop now?

At this crucial moment?

Yes - *stop* !

(don't worry, I'll not move a muscle).

Moisten the tip of a finger, and smooth the lids of her eyes.

Why?

To feel the shape *that* fold of skin contains.

(and all this, while remaining still?).

Not quite - you can rub her behind the ears, run the tips of your fingers up and down her spine (there's no fear she'll not like it).

Span her waist.

Massage her bottom, and as you grasp her, feel the catastrophic tremor start somewhere in your loins. A tightening of hamstrings, ruthlessly yet deliciously conveying the sweet but bitter knowledge that love's lipped dam is soon about to burst; because as you gripped her by the tightly fisted buttock, the serious business of copulation has certainly begun.

Not in Waltz Time, with its reciprocating rhythm; but with an urgency lacking all trace of a sophisticated beat.

No longer the delicate arrangement meant to tickle her fancy, or even the lance thrust which thrilled her to the core.

That play is over.

This is business for the unsheathed sword, which is going to be used, as all swords are, when leapt from scabbards, as a weapon that is ruthlessly deployed and without a hint of mercy.

Not that you're intent on destroying her.

To the contrary, you have both been engaged, have scaled the heights, and up to this point in the breathtaking ascent have been all consideration; able to compliment each other while she fashioned this gorgeous scabbard into which you are plunging yourself, again, and again, and again.

And even as you do so, you know the sword is yours to lay about you, that you have no choice now, but act-out Man's roughly shouldered part.

Not offering her one avenue of escape.

Unaware, that escape is the last thing she is seeking, with your arms about her, squeezing the life out of her, in a rush to deposit your seed, with its 'oh' for the filling, and gasping ah's for the sperm that's now brimming, before you are felled (it seems too soon, all too soon) by the ball-sapping slash, brought low by the act, which Nature administers from the sperm-dripping tip of your blade.

And then.....and then.

And then - after *your* trip to the moon - the emasculated return to earth, with now and again a reactionary gasp, as you are forced to make (sometimes, it seems, against your will) another stout-hearted thrust that attempts to spurt up to, what you are mistakenly convinced is the unlaced neck of her womb.

But the spring has unwound - what you are experiencing now is the backlash.

The delayed reflex, which can lull you into thinking it's all over; until your loins contract again, an involuntary movement, precipitating yet another penetrating thrust, that provides the impetus for the last - the very last bugle-called rally.

The call specifically marshalled to drum-on the march of your sperm.

By this time, you (who cares about the bosun?) are well enough in control of your perceptive senses (or hoping you soon will be) to wonder what effect these sword thrusts are having. But it would be foolish to claim there's the slightest hint of compassion, or even an echo of the well intentioned finesse with which you negotiated the early path of this relationship.

And you know this to be true, no matter in what regard you hold her.

Yet you wonder about it.

You wonder if - by, in the end, so ruthlessly shouldering your way into her, you may have destroyed what you previously took such care to sustain?

Then again, it must be conceded, that while the thought occurs, it doesn't carry with it any sense of pity, or even a tinge of regret (during the final cut and thrust of the encounter there was no room for such niceties). And you are still much too close to the act to worry about anything else.

This is not a personal inquisition which afflicts you.

Merely a sense of breathless wonder.

You started by wooing her ....

But has she finally been plundered?

And when this relentless little thicket finally encompasses you (you must open your eyes, just to ascertain what you fear may be the remorseless tip of the scales). But when you do, you know, immediately, there's no need to entertain such doubts.

How do you know?

Because *nobody* could look like this - if they had just been, plundered.

What you encounter is a level-headed gaze, that's not cool, not saucy, not limpid, not superior, not anything but, serene; and you know, accompanied by no small degree of admiration, that she's not been in any way scared by the tumultuous call to arms.

If you're cautious of the judgement, you can test this thesis in the most practical, and also the most delightful way, known to doubting man.

Before it's too late, while you still have worthwhile use of your flag-staffed erection (your personal ensign, hauled down now, to grace little more than half the original mast) you can put what's left of it to the ever-loving test.

A deliberate withdrawal, followed by a bold thrust, upward, right to the root of the ball-bouncing hilt, and again, as forcefully *up* as ever you can.

You think you may hurt her?

(take a surreptitious glance) while driving your cock yet again through the gorgeous felt front of that moist-dripping mound.

She doesn't bat an eyelid - doesn't even blink.

You don't believe me?

Then try again; but if you do, she'll know you're just arsing about. And now she'll smile, the indulgent smile she might bestow - not on an erring lover, but on a *boy*, who's been caught indulging in a boyish prank.

So this is what you've been reduced to?

You (the hairy-arsed old seaman) who thought he knew a thing or two about it - put in your place by this slip of a girl?

And in a way, it's true enough.

The war is over (never mind who blew the bugle) you have both responded, as you must, to the irresistible call to arms; have willingly submitted to the tide and stress of unbridled emotion; have fought, and sometimes wheedled your way to the ramparts, feigning withdrawal, only for the pleasure of being able to mount yet another thrilling attack.

And you would have to admit (with a slight swelling of the chest) that you were able to respond so effectively to the age-old rallying cry.

The call to the scabbard-slid charge, so well led by *your* boldly flashing blade; because it was you - none other than *you* - who risked everything, dashing gallantly forward to plant the heroic standard on what must be, if it's the most *fought over* mound in the world - it has to be the most *desirable* mound in the world?

And you have had the pleasure of not only watching a standard unfurl, but *feeling* a standard unfurl.

So aren't you now convinced, after such a well-fought campaign, that you are bound to be the victor?

But when you look into her brave blue eyes, you know only too well the case has been wrongly stated.

There has been no war.

There's no hint of askance in her look, it's perfectly direct, and for that you should be thankful; those fine blue eyes, which a short time since were screwed tight shut (and you should do your best to suppress a chauvinistic snigger) because those fine blue eyes are now *wide open*, and they have, you should be warned, a different look about them.

An altered depth of focus.

Because she ....

Is now looking at - *you.*

And if you are man enough, it might be as well to consider the person who lies beneath, not only her dispassionate gaze, but rather more subtly, the gaze that follows passion.

You may wonder what she's looking at.

Can she see a loud-mouthed Jock, who, sooner rather than later will be up on some bar stool, letting ring the tale (the archetypal yob) of how often and tough he has tailed her?

Or can she see - not Neanderthal Man (who may indeed have dragged a terrified captive to his cave) not that brute - but Philandering Man, who may be more sophisticated, but only marginally so, as he ostentatiously displays the scalps that are hanging from the rude-tooled leather of his belt.

Or can she see, the selfish brute himself?

Someone who's just had a good fuck.

The smart-arsed lad who got the dirty water off his chest (as they take such delight in saying) leaving her to get on with it, as he zips up his fly and strolls boastfully off to the pub.

But it's no use pretending these are the thoughts that meander through your mind, when you find yourself subjected to the Womanly Gaze, because, if they were, and you were agile enough, you might be able to avoid them. Now, there's not the slightest possibility of dodging the issue, because the sort of man you are has long since been established.

You may feel the necessity of altering (or appearing to alter, because you have nefarious ends) the category you fall into; but you're wasting your time, because at this crucial moment ....

You are not only who you are, and what you are, but *where* you are, regardless of the roses; and it comes as a sobering thought (if only because some of us have been led to believe a rose, is a rose, is a rose). [2]

But take heart, because if you're fortunate enough, wise enough, or merely capable of being educated, you may be able to alter, hopefully for the better, the person she's now looking at. And whatever the outcome of this intimate debate you are in any case about to be helped by one of the practicalities of the situation, because; while she may or may not have been subjecting you to the emotional critique, there are other things that are running their inevitable course.

Apart from the fact that your erection is now little more than a wand (but surely the fondest, of all your fond memories?); while she's been day-dreaming above you, things have moved on, and you are about to be subjected to one of Nature's more ironic little jokes.

Now (shipmates), there's no mistaking the observation that you have just experienced, thankfully together, one of the more sublime moments available to Man and Womankind.

Moralists dispute it, theologians decry it - particularly if they profess a Faith which requires celibacy as one of the requisites before they can bestow, usually on themselves, the accolade of having attained the *truly* Holy State.

But there can be little doubt, in your own mind, that you have just experienced the apogee of your purely physical existence, [3] and that this can be defined as the point in the orbit of the Moon which is furthest from the Earth (and we can let the moralists and the theologians do what they can to skate around this awkward little fact).

But what does it *really* feel like?

And whatever is said, it must be said honestly, because this is the only way the matter can be approached - it's much too serious to be the subject of a jest.

It has *got* to be straight down the middle.

So, what then is it like?

In a word?

Sticky.

All this time, while you've been rapt, first in each other, then each other's thoughts, she's been leaking (some of you, and some of her, on you); nothing more nor less than the sticky effluent of Love's Long Labour Lost, that's now running down the flaccid stem of your penis, gathering in a gunjee mess about the squishy roots of slippery pubic hair.

This is also the moment when, in this position, a gentleman would be taking the weight on his elbows (but women are more intimately inclined) they lie close, even nibbling the lobe of your ear, whispering ....

Am I getting heavy?

Now, after all the pumped-up razzle dazzle, *nobody* is going to admit his partner is getting heavy; but she is, and no mistake - not the weight of her (this slip of a girl?) it's just the presence of her, lying on your chest, not affecting your breathing - but, somehow, hindering.

Or is it because you are being forced to depart the bugle-blown field of action?

You haven't much time to reflect on this demanding situation, because, as she's on top, you're slipping out of her - and there's nothing you can do about it.

You would have to be *Superman*, before you could do anything about it.

And you are quite sure, now, you're not Superman (a little earlier, maybe, you could have entertained the thought?).

But not now ....

Right now, you are just an ordinary man, who has shot his own particular bolt.

You have done your best (you *should* have done your best) and you can draw comfort from the fact that you *have* done your best. But you can do no more; and it's no use pretending - she knows it.

She can feel it.

Previously, you may have filled her being in more delightful ways than one; yet now, to her, you are Man Just Spent. The boldly flashing blade has been reduced - fails to raise a twinkle in the charm of your smile-set eye - an eye which dims, then sighs farewell to the lowered pass of love.

Even if you produced a grin, it would appear as your own rueful little smile, as you ease the weight of her, slipping at last out of her, to experience the chill you feel as you leave the blood-red heat of her, to fall, not much better than a miserable worm, into the sticky pool - which you really must do something about.

'Do you want a towel?' (good girl).

So you share a corner of the towel she previously used to dry herself - it seems such an age ago. A towel still damp from the salt from the sea, and none the worse for that, because the texture of the cloth provides its own pleasant effect. A fine thing to wipe with, when you're mopping the slip and the drip of your sprayed-about sperm mixed in with slithering great dollops of spunk. [4]

And when you've finished, she lies alongside you, which is so much more than merely adjacent to you; her head and shoulders settled comfortably within the crook of your fondly cradling arm; breasts nicely parted, one firm tit pressed on the hairy rub of your chest.

Her belly on your flank.

A leg partly over yours, applying damp pressure on the firm muscle of your thigh.

Feel the calf of her leg?

The bone in her ankle?

And there's the smell, the sweaty sexual odour you've both been manufacturing (of which you're unaware, until the quiet of this moment).

A sweating woman.

The damp patch on your leg.

The stickiness between her thighs.

The musky vapour, wafted to your nostrils.

The rivulet of sweat, oiling the feel of her breast.

Doesn't all this lead, even the least prurient amongst us (let alone the Mitred Gentlemen) to some degree of revulsion?

No: you are lying together as so much more than erstwhile partners, you are lying as puppies in a litter (and if you can bring the sight to mind, you'll notice how they do so).

Not separately - but in amongst each other - as if, not long from the womb, they retain the imprint of fecundity, which, as they grow, they'll inevitably lose when idiosyncrasies develop; but now, they come as close to being a homogeneous group as can individuals aspire to.

And so it is with you.

And notice how the word 'you', naturally assumes the mantle of you both.

Because you have been part of her, and she of you, there's been a carry over of congress.

You are lying together (and who can miss the warm caress that's tenderly involved in the phrase?).

Breathing quietly, not in unison ....

In harmony.

Her head rising on your chest, as you luxuriously inhale.

Her hair floating about your being, as a trickle of air runs tremulously over your skin.

An experience which may be thought too trivial for words.

It's not too trivial for words.

It's the very life of her - so much part of your shared existence that you find it quite delightful.

A tickle, as she breathes.

A breath, as sensual and warm as the press and gorgeous length of her, which you can feel - belly, hip and thigh - as well as the patch between her legs, while she gives a little wriggle, unselfconsciously settling herself (and you are happy to share the unbecoming tackiness).

So where now is revulsion?

Maybe in the minds of prudes - *never on the lips of lovers.*

And because this is so, you find you still have yourselves to enjoy. By running a hand over her hair, stroking her shoulder (it feels finely muscled) by the quiet light of the lamp that's darkening her skin and deepening her sunburn ....

And you're not surprised to find she's sweating.

Nothing you can see.

Something you can *feel.*

And *taste* - as you run the tips of your fingers in her armpit, finding a dew there as salt as the sea itself; and you know that this is so, because whatever else you've done together, you have equipped each other with a sense of intimate perception - an understanding, which finds ease of expression in this physical proximity, so that your fingers ....

The extremity of the arm she's now lying on ....

Those fingers, have no ulterior motive as they move thoughtfully over the surface of her skin.

They are not exploratory fingers - concerned with eroticism.

They are not applying a touch meant to stimulate - even though they move from her shoulders to the swelling of her breasts.

They are not involved with reminiscence - the sort of fingers which question there's an intimate contour left primly unexplored.

And they are not desultory fingers, having nothing better to do than convey a mood (a mood which could be described as Mood Indigo) if you felt the necessity of avoiding the first sad pang of post-coital remorse.

They are not any of those fingers.

They are not part of a *caressing* hand, because the mood has changed, has slipped from passion to *compassion*, and what's passing between you now is not being conveyed by the pressure of your palm.

These caressing fingertips are not the means ....

But the *acknowledgement*, of something much too tender and intimate to be physically conveyed.

And so it is with words.

You don't believe me?

Why then is she crying?

While I try and comfort her ....

you answer me that [5]

CHAPTER ELEVEN: PAGE NOTES

(1) Page 353. Line 30 ………. *'not only rampant, but Minotaured as well'*.

An obscure, but still relevant reference to the Greek mythological monster, half man, half bull, reputedly housed in a labyrinth and fed on human flesh. Associated with *Cnossus*, ancient city of Crete, situated on the river Caeratus, 3 miles from the harbour of Candia.

The work of the archaeologist Sir **Arthur EVANS** has revealed details of fresco paintings, ceramics, sculpture and metal work, indicating a civilization of high order.

The modern name for Cnossus is *Katsabas*.

(2) Page 359 Line 16 ………. *'a rose, is a rose, is a rose'*.

Witticism coined by **Gertrude STEIN** (1874-1946) the American novelist born in Allegheny, Pennsylvania, educated at Radcliffe College and Johns Hopkins Medical School, Baltimore.

William James, her university tutor, declared she was among the brightest students he ever met .... let alone taught.

Her own writing, notably *The Making of Americans* and *Being a History of a Family's Progress,* established her as a leading literary figure. And during the second World War, her care of American servicemen brought further public recognition.

In the 1930s she was a luminary of artistic life in Paris, establishing friendships with, amongst others, Roger Fry, Clive Bell, Wyndham Lewis, Ezra Pound, Sherwood Anderson, Ernest Hemingway, and Scott Fitzgerald.

She was undoubtedly an influence on the artistic development that took place in the 1930s, and was concerned, not only with the surrealist movement, but she actively collected paintings, notably by Braque, Cézanne, Matisse, and Picasso, who produced a distinguished portrait of Ms Stein.

When she parted from her brother, in 1912, she lived for many years with Alice Toklas, who received mirrored recognition in Stein's work, *The Autobiography of Alice B. Toklas.*

There are valuable anthologies edited by **Carl Van VETCHEN** (1946) and **Patricia MEYEROWITZ** (1967); also two biographies, one by **Elizabeth SPRIGGE** (1957) and another by **Frederick HOFFMAN** (1961).

(3) Page 359. Line 36 ………. *'the apogee of your purely physical existence'*.

It would be hard for anyone to deny that the act of reproduction is apt to give us all a bit of a lift; but for every 'up' there must be a *'down'* (for every apogee, a *perigee?*) for every height to scale, there are depths to plumb? This well illustrated by the

Liverpool, Lime Street whore, when she was being given a brutal time by a drunken lout, who was determined to *'get his money's worth'*. She decided to cut him down to size (not all that easy to do, when he was on top of her) nevertheless, she kept her end-up by feigning indifference, as she delivered the immortal put-down ....

'haven't you slimed .... **yet** *....Johnny?'*

(gor' Blimey O'Reilly)

isn't this about as low as it's possible to go?
but then, given the circumstances
isn't it just about as high
as she could reasonably expect to get?

(4) Page 361. Line 13 .... *'mopping ... your sprayed-about sperm, mixed in with slithering great dollops of spunk'.*

The interesting thing here, surely (says the bosun with a wink of his lecherous eye) the significant thing is, these commodities are both vehicles, regardless that the Shorter Oxford Dictionary defines spunk as ... *spirit, mettle, courage, or pluck*. But objectively considered, the ejaculatory substance our rude old shipmate knows as 'spunk' is the part of the seminal fluid, protecting, supporting and conveying the essential element, which is also a vehicle, carrying our genetic make-up ....

Who knows where?

(5) Page 363. Line 19 ………. *'why then is she crying? … you answer me that'.*

The lady in question is visibly upset because she's been struck with remorse; she now regrets her swim in the night, even though she enjoyed the outcome.	
She doesn't regret a minute of it, but is worried about tomorrow morning's consequences, which could be difficult to handle.	
This lady has been roughly treated in the past, but has had her confidence in human nature at least partly restored, by the move from 'passion' to 'compassion' which is a genuine first for her.	
She isn't crying . . . she's actually having trouble with her contact lenses, but was too well-mannered (or otherwise engaged) to deal with the problem before.	

(tick where appropriate)

As this is an experimental questionnaire, the correct answer may have been overlooked (feel free to complete the spare box), bearing in mind there's the possibility that a dream-time relationship may be more complex than it first appears.

LIGHT AT THE END OF THE TUNNEL

(aren't dreams astonishing?)

To be able to spend a day out hunting with the South - when you're actually wallowing about in the middle of an ocean; then find yourself involved in a midnight frolic with a lass, who provides the type of entertainment that poses not only questions regarding the *content* of our dreams, but *why* we dream - and what relevance do dreams have to our everyday experience? And this is barely glancing at the surface of a mirror which is often fogged with the guilt of mists that are sometimes elevated to the status of inhibiting taboos.

THE man to sort this thicket out is not aboard the tub right now, [1] and while this might be a matter of regret, we can't do anything about it, so on this particular morning, as on every other, it's no bad thing that brazen old Sol has decided it's time to pop over the eastern horizon.

To flood the world with the light of a brand new day, which encourages the skipper to climb the companionway steps and feel the clean sea breeze on his weather beaten features - relieved to find the boat's still lying across the trade, bobbing innocently about, well above those unlit depths that double-dealing Davy (and not only Davy) uses as his place of surreptitious entertainment.

To step out further, from what could be classed as navel gazing, let's hope it's not necessary to draw attention to the fact that it's the seafaring situation which now delights the seaman's eye, as a swell elevates the boat, and when she's balanced on the Old Man's ample shoulders, observe that westward goes the crest, leaving the tub to slide dry decked, down the smooth-backed wave, while others curl and break around the vessel in a froth of bubbles and a scattering of spray that rainbows its way about the surface of the ocean.

To bring it down to practicalities, shorn of every scrap of day or night-time dreaming, what we're *trying* to concentrate on, is an attractive, absolutely normal ocean going morning (but when you've spent weeks aboard a hooker, *drifting* across an ocean) wouldn't you *expect* the situation to develop vignettes with a flavour all their own?

True enough, the days drift by, but without the discipline of regularly fixing the vessel's position, and the absence of day-to-day decision taking (the sailing management of the boat) it's easy to become sloppy about the conduct of affairs.

This is of course a development that should be guarded against, and perhaps it's fortunate that one of the milestones of this particular voyage is looming over the horizon, with its arrival bound to sharpen up the crew.

The trade seems to have eased a knot or two, but there's still plenty of wind about, certainly enough to keep the tub plodding along in roughly the right direction, and while the fall-off in wind-speed has marginally reduced the height of the swell, there's still puff enough to roll the occasional crest, and these tumbled about lumps of 'oggin are leaving patches of froth on the otherwise blue of the ocean.

Overhead, the puff-balled clouds are scudding happily about, rarely obscuring the sun, and taking an AM sight will be easy enough. If the bosun gets his act together, rubs his rheumy eyes, and reads the ship's chronometer, there will only be the usual odds and ends of the mathematics to attend to, and we'll know exactly where we are.

This navigational requirement is one of the items that's been allowed to slovenly let slip, because up to now it's been assumed that to keep worrying about the rate of progress, or lack of it, is not much more than a knicker-twisting exercise.

Previously, the stance has been - make sure the crew go easy on the stores, ration the fresh water, acknowledge the fact that it would be better to stay out of the sun, and if this sounds something that's easily accomplished, it ain't necessarily so, because a flush-deck, thirty-eight foot, sparsely fitted ocean-racing cutter doesn't offer much in the way of a shaded promenade.

The 'awning' does help, but during the early part of the forenoon and late in the afternoon, with the sun low in the sky, it doesn't offer much protection. And further than that, I've become careless to the extent that I've taken to strolling about the boat without even bothering to pull on a pair of shorts, let alone a shirt, having taken the view that consequential happening are too far down the track to worry about. [2]

There's also the fact that when you've spent the previous night in your bunk (a twelve hour, sweated stint in these latitudes) with a flush-raising dream thrown in, it's difficult to resist the dawn move from the cabin to the relative cool of the cockpit, in order to enjoy a cup of coffee and an apple, regardless that relentlessly sizzlin' Sol is zooming up from the eastern horizon and will soon be subjecting the crew to the usual blistering fry-out.

What this argument's skating around is - that the previously mentioned 'major milestone of the voyage' is not only just around the corner, but has in fact arrived.

It's the 25th of December: Christmas Day

And while the Barbadian rendezvous with the Australian yacht *Out From Under* has been occasionally mulled over, in the relative cool of a contemplative evening (with the crew enjoying a cup of tea in the cockpit) I would have to admit, it's no longer possible to ignore the fact that there will be people, and not only in Barbados, who will be wondering what's happened to our overdue boat, with some of them edging towards the gloomy conclusion that Davy's claimed yet another victim.

But I hope there are others (I'm sure there are) who will take a more optimistic stance, and while they've got an elbow up on the Yacht Club bar, will treat a 'no-show' as nothing much to worry about, until, say, another month drifts by; with this idle speculation prompting me to get the sextant out, in order to find out not only where we are, but when we can expect to arrive.

The last fix, on 15th December, put the vessel at 16 degrees 52 minutes north, and 47 degrees, 42 minutes west; since that date we've been drifting to the west'ard (and let's hope the Old Man's been feeling generous).

However, when the new figures are worked out, the wishful thinking does take a bit of a knock, because the position at 15 degrees, 21 minutes north and 53 degrees, 48 minutes west, puts us about 400 miles from Barbados, and well to the nor'ard of the track; so taking one set of figures with another, we must look forward to several more weeks of sliding across the ocean.

In a way, this is a blessing in disguise (not the fact we're to the nor'ard of the track, and may not *get* to Barbados) but the inescapable nudge - that this odd drift across an ocean still has some way to go, and there are bound to be difficulties of one unexpected sort or another to be negotiated before the escapade is over, with perhaps the question of *attitude* being something that can't be put lightly aside.

There was of course the severe attack of the glums which occurred not long after the rudder fell off the boat, but since that date, things have improved, and taking one unusual thing with another, I could perhaps big-headedly claim to have adjusted reasonably well to what is, by any standard, an awkward situation - able to adjust to the fact that we are going to miss the Christmas rendezvous. And then go on to debate whether or not we should celebrate the event itself, with the question now being - are we going to have a nosh-up, [3] regardless of where we are on this crazy old planet, or in which direction we're heading?

As far as the vessel herself is concerned, it's a wonderfully bright tropical afternoon.

We're hove-to across a 15 knot trade, leaning away from the oncoming swells, dragging a well-defined slick, so even when the occasional wave breaks near the boat, she stays dry-decked, providing a passable imitation of a corked bottle, afloat on a deceptively somnolent ocean.

As the afternoon's progressed, with the sun heading towards the western horizon, I've been intrigued by the appearance of what look like shadows, drifting about in the tops of the swells, with an occasional better-drawn silhouette offered when a toppling crest is pierced by the lowering rays of the sun.

From where I'm situated (lounged idly in the cockpit) most of these wraiths look like blues, *Prionace glauca*, but there's also what could be a wandering Porbeagle. [4]

I may be wrong about this, and will have to wait until he ventures close to the boat. But we're not without other close-aboard companions right now, because a glance over the side, and then on down to the depths, reveals that our fine example of *Coryphaena hippuris* is still hanging about the keel - still enjoying *his* lounge in the shade.

On the run up to Christmas, I've spent hours watching this dorado (Percy) hunt down his matchboxed-sized companions - noting that he darts off to join in the fun when a school of flying fish stream past, trying to outrun their predators.

Observing the game, and given the nudge, I have of course been mulling over the possibility of despatching this very good to eat but nevertheless heartless companion, with the balance of probabilities previously being, that poor old Perce will eventually meet his come-uppance and end up gracing the pot.

Armed with the evidence, and feeling judicial, I went to the trouble of overhauling the boat's speargun, and there's now a needle-sharp point on the business end of the contrivance. Thus, it may appear, it's only the matter of getting the kit together, leaning outboard of the hull, and lining up the unsuspecting target, while not forgetting refraction.

Yet here I am, lounging about, sheltered by the awning.

Busy enough (toying with the idea of how to organise what's left of the idle part of the day), but I might as well admit - this is unlikely to include pulling the trigger on Percy.

Why slaughter the innocent?

Even though it is Christmas Day.

There's plenty of grub aboard the boat, dozens of tins of one rusty sort or another - odds and ends of not-far-from-rotting stuff in the vegetable locker; so, taking one thing with another, knocking the evening meal together shouldn't present a problem.

The afternoon drifts on, until it's time to start cooking, with the plan being, to split the task into two sessions (essential anyway, because there's only a single-burner primus available), even though there are two saucepans aboard the boat, - so what I'm going to do now is, sort the spuds out.

Most of them are sprouted and soft, but I've managed to find a few that are edible, and intend to boil these up in time to allow them to cool, well before Sol has even thought about setting.

The spuds will be sliced and mixed with diced raw onions, also beginning to sprout, and the salad will be dressed with what's left of Hellman's mayonnaise (a supermarket marked-down item) which has admittedly become runny in this tropical environment. But taking one eye and mouth watering thing with another - everything's under control, and while the spuds are cooling, I can while away the time by sorting out the books.

The Dick Francis novels have been read several times; nevertheless, I'm going to keep them, just in case they'll have to be recycled again, and again, and again.

The reference books are useful, while Rachel Carson's *The Sea Around Us* is still a delightful read (particularly for someone stuck in the middle of an endless stretch of ocean?).

Arthur Beiser's *The Proper Yacht* is something to dream over, while the *New Standard Encyclopaedia* offers not only interesting, but endless avenues for a seaman with plenty of time on his hands (20,000 references relating to Biography, History, Geography, Science, Literature, Sociology, Medicine, Law and Human Knowledge in all its fascinating diversity).

So we've come now, to the last volume to be found in the tub's lending library; *The Book of Common Prayer,* and surely this must be the volume best

373

suited to this ocean-going Christmas afternoon? [5]

I'm lounged on the coach-roof, under the awning, leafing over the pages, having a certain amount of difficulty, because of the miniscule size of the print. The problem derives from the glare associated with this tropical afternoon. It's astonishingly hot, even under the awning, and I've had to bring up a towel to lie on, because a bare bum would certainly be blistered if I was foolish enough to plonk it down on the deck. Also, the reflective glare, from the surface of the ocean, is bad enough to require the use of sunglasses; but the trouble is, those I do have available don't have prescription lenses, and I'm reduced to peering short-sightedly at the Book of Common Prayer.

The page designated *General Tables, for finding the Dominical or Sunday Letter* demands attention. And then *Table 2* illustrates how to find the month, and the days of the month, to which the Golden Numbers ought to be prefixed; starting with 1600 AD and going on to the year 8500 (which demonstrates a welcome confidence in the future of the planet?).

Nevertheless, the book is fascinating, particularly the prayers to be used at sea, which also seem appropriate for someone adrift on an ocean.

Then there are the *Psalms of David* (150 in number), so even a sun-fried seaman may find something to ponder on during this tropical afternoon, which drifts along, as all afternoon's do, until it's time for the evening meal.

The main course, to be served alongside the potato and onion salad, is going to be pasta, spiked with the last remaining bottle of Dolmio sauce. This means a trip below to fire up the primus - and then keep popping up and down the companionway steps, between the Psalms of David, just to make sure the chef's on top of the job.

The cooking doesn't take long, then it's only the matter of fixing a drink; all the tonic's gone, and there's only enough booze for one snort, admittedly a large one.

So here I am, lounged in the cockpit.

Enjoying a sip of Mother's Ruin, [6] followed by a spoonful of pasta, a fork-full of salad, a second slurp of warm drink; an appreciative stare at the ocean, followed by another fork-full of salad and one more tincture of ruin.

Sounds simple enough?

But I reckon I'm in the very best of company.

The sun is approaching the western horizon.

The trade is sighing in the rigging.

The sea is blue.

There's a storm petrel swooping along, soaring effortlessly in and out from under white-splashed tumbling crests.

The porbeagle I noticed earlier has come alongside, and is looking up at me (the cheeky bugger) with the sort of look you get from a predator who's been weighing up the chances (Percy's already taken a powder).

The Psalms of David are turning out their usual blast, with Number 23 as beautiful as ever.

(Dominus regit me)

the Lord is my shepherd, therefore I can lack nothing
he shall feed me in a green pasture, and lead me forth beside the waters of comfort
he shall convert my soul
and bring me forth in the paths of righteousness for his Name's sake
yea, though I walk through the valley of the shadow of death
I will fear no evil
for thou art with me; thy rod and thy staff comfort me
thou shall prepare a table before me against them that trouble me
thou hast anointed my head with oil, and my cup will be full
thy loving kindness and mercy shall follow me all the days of my life
and I will dwell in the house of the Lord for ever

Quite a statement.

And I'm impressed ....

By the beauty of the language.

The confidence of tone.

The *absolute* assurance there's a direct line - to and from the Almighty (just the sort of devotion my dear old Grandmother taught me as she shawled me to and fro).

The light's fading, so it's a question now of enjoying the end of the evening meal, savouring the last of the ruin, taking a look around the darkening horizon (with a glance aloft, to make out the first of the twinkling stars) and I'm on my way below.

The cabin's small (compared with the size of the firmament, it now seems even smaller than that) so I'm rather glad I've got the Book of Common Prayer safely in my hand.

However, before I stow it away, there's something I must do, because the recollection of my Grandmother's image has brought to mind the hymns she used to sing.

She'd been blessed with a fine contralto - knew the hymnal intimately, well familiar with the names of those who'd penned the words and composed the tunes she sang.

Some of her favourites were the work of the Wesley brothers, [7] so I'm searching the index of 'first lines', trying to trace them back.

The one I'm looking for is Charles Wesley's most famous composition, *Jesu, Lover of my Soul*, but it's just about dark. The print in The Book of Common Prayer is so small, that I have to use the ship's torch, and even with the light of the torch, it still requires an effort to actually decipher the words.

> *Jesu, lover of my soul*
> *let me to thy bosom fly*
> *while the gathering waters roll*
> *while the tempest still is high*
> *hide me*
> *oh*
> *my Saviour, hide*
> *till the storm of life is past*
> *safe into the haven guide*
> *oh*
> *receive my soul at last*

And two more verses, perhaps not quite as good as the opening stanza, but what I'm trying to remember is the tune the words were set to.

I can make a stab at it, but my own voice offers a disturbing echo of a Jack donkey who, having aired his views, [8] is now embarked on drawing attention to the blessing with his ear-piercing horn of a voice - so perhaps it's fortunate I'm alone on the ocean.

Either way, prompted by that emboldening spur (the slurp of Mother's Ruin) I can stand on the companionway steps, delivering *my* message.

Prayer book in one hand and torch in the other.

> *(fortissimo)*
> *other refuge I have none*
> *hangs my helpless soul on thee*
> *leave, oh! leave me not alone*

376

still support and comfort me
all my trust in thee is stayed
all my help from thee I bring
cover my defenceless head
with the shadow of thy wing

While I'm about this heart-rending bellow, there's an expiration of air near the boat; a *whoooosh* that can only have come from a close-aboard cetacean. But I've got the bit firmly in my teeth, and no damned whale, with or without Ahab (the Captain, not the King), [9] is going to put me off my strut across the boards with Wesley - so on I go.

(espressivo)

plenteous grace with thee is found
grace to cleanse from every sin
let the healing streams abound
make and keep me pure within
thou of life the fountain art
freely let me take of thee
spring thou up within my heart
rise to all eternity

There's another great *whooooooosh,* much longer and louder than the first, and perhaps it's providential (secular meaning only) there was only one snort left aboard the vessel. In any case, I've shot my bolt; and now I've stopped 'singing', the accompanying sigh of the trade is more than enough to put me in my place.

I don't know the colour of the whale (I doubt if he's a white'un) but it's more than time to go below.

Stow the torch.

Put the *Book of Common Prayer* in the waterproof 'secure' locker (wrapped in oiled silk) and it's time to take to my bunk.

This bit of a hoo-haa does have a tacky side to it, and perhaps I should apologise for that. But I can also put forward the view that this is only half the argument; the other half, is the admission that a sense of isolation *is* a real experience; that it can, prompted by a variety of recollections, eventually get to you - and there are all sorts of ways of letting-off-steam (with apologies to Wesley). But whatever the truth of the matter, it's time to turn-in and listen to the radio.

This bit of equipment is conveniently arranged, so that when I'm ensconced in my cart, the knobs are handy-by, with the loudspeaker only a few inches from (on this particular tack) my right ear. In bad weather, in the midst of a howling gale, the slam and bang of survival necessitates the use of headphones; but tonight, the sigh of the trade and the murmur of the ocean can't be heard below.

The cabin *is* small, and as dark as the inside of a cow, so it may seem that this confined space could have a claustrophobic side to it (and indeed it has, in a different set of circumstances). But while the cabin *is* small - *and as dark as the inside of a cow*, the other thing that demands attention is, that whoever occupies this living space, has access to a beast with extraordinarily sensitive ears.

The Sanyo-designed radio has band-spread throughout the shortwave spectrum, and I've been twiddling with it so long I know to a fraction of a revolution how far to rotate the knob to bring in God's Own Country. There's another spot, where European stations are predominant. And then again, on a different spread, a place on the dial where the Orient holds sway, with this geographical and cultural range influenced by the spin of the planet (broadly speaking; how much darkness there is between the boat and the transmitting country at the particular time of night).

No doubt choice of station is influenced by accident of birth (there would be little point in listening to China, if you didn't have a passable command of Mandarin?) so I have, without doubt from necessity, become used to tuning in to the BBC.

It's not a bad service.

Standard English is still the medium of the message, and even though the quality of shortwave reception is often adversely influenced by the condition of the Layer (a leaky lid, sun spot activity and so on) I'm usually able to absorb some of the grist from the endlessly grinding mill.

On this occasion, and particularly yesterday, a lot of the stuff bouncing around the ether has been involved with the Nativity.

Crosby's [10] *I'm Dreaming of a White Christmas*, (5 delivered croons from 3 different stations).

Andy Williams [11] warbling away with *Silent Night, Holy Night*.

Then there's *Amahl and the Night Visitors*, [12] with its specific view of the world; followed by a wonderful rendering of *The Creed*, set to music by Alexander Grechaninov and sung by the choir of the Russian

Metropolitan Church in Paris (surely there's no need to add - 'France'?)

There have also been lots of hymns, some preaching (good in places; like the curate's egg) and, of course, a marvellous *Midnight Mass*.[13]

That was yesterday: today, even before Christmas is even half-way over in this particular part of the placid Western Ocean, we're back to the future, and what's on offer also has a flavour of its own.

I've tuned in towards the end of a BBC news broadcast, and what I'm getting now is a rundown on the rest of the holiday's activities, with these centring largely around sporting fixtures.

Horse racing at half a dozen tracks.

Association football at scores of venues scattered throughout the length and breadth of the country.

The traditional Boxing Day meets of foxhounds, which members of the 'Volvo & welly brigade' have absolutely no need to pencil-in on their Harrods [14] complimentary calendars.

The list isn't endless, but there's quite a lot of it - followed by a brief résumé of what's been aired before. This includes details of the arrest of an African Corps Commander (a tribal warlord) who's been on the 'wanted' list ever since the troops under his command slaughtered 5,000 non-combatant prisoners, and went on to rape their widows and burn their houses to the ground. This monumental blot on humanity followed by details of an attack in Palestine, prompted by the (claimed as *non-provocative?*) enlargement of Israeli settlements into traditional Arab territory. The bomber set off the charge at a school bus stop and the carnage claimed 10 lives and left a score of children injured, resulting in a retaliatory Israeli helicopter-gunship attack which slaughtered thirty more. The Palestinians have announced - they will never rest until their flag flies over *their* holy sites - located in Jerusalem; while the Israelis claim the city is their territory - on the basis that *God has given them the land*.

So what's new?

And do you *really* have to be familiar with Feuerbach, [13] to harbour honest doubt?

Please Sir: all I've been doing, Honest Injun, is listen to the radio in my small boat, adrift on the Western Ocean. But I've had enough of it - have switched the damned thing off, having decided we've all been below far too long already (in more ways than one, Sir - if you follow the drift of the argument?).

On deck (having stood up to be counted) I can hear the black water gurgling around the slick we're leaving on the ocean, as we drift through patches of silver phosphorescence, surrounded by a school of leaping porpoise, cutting glittering swathes of ring-a-ring-a-rosie around the idling boat.

There's no moon (due in half an hour) and I can enjoy the sky at night.

Looking at the Milky Way, [14] and those many hundreds of billions of twinkles bobbing along to infinity.

The porps have stopped chasing each other around the boat.

They're swimming in a larger circle, with the tub located on the periphery, coming alongside in line-astern formation, and as they pass, they leap into the air, and then re-enter the 'oggin, barely raising a ripple.

Off they go - swimming into the night.

Nevertheless, cunning old Davy's still got plenty of shots in his locker, because now the scene-stealers have gone, I can look over the side, down to those pitch black depths that spiral below the keel.

The squid are back.

Zooming through the phosphorescence with the jet-propelled assurance of rocket-fuelled space ships - leaving silver-bubbled passage trails that herald earth-arriving meteors. In amongst these super-active lads there are other (perhaps not quite so delightful) denizens of the deep. Tight-arsed, clichéd, dozing jellyfish types, who drift along, apparently unaffected by their darting-about companions.

While I've been mooning over the side, the real moon's come up, and we're now drifting across a different sort of seascape. The trade has fallen away to little more than an air, and instead of tumbling crests, we've got patches of golden phosphorescence, plashing about the ocean with a narrow path - a sliver of silver - glinting to this seaman's eye, from the tops of somnambulant swells to an appreciative point, just below the moon.

So I reckon, this may be as good a night as any to stay on deck.

The trouble is, the cockpit's too short to enable a longish sort of seaman to lie comfortably stretched out in it. The only other place is the coachroof, which does offer the benefit of the rearranged upholstery; but this may not be too clever either, because, as the tub hasn't got much of a breeze to lean on, she's inclined to indulge in the occasional lurch, and there's the chance of a nodding dog being tipped off the settee and ending up in the scuppers.

With this in mind, I'm sitting in the cockpit, and this turns out a fortunate decision because, although I'm not actually keeping a lookout,

I'm not asleep either, and I've just noticed the masthead lights of a vessel, three points on the starboard bow and crossing to the south'ard. There's not much sense in trying to make contact, because she's too far away to signal with the torch, nevertheless, sight of this vessel does raise an interesting point.

Wondering how many ships have passed close-aboard, while we've been drifting across the ocean?

I would have to admit that the single-hander's watch keeping schedule (popping up at 30 minute intervals) has long since been abandoned, with the result that we may have missed the threat of being run down on several occasions in the past. Not that it bothers me (because we *haven't* been run down), but this sort of idle thought does jog the conscience a bit, and perhaps we (the bosun and I) should arrange a conflab when convenient in the morning.

The idea of bouncing things off the bosun may seem a bit odd, yet it shouldn't be dismissed, because having an old-fashioned seaman on hand can be convenient at times.

Comes the morning, and this same gent has drawn attention to the fact that the halyards, guys and braces which are involved with the rig we're 'sailing' under, haven't been given the attention they deserve. Like the sloppy navigation, the day-to-day seafaring maintenance of the tub hasn't been what it should be, so the first job, after breakfast, will be to take care of this small chore.

All this means is, that the ropes involved with the guys, braces, and halyards must be eased, or hauled in a bit. Only a few inches either way, but that's enough to move the job on (put a 'new' bit of rope at the place which might be chaffing) and I must say that this display of elementary seamanship does leave a disproportionate glow.

The other thing the bosun's been on about is - the little matter of sunburn.

I've certainly been careless - have spent far too long in the sun, with the result that I'm not only as brown as a berry - even my balls are brown, [15] and this hasn't been easy to accomplish. Nevertheless, there are problems here, because it's all very well saying *keep out of the sun* (in a shore-going world that's good advice). Aboard a small boat, trade-winding across the tropics, it's easier said than done.

So what we've agreed on, is a sensible compromise.

I'm going to take a few more sights, certainly more than one every seven days; and as far as the sunburn's concerned - I'm not going on deck without a shirt, shorts and some sort of a hat.

The other bone of contention is - it's getting a bit niffy down below.

The bedding hasn't been changed often enough (only one spare set of sheets) and the sweating body not so beautiful could also do with a wash.

Another example of carelessness, because there *have* been the occasional rain showers, and anyone with a sense of communal responsibility would have soaped-up just before one arrived, and then used the needle-sharp and relatively ice-cold deluge to sluice the bubbles off. [16]

So, having taken these sensible decisions, the days are drifting by.

We haven't yet passed Barbados, but I suppose the time has come to think about our ultimate destination.

The ocean's undergoing a sea change.

Because the trade hasn't picked up from last night's falling away of the breeze, the swell is as substantial as ever, but there's a dearth of tumbling crests and we're drifting lazily though the sort of junk that's found floating about on an ocean.

Hatch boards.

Plastic items of one everlasting sort or another.

And occasionally, the sort of massive steel box, [17] that's 'fallen off' a 50,000 ton 'container' vessel.

But since we've moved into this particular part of the ocean, other rather less than delectable items have put in an unwanted appearance.

These appear to be blobs of gunk (for want of a better word) sticky, dark-brown fist-sized lumps of rubbery consistency.

When you pick the stuff out of the ocean and examine it (and you *can* do that aboard our hooker, because we've got plenty of time to fish about in the 'oggin) these bits of flotsam or jetsam of one irresponsible sort or another seem be associated with the oil industry, and I suppose provide yet another indication of the way we're messing up the planet.

But there is a bright side to this nasty looking muck, because I've noticed, on the underside of these bits of gunk, there are what seem to be eggs (?) laid by our old friends Halobates (?) so at least Mother Nature's making the best she can of Man's reprehensible behaviour.

The other eye-catching thing is - we're drifting through a lot of weed.

We're way south of the Sargasso Sea, [18] but I wouldn't mind betting a stiff quid that's where this stuff hails from (a bit 'broken off' from the hundreds of square miles of the slowly rotating 'sea' itself), brought down here by an eddy in the current?

When you look at it closely, it's providing a habitat for all sorts of creatures, some of which are small, colour-coordinated and not all that easy to see.

There are others where it doesn't matter a damn, because they turn out to be the empty shells of the cephalopod *Spirula*, [19] so taking one thing with another, we've got plenty to occupy our time.

The deployment of the weed is interesting.

The rolling action of the swell has created counter-rotating cylinders, with the result being, that the Sargassum is arranged in neat windrows, extending miles in either direction.

These rows are being patrolled by a Hawksbill turtle. [20]

This gent is swimming amongst the weed, and apparently feeding on whatever he finds there to suit him; while groups of petrels are skittering about, a few inches above the surface of the 'oggin, pecking at whatever *they* fancy - so its feeding time for everyone concerned.

The vessel's crew included.

On this particular occasion, I'm enjoying the very last apple, *and* a cup of weak coffee, which is an epoch-making event in ship-drifting small-boat terms - because it marks the end of the fresh grub (and, perhaps equally important), the jar of Nescafé *'instant'* ain't as full as it used to be.

However, the drinking water's holding out well, and of course there's plenty of tinned food available - but it does bring to the fore ....

How much longer are we going to drift through the upper reaches of the Old Man's kingdom - before we'll be in sight of the shore?

The last noon position (Jan 4) turned out to be 14 degrees, 8 minutes North; 57 degrees 56 minutes West; which puts us about 180 miles from the curve of the Lesser Antilles. [21]

So, at the present rate of undoubtedly slowing progress, we'll be sculling around the windward side of - which island?

And in how many days time?

It's not all that easy to figure out.

The landfall could be almost anywhere.

The only sure thing is, we're going to pass to the nor'ard of Barbados and could end up at St Lucia, so it's fortunate the bosun's bobbing about in the background (he's got a working knowledge of the area, and between us, we should manage to scrape through somehow). [22]

What the paragon of seagoing virtue has been on about lately, is the necessity of devising the sort of plan which will offer a reasonable chance of survival. This may sound a bit simplistic, because anyone who knows the West Indies is aware that many of the islands have off-lying reefs, with all this entails in the way of jagged coral, topped with a thunder of surf. The sort of place where the crew, minus the boat, *may* be able to struggle ashore - so it really *is* time to sit down and think the thing out.

The last attempt to steer the vessel turned out an absolute disaster, with whoever was at the helm at the time standing a fair chance of being dumped overboard.

Part of the trouble was associated with the diameter of the spinnaker pole (modified to provide a rough sort of 'sweep') so there's an obvious need to tackle this - 'size of hand and finger' problem, (relative to the diameter of the pole), sooner, rather than later.

What we've decided to do is make two handles.

One of these will be fitted into the end of the pole, then whittled down to finger-fitting size. The other handle will be slotted into the pole in a way that offers the leverage necessary to make sure the business end of the pole (the 'blade' of the sweep) can be kept upright, when it's dipping in and out of the 'oggin.

This may sound easy - but there are practical difficulties.

First up, there's very little timber available.

It's a question of cutting what's left of the plywood cabin sole into strips, and then gluing these bits together in order to manufacture the right sized piece. The trouble is, the cabin sole has been coated with non-slip polyurethane varnish (mixed with a little wind blown sand), and the under-side of the sole has been sealed with the same stuff, with the akward end-result being - we've got to scrape the varnish off the ply before being able to glue the strips of timber together.

This job is taking ages.

Hampered by the lack of a proper scraper, one of the ship's knives has been pressed into service. But it isn't the best of implements, because there's a pronounced curve in the blade (when used as a scraper, it's apt to leave miniature hills and valleys) which then lead to problems regarding the glue-up of the material.

But needs must when the bosun drives, and with a little care and attention it's possible to produce two faying surfaces that can be stuck together, with odd pieces of timber sandwiched between them (to make up the thickness required).

Admittedly, the process is helped by the fact that the glue does have gap-filling properties, and the item we're trying to manufacture doesn't have to

384

be up to Tom Chippendale's cabinet-making standards. [23] Nevertheless, it takes a day to complete the job, followed by an overnight cure for the glue, with the process being facilitated by the ability to clamp the pieces together (a stroke of luck: having those 'G' clamps on board).

With the necessary bits and pieces, what we've got to do now is ....

Take the cast alloy end out of the spinnaker pole.

Cut a slot in the tube that will accommodate the second of the handles.

Complete the job by fitting the wooden plug back into the end of the pole, and when that's done, whittle the timber down to the required finger-fitting diameter.

Time for yet another cup of coffee (which turns out to be the last-but-one cup) and then formulate some sort of plan to see if the lash-up will work.

This involves fixing the modified spinnaker pole into what's left of the self-steering cradle, in a manner that will allow whoever takes a turn at the oar (guess who this turns out to be) at least some hope of (A), not being pitched overboard, and (B), gaining control of the boat.

There's nothing too difficult involved in altering the rig we're using to drift across the ocean. The bosun's suggestion is, that we make neat whippings, to mark the positions where the ropes concerned with the guys, lifts, and braces leave the cleats and pass through the blocks, in order that they can be returned to the precise place, even in the dark.

Then it's just the matter of handing the hove-to rig, and setting a small jib, to see how the contraption will work.

Quite well, is the short answer to that.

Having a handle you can get your fingers around is a vast improvement on the previous model, and being able to keep the blade of the contrivance *upright* is also another very large plus.

But there's always a snag somewhere, and, in this case, it's the amount of physical effort that's required to keep the vessel on course, allied to the fact that the pole still kicks like a mule and must be treated with respect.

The latter point can be at least partially remedied by setting up restraining shock cords, backed up by 'stopper' lanyards (in order that the shock cords don't get over-stretched and carried away). So we're beginning to make progress, with the decision taken that we'll be putting in some practice, say half an hour a day, just to make sure we've got the hang of the job before we're in a desperate all-or-nothing situation.

These sessions were at the prompting of the bosun, who really is turning out to be the most appalling know-all. The sort of irritating buffoon who *must* get his own way - who can't rest until every little item's been trawled over, and the worst-case scenario dug out and aired on every possible occasion.

What he's endlessly on about now is - the sloppy navigation.

Even the improved regime (sights every couple of days) hasn't satisfied him, because he's got it into his noddle there's unlikely to be a straight-forward approach to the Windies. More than likely, according to the worrisome old sod, we'll encounter the sort of eddies that usually occur when an ocean stream (particularly a colossal body of water like the North Equatorial Current) bumps against a substantial land mass. In this regard, there may *seem* to be plenty of room between the islands for the current to flow *through,* but these dotted about bits of greenery are really the tops of a diverting mountain range, which is more than capable of altering the course of the current.

On Christmas Day, we were in over two thousand fathoms of water, drifting over the abyssal plain. As we moved to the nor'ard of Barbados and approached the thousand fathom line, we've left the plain, and are now floating over an area that offers depths of about two hundred fathoms - from the rolling top of the 'oggin - to the floor of the ocean itself. Hereabouts, there are gigantic platforms of rock, some sheer-faced and a mile or more in extent, rising to within less than a hundred fathoms of the surface; so taking one quick up and down with another, there are plenty of reasons for the swirling-about of the current the bosun's persistently on about.

To try and keep him quiet, we've moved from the normal sequence of an AM sight, followed by the run-up to a meridian altitude and the resultant noon position, because if you're not too sure of how far you've 'run' (and particularly taking into account the possibility that you may have been inadvertently shifted in the wrong direction) then this simple navigational method will have to be improved on - which means transferring from relying on the sun, to stellar observations at dawn and dusk, [24] in order that we really do have an accurate position of - where we've been, which may help us anticipate where we're likely to eventually end up.

While the bosun's been strutting his stuff, I've done what I can to make myself scarce (not all that easy to do on a 38 foot cutter) and have been spending a deal of time under the awning, keeping as far out of the sun and strife as I can - passing the best part of the day with the books that are available.

As far as sheer quantity is concerned, the Standard Encyclopaedia (published in 1932) offers endless entertainment.

As an example: I now know, with absolute certainty, that Fermoy is a market town *and* an urban district, located in the Irish Free State, on the river Blackwater. The general railway system provides a service to Mallow (15 miles) and the City of Cork (8 miles further down the track). The local industries include agriculture and some fishing, and (this being the emerald isle) horse races are regularly held here. In 1920 there was serious rioting in Fermoy (presumably connected with 'the troubles'?) [27], and in 1927 the population amounted to some 7,000 Irish, Tricolour-waving, probably full of Guinness-burping souls; which is a fact not *actually* mentioned in the encyclopaedia. A volume that kicks off with an introduction by the Reverend C. A. Alington, D.D., the headmaster of Eton,[28] which as everyone knows, is *the* heartland, of the fee-paying, class-conscious, cradle-of-the-establishment, archetypal, English 'public' school.

Isn't that fascinating?

Just the sort of information the sharp navigator needs when he's drifting towards possible shipwreck in the Windies, and is trying his best to stay relaxed about it.

I also know that Carl Milles is a Swedish sculptor, born at Stockholm in 1875. He was for a time Professor at the Royal Akadamie at Stockholm, but is now (being reported on in 1929) teaching at the University of Cranbrook, Michigan, U.S.A. His work is represented in the principal galleries of Europe and America.

This leading to another lucky dip in the bran tub, which delivers the information that the *Mikado* is the sovereign of Japan, although the Japanese don't use this title, preferring to call their ruler *Tenshi* (the Son of Heaven). And, just in passing - The *Mikado* is also one of Gilbert & Sullivan's [29] most popular operas, first produced in 1885.

The turn of another page reveals the fact that Cecil B. de Mille [30] was born in Ashfield, Massachusetts, and made his mark in the cinema, becoming progressively, actor, playwright, manager, and producer. He directed his first big picture in 1912; *The Squaw Man*, with Jesse Lasky, [31] and has since produced many famous movies. *The Volga Boatmen; The Ten Commandments; The King of Kings*; and lots of others, which leaves just nineteen thousand, nine hundred and ninety six other entries in the *New Standard Encyclopaedia* that the concerned seaman can delve into.

So taking one informative item with another, we're not in any danger of running out of print.

Or patience: in marked contrast to the still worrisome sod (aka 'the bosun') because I've been at this game long enough to know we're actually making progress.

Just after dawn this morning, I spotted a bunch of brown Noddies. [25]

They range far and wide about the Caribbean, but I have a hunch that they're another indication that we are, at last, approaching the curve of the Lesser Antilles.

The star sights have confirmed that we are being mucked about by the current, which doesn't seem to be flowing in a westerly direction, but apparently swirling in (I expect) huge circles, within the mass of water that's bumped against the gigantic uprising from the ocean floor (that *the seamn* sees) as a relatively-small chain of volcanic islands.

But we're not talking about a major alteration in the current flow, on the scale of the Niño effect. [26]

A few days ago, the plot showed the tub is being *edged* to the nor'ard, with just the possibility (not anywhere near the probability) that our landfall will be somewhere around Guadeloupe.

Then the next set of sights seemed to indicate a further northerly push, without even a westerly component, thus offering, believe or not, Antigua as the landfall. However, all this is mere speculation - we're still too far offshore to know where we'll end up, so we've got plenty of time to explore more encyclopaedic items.

Do you know that?

Ulrich **Zwingli** was a Swiss reformer, born on January 1st 1484.

He was educated at Berne & Basel and became a priest.

In 1516 he settled at Einsiedeln and in 1518 at Zürich, where he denounced the sale of indulgences and other abuses of the Church of Rome.

He married, and in other ways broke away from the old faith.

Under his direction, the citizens accepted the reformed teaching and Zürich became a Protestant centre.

In 1531, the canton of Zürich became involved in a war with other cantons and in a battle at Kappel; Zwingli, who was with the troops as a chaplain, was killed on October 11th, 1531.

This is followed by the last item in the encyclopaedia.

So I now know that Zygote is a term used in biology.

It's the cell that results from the fusion of two others (gametes) from which a new individual develops.

Strike me a light (on second thoughts, don't bother, there's light a'plenty already), all we have got to do is direct it; while out of the corner of my other winking eye, I can see what looks like a friendly Humpy, [27] mooching about in the ocean (probably fed up having to play wallflower) if a 5 ton cetacean with an 6 foot dick and looking for somewhere to put it doesn't mind being described in these rather unromantic terms.

The other thing of interest is - the Bosun's showing signs of skittishness (he won't bless me for mentioning this; but he's definitely got a touch of the channels). [28]

The silly old coot is almost floating *above* the deck (mucking about with things that don't *really* need mucking about with), while I, although certainly interested in the progress we're making, prefer to adopt a more relaxed attitude - paying attention to things that *do* need doing - with a haircut on top of the list.

When I looked in the mirror this morning, I could see what the bosun's been on about.

Talk about the Tatty Old Man Of The Sea (if I ain't 'im - I gotta be 'is ugly bruvver) and I really must do something about it.

This means getting the scissors out (hope they're not too rusty) and then start hacking away at a beard that's grown an amazing extent since we departed Tenerife. My hair is just as bad, and it's harder to trim (I'm a bit thin on top, but there's still plenty falling over my collar) and it's not all that easy to cut.

The other thing I'm going to indulge in is - a shower, a *shower*, a ***shower***.

There's enough fresh water available (because we've been really careful with it) and following-on from the progress we're making, it now seems reasonable to assume we'll be ashore - sooner, rather than later.

The trick here (referring to a shower) is to put a few water jugs out in the sun, for as long as you're prepared to wait, because it's amazing how much heat Sol is prepared to slip into the container. As it happens, all our jugs are made of white plastic, which does frustrate the job a bit (a matt-black surface is tops); nevertheless, what we've been provided with is not far removed from a hot shower. A reasonable outcome in a boat without an engine, and only one oil lamp, even though we've still got plenty of matches.

So things are looking good.

Body burnished.

Teeth clean.

Hair and fingernails cut.

A decent pair of shorts laundered (and then put carefully aside).

A shirt dug out of the locker, and given the same treatment.

What more can the capricious idiot ask for?

He's still on about the variations in the current (as if we could do anything about it) while lounged under the awning, occasionally dipping into '*The Sea Around Us*' (the book, yer fool, not the endless breadth of the ocean). [29]

This volume is a beautiful read; just the thing to occupy a perplexed navigator who is being humbugged by a maze of contrary currents.

It really is astonishing - yesterday, we were being set to the nor'ard, at a trickling rate of knots - now, it seems we're on our way down south again.

But there *are* one or two encouraging signs.

We are still making westerly progress - several frigate birds have been giving us the once-over, [30] and there are boobies about; [31] but even with sight of these attractive straws in the wind, the bosun is still mooching and moaning away.

To ease the pain I've decided to ....

(A) to keep the newly-modified steering gear (aka, a spinnaker pole) permanently rigged.

(B) get down to the task of *steering* the boat, because now the 'distance to go' has been reduced to less than a hundred nautical miles, even ten extra westerly miles made good, on top of the favourable current, could influence the course of events.

However, that's somewhat easier said than done, when standing on the afterdeck of a 38 foot cutter, which is being coaxed along under a boomed-out headsail, while running before a breeze that's freshened enough to massage the tops off the swells.

This isn't any easier now, than it was when the same exercise (mucking about with a steering oar) was previously attempted.

The tub's still inclined to pick up speed as she lifts her arse to the swell, and it's difficult to keep her pointing in the right direction.

But *now* - the significant thing is - it's an '*almost*' manageable task !

And anyone who doubts the veracity of the argument should weigh-up the change in attitude when 'distance to go' is considered.

For the crew - whether steering or lounging about arguing the toss with the bosun - the Old Man's kingdom is as enticing as ever it's been.

The blue seas continue their march to leeward.

The sun highlights the crests, while shadows from the puff-balled clouds dapple the face of the ocean - as the boat lifts to the surge of the deep, with the crew plying his trade at the oar.

When engaged on this task, you soon appreciate the rhythm that a sensible coxswain can turn to his advantage. The trick being - to *study* the face of the wave that's bearing down on the boat - and while she's still in the trough, and *before* she starts to climb the crest-topped slope, give her an appropriate *nudge*.

With a bit of luck she stays on course.

And that's another fractional part of a nautical mile made good in roughly the right direction.

There's no denying this is a tough job.

Not only the balancing-act required of the crew. The fact that we're in the high tropics means it's blisteringly hot on the blunt end of this hooker, where it's impossible to rig an effective awning, unless you happen to possess several convenient sky hooks.

The solution to the problem is a reduction of the number of *daytime* tricks at the helm, and have another stab at steering at night. So after this evening's star sights, I'm going to give it a go, while making damned sure I'm well attached to the boat (just in case Davy catches me out) and I end up being dragged along by my safety harness.

The twilight sights have revealed that we're now being set in a nor'westerly direction, and if we project the course-made-good over the past twelve hours, the anticipated (read this as - the *definitely* pie-in-the-sky track) is indicating there's the possibility of making a landfall on Antigua; which wouldn't be a bad outcome, as English Harbour offers all the things a seafarer needs; [32] but we're still too far offshore to be certain of where we will eventually come within sight of a beach.

Steering at night, even with a sliver of moon, is certainly more difficult than a daytime trick at the helm.

When the principle source of the light that's available is low in the eastern quadrant, there are shadows on the advancing face of the swell, and these black holes can pose a problem, even if the elevating spin of the planet will sooner or later take care of it. However, the good thing about steering at night is (apart from the fact that it's cooler) the crew's awake, and on deck most of the time, so the chances of being run down have been reduced, which may be important, now we're close to a landfall and the near-certainty of coming across inter-island traffic.

As a matter of fact, the bosun and I have been discussing this very subject, and have come to the conclusion, that while we are to windward of the islands, the only thing we'll be likely to come across will be a steamer of one sort or another. But if we get swept *through* the chain of the Antilles, then we'll be amongst the yachts and charter-boats that cruise the Caribbean, and this is a development that may be only just around the corner.

After a hard night's graft on deck, keeping the hooker trickling along to the west'ard (2 hour tricks at the helm, with about an hour of exhausted watch-below and cups of tea between each trick) the morning star sights have revealed that we can forget about Antigua as a landfall, because, believe it or not, we are now being swept in a *sou'westerly* direction.

This really is amazing, almost unbelievable.

But there's no doubt about it.

Right now we're at the latitude of Marie Galante, heading towards Dominica, and the way things are shaping up, there's the possibility of actually making a landfall just before dark this evening.

The evening sights have given a position twenty miles due east of St David Bay, about half way down the eastern seaboard of the island, and there is a bit of a smudge, low on the horizon, that seems to confirm this result.

The other interesting thing is, we are making over two knots in the right direction, with this figure no doubt mostly Neptune's gift; but also including some component that can be credited to the crew's labour on the steering oar.

But of all the places in the Caribbean that you *wouldn't* make for, aboard a disabled hooker - the island of Dominica just about takes the biscuit.

It is of course an attractive location, as far as mountainous scenery is concerned. And there *is* a relatively sheltered anchorage in the North West corner of the island (Prince Rupert Bay). But Dominica is probably the most rustic of the West Indian islands, with the significant point being, that it lacks a harbour equipped with the sort of small-boat dockyard facilities that will be needed to put our wreck back together again - which leads to the conclusion that we should bow to the inevitable - forget about Dominica, and shape what course we can for Martinique, the next island in line to the south'ard.

Comes the dawn.

And we're north of the northern-most point of Martinique, about five miles offshore, with the peak of Mount Pelée showing up a further five or six miles inland. And this is handy, because it means we can make use of transits between the mountain top and prominent places on the shoreline. This simple navigational tool indicating that we're not only being carried along by the west-going current - we'll have to set as much canvas as we can manage to have any chance of avoiding the worst-case scenario; which is, being swept through the chain of the Lesser Antilles and out into the Caribbean proper before we can close the shore.

To have any chance of avoiding this unfortunate outcome, we need to make good a course that will slant *across* the current - enable us to tuck under the lee of the island - and this means bringing the nor'easterly trade over the port quarter, a point of sailing that normally provides a comfortable reach.

But the hoisting of a little more canvas (a small staysail and the peak of the fully reefed mainsail) although it's provided more boat speed, has presented the struggling coxswain with an awkward problem (even with the extra handle on the spinnaker pole, and the lash-up of shock cord and stopper-lanyards, it's impossible to retain 100% control of the boat). She occasionally takes it into her head to round-up, which is a frustrating state of affairs, and one that could have serious consequences, as the Mount Pelée transits are revealing that we're still losing the battle with Davy (being swept *past* the island). The outcome the worry-guts bosun's been endlessly on about.

If we had a *serviceable* radio transmitter (the battery we have is absolutely flat) this would certainly be the time to use it - but as we haven't got that handy bit of equipment, we'll have to do without it.

We do have parachute rockets and smoke flares on board; but the chances of anyone seeing them are just about zero.

There's also the emergency radio beacon which transmits a distress signal on the international frequencies which are monitored twenty-four hours a day (121 & 242 mhz). But whether there's a rescue service hereabouts on the scale of the USA Coastguard; or, similarly, the U.K. based RNLI, [33] is probably too much to hope for. In any case, by the time the helping hand could arrive we would be miles past the island.

While I've been struggling to control the tub, and weighing up the chances, I've noticed, away to the nor'ard, what looks like a sail on the distant horizon, apparently heading in our direction.

A light aircraft has also put in an appearance, droning its way towards Dominica.

This means a quick dash below to get the screw-topped tin that contains the parachute flares. And I'm also debating whether to switch the emergency radio beacon on, in the hope that the plane is monitoring the frequencies (I must also reveal that at this critical stage in proceedings, the bosun has decided to contribute his two pennyworth).

What the meddlesome idiot's on about now - is concerned with the question of 'asking for help'.

Can you believe it?

He's actually putting forward the view - that we've been aboard the hooker for the best part of two months (a fortnight with a rudder, and six weeks without that useful bit of equipment) and during this time there has been at least one opportunity to pull the plug, abandon the tub, and hop aboard a passing vessel. So having got this far - it seems a pity we can't bring the adventure to a satisfactory conclusion 'under our own steam'.

Make no mistake about it - what the crazy old dog is on about is - *his* preference, for an *ego-boosting* conclusion.

In the meantime, the aircraft has burbled its way towards Dominica and is almost out of sight.

As far as I'm concerned, the bosun's barmy (the switch on the emergency radio beacon has *already* been switched on) so the main item of interest now is - the sail that's shown up to the nor'ard.

Viewed through the binoculars, she's a small vessel, broad reaching under a mainsail and a coloured spinnaker - making best use of the trade, looking to pass well to windward of our present position, no doubt on passage to Martinique and maybe further south.

Within twenty minutes she's abeam, though still upwind, and through the binoculars I can see two people in her cockpit, so it's a question of how best to attract their attention.

The parachute rockets are fine, they hang in the sky in a reassuring manner and, at night, are visible for miles; but how effective they'll be during a sparkle-bright tropical morning might be the matter of debate.

The smoke floats are probably a better bet, and it's not long before I've activated one of the canisters.

They certainly produce plenty of orange smoke, dense and heavy enough to provide an eye-catching signal. The trouble is, it's being blown downwind, and this means, that as the other vessel is upwind of our present position, only a relatively narrow ('end-on') plume would be visible.

This is a problem that will of course be corrected as she passes ahead and alters the relative bearing, when her crew (if they look astern) will have thebenefit of a longer plume of smoke to attract their attention.

Whatever else it is - this is a belt and braces situation, so I've fired a rocket.

Watching it arc gracefully into the sky, to ignite with a distinctive 'pop', and then float slowly down towards the 'oggin.

It would be foolish to claim that the crew are in any way blasé regarding the outcome of these manoeuvres, because if the people on the other vessel *don't* see the signal, the tub's going to be swept away from the island, to end up ....

Who knows where?

The Caribbean is a big place.

We could be sculling around for weeks before making a safe landfall, and although there's probably enough grub on board, the amount of fresh water remaining is quite another matter.

The first parachute flare only has a few more moments of useful life before dropping into the sea.

The smoke float is still doing its stuff, but there doesn't seem to be any sign of acknowledgement from the people aboard the passing yacht.

We've got plenty of rockets (there were 12 in the watertight box) so I've decided to fire a series of signals, timed to get the next flare airborne before the last has run its course.

I'm also trying to 'angle' the rockets upwind.

Aiming the metal tube the necessary few degrees in the right direction, in order that the flares will hang between the two vessels and thus be perhaps easier to see.

We've also got another smoke float going, not only to produce more of the orange stuff - to make sure the second gadget is producing smoke before the first runs out of puff.

In between this hectic activity, I'm keeping a sharp eye lifted to see if there's any response from the windward craft, now bearing about three points on our weather bow.

Through the binoculars, I can see one of her crew moving from the cockpit, gaining the foredeck, then handing the spinnaker.

The vessel's altering course - running down towards our tub, under her mainsail.

In a few minutes she'll be close enough to shout some sort of a greeting.

There's also been another encouraging development.

It seems the people on the other vessel know what they're doing, because the foredeck hand, having handed their spinnaker, is now hoisting a small jib, and having done so, has returned to the cockpit where he's taken over the tiller - shaping a course to pass astern of our tub.

A small vessel, but expertly handled.

Executing a neat gybe, and then coming up on our quarter where they're spilling wind, intending to maintain station about three boat lengths to leeward of the hooker.

The guy at the helm is standing up, he's got the tiller between his legs.

Hands free, he's 'playing' the main and jib sheets, making sure he retains control, by keeping the mainsail fluttering as he takes way off the vessel.

He's saying something, but the words are carrying away on the breeze, making it difficult to hear exactly what he's trying to convey.

In any case, I reckon he's speaking French - and this presents a problem. What am I to say?

My command of the language is to no more than modest schoolboy standard, but I've got to make some sort of reply, so having dredged up the unlikely residue of ill-assorted and, up 'till now, long-forgotten phrases, I'm bellowing across the water.

'Le gouvernail.'

Shouts I, with a wave of an arm, indicating the lash-up of spinnaker pole, shock cords and stopper lanyards that have been set up to replace a conventional rudder.

'Le gouvernail.'

Says I, again, with what I hope is a friendly smile.

'Le gouvernail.'

Shouts I, yet again (desperately trying to think of a suitable phrase).

'Le gouvernail.'

Mumbles I, once more (failing to come up with the business).

The *rudder*, the bloody rudder - is absolutely buggered.'

Reverting to my native tongue - and while the choice of words may be judged a poor way of describing the state of the vessel, they do offer the saving grace of being an accurate assessment of the skipper's physical condition ....

after two days, and two nights
of just about non-stop battle with the steering oar

CHAPTER TWELVE: PAGE NOTES

---

(1) Page 369. Line 12 .... *'the man to sort this thicket out is not aboard the tub right now'*.

Sigmund FREUD (1856-1939) the Austrian scientist whose investigations into hysteria and dreams led to his becoming Professor of Neurotic Diseases and Neurology in Vienna in 1902. He put forward the now familiar thesis that dreams are influenced by repressions in the unconscious mind, which are subconsciously seeking an outlet. His published works include the ground-breaking *The Interpretation of Dreams* (1900); *The Psychopathology of Everyday Life* (1904); *Three Essays on the Theory of Sexuality* (1905), which met with intense opposition. Later work included *Totem and Taboo* (1913); *Beyond the Pleasure Principle* (1920); and *Ego and Id* (1923), in which he discussed the division of the unconscious mind into the *'Id'*, the *'Ego'*, and the *'Super-Ego'*. He also edited and contributed to *The International Journal of Psycho-analysis*, and in 1927 published *The Future of an Illusion* which argued a controversial view of religion and the religious experience. He was awarded the prestigious *Goethe* prize in 1930.

Before leaving the subject of dreams it's worth noting that Freud used the term *Id* to denote those primitive forces present in every individual, some of which are associated with wishful thinking and form a significant part of our unconscious minds.

The *Ego*, in contrast to the *Id*, represents reason and common sense, attributes that accumulate in childhood and adolescence as we grow up and become aware of our social and physical environment. The *Super-Ego* represents that part of our personality which has been formed by, amongst other things, parental influence and includes the not always easily acquired attributes of self-criticism and self-awareness.

But, it should be noted, these implanted judgements are sometimes at odds with our conscious values and so give rise to problems of adjustment.

(2) Page 370. Line 35 .... *'too far down the track to worry about'*.

A reference to one of the problems all small-boat sailors face when spending time in the tropics. The argument here being - that for a fair-skinned person to ignore the threat posed by exposure to the sun's rays, and then go on to say that the risk of skin cancer is *'too far down the track to worry about'*- not only comes close to, but *is*, a foolish statement (however, for someone stuck in the middle of an ocean, perhaps priorities are apt to fluctuate a bit?).

Nevertheless, that still leaves Bondi beach and the deliciously seductive curve of the Copacabana, with those *hectares* of sizzling tit on display, gorgeous though it may be.

(3) Page 372. Line 4 .... ' *are we going to have a nosh-up?'*.

The 'nosh-up' is a reference to the festival celebrating the birth of Jesus Christ, which has as its secular centrepiece the traditional Christmas Dinner, usually involving turkey, plum pudding, lashings of brandy sauce, and an exchange of expensive presents, with this activity well on its way to out-performing the prayers.

The real tradition (the nativity) dates back to approximately the year 400 A.D., with the present-day extravaganza deteriorated to a marketing exercise that does nothing to support (indeed, is more than likely damaging) the Faith on which it was founded.

(4) Page 372. Line 20 .... *'wandering Porbeagle'.*

These lads are also known as 'mackerel' sharks *(Lamna cornubica)* and are usually bigger than their 'blue' cousins, sometimes reaching 10 feet overall. They are recognised not only by their size, but also by their pointed snouts. Fast and aggressive, they are a magnificent example of the superbly outfitted predator.

(5) Page 374. Line 1 .... *'the volume best suited to an ocean-going Christmas afternoon'.*

The Cambridge University Press edition of *The Book of Common Prayer* (c 1916) carried in the vessel's library is bound in leather and measures 5 inches long, by 3 inches wide. It is merely three quarters of an inch thick (19mm) yet it offers over 500 pages that contain, apart from the prayers and psalms, an amazing amount of ecclesiastical information, with some of the print being almost too small to be read by the naked eye.

FORMS OF PRAYER TO BE USED AT SEA

IN STORMS

O most powerful and glorious Lord God, at whose command the winds blow, and lift up the waves of the sea, and who stillest the rage thereof. We thy creatures, but miserable sinners, do this in our great distress cry unto thee for help. Save, Lord, or else we perish. We confess, when we have been safe, and seen all things quiet about us, we have forgot thee our God, and refused to harken to the still voice of thy word, and to obey thy commandments. But now we see how terrible thou art, in all thy works of wonder; the great God to be feared above all. And therefore we adore thy Divine Majesty, acknowledging thy power, and imploring thy goodness. Help, Lord, and save us for thy mercy's sake, in Jesus Christ thy Son, our Lord: Amen.

BEFORE A FIGHT AT SEA, AGAINST ANY ENEMY

Oh, most powerful and glorious Lord God, the Lord of hosts, that rulest and commandest all things. Thou sittest in the throne judging right, and therefore we make our address to your Divine Majesty in this our necessity, that thou wouldest take the cause into thine own hand, and judge between us and our enemies. Stir up thy strength, O Lord, and come and help us, for thou givest not always the battle to the strong, but canst save by many and by few. O let not our sins now cry against us for vengeance, but hear us, thy poor servants begging mercy and imploring thy help, and that thou wouldest be a defence unto us against the face of the enemy. Make it appear that thou art our Saviour and Deliverer; through Jesus Christ our Lord: Amen.

(6) Page 374. Line 33 ………. *'enjoying a sip of Mother's Ruin'*.

Slang for the alcoholic beverage marketed as Gin, dating back to Victorian times when its chronic misuse no doubt merited the pejorative description.

(7) Page 376. Line 6 ………. *'the Wesley brothers'*.

The elder brother, **John WESLEY** (1703-1791) was the founder of the religious movement which became known as Methodists. His brother Charles (1707-1788) is recognised today as one of the greatest hymn writers of the 18th century; both brothers were graduates of Oxford University, with John taking Holy Orders and returning to Oxford in 1729 as tutor at Lincoln College. He and his brother visited America in 1735 and on their return from Georgia, began 'field-preaching'; the amazingly successful evangelical work that continued unbroken for over 50 years.

(8) Page 376. Line 29 ………. *'aired his views'*.

The countryman's polite description of even a small Jack donkey's boastful habit of extending his disproportionate dick, which is usually kept modestly stowed in an unpretentious sheath.

(9) Page 377. Line 10 ………. *'Ahab (the Captain, not the King)'*.

The historical figure Ahab, was a son of Omri, who succeeded his father and reigned over Israel for 22 years (875-853 B.C.). His story is recounted in the Bible (2 Kings).

Captain AHAB: the fictional character brought to life by the American author, Herman Melville, who put the old reprobate in charge of the *Pequod*, a whaling vessel which provides the vehicle for a seafaring yarn; searching the oceans for Moby Dick - the Great White Whale, which turned out to be (on some, but not all assessments of the work) one of the great metaphysical books of the age.

Herman MELVILLE: was born in New York on the 1st of August 1819, of a well known but impoverished family (his father was overcome by bankruptcy, became insane, and died when his son was 12 years old). The young Melville left school early in order to help support his mother; first working as a clerk, then as a farm labourer. He later found employment as an engineering student. When aged 20 he shipped aboard a merchantman (the packet *St Lawrence*) on a voyage to Liverpool and back to New York. In 1841 he joined a New Bedford whaler (*Acushnet*) and served aboard that vessel until, having arrived at the Marquesas, he deserted. On his way to Tahiti aboard another whaler he was involved in what amounted to a failed mutiny, and this misdemeanour earned him a short jail sentence, served in Papeete. On release, he wandered around the Pacific for a while, ending up in Honolulu, where he enlisted in the United States Navy, returning to Boston on the frigate *United States*.

Back home in New York he began writing, using his varied seafaring experience as a basis for his first book, *Typee* (1846). The volume recounted his adventures amongst cannibals in the Marquesas, and the work sold well enough to hold out the prospect of a literary career, with *Omoo* (1847); *Mardi* (1849); *Redburn* (1849), and *White-Jacket* (1850) following in relatively quick succession. These volumes were not all well received, particularly *Mardi*, possibly because he had moved away from utilizing his seafaring experience and become what amounted to a contemporary novelist, expressing a degree of contempt for established western attitudes; nevertheless, in the field of literature, apart from earning a living, he made sufficient mark to influence the abolition of corporal punishment in the United States Navy.

At about this time he embarked on his own mind-furnishing programme; studying and reading widely. During this period, and after he and his wife had moved from New York to Pittsfield, Massachusetts, they became neighbours of **Nathaniel HAWTHORNE** whose influential friends included **LONGFELLOW** and **Franklin PIERCE** (elected the 14th President of the United States of America in 1853). No doubt encouraged and perhaps influenced by his well-connected neighbour, Melville began work on *Moby Dick* (1851); published in London as *The Whale*, and now generally recognised as a major contribution to 19th century American literature. The work is complicated, extends to 135 chapters, not all of which fit easily together, partly because the plot moves from descriptions of the practicalities of commercial whaling (an unwholesome bloody mess) to moral and metaphysical issues the average reader (engaged as he might think on seafaring adventure) would normally choose to avoid, or at least postpone until a perhaps more suitable occasion. However, *Moby Dick* has been acclaimed a masterpiece; demonstrating a command of language and the ability to weave allegory with symbolism that illuminates the power of the author's mind and, incidentally, the scope of his ambition.

Melville's literary career suffered a setback after the publication of *Moby Dick*. The book was not generally well received, and his next work, *Pierre* (1852) was hardly read at all during his lifetime. Nevertheless, he continued writing, producing three more novels, *Israel Potter* (1855); *The Piazza Tales* (1856), and *The Confidence Man* (1857). Shortly after this date he all but abandoned the genre, and having obtained a post as an Inspector of Customs in New York, turned almost exclusively to poetry, not with a great deal of success. All his later works were printed privately and distributed amongst his friends. However, long after his death, his reputation recovered and four more volumes were published, the most notable being *Billy Budd* (1924); an unfinished sketch that later became source material for **Benjamin BRITTEN'S** opera of the same name, published in 1951.

When Melville died, in 1891, only one American newspaper recorded the event, producing a three line obituary that barely mentioned his literary achievements.

Nathaniel HAWTHORNE (1804-1864); born in Salem, Massachusetts. His literary career varied from writing novels and short stories, together with historical and allegorical tales, to working for the publisher Samuel Goodrich both as editor and writer, until he accepted a post in the Boston Custom House in 1839. He resigned from this position when he made his way in literary circles, later becoming involved with his wife in the Transcendentalist movement. His *The Scarlet Letter* (1850) is considered a major work, followed by *The House of the Seven Gables* (1851) and *The Blithedale Romance* (1852). There were subsequently other novels (an earlier work, *Young Goodman Brown* had been very well received) but he was apparently unable to reproduce this quality later in his life. His friendship with President Pierce led to preferment as US consul at Liverpool, and he travelled about Europe for several years after that appointment.

Transcendentalism: associated with the New England school of thought represented by **EMMERSON,** but derived from the philosophy of **KANT** and the idealism of **SCHELLING.** The movement favoured the use of exalted characterisation, together with a certain vagueness, combined with visionary intent (all to be found, in one form or another, in the plot of *Moby Dick*).

(10) Page 378 Line 34 .... *'Harry Lillis Crosby', known as 'Bing'.*

Born May 3 1902, in the town of Tacoma, Washington, USA; died October 14 1977, in Madrid, the capital city of Spain. As a singer of popular songs, his smooth bass/baritone voice, beautifully delivered, with carefull attention to the clarity of diction, enabled him to become the leading performer of this type of entertainment in America in the 1930s. But he was very much more than what was known at the time as a 'crooner', as he appeared in 79 motion pictures, receiving top billing in the majority of them. He was also involved with the technical developments that took place during that era and, as a perceptive businessman, was in a position to construct what became, in effect, an influential position in the music industry.

He was not only interested in sport (for many years he was part-owner of professional baseball's *Pittsburgh Pirates)* but was a talented golfer, playing off a 'two' handicap. His other major interest was professional tennis, and he became, over the years, a regular attender at the Wimbledon Tournament, being treated there in a manner which he thoroughly deserved ....

> *'Shall we serve your guests the strawberries and cream, now, Mr Crosby ?*
> *Or, perhaps, after a little more champaigne ?'*

Wimbledon: accepted shorthand for the '*All England Club*', founded in 1877, with it now hosting the only tennis 'major' to be played on the original surface; which, at the time, and now, is the hard to maintain and sometimes difficult to master plain old natural grass.

(11) Page 378..Line 36 ....'*Andy Williams*'.

Howard Andrew (Andy) Williams was born on December 3rd., 1927, in Wall Lake, Iowa, USA. From his early years he was involved with a childrens choir at his local Presbyterian church, and from that promising start became a major figure in the development and professional delivery of the Amercan popular song. From the late 1950s onward he became one of the most marketable of vocalists, and had the distinction of signing what was described at the time as the biggest recording contract that had ever been drawn up. His political stance is interesting because, as a lifelong Republican, he was on intimate terms with JFK; and yet, when Barak Obama first won the Democratic nomination, and then went on to become the first black president of the United States, Williams accused him of following Marxist theory, and of actually '*wanting the country to fail*'; which is a remark that's difficult to reconcile with a Christian stance, if only because it is demonstratably untrue.

(12) Page 378. Line 37 .... '*Amahl and the Night Visitors*'.

The One Act Opera by **Gian-Carlo MENOTTI** (1911-2007) to his own libretto, which was inspired by a painting by **Hieronymous BOSCH**. The work is centred about a crippled boy (Amahl) who is cured when he gives his crutch to the Three Kings as a gift for the Christmas Child.

(13) Page 379. Line 32 .... '*Feuerbach*'.

Ludwig Andreas FEUERBACH (1804-1872) German philosopher. His major work, *Das Wesen des Christentums* (1841) was translated by **George ELIOT** (nom de plume for the English novelist) **Mary Ann EVANS** (1819-1880) and reprinted as *The Essence of Christianity*. The book advanced the view that religion is 'the dream of the human mind' and 'God' an imaginary figure which men and women have endowed with their own ideals and aspirations. That the dogmas involved with Christianity fulfil a need in human nature (for example: for those who embrace the Faith - the fear of death assuaged by the promise of eternal life). Although Feuerbach's hypothesis was greeted with vehement rebuttal at the time of publication, and is still stubbornly opposed, it would seem the argument has gained adherents. The trickle swollen to a stream; not large, nevertheless with the power to erode, because it can hardly be disputed that exponents of the strictly religious stance now find themselves challenged by a significant fall in church attendance; starting, and then rippling outward from the halls of Western Europe, where the quest now is - to explore not only the intricacies of *what* we think, but *how* we think, in the belief this knowledge will offer mankind the opportunity of recognising that the sight of people preaching universal love, while at the same time indulging sectarian hatreds, should be confined to the context of the stage (footlights, daubs of greasepaint, and the embarrassed silence when a supposedly enlightened company presents an ugly, as well as a regressive performance).

To carry the argument a short navigational stage further: the manner in which The Church has shifted its ground; been forced to abandon its defence of the indefensible (for example - the trial and imprisonment of Galileo, because he supported the Copernican view of the universe) has left an indelible mark which, even if it is threadbare, is still capable of driving the questioning individual to the view that despite the supportive secular achievements (in music, literature, architecture, the arts in general devoted to the Faith) the authoritative base has shrunk to the extent that the whole colossal edifice may come crashing to the ground. A sorry state of affairs for an organisation that at one time could afford to face the future with magnanimity (which prompts the bosun to the view that the world might be a happier, certainly a more peaceful place, if some of the stuff being fed as *Scripture* was loaded into a barrow and wheeled quietly off to a convenient museum).

On his bad days, the old bosun is inclined to the more radical stance - that religion is in danger of being transposed by Christian Fundamentalists, Islamic Militants, and other fanatics - from what used to be described as, *'the Light of the World'*, to something that will be come to be recognised as the curse of humanity.

Galileo GALILEI; known as Galileo was born at Pisa in 1564. Having entered the university there, his studies led to discoveries that advanced physical science. He became a professor - but was soon compelled to resign. He moved to Padua, and became professor of mathematics at the university there; but moved again in 1610, to Florence, where he remained until he died in 1642. It is generally recognised that his abilities were such that they place him amongst the first rank as a scientist, with his development of the telescope (a Dutch invention) allowing him to discover the satellites of Jupiter and the phenomenon known as sun-spots.

His extensive astronomical research led him to support the Copernican view of the universe (that the planets move around the sun) but this sensible stance, and the publication of his work, drew objections from the church and he was hauled before the Inquisition and not only compelled to renounce his position but sentenced to indefinite imprisonment. He was ultimately spared this fate by the reluctant intervention of Pope Urban V111 (the august and infallible personage believed that the scientist had belittled him with his own particular brand of obloquy).

Galileo suffered failing sight for the last years of his life, but before becoming totally blind (1637) was able to add to the immense body of work he had already accomplished by establishing the Moon's monthly and annual librations.

(14) Page 380. Line 7 ………. *'Milky Way'*.

The group of stars that stretch in a noticeable band across the sky. It consists of a dense belt, having darker patches that shade into areas of greater luminosity. In the vicinity of *Alpha Centauri*, the Milky Way divides into two branches which reunite near *Eta Cygni*.

Alpha Centauri (aka: Rigil Kentaurus) a first-magnitude multiple star in the constellation *Centaurus*. It consists of two dwarf stars which orbit each other every 80 years. A third member of the system, *Proxima Centauri* (because of its nearness to our own sun) takes about two million years to orbit Alpha Centauri.

(15) Page 381. Line 32 ………. *'even my balls are brown'*.

There's an error of description here, because my balls are *not* brown. My balls are the same colour as everyone else's on the planet (with the obvious limitation tucked away in the trousered shape of the phrase). So what I'm trying to say is - my **scrotum** is brown - and this hasn't been easy to accomplish, because, as everyone knows, the male appendage hangs down, even when the proud owner is prone on deck, and this means you have to succumb to an idée fixe (to become sunburnt *all* over) before you take the trouble to make the necessary dick-positioning re-adjustment when lounged on the coachroof of even *this* ocean-going vessel, where the objective has been - try to look truth boldly in the face, and then go on to call it as it is.

(16) Page 382. Line 8 ………. *'to sluice the bubbles off'*.

The procedure of waiting until a rain squall can be seen on the distant horizon, and then using the minimum amount of precious fresh water to soap-up just before the shower passes over the boat (a well established water-saving small-boat procedure) does have a cautionary side to it. True enough, you can see the rain-bearing cloud, and it's not all that difficult to assess the possibility of any particular cloud passing over the boat; but occasionally, what seems to have promised a downpour only provides a dribble, with the result that the bollock-naked, ablution-indulging mariner **remains** soaped all over - looking and feeling something of a fool.

(17) Page 382. Line 20 ………. *'massive steel box'*.

Unlikely though it may seem, there are not hundreds, but *thousands* of these damned things sculling around the world's oceans. They are substantial items; measure approximately 30' x 10' x 10' and are presumably floating because they contain buoyant material. Most are just awash and thus difficult to see, even in daylight, so it would seem that at least some of the 'unexplained' small-boat disappearances could be attributed to these navigational hazards.

(18) Page 382. Line 36 ………. *Sargasso Sea'*.

Located to the south'ard of the 36th parallel of latitude, on the western side of the North Atlantic, the mass of floating weed (*Sargassum bacciferum*) was first reported by Columbus, who encountered the plant during his outward voyage in 1492. At the time, seamen associated weed with coastal waters, so it was assumed the ships in the squadron were either approaching land, or dangerous off-lying reefs. The gallant captain wanted to press on - but the crew deferred; the dispute adding another dimension to the many disagreements that had already taken place, with the outcome being a mutiny which almost brought the historic voyage to a less than glorious conclusion.

On a scientific note: the area is of interest because, amongst other things, it provides a gathering ground for countless billions of eels, who die after they have spawned (some in European river systems) while the resulting progeny ultimately retrace their parents 3000 mile ocean passage; but on this amazing occasion, *back* to coastal Europe.

(19) Page 383. Line 5 .... *'the cephalopod Spirula'.*

Cephalopods are the most highly organised of the molluscs which count amongst their number *Cuttlefishes* and *Nautilus*. Spirula are relatives of squid and octopus; they live at depths of 1,000 metres and have a gas-filled shell that provides a variable degree of buoyancy. When the animal dies, its soft tissue decays and the empty husk comes to the surface, where they can be found amongst the saragassum, together with many other planktonic animals, amongst them being *Sappharina:* small copepods that resemble flakes of mica suspended in the sea.

(20) Page 383. Line 11 .... *'a massive Hawksbill turtle'.*

These animals are reptiles with fossil remains that date back to the Triassic period, which places them prior to the dinosaurs in the overall scheme of things. The Hawksbill (*Chelone imbricata*) is one of group of 250 species that are listed under 12 families, nearly all of which are found in either terrestrial or freshwater locations.
Triassic: the geological age between Permian and Jurassic: the oldest period of the Mesozoic era, having a time span of approximately 250 million years.

(21) Page 383. Line 27 .... *'the curve of the Lesser Antilles'.*

The group of islands known as The Antilles run down to the south'ard from the Bahamas, with the Greater Antilles comprising Cuba, Jamaica, Haiti, the Dominican Republic, Porto Rico, and some smaller islands.

The *Lesser* Antilles have leeward and windward groups, with the former comprising those islands that lie between the British Virgin Islands and Guadeloupe, while the windward islands range from Dominica on down to Grenada.

Another group, also classified with the Lesser Antilles include the islands of Aruba, Curaçao, and Bonaire - collectively known as the Netherlands Antilles.

(22) Page 383. Line 36 ......*'he's got a working knowledge of the area, so between us we should scrape through somehow'.*

In this particular instance I can pull rank on the bosun, because not all that long ago I spent a season in the Windies as skipper of a large staysail schooner (70 passengers and 15 men in the crew) so I know the area fairly well.

(23) Page 385. Line 1 .... *'Tom Chippendale's cabinet-making standards'*.

The English craftsman **Thomas CHIPPENDALE** (1718-1779) was born in Otley, Yorkshire, and later set up his own cabinet making business in the 1750s. His work soon attracted a perceptive clientele, but apart from the quality of the furniture, his book, *The Gentleman and Cabinet-maker's Director (1754)*, displayed a profound knowledge of his subject and became recognised as the first and certainly the most influential volume in its field. Chippendale was indebted to French furniture makers, but developed his own technique, which combined strength with a lightness of touch that captivated the connoisseur, both in Europe and America.

(24) Page 386. Line 31 .... *'Stellar Observations at dawn and dusk'*.

There's nothing too difficult about working out a star sight, even if the navigator is in some doubt regarding the identity of the object he's observing. The hard graft of the exercise has been taken out of it by the navigational tables (Volume 1 of AP 3270) while the mathematics involved shouldn't present a problem to anyone who can add and subtract. The practical difficulties centre about the time you have available - when the star is visible, and there's sufficient light remaining to see the horizon. But any competent mate with a sextant should be able to haul down four or five stars within the space of fifteen or twenty minutes; this multiple observation then provides a series of position lines, leading to a nice 'cocked-hat' on the plotting chart, which the proud navigator can display to all concerned (in this case; our fussy old bosun, who has been obliged to play his part by supposedly reading the ship's chronometer).

(25) Page 388. Line 4 .... *'brown Noddies'*.

These chaps (*Anous stolidus*) are common noddies and there are lots of them. They are Terns, belonging to the genera *Procelsterna, Anous, or Gygis*. In addition to brown noddies, there are also white terns (*G. alba*) and blue-grey terns (*P. cerulea*) all of which are widely distributed in tropic seas.

(26) Page 388. Line 18 .... *'the El Niño effect'*.

A reference to the phenomenon (the southern oscillation) that occurs in the tropical Pacific when a natural change in the global weather system leads to a weakening of the trade winds. Normally, the south easterly trades drive the ocean current, that in turn provides an up-welling of cold, nutritionally luxuriant water (the Humbolt current) along the tropical coast of South America. When the trade weakens (occasionally reverses) not only is this up-welling reduced, but a complicated sequence of consequential events takes place, which create sometimes catastrophic weather patterns - provide torrential rainfall in Peru and the southern areas of the 'States, combined with drought and forest fires in Indonesia and Australia.

The term El Niño derives from the initial timing of the climatic changes (assumed to be around Christmas) and is referred to, in colloquial Spanish, as belonging to the Christ Child.

(27) Page 389. Line 2 ………. *'what looks like a friendly old Humpy'.*

A familiarisation accorded to the Humpback whale *(Megaptera novaeangliae)* which has been awarded this title not because it in any way resembles a 'hunchback', but because it arches its back prior to rolling over at the beginning of its dive. These are large animals, up to 50 feet in length and weighing-in at 100,000 pounds or more. They are found in every ocean and follow regular migratory routes. Solitary males 'sing', sometimes for half an hour or more without repeating the refrain, presumably using this method of communication to attract an unattached female.

The whales, as a group, have been treated abominably, some species hunted to near-extinction; only saved by the lack of economic return. That is (and its worth repeating) the lack of *economic* return - *not* the establishment of the International Whaling Commission - a body that *attempted* to regulate the butchery, but met with determined opposition from most sections of the industry (hardly one of Man's honourable episodes in the saga of his on-going exploitation of the planet).

(28) Page 389 Line 8 ………. *'definitely got a touch of 'the channels'.*

This is a reference to the long-gone days when seamen were obliged to sign articles that necessitated prolonged service overseas, with a four year stint being somewhere near the norm. Having been away from kith and kin for these substantial periods of time (without the benefit of quick, relieving flights back home) it was perhaps understandable that the eventual return to the U.K. became a red-letter affair for the crew, with *'The Channels'* being bosun-speak for the sense of euphoria which manifested itself when the homeward-bound vessels entered the Western Approaches.

The channels referred to are; the English Channel (for ships bound to Southampton and the Port of London); Saint Georges Channel for craft going 'south-about' to Liverpool; the North Channel (between Belfast and Galloway) for those engaged in the North American trade, when bound for the same port. And the Bristol Channel when trading to Cardiff, Newport, and Bristol. All these places being mere shorthand for the scores of other seaports that were in use during the colonial days of exploitive commercial activity, when the red ensign fluttered proudly over those thousands of vessels that were, *'plugging down The Channel, with salt-caked smoke stacks; outward-bound; full to the gunnels with their profitable cargoes of cheap tin trays.'* (no doubt incorrectly quoted, but the gist of the thing's conveyed).

(29) Page 390 Line 6 …. *'The Sea Around Us (the book, yer fool) not the blasted ocean'.*

The work of **Rachel Louise CARSON** (1907-1964) the American naturalist who was born in Springdale, Pennsylvania; studied at Johns Hopkins University and served in the US Wildlife Service 1936-1949. In addition to *The Sea Around Us*, she also wrote *Under The Sea Wind,* as well as contributing various articles and pamphlets concerning marine ecology. Her influential book *Silent Spring* (1962) led directly to an increasing awareness of the dangers posed by the misuse of agricultural pesticides.

Having gained a world-wide audience, she played a significant role in the establishment of the conservation movement, linked with sustainable development.

All her books are well written, with the opening page of *Silent Spring* being particularly memorable.

(30) Page 390. Line 13 ………. *'Frigate birds have been giving us the once-over'.*

There are five species of tropical birds of the genus *Fregata* (of the family *Fregatidae*). Their name derives from their combatative habit of attacking other birds (specialised aerial predation) with the object of forcing them to disgorge the food they have gathered. But they also do their own hunting, being agile enough to catch flying fish 'on the wing'. All five species are black in colour, have forked tails, and distinctive pointed wings, with spans of up to 7 feet.

Frigate: a type of warship, developed by the French about 1730; initially they were close-winded, fast, and lightly armed, but later developed to carry increased fire-power. In our modern age the term Frigate describes a small to medium sized fighting ship, a jack of all trades, but technically proficient, often used (particularly in WW2) for anti-submarine work.

(31) Page 390. Line 13 ………. *'there are Boobies about'.*

A seabird of the family *Sulidae*. There are six species (genus *Sula*) three of which are wide ranging; the other three are confined to parts of South America. These Caribbean lads have sharp, conical bills, and are adept at plunging into the sea in search of food.

They are the tropical equivalent of the Gannet (*Sula bassana*) the white seabird common in European waters, recognised by its long neck, slender wings with black tips, grey dagger-like beak, and the splash of yellow colouring on its head and neck combined with a spectacular dive into the ocean in its endless search for food.

(32) Page 391. Line 26 ………. *'English Harbour offers all the things a seafarer needs'.*

The island of Antigua lies to the nor'ard of Guadeloupe and has as its commercial centre the town of St John, which at one time was the capital of the group know as the Leeward Islands; but for the seafarer, English Harbour provides better small-boat anchorage. It also offers the historical association with Lord Nelson who, while serving in the West Indies, used E.H. as his base.

(33) Page 393. Line 32 .... 'U.K. based R.N.L.I.'

The Royal National Lifeboat service is one of the institutions of which the British people (and those citizens of the Republic of Ireland) can be legitimately proud. It has a magnificent tradition, dating back to 1824, when the United Kingdom began building the first dedicated lifesaving vessels to be found anywhere in the world.

The R.N.L.I. stands apart from similar organisations (for instance: the U.S. Coast Guard) in that it is financed by public donation and manned by volunteers, although the professional coxswains and engineers are usually seamen who have previously spent their working lives at sea.

Epiloque

While a rather unusual transatlantic passage has been recorded, there remains by far the greater part of a fascinating circumnavigation, which involves a season cruising the South Pacific; visiting, amongst other places, the Marquesas, Ahe (located in the so-called 'dangerous archipelago), then the Society Isles, as well as the islands of Suwarrow, Samoa, Tonga, and Fiji.

A passage to Sydney, and time spent in Australia, working in the boat building industry (without a work permit) in order to save enough money to have time enough to cruise the length of the truly magnificent Great Barrier Reef.

From Cape York and Thursday Island, across the Indian Ocean, calling at Cocos Keeling and Mauritious on the way to Durban.

Time spent in South Africa; back-packing about, not only some of the game reserves, but also hiking in the Drakensburgs, enjoying what surely must be some of the most rugged scenery in the world.

After leaving Durban, sailing around the Cape, visiting Port Elizabeth, East London, and Mosel Bay, before spending time in Cape Town, preparing the old tub for the South Atlantic trip with stops at Saint Helena and Ascension.

From that cinder of an island; negotiating the doldrums, which, in some seasons can be an interesting interlude in a boat without an engine; but once through, a call at the Azores, with the unexpected and disturbing opportunity of observing the hunting of sperm whales, which was supposedly legal at the time.

From that conscience-driven scene, back to the home port of Milford, having completed the trip now described as *Martinique to Milford (the right way around)*; the third volume of a seafaring trilogy which it has been a pleasure to produce.

Valentine Howells

23:06:12

www.valhowells.com

411

BIBLIOGRAPHY

(indicative volumes only of the authors concerned)

Ashley, Clifford. *The Ashley Book of Knots.*

Ashmole, Philip. *Natural History Excursions in Tenerife.*

Beiser, Arthur. *The Proper yacht.*

Bigon, Mario & **Regazzonie**, Guido. *The Guide to Knots.*

Blewitt, Mary. *Celestial Navigation for Yachtsmen.*

Book of Common Prayer.

Brook-Hart, Denys. *20th Century British Marine Painting.*

Burns, Robert. *Holy Willie's Prayer.*

Butler, Dr T. Harrison. *Cruising Yachts: Design & Performance.*

Carroll, Lewis. *Alice in Wonderland.*

Carson, Rachel. *The Sea Around Us.*

Cheng, Lanna. *Marine Insects.*

Chichester, Francis. *The Lonely Sea and the Sky.*

Chippendale, Thomas. *The Gentleman & Cabinet Maker's Directory.*

Churchill. *Marlborough.*

Clarke, M.R. & **Herring**, P.J. *Deep Oceans.*

Clark, Kenneth. *Civilisation.*

Corkhill, Thomas. *A Glossary of Wood.*

Cunliffe, Tom. *Celestial Navigation.*

Cupitt, Don. *The Sea of Faith.*

Dana, Richard Henry. *Two Years Before the Mast.*

Dijkstra, Gerard. *Self-steering for Sailboats.*

Doyle, Arthur Conan. *A Study in Scarlet.*

Edmunds, C. *Marine Animal Injuries to Man.*

Feuerbach, Ludwig Andreas. *The Essence of Christianity.*

Fishlock, Trevor. *Conquerors of Time.*

Fordred, Liz, with Suzie **Blackmun.** *An Ocean to Cross.*

Francis, Dick. *Dead Cert.*

Freud, Sigmund. *The Future of an Illusion.*

Gerbault, Alain. *The Fight of the Firecrest.*

Gielgud, Arthur John. *An Actor in his Time.*

Gombrich. *Art & Illusion.*

Hawthorne, Nathaniel. *The House of Seven Gables.*

Hiscock, Eric. *Cruising Under Sail.*

Hocking, Charles. *Directory of Disasters at Sea during the Age of Steam.*

Horsman, Paul. *The Searfarer's Guide to Marine Life.*

Huxley, Julian. *Religion without Revelation.*

Joyce, James. *Portrait of the Artist as a Young Man.*

Kent, Charles. *Poetical Works of Robert Burns.*

Kinney, Francis & **Bourne**, Russell. *The Best of the Best.*

Leather, John. *Colin Archer & the Seaworthy Double Ender.*

Letcher, John, S. *Self Steering for Sailing Craft.*

Lewis, David. *The Ship Would Not Travel Due West.*

Little, Capt. E.N. *Log Book Notes.*

Long, Dwight. *Cruising All Seas in the Idle Hour.*

Macaulay. *Lays of Ancient Rome.*

Manrique, César. *In His Own Words.*

Maugham, Somerset. *The Moon & Sixpence.*

Melville, Herman. *Moby Dick.*

Menotti, Gian-Carlo. *Amahl and the Night Visitors.*

Moeller, Herbert. *What's Blooming Where on Tenerife.*

Neale, Tom. *An Island to Oneself.*

Norrie, J.W., *Practical Navigation.*

Ormand, John. *Requiem and Celebration.*

Oxford Companion to Music.

Robinson, Bishop John. *Honest to God.*

Rogers, Dr N.A.M. *The Wooden World, an Anatomy of the Georgian Navy.*

Shackleton. *The Heart of the Antarctic.*

Shakespeare, William. *The Tempest.*

Slocum, Joshua. *Sailing Alone Around the World.*

Southby-Tailyour, Ewen. *Blondie.*

Stein, Gertrude. *The Making of Americans.*

Stephens, Olin. *All this and Sailing too.*

Summerhayes, C.P. & **Thorpe** S.A., *Oceanography.*

Sutherland, Struan, K. *Venomous Creatures of Australia.*

Tabarly, Eric. *Lonely Victory.*

Tambs, Erling. *The Cruise of the Teddy.*

Taylor, E.G.R. *The Haven-Finding Art.*

Thomas, Dylan. *Portrait of the Artist as a Young Dog.*

Tickell, Crispin. *Climate Change and World Affairs.*

Tillich. *Systematic Theology.*

Tuck, Capt. Gerald. *A Guide to Seabirds on the Ocean Routes.*

White, Amber Blanco. *Ethics for Unbelievers.*

Williams, J.E.D. *From Sails to Satellites.*

Woodham-Smith, Cecil. *Florence Nightingale.*

Voss, Captain. *The Venturesome Voyages of Captain Voss.*

ACKNOWLEDGEMENT

Mr Simon Trice

D & D
Computers
Narberth
SA67 7AA

not only for the
software and hardware
but the essential technical support
that old buffers need
when they are trying hard to just
keep up
with this galloping digital age

V.N.H

28-08-12